THE UNITED NATIONS AND COLLECTIVE SECURITY

AF737023

Updated throughout for its second edition, this book explores collective security as practised within the legal framework provided by the United Nations Charter, with a particular focus upon activity undertaken under the auspices of the UN Security Council for the maintenance of international peace and security.

This new edition follows a decade of new developments in the areas covered by the first edition, both in respect of the UN's practices under its collective security system and the wider international context within which it operates. Taking account of the Russia–Ukraine conflict and Syrian Civil War, the book additionally covers debates over UNSC reform and conceptualisations of the collective security concept. Offering a comprehensive analysis, it considers the full range of measures which can be utilised by the UN in the performance of its collective security remit, including military enforcement action, peacekeeping, non-military sanctions and diplomacy. The book considers each of these measures in detail, assessing the legal framework applicable to the form of action, the main legal controversies which arise in respect of their appropriate utilisation and the UN's use of this collective security 'tool' in practice. The book draws conclusions about the main strengths and shortcomings of the various means through which the UN can attempt to prevent, minimise or end conflict.

The book will be of interest to researchers in the fields of international law, international relations and modern international history.

Gary Wilson is Principal Lecturer and Undergraduate Programme Leader at Liverpool John Moores University. His main research interests centre on the UN collective security system, the use of force in international law, self-determination and constitutional reform. He has published widely in these areas, and in addition to the first edition of *The United Nations and Collective Security*, he is the author of *Constitutional Reform and Brexit*, also published by Routledge. Gary is also editor-in-chief of the peer-reviewed journal *Liverpool Law Review*.

Routledge Research in International Law

The Social Contract Rediscovered
Consent's Onto-Epistemological Integrity in the Late 20th Century
Wenwei Guan

Legal Perspectives on the Russia-Ukraine War
International and Polish Approaches
Edited by Michał Balcerzak and Ewelina Cała-Wacinkiewicz

Legal Challenges of China's One Belt One Road Initiative
Private International Law Considerations
Edited by Poomintr Sooksripaisarnkit and Sai Ramani Garimella

International Law After the Ukraine War
Edited by Jennifer Giblin, Olena Chub, Patrick Butchard and Oksana Senatorova

EU Sanctions Litigation
Fundamental Rights and International Security
Alexandre Sztulman

WTO Law and Dispute Settlement
Least Developed Countries
Ronald Welsh

The United Nations and Collective Security
Gary Wilson

Relational Normativity of International Law
General International Law and the International Legal Order
Roman Kwiecień

For more information about this series, please visit www.routledge.com/Routledge-Research-in-International-Law/book-series/INTNLLAW

THE UNITED NATIONS AND COLLECTIVE SECURITY

Second Edition

Gary Wilson

Routledge
Taylor & Francis Group
LONDON AND NEW YORK

Designed cover image: Getty Images

Second edition published 2026
by Routledge
4 Park Square, Milton Park, Abingdon, Oxon OX14 4RN

and by Routledge
605 Third Avenue, New York, NY 10158

Routledge is an imprint of the Taylor & Francis Group, an informa business

© 2026 Gary Wilson

The right of Gary Wilson to be identified as author of this work has been asserted in accordance with sections 77 and 78 of the Copyright, Designs and Patents Act 1988.

All rights reserved. No part of this book may be reprinted or reproduced or utilised in any form or by any electronic, mechanical, or other means, now known or hereafter invented, including photocopying and recording, or in any information storage or retrieval system, without permission in writing from the publishers.

For Product Safety Concerns and Information please contact our EU representative GPSR@taylorandfrancis.com. Taylor & Francis Verlag GmbH, Kaufingerstraße 24, 80331 München, Germany.

Trademark notice: Product or corporate names may be trademarks or registered trademarks, and are used only for identification and explanation without intent to infringe.

First edition published by Routledge 2014

British Library Cataloguing-in-Publication Data
A catalogue record for this book is available from the British Library

ISBN: 978-1-032-84980-5 (hbk)
ISBN: 978-1-032-85424-3 (pbk)
ISBN: 978-1-003-51810-5 (ebk)

DOI: 10.4324/9781003518105

Typeset in Times New Roman
by Deanta Global Publishing Services, Chennai, India

For Katie Discere ne cessa

CONTENTS

ACKNOWLEDGEMENTS

Since this book was first published over a decade ago, the UN collective security system – and the world within which it must operate – has continued to evolve. Although the fundamental features of the system remain, in the course of teaching the UN system to my students, it became increasingly necessary to supplement the content of sessions with reference to developments not covered in the book. A decade seemed an appropriate time to revise it and bring it up to date, not only with the incorporation of reference to more recent events but also to develop some lines of enquiry which I felt warranted further attention. A recent visit to the UN headquarters in New York reinforced why the project begun all those years ago remains as worthwhile as ever.

I would like to thank Routledge, in particular my editor Nicola Sharpe, for commissioning this second edition. As always, the publication process has been smooth. Thanks also to my fantastic colleagues at Liverpool John Moores University who have patiently indulged numerous discussions centred on the subject matter of the book, and to the students whose interest and curiosity over the years have only served to reinvigorate my own.

Most importantly, however, I must acknowledge the encouragement, patience and love shown at home by Jenny and Katie, essential to keeping me both grounded and on track during the course of writing the book. It would also be remiss to omit mentioning the daily contribution of my feline family, Arabella and Timothy, in bringing calm and stress relief, perfect ingredients for success.

Gary Wilson
November 2025

LIST OF ACRONYMS AND ABBREVIATIONS

ACT	Accountability, Coherence and Transparency Group
AFISMA	African International Support Mission to Mali
AMIB	African Mission in Burundi
AMIS	African Mission in Sudan
AMISOM	African Mission in Somalia
AOSIS	Alliance of Small Island States
ASEAN	Association of South-East Asian Nations
CFSP	Common Foreign and Security Policy
CIS	Commonwealth of Independent States
CSCE	Conference on Security and Co-operation in Europe
CSRC	Crisis States Research Centre
ECHR	European Convention on Human Rights
ECOMOG	Economic Community of West African States Monitoring Group
ECOWAS	Economic Community of West African States
EU	European Union
EUFOR	European Union Force
FORD	Friends of Rapid Deployment
FRY	Federal Republic of Yugoslavia
G77	Group of 77
HIPPO	High-Level Independent Panel on UN Peace Operations
ICCPR	International Covenant on Civil and Political Rights
ICESCR	International Covenant on Economic, Social and Cultural Rights
ICJ	International Court of Justice
ICTY	International Criminal Tribunal for Yugoslavia
IFOR	Implementation Force
IGAD	Intergovernmental Authority on Development
IHL	International Humanitarian Law

IHRL	International Human Rights Law
INTERFET	International Force for East Timor
ISAF	International Security Assistance Force
ISIL	Islamic State in Iraq and the Levant
KFOR	Kosovo Force
LON	League of Nations
MAES	Security Assistance Mission in the Comoros
MINURCAT	United Nations Mission in the Central African Republic
MINURSO	United Nations Mission for the Referendum in Western Sahara
MINUSCA	United Nations Multidimensional Integrated Stabilisation Mission in the Central African Republic
MINUSMA	United Nations Multidimensional Integrated Stabilisation Mission in Mali
MINUSTAH	United Nations Stabilization Mission in Haiti
MONUC	United Nations Organization Mission in the Democratic Republic of the Congo
MONUSCO	United Nations Organization Stabilization Mission in the Democratic Republic of the Congo
MSC	Military Staff Committee
NAM	Non-Aligned Movement
NATO	North Atlantic Treaty Organization
NGO	Non-Governmental Organization
OAS	Organization of American States
OAU	Organization of African Unity
OCHA	Office for the Coordination of Humanitarian Affairs
OECS	Organization of Eastern Caribbean States
ONUB	United Nations Operation in Burundi
ONUC	United Nations Operation in Congo
ONUCA	United Nations Observer Group in Central America
ONUMOZ	United Nations Operation in Mozambique
ONUSAL	United Nations Observer Mission in El Salvador
OSCE	Organization for Security and Co-operation in Europe
P5	Permanent Five
PCRS	Peacekeeping Capability Readiness System
POLISARIO	Popular Front for the Liberation of Saguia el-Hamra and Río de Oro (Western Sahara)
RUF	Revolutionary United Front
SAARC	South Asian Association for Regional Cooperation
SADC	Southern African Development Community
SFOR	Stabilization Force
SHIRBRIG	Standby High Readiness Brigade
UK	United Kingdom
UN	United Nations
UNAMID	United Nations/African Union Mission in Darfur
UNAMIR	United Nations Assistance Mission for Rwanda
UNAMSIL	United Nations Assistance Mission in Sierra Leone
UNAVEM	United Nations Angola Verification Mission
UNCIO	United Nations Conference on International Organisation

UNDOF	United Nations Disengagement Observer Force
UNEF I	United Nations Emergency Force I
UNEF II	United Nations Emergency Force II
UNFICYP	United Nations Force in Cyprus
UNHCR	United Nations High Commissioner for Refugees
UNICOI	United Nations International Commission of Investigation (for Rwanda/Zaire)
UNIFIL	United Nations Interim Force in Lebanon
UNIPOM	United Nations India–Pakistan Observer Mission
UNISFA	United Nations Interim Security Force for Abyei
UNITA	National Union for the Total Independence of Angola
UNITAF	Unified Task Force
UNMIK	United Nations Mission in Kosovo
UNMIL	United Nations Mission in Liberia
UNMIS	United Nations Mission in Sudan
UNMISS	United Nations Mission in South Sudan
UNMIT	United Nations Integrated Mission in Timor-Leste
UNMOGIP	United Nations Military Observer Group in India and Pakistan
UNOCI	United Nations Operation in Côte d'Ivoire
UNOSOM I	United Nations Operation in Somalia I
UNOSOM II	United Nations Operation in Somalia II
UNPROFOR	United Nations Protection Force
UNSAS	United Nations Standby Arrangements System
UNSCOB	United Nations Special Committee on the Balkans
UNTAC	United Nations Transitional Authority in Cambodia
UNTAET	United Nations Transitional Administration in East Timor
UNTAG	United Nations Transition Assistance Group
UNTSO	United Nations Treaty Supervision Organization
US	United States of America
USSR	Union of Socialist Soviet Republics (Soviet Union)
WMD	Weapons of Mass Destruction

INTRODUCTION

The United Nations (UN) was created, as the preamble to its Charter quite clearly states, 'to save succeeding generations from the scourge of war.' The events of World War II served as the key motivating influence for the major powers who laid the foundations for the UN's creation. Their earlier attempt at the creation of a global collective security system, the League of Nations, was widely perceived as having failed in light of its inability to prevent the drift towards war in the 1930s, an experience which undoubtedly provided some key lessons to inform the process of drafting the United Nations Charter. In legal terms, the UN Charter marked a major improvement upon the Covenant of the League of Nations. An executive-styled body, in which the major powers were given a special role, was entrusted with wide-ranging powers to respond to any situation which it deemed threatened international peace and security, through the utilisation of robust measures extending to military enforcement action. Significantly, the powers afforded to this body – the Security Council – extended beyond facilitating responses to armed attacks upon states, to embrace addressing security challenges more broadly conceived. This has resulted in a wide range of circumstances and phenomena being brought within the ambit of the UN collective security system, and since the publication of the first edition of this book attention has been directed, for example, towards the implications for international peace and security of the COVID-19 pandemic, while debates over the effects of climate change upon the global security agenda have only escalated. As set out on paper, the UN's collective security mechanisms could not conceivably be any stronger than they are. However, the relative success or failure of the UN system cannot be assessed simply through an assessment of

DOI: 10.4324/9781003518105-1

the provisions of its Charter, but requires an appreciation of the manner in which they have been effected in practice. It is the overriding objective of this book to provide this, this revised second edition bringing developments within the UN's collective security practice up to date.

If the performance of the UN since 1945 is judged simply against the grand proclamation contained in the preamble to its Charter, then it can clearly be considered to have failed. Subsequent generations have not been spared the 'scourge of war.' It rages to this very day in various parts of the world, with the most recent prominent examples of armed conflict at the time of writing including those in Ukraine and Israel/Gaza. The efforts of the UN have not been sufficient to eradicate conflict wherever it has broken out. The weakness of responses offered under UN auspices to crises such as those which occurred in the former Yugoslavia, Somalia and Rwanda during the 1990s in particular presented the organisation's collective security apparatus in a bad light, while the vested interests of the P5 and/or deadlock between them have undermined the prospects of the Security Council being able to address conflict in Syria and the aforementioned situations in Ukraine and Israel/Gaza amongst others. However, while the UN has been the subject of much criticism over time – some of it justified – to write it off as a failure as a collective security actor is naïve and neglects to appreciate the important contribution which it has made to the advancement of peace and security in the world.

While the UN Charter provides its pre-eminent body, the Security Council, with theoretically robust powers to respond to conflict situations, these must be exercised in accordance with political realities, and the agendas of the permanent members within that body are of paramount importance. The need to be realistic about the prospects for the UN was recognised by its second secretary-general, Dag Hammarskjold, when he famously commented that the UN was 'not created in order to bring us to heaven but in order to save us from Hell.'[1] The legal framework within which the UN operates is sufficiently broad to enable it to take the necessary steps to respond to any situation which threatens international peace and security, but it is unrealistic to expect that it will always be able to do so given the political environment within which it must operate. The dynamics of the P5 within the Security Council's decision-making processes are particularly significant, especially given the power of veto which means that action does not proceed where the interests of one or more of these states militate against it. That notwithstanding, as one commentator has written, the 'remarkable record of the UN … is a case of adapting to new challenges and opportunities without rethinking the basic rules of international life or considering the very foundations of international order.'[2] Throughout its history, the organisation has proven adept at

1 Quoted in Urquhart, B., *Hammarskjold* (New York: W.W. Norton, 1994), p.48.
2 Haas, E.B., 'Collective conflict management: Evidence for a new world order?' in Weiss, T.G. (ed.), *Collective Security in a Changing World* (Boulder: Lynne Rienner, 1993), pp.63–117, at p.84.

rising to meet new challenges, overseeing an evolution in the interpretation and execution of its powers to further advance its collective security remit. A major objective of the book is to illustrate the extent to which the UN has proven adaptable and creative in its development as a collective security actor in response to changing circumstances and pressures.

The book is written primarily from the perspective of an international lawyer and seeks to explain how in different forms of activity, the organisation and its principal actors – in particular the Security Council – have been able to utilise its legal framework to effect responses to situations threatening international peace and security, and the relative perceived success or failure of these responses. The wider political environment within which the UN operates is nonetheless recognised, and the extent to which it serves to restrict the potential of its collective security mechanisms is identified where relevant. Two themes already alluded to run throughout the book. On one hand, it is apparent that the effective utilisation of the UN collective security mechanisms has been considerably hindered by political considerations which have informed the approaches of the UN membership, in particular the permanent members of the Security Council, to action in given situations. This accounts for the perceived failures with which the UN has been charged. On the other hand, however, in the UN's collective security practice, its membership has demonstrated the ability to develop and utilise its powers with sufficient flexibility to respond to new challenges and circumstances. The creation and subsequent evolution of UN peacekeeping, and the move towards tailored sanctions which came to take on a more targeted form in light of the perceived limitations of widespread conventional economic sanctions, are two of the most striking examples of this. Underlining all of this has been the conceptual evolution of collective security, as the UN has increasingly approached this in terms which place the protection of the human being against all existential and tangible threats at the centre of its responses to situations of international concern.

It is important to clarify what the book is not intended to be. It is not a doctrinal analysis of the content and scope of the various provisions of the UN collective security system. Although some attention is given to these issues, the primary aim is to shed light upon the utilisation of these powers in practice and their evolution through the activities of the UN organs, in particular the Security Council. Nor does the book purport to provide a comprehensive historical overview of the UN's experience as a collective security actor. While relevant examples are drawn upon throughout to illustrate the various measures of the UN collective security system in operation, it does not aim to provide a detailed overview of the various instances of the UN's utilisation of these measures.

The approach followed in the book becomes clearer when its structure is set out. The first three chapters provide important contextual background for the subsequent consideration of the specific collective security measures of the UN system. Chapter 1 considers how perspectives upon the concept of security have evolved during the course of the UN era, introducing the concept of collective security more specifically and explaining its underlying rationale and the requirements that must be satisfied for it to function effectively. The legal and political dimensions to the concept are explained, underpinning the fact that while within the UN system there is a clear legal concept of collective security, this operates within a political environment upon which its effective implementation is contingent. These legal and political dimensions intertwine; while the legal framework provided by the UN Charter prescribes the parameters within which essentially political decisions and actions are taken, political considerations simultaneously influence the development in practice of the Charter provisions. Chapter 2 adds to this theoretical background by explaining the main collective security provisions of the UN Charter and the factors which shaped their content after having provided a brief account of the implementation of collective security within the League of Nations system and the factors which resulted in its ultimate downfall. A key contribution of the chapter is to illustrate the extent to which the UN's founders envisaged that a selective form of collective security would be practised by the organisation, demonstrating the extent to which political considerations have shaped collective security within the UN system from its very inception. In so doing, particular attention is paid to the P5's role within the Security Council's decision-making processes, questioning the perceived legitimacy of the Council within the context of pressures for reform. Chapter 3 adds useful context for the subsequent chapters by providing a brief historical overview of the key stages in the development of the UN as a collective security actor, demonstrating the main challenges which it has faced and how it has responded to these. Important developments that have taken place since the publication of the first edition of this book are highlighted.

In the subsequent chapters, the contribution of the various tools of the UN system towards tackling threats to international peace and security is considered. Chapter 4 considers the use of diplomacy as a collective security technique, with specific emphasis upon the good offices of the UN Secretary-General. The office is defined in very general language in the relevant Charter provisions, but as will become apparent, the various individuals to have held the position have interpreted their powers sufficiently flexibly to make a meaningful contribution to the peaceful settlement of disputes. The measures provided for the peaceful settlement of disputes by Chapter VI of the UN Charter are considered, their relationship to Chapter VII – typically regarded as the core collective security chapter of the Charter – being explored in so doing. We then move on to consider the application of non-military sanctions by the UN Security Council in Chapter 5. The underlying theory of sanctions was that they may prevent the need for recourse to more robust military measures. As will be seen, the generality of Article 41 gives the Council considerable discretion in choosing to apply them, and historically, they have arguably given rise to more problems than solutions. Although their utilisation has become more carefully considered in the post-millennium era, questions remain as to their practical effectiveness. Peacekeeping, the subject of Chapter 6, is not mentioned at any point within the UN Charter, yet its creation by the UN as a means of responding to low-key conflict situations during the Cold War represented one of its greatest contributions to collective security. Since then, its legal framework has evolved to allow its use in a wider range of circumstances, but this has not been without resulting difficulties. The fact that no new UN peacekeeping operations have been created in over a decade forces reconsideration of their future role within the UN's practice of collective security. The final technique of the UN collective security system, military enforcement, is considered in Chapter 7. This represents collective security in its most traditional form. However, while the Charter set out an elaborate framework to govern its operation, this soon gave way to a system of 'subcontracting,' whereby military operations were entrusted to 'able and willing' actors. This approach gives rise to dangers of abuse, necessitating the imposition of strict controls over military enforcement operations. Furthermore, their utility is contingent upon the willingness of suitably equipped actors to undertake them. Although there are indications of declining support for military enforcement action, these issues will be addressed in Chapter 7 before alternative approaches to military enforcement action are briefly mooted.

In light of the extent to which the UN system has increasingly become overburdened in the post–Cold War era, calls have been made for regional bodies to be used on a larger scale to support the work of the UN. At the same time, developments within some regional organisations have arguably posed potential challenges to the primacy of the UN within the maintenance of international peace and security, amid claims to greater autonomy on their part. The viability of the 'regional option' within the framework provided by the Charter is considered in Chapter 8 with reference to both the Charter framework and the constituent frameworks and agendas of regional organisations themselves.

1

THE CONCEPT OF COLLECTIVE SECURITY

Introduction

The purpose of this chapter is to provide an understanding of the concept of collective security. Although this book is concerned specifically with the collective security system established by the United Nations Charter, we can only fully appreciate the manner in which this has functioned and the factors which have impacted upon its perceived successes and failures by considering at the outset what collective security entails as a concept, and how understandings of it have changed over time in accordance with shifting perspectives upon the idea of security more generally. Making sense of collective security also necessitates an appreciation of the conditions upon which its effective implementation depends. In advancing these objectives, this chapter provides a necessary theoretical foundation for the remainder of the book.

We begin by exploring the idea of collective security, unpicking in so doing developments in perspectives on the sources and nature of security threats, demonstrating that it is a potentially broad concept, which has evolved considerably within the UN era to embrace concern for a wide range of threats posed to human well-being arising from multiple sources. We then appraise the various requirements that must be satisfied if any collective security system is to have the optimum prospect of success, relating these to the system of collective security enshrined within the UN Charter. These reinforce the political contingencies upon which the operation of collective security hinges. That they have never been fully satisfied in practice reinforces the practical limits to collective security. In acknowledging the political dynamics of collective security, we move on to consider the relevant role of legal and political perspectives in evaluating its practice. Finally, a case is made

DOI: 10.4324/9781003518105-2

for collective security that justifies the contribution of this book to contemporary discourse on the evolution of the United Nations as a collective security actor.

The evolution of perspectives on security and the concept of collective security

The term 'collective security' implies an arrangement by which states act collectively to guarantee one another's security. Defined in general terms, in an ideal collective security system, each state 'accepts that the security of one is the concern of all, and agrees to join in a collective response to threats to, and breaches of, the peace.'[1] Before seeking to understand collective security as a concept, it is necessary to appreciate that broad and varying perspectives have been offered in respect of what constitute matters of security within an international context. The scope of what are considered to pose security threats will ultimately depend upon the dynamics of the particular collective system in place, and the view that it adopts of what constitutes 'security.'

Historically, collective security was largely deemed to concern the protection of states from external attack. As the Commission on Global Governance noted, 'Since the seventeenth century, international security has been defined almost entirely in terms of national survival needs. Security has meant the protection of the state … from external attack.'[2] Similarly, Hemmings et al suggested that 'traditional view[s] of security define it in military terms with the primary focus on state protection from threats to national interests.'[3] Within these more traditional understandings, the referent object of security discourse was the state: the state was the actor which needed protection, the identifiable threat being an attack against it, undertaken by another state or group of states, using military means. Little attention was given to the security of human populations against other challenges to their existence or well-being, which may not have their origin in the application of military force or even any intentional human-orchestrated action, for example, where these are the result of natural disaster or disease. The notion of security can, however, be conceived more broadly and has been discussed in terms of 'a self-referential practice to construct a shared understanding of an existential threat and the collective response to [it].'[4] Such existential threats may be

1 Roberts, A. and Zaum, D., *Selective Security: War and the United Nations Security Council since 1945* (London: Routledge, 2008), p.11.

2 Commission on Global Governance, *Our Global Neighbourhood* (Oxford and New York: Oxford University Press, 1995), p.78.

3 Hemmings, A.D., Rothwell, D.R. and Scott, K.N., 'The Search for Antarctic Security,' in Hemmings, A.D., Rothwell, D.R. and Scott, K.N. (eds), *Antarctic Security in the Twenty-First Century: Legal and Policy Perspectives* (London: Routledge, 2012), pp.1–17, at p.3.

4 Nasu, H., 'The Global Security Agenda: Securitization of Everything?,' in GeiB, R. and Melzer, N. (eds), *The Oxford Handbook of the International Law of Global Security* (Oxford: OUP, 2021), pp.37–53, at p.38.

posed not only to states, but also to other security actors, groups of people or individuals.[5] As asserted by Schroeder, 'Today, security challenges are diverse, often transnational and not necessarily military or state-based in nature.'[6]

As will be seen in subsequent chapters, the history of activity by the UN Security Council, especially in the post–Cold War era, has evidenced a broader understanding of the nature of security threats. The provisions of the UN Charter permit collective measures to be employed to maintain or restore international peace and security, following a determination by the Security Council that there exists a threat to the peace, breach of the peace or act of aggression, under Article 39. The flexible language used has allowed for the implementation of a form of collective security going beyond simply responding to external aggression to embrace concern for human security, Shraga noting correctly that 'more than six decades after the adoption of the UN Charter, the concept of "peace" and of what constitutes a "threat to the peace" has fundamentally changed.'[7] Receiving its first significant treatment at UN level in the UNDP's 1994 Human Development Report,[8] human security entails 'A human or people-centred and multisectoral approach to security, which entails the protection of people from critical and pervasive threats and situations.'[9] The primary focus of human security is 'on protecting the integral worth of people against insecurities rather than protecting the state.'[10] The human security agenda soon came to inform the activities of the UN's principal political organs. As asserted in one study, 'Global security was redefined … and the tasks undertaken to provide security widened to protecting civilians from massacre by their own governments as well as shoring up weak states threatened by struggles among factional militias.'[11] The Security Council's debates have increasingly centred on a wide range of actual and potential security threats extending to health pandemics, terrorism, proliferation of weapons of mass destruction, drug trafficking, food security and climate change.[12] The latter

5 Buzan, B., Waever, O. and de Wilde, J., *Security: A New Framework for Analysis* (Boulder: Lynne Rienner, 1998), p.5, cited in White, N.D. and Davies-Bright, A., 'The Concept of Security in International Law,' in GeiB and Melzer, ibid, pp.19–36, at p.21.

6 Schroeder, U., 'The Transformation of Security Concepts: Beyond the State,' in GeiB and Melzer, supra n4, pp.54–68, at p.61.

7 Shraga, D., 'The Security Council and human rights – from discretion to promote to obligation to protect,' in Fassbender, B. (ed.), *Securing Human Rights?* (Oxford: Oxford University Press, 2011), pp.8–35, at p.12. See in general MacFarlane, S.N., 'Human security and the law of states,' in Goold, B.J. and Lazarus, L. (eds), *Security and Human Rights* (Oxford: Hart, 2007), pp.347–361.

8 UNDP, *Human Development Report: New Dimensions of Human Security* (Oxford: OUP, 1994).

9 Final Report of the Commission on Human Security, *Human Security Now* (New York: Commission on Human Security, 2003).

10 Louw, L.-A. and Lubbe, H.J., 'Threats to Security Posed by ISIS in Syria: A Human Security Approach,' *Journal of Human Security*, 2017, v.13, n.1, pp.16–21, at p.17.

11 Crocker, C.A., Hampson, F.O. and Aall, P., 'Collective conflict management: A new formula for global peace and security cooperation?,' *International Affairs*, 2011, v.87, n.1, pp.39–58, at p.42.

12 See, eg., Nasu, supra n4, pp.41–44.

two issues are particularly profound examples of 'new' security challenges, climate change having been at the centre of debates both within and beyond the Council for a number of years for its implications for the maintenance of international peace and security,[13] while the consequences of food insecurity have been addressed relatively recently by the Council.[14] Significantly, several of these new threats have their sources in the actions of non-state actors or natural phenomena, and while states remain the principal actors responsible for the utilisation of the UN's collective security apparatus, it has become increasingly necessary to acknowledge the challenges posed by the need to take action to exert coercion over the activities of non-state actors.

Opportunities have been taken at successive intervals to formally restate the importance of conceptualising security in terms which extend beyond concern only for the protection of states. The report of the *High-level Panel on Threats, Challenges and Change* stressed the importance of adopting a 'comprehensive' conception of collective security.[15] It noted in particular that, in the modern world, security threats are interrelated[16] and that their nature is such that no state alone can make itself invulnerable.[17] Importantly, however, it acknowledged that

> the biggest security threats we face now … go far beyond states waging aggressive war. They extend to poverty, infectious disease and environmental degradation. The threats are from non-state actors as well as states, and to human security as well as state security.[18]

It is also worth noting the emergence of the Responsibility to Protect doctrine,[19] under which states have a duty to protect their civilian populations from harm, and the international community has a duty to intervene where a state is unable or unwilling to meet its obligation to protect its people.[20] The doctrine received the support of the UN General Assembly at the 2005 World Summit,[21] evidencing the extent to which contemporary conceptions of security have human security at their core. The General Assembly returned to human security in 2012, setting out

13 See, e.g., Wilson, G., 'Climate Change as a "Threat to the Peace": Responding to Climate Change through the UN Collective Security System,' *International Journal of Climate Change: Impacts and Responses*, 2020, v.12, n.3, pp.33–44.

14 See UN Docs. S/PRST/2017/14, S/PRST/2023/4.

15 Report of the *High-Level Panel on Threats, Challenges and Change*, *A More Secure World: Our Shared Responsibility*, UN Doc. A/59/565, Pt.II.

16 High-level panel, ibid, para.17.

17 High-level panel, supra n15, para.24.

18 High-level panel, supra n15, p.1.

19 *The Responsibility to Protect: Report of the International Commission on Intervention and State Sovereignty*, available at http://responsibilitytoprotect.org/ICISS%20Report.pdf.

20 See further Chapter 3.

21 UN GA Res. 60/1, paras.138–140.

a common understanding of the concept and emphasising the importance of interlinkages between human rights, development and security in calling for people-centred comprehensive responses to challenges of these kinds.[22]

In line with developments in UN security discourse, regional bodies have also evidenced a broadened conception of what amount to security threats. For example, the Organization for Security and Co-operation in Europe (OSCE) was one of the first bodies to employ a broad conception of security threats centred on human security,[23] and in its 2003 *European Security Strategy*, the EU made reference to the emergence of new security threats including terrorism, the proliferation of weapons of mass destruction, state failure and organised crime.[24] Indeed, it is suggested that all EU member states have individually adopted broadened understandings of security which encompass 'dimensions of economic, societal, environmental, energy, food, health, and human security.'[25] Similarly, around the same time, organisations such as the African Union and the Association of South-East Asian Nations (ASEAN) adopted comprehensive security concepts. The AU acknowledged protection against poverty and environmental degradation, among other matters, as components of security,[26] while ASEAN's 2007 Charter recognised various sources of potential instability.[27] A survey of some of the key security pronouncements of the UN Security Council's dominant permanent members during recent years also reveals that all have, to varying extents, adopted comprehensive concepts of security. The US National Security Strategy alludes to a wide range of security concerns,[28] while the other Western powers – the UK and France – have demonstrated the importance attached to a human security approach within their own national security strategies.[29] Although often associated with more traditional conceptions of security, Russia and China nonetheless

22 UN GA Res. 66/290.

23 Odello, M., 'The Organization for Security and Co-operation in Europe and European Security Law,' in Trybus, M. and White, N.D (eds), *European Security Law* (Oxford: Oxford University Press, 2007), pp.295–328, at p.297, 313–315.

24 European Union, *European Security Strategy: A Secure Europe in a Better World* (Brussels: EU, 2003).

25 Methymaki, E. and Ozcelik, A., 'Europe,' in GeiB and Melzer, supra n4, pp.857–877, at p.862.

26 Solemn Declaration on a Common African Defence and Security Policy 2004, para 6, available at https://au.int/en/documents/20110728/solemn-declaration-common-african-defence-and-security-policy.

27 ASEAN Charter 2007, available at https://asean.org/book/asean-charter-29th-reprint/.

28 See US National Security Strategy 2022, available at https://www.whitehouse.gov/wp-content/uploads/2022/10/Biden-Harris-Administrations-National-Security-Strategy-10.2022.pdf.

29 See the UK's Integrated Review Refresh 2023, available at https://www.gov.uk/government/publications/integrated-review-refresh-2023-responding-to-a-more-contested-and-volatile-world, and France's National Strategic Review 2022, available at https://www.sgdsn.gouv.fr/files/files/rns-uk-20221202.pdf. On the place of human security within these strategies, see respectively Marhia, N. and Davies, C., 'A "force for good"? British national security and human security in an age of counterterrorism,' in Kaldor, M., Martin, M. and Serra, N. (eds), *National, European and Human Security: From Co-Existence to Convergence* (London: Routledge, 2012), pp.64–88;

have also demonstrated that their approaches to matters of international security have evolved over time. Russia's 2023 *Foreign Policy Concept*, for example, refers to transnational challenges including trafficking, terrorism, infectious diseases, natural disasters and environmental degradation,[30] acknowledging that there has been a 'blurring of the line between military and non-military means of interstate confrontation.'[31] Meanwhile, China's *Global Security Initiative Concept Paper* of the same year asserts that traditional and non-traditional security threats are intertwined and commits China to a vision of 'comprehensive security,'[32] while China has previously evidenced engagement with the human security agenda.[33]

The scope of the concerns of a collective security system is potentially as broad as are prevailing understandings of the concept of security more generally, and as will become apparent in subsequent chapters, the UN's collective security system itself has proved to be flexible and evolutionary in its capacity to respond to a diverse range of threats, including from newly emergent sources of insecurity. While the focus of the present book is the UN system specifically, it is important to note that there is no singular template through which collective security must be affected.[34] It may, for example, involve a universal legal obligation among states to provide mutual assistance to one another in the event of their being a victim of external aggression or some other predefined occurrence. Such a form was evident within the system established by the League of Nations Covenant and represents the most traditional means for describing collective security.[35] Article 10 of the

Schmeder, G., 'French security policy: A human security perspective,' in Kaldor et al, infra, pp.18–40.

30 The Concept of the Foreign Policy of the Russian Federation 2023, para 9, available at https://mid.ru/en/foreign_policy/fundamental_documents/1860586/.

31 Ibid, para 11. For further discussion of Russia's conception of security, see Tuzmukhamedov, B., 'The Russian Federation,' in GeiB and Melzer, supra n4, pp.913–925; Makarychev, A.S., 'Human security as a 'floating signifier': Russia's reinterpretation of the concept,' in Kaldor et al, supra n29, pp.152–166.

32 The Global Security Initiative Concept Paper 2023, available at https://www.mfa.gov.cn/eng/wjbxw/202302/t20230221_11028348.html.

33 See, eg., Ren, X., 'Human Security: China's Discourses and Experience,' *Journal of Human Security*, 2016, v.12, n.1, pp.112–120; Jia, L. and Xiaofeng, Y., 'Human Security: China's Conceptual Approaches and Policymaking Patterns,' in Walton, D. and Tow, W.T. (eds), *New Approaches to Human Security in the Asia-Pacific: China, Japan and Australia* (Taylor & Francis, 2013), pp.15–30.

34 See Kupchan, C.A. and Kupchan, C.A., 'The promise of collective security,' *International Security*, 1995, v.20, n.1, pp.52–61, at pp.52–54; Haas, E.B., 'Types of collective security: An examination of operational concepts,' *American Political Science Review*, 1955, v.49, n.1, pp.40–62.

35 Such a definition has been employed in many of the theoretical discussions of collective security. See, for example, Claude, I.L., *Swords into Plowshares* (3rd ed.) (London: University of London Press, 1964), p.224; Johnson, H.C. and Niemeyer, G., 'Collective security: The validity of an ideal,' *International Organization*, 1954, v.8, pp.19–35, at p.20; Kupchan, C.A. and Kupchan, C.A., 'Concerts, collective security and the future of Europe,' *International Security*, 1991, v.16, n.1, pp.114–161, at p.118.

League Covenant provided that 'The Members of the League undertake to respect and preserve as against external aggression the territorial integrity and existing political independence of all Members of the League.' The Covenant made no express reference to other possible forms of security threats. However, collective security should not be viewed purely in terms of an arrangement among states to join in fighting external aggression. This is too narrow and fails to recognise the potentially broader nature of collective security. An alternative approach is that of the 'concert' system, in which major powers take on a special role and cooperate to address security threats, using more flexible procedures in adopting collective measures to respond to them. The 'concert' system inherently leads to a selective form of collective security. Such characteristics can be identified within the UN Charter's collective security system, in which the Security Council – and in particular its five permanent (P5) members – is conferred with the primary responsibility for the maintenance of international peace and security.[36] The Council enjoys discretion in determining the existence of a threat to the peace, breach of the peace or act of aggression under Article 39, and in choosing upon the course of action, if any, to be taken in response. Collective security may also operate on a regional basis, the states of a particular region creating and using collective mechanisms for addressing security threats within that region.[37]

A system of collective security must not be confused with one of collective defence. While both are predicated on the adoption of a collective approach by states to guarantee the security of their number, there the similarities largely end. Collective defence arrangements are more exclusive in nature, formed by a select group of states to afford protection against threats posed by (often pre-identified) states outside of their number. By contrast, a system of collective security strives for inclusivity, envisaging that any threat will arise from within its number.[38] It is important to note also that not only can a system of collective security be concerned with a wide range of security threats, but that the means available for it to respond to these are not confined to the use of military force. As Orakhelashvili notes,

> the concept of collective security is broad, and can include in itself a variety of tasks such as conflict prevention, crisis management, peace-keeping, or peace enforcement, as required to enable the relevant institution to deal with threats as their gravity and magnitude require.[39]

36 Article 24 (1). See Chapter 2.

37 See, for example, McCoubrey, H. and Morris, J., *Regional Peacekeeping in the Post-Cold War Era* (The Hague: Kluwer, 2000); Tavares, R., *Regional Security* (London: Routledge, 2010).

38 On the distinctions, see Butfoy, A., 'Collective Security: Theory, Problems and Reformulations,' *Australian Journal of International Affairs*, 1993, v.47, n.1, pp.1–14, at p.2.

39 Orakhelashvili, A., *Collective Security* (Oxford: Oxford University Press, 2011), p.15. See also Abass, A., *Regional Organisations and the Development of Collective Security* (Oxford: Hart, 2004), pp.112–114, for the distinction between collective security and enforcement action.

In recognising that the UN collective security system is provided with a number of tools for tackling security threats, this book gives attention in turn to pacific settlement, sanctions, peacekeeping and military enforcement action as means of effecting collective security.

The requirements of collective security

Commentators on collective security have set out a series of requirements that must be satisfied for its effective implementation.[40] It should be noted that these have largely been devised with the most traditionally understood form of collective security in mind: a collective military response to an attack on one state by another state. Nonetheless, it remains possible to apply these requirements to broader, more comprehensive forms of collective security, such as that represented by the system created and developed in practice under the UN Charter. However, the satisfaction of all of these requirements ought to be regarded as the necessary condition for the operation of an ideal form of collective security. In practice, these have never been satisfied in their entirety, reinforcing the political dynamics of collective security.

First, collective security requires that some kind of institutional system be in place through which it can operate. As Claude suggests, the system is the institutional component that allows the means (a collective approach) to serve the end (security).[41] If collective security is to be meaningful, there needs to be some certainty as to when a particular situation will be regarded as being of concern to the wider international community, and how it will respond collectively to deal with it. While there is no one template of a collective security system, as the preceding discussion of the nature of collective security illustrated, it is essential that means are in place to determine what situations will trigger collective action and what form that collective action will take. This necessitates a series of norms and procedures and underlines the centrality of principles of law to collective security.[42] As Miller puts it, '[what is] demanded is some kind of institutional structure in which the members of the community can determine when conditions requiring their collective action have arisen.'[43] An institutional framework is also needed for the purpose of coordinating collective action. With an international community in the

40 See Claude, supra n35, pp.227–238; Kupchan and Kupchan, supra n35, pp.124–125; Naidu, M.V., *Collective Security and the United Nations* (London: Macmillan, 1975), pp.17–27; Thompson, K.W., 'Collective security reexamined,' *American Political Science Review*, 1953, v.47, n.3, pp.753–772, at pp.758–762; Bennett, A. and Lepgold, J., 'Reinventing collective security after the cold war and Gulf conflict,' *Political Science Quarterly*, 1993, v.108, n.2, pp.213–237, at pp.215–222.

41 Claude, supra n35, p.223.

42 See below.

43 Miller, L.H., 'The idea and the reality of collective security,' *Global Governance*, 1999, v.5, pp.303–332, at p.304.

region of 200 states, it must be questioned how effectively collective action could be conducted in the absence of any coordinating mechanism. It would clearly be impractical for states to take action, whether militarily or otherwise, in isolation, making the need for an institutional framework fundamental to the operation of collective security. As will be detailed in the next chapter, the application of collective security measures within the UN system rests largely on the decision-making processes of the Security Council. While this gives rise to a discretionary system, in which there may arise an inconsistency in approaches and outcomes, there are nonetheless clearly recognisable procedures by which collective action can be pursued.

Second are the related requirements of universality, preponderance and diffusion of power.[44] Any collective security system's effectiveness rests upon its membership being substantially universal, taking in the vast majority of the international community. This is because the collective might of the members of the system must be sufficient to remove any security threat. Where military action is to be taken, its success in achieving its objectives is contingent upon the force deployed being sufficiently preponderant to enable it to overcome the problem with which it is mandated to deal.[45] Even where the collective response chosen is non-military in nature, its effectiveness will still be dependent upon the willingness of a sufficient number of states to, for example, apply sanctions or exert diplomatic pressure against those responsible for threatening international peace and security. The less universal a collective security system is, the weaker its collective resources, and thus its capacity to effectively tackle security threats. While the absence of a handful of relatively minor powers may be of no huge consequence, if a number of major states abstain from participation, collective security's potential may be seriously undermined. Any system lacking the participation of a number of major states may find it difficult to muster the overwhelming power that would be essential to its ability to engage in collective action against identified security threats. An often-advanced criticism of the League of Nations is that it never enjoyed the membership of the United States (US), and prior to the outbreak of World War II other major powers such as the Union of Soviet Socialist Republics (USSR), Germany, Italy and Japan all left the League.[46] By contrast, the UN has enjoyed a relatively universal membership throughout its lifetime. However, as shall become apparent, it is one thing to enjoy universal membership and another to benefit from the universal commitment of that membership to collective security ideals.

To ensure that the collective strength of the members of the system will be preponderant over any threat with which it is faced, it has been suggested that

44 Claude, supra n35, pp.234–236.
45 Thompson, supra n40, p.760–761.
46 Claude, supra n35, pp.80–81.

collective security ideally requires the existence of a world in which power is diffused among a number of states.[47] The basis for this is that should one or two states enjoy power disproportionately superior to that of other states, it will not be possible for collective security to serve as a deterrent against such states engaging in acts of aggression or behaviour which otherwise endanger international security. Collective security's value as a deterrent against such kinds of behaviour is best guaranteed if all states are considered vulnerable to collective action. A state enjoying power equivalent to, or greater than, that of most other states combined will probably not feel threatened by the possibility of collective action. This theoretical requirement of collective security arguably represents something of a utopian ideal. Although over the course of history, the identity of the world's most powerful states has changed, certainly throughout the League of Nations and United Nations eras, there have always been a small number of states enjoying disproportionate levels of global power and influence. Most prominently, the dominant position of the US and USSR during the Cold War effectively left them immune from any international criticism for their actions, while their privileged status within the UN's collective security system allowed them to keep off the UN's collective security agenda any matters they chose to.[48] Although a world in which power is relatively widely dispersed need not be absolutely essential to collective security's effectiveness, this is contingent upon a third requirement being satisfied.

The third requirement of collective security is that major powers are committed to the system of collective security in operation. Given that collective security's application to any given situation is unlikely to be possible in the face of the opposition of a major power, it is imperative that major powers are agreed upon the status quo which the particular collective security system is intended to preserve, or what has been referred to as their enjoyment of a 'minimum degree of political solidarity and moral community.'[49] This is arguably recognised by the UN Charter system's conferment of special status upon the major powers with permanent membership of the Security Council.[50] According to Anderson, this reflects the realist recognition that collective security must be enforced by the great powers and be consonant with their interests, and takes account of the unrealistic idealism of the League of Nations in affording equal status to all states irrespective of their capacities.[51] The major cause of inaction on the part of the UN during the Cold War was the existence of the superpower struggle between the US and USSR, with the two superpowers lacking a great

47 Claude, supra n35, p.234; Naidu, supra n19, pp.24–25.

48 See further ch.2.

49 Thompson, supra n40, p.761.

50 Article 23 (1).

51 Anderson, K., 'United Nations collective security and the United States security guarantee in an age of rising multipolarity: The Security Council as the talking shop of the nations,' *Chicago Journal of International Law*, 2009–2010, v.10, pp.55–90, at p.59.

deal of consensus upon the manner in which the UN collective security system should function and the priorities which should underpin its work. The Cold War effectively saw them bypass the UN to serve their own individual policy objectives, there being no commitment to any shared collective security ideal. Disagreements among the P5 continued to manifest themselves in the post–Cold War era as the fallout over the US/UK-led invasion of Iraq served to demonstrate particularly well,[52] while intense divisions later prevented the adoption of robust measures in response to the civil war situation that came to grip Syria during 2012 and its horrific humanitarian consequences.[53] More recently, the UN Security Council was unable to meaningfully address the Russian invasion of Ukraine, the invading state being a veto-wielding permanent member of that body,[54] while the Council's inability to formally label climate change a threat to international peace and security – despite widespread recognition of it in such terms – stemmed from a difference of opinion between the Council's permanent members.[55]

The final cornerstone of collective security is states' acceptance of the principle of the 'indivisibility of peace,'[56] the idea that a threat to the security of one state or group of people is a threat to the international community as a whole, regardless of where the threat arises. This is the very basis of collective security. Without this shared attitude, it will be difficult to persuade states to participate in collective action – particularly where the deployment of military forces is envisaged – in response to a situation in a distant part of the world where they may feel that they have no immediate national interests at stake, or which they might feel compromises these, for example, by imposing trade sanctions that are detrimental to their own economic well-being. Thus, states must subordinate what they may regard as their immediate national interests to the longer-term good of the international community as a whole. They must be willing to take action anywhere, and against anyone, in accordance with whatever procedures are laid down for collective action to maintain or restore security when it is endangered. Acceptance of this principle must be regarded as the most important requirement of collective security, as satisfaction of this is likely to ensure satisfaction of other requirements.

52 See Malone, D.M., *The International Struggle over Iraq: Politics in the UN Security Council 1980–2005* (Oxford: Oxford University Press, 2006), Chapter 7.

53 This included the use of the veto by Russia and China to prevent the adoption of a resolution critical of the Assad regime; UN Doc. S/2012/538. On the Council's debate, see UN Doc. S/PV.6810.

54 See ch.3.

55 See Wilson, supra n13.

56 Claude, supra n35, pp.229–232; Naidu, supra n40, pp.21–22.

Legal and political elements of collective security

Collective security must be approached from both political and legal perspectives. These tend to afford understandings of international events, actors and processes which stem from different starting points. Whereas international relations (IR) scholars concern themselves primarily with the viability of collective security, seeking to establish the *why* and *how* in explaining the causation of events and their consequences, international lawyers focus on evaluating the legitimacy of the same events in terms of their compliance with established legal norms. Both functions are undoubtedly important. As an abstract ideal, collective security may appear to be prima facie a political concept, the foregoing discussion of its requirements demonstrating the extent to which its effective operation ultimately hinges on key political factors. However, when implemented in any given form, collective security becomes a legal concept as it becomes governed by the series of norms and procedures that particular system lays down. In the case of the UN, the legal concept of collective security can be found in the various principles and norms contained within the UN Charter to regulate its operation.

Although a wealth of literature has been produced on legal issues pertaining to the practice of collective security under the auspices of the UN, very little has been written on the more general question of the role which law is capable of performing within collective security systems in conceptual terms. This is not, perhaps, surprising. Collective security is a potentially broad concept, and thus its conceptualisation in legal terms will vary with the particular system of collective security in place. Certainly, the collective security system enshrined within the UN system differs in legal terms from that which existed during the League of Nations era.

It will be recalled that the effective functioning of collective security ideally requires the existence of an institutional framework through which it can operate. Law is capable of providing this, contributing to collective security by establishing a series of norms, standards and institutions to govern its operation, and which can thus give effect to the shared values of the international community. Such a function of law can be seen as performed within the context of the UN, where rules and principles contained in the UN Charter and developed subsequently in practice specify procedures and considerations which should determine matters such as decision-making, the forms of action which may be taken, when such action is permitted and by whom. Thus, law serves an important role in the construction of an institutional and normative framework through which collective security will function.

More generally, law seeks to normalise international relations between states. Higgins, for example, has described international law as a normative system that provides an operational system for securing shared values which all desire, including security.[57] Similarly, Barker views international law as a cooperative enterprise aimed at identifying common interests and developing norms and principles to advance common aims.[58] However, the very idea that law has a place within collective security has been criticised by those belonging to the realist school of international relations thought. Although in disagreement with this attack on law, the realist argument is well set out by Koskenniemi,[59] and can essentially be summarised in the proposition that law is irrelevant in the context of collective security arrangements, as the perceived political interests of states will ultimately dictate how they act. Action will take place in accordance with political calculations regardless of the existence of a body of law which conflicts with these. Power will dictate outcomes, not law. This leads to the conclusion that any notion of law becomes meaningless.

Few international lawyers would deny that international law has its limitations in terms of its ability to regulate the behaviour of states. On occasions, actions do take place that are in violation of international legal rules. States do not always abide by treaty commitments. However, as Barker points out, no system of law can eliminate breaches altogether. Law is just one force among others that also have a bearing on states' behaviour.[60] Domestic law likewise suffers from violations, sometimes on a large scale, yet it is not generally suggested that it is irrelevant. Generally, international law is observed by states, arguably reflecting the fact that it embodies their shared values. Even if the view is taken that political factors are the principal motivation for states' conduct, it is contended that law remains vital to collective security. A strong case for the importance of law has been advanced by Koskenniemi.

Koskenniemi argues that the realist explanation of events is purely causal and devoid of any normative element.[61] Put simply, the realist view that states act as they do out of political considerations merely attempts to explain why certain events happen without providing any justification for them. The rejection of the relevance of law means that everything is viewed purely in terms of causation. Arguably, this is unsatisfactory. To say that state A uses military force against state B for reason X, for example, may accurately explain the reason the action has taken place but fails to provide standards by which it can be evaluated in terms of acceptability. As Koskenniemi goes on to argue, law fills this void by providing standards by which it is possible to attempt to justify or criticise actions. It insists

57 Higgins, R., *Problems and Processes: International Law and How We Use It* (Oxford: Clarendon Press, 1994), p.1.

58 Barker, J.C., *International Law and International Relations* (London and New York: Continuum, 2000), p.75.

59 Koskenniemi, M., 'The place of law in collective security,' *Michigan Journal of International Law*, 1996, v.17, pp.454–490, at pp.463–464.

60 Barker, supra n58, p.30.

61 Koskenniemi, supra n59, pp.465–480.

> on their justification in terms of [the] historical practices and proclaimed standards ... the formalism of the legal argument inevitably makes public the normative basis and objectives of one's actions and assumes the actor's communal accountability for what it is that one is justifying.[62]

Without the existence of legal norms by which action can be evaluated, everything becomes subject to the individual interpretation of states, thus negating the fundamentally collective nature of collective security, which is intended to embody a universal enterprise built upon shared values.[63]

We only have to consider certain events in which action has been taken involving the use of force in order to identify the importance of law in the attitudes displayed by states towards the use of force and its perceived legitimacy. A comparison of the US-led military action against Iraq in 1991 with that of 2003 is particularly instructive in this respect. The action taken in 1991 to force Iraq from Kuwait enjoyed wide international support. This can, arguably, be attributed to the fact that Iraq had violated a fundamental principle of the UN Charter by invading Kuwait in violation of Article 2 (4), and that the military response had been authorised by the UN Security Council in accordance with other accepted rules of the collective security system.[64] That the US invasion of Iraq in 2003 met with much opposition can, arguably, be attributed to the existence of doubts on the part of many states that this operation was in accordance with accepted legal norms, given the evident lack of support within the Security Council for authorisation of the action.[65] Thus, even if political factors might have been the ultimate cause of the decisions of the intervening states to take the military actions in 1991 and 2003, the importance of international law for many states as a means by which these actions were evaluated is apparent. Furthermore, it is significant that even when states act in a manner that is of dubious legality, they still usually seek to justify their actions in legal terms, suggesting recognition on their part of the importance of law. Certainly, the US and UK sought to provide legal justification for their invasion of Iraq which paid close regard to the UN Charter framework.[66] Similarly, Russia sought to justify its invasion of Ukraine in February 2022 on legal grounds, even if these were clumsily invoked and met with very limited acceptance internationally.[67] It is also worth noting that states invest consider-

62 Koskenniemi, supra n59, p.478.

63 Koskenniemi, supra n59, pp.477–478.

64 SC Res 678 (1990); Koskenniemi, supra n59, p.472.

65 White, N.D. and Myjer, E.P.J., 'The use of force against Iraq,' *Journal of Conflict and Security Law*, 2003, v.8, n.1, pp.1–14; Sands, P., *Lawless World: America and the Making and Breaking of Global Rules* (London: Allen Lane, 2005), Chapter 8.

66 Ibid.

67 See, eg., Cavandoli, S. and Wilson, G., 'Distorting Fundamental Norms of International Law to Resurrect the Soviet Union: The International Law Context of Russia's Invasion of Ukraine,' *Netherlands International Law Review*, 2022, v.69, pp.383–410, at pp.387–88.

ably in international legal advisers, membership of international bodies and treaty negotiation, an indicator that international law is an important factor in guiding their actions within the international arena.[68]

Collective security, then, needs to be approached from both legal and political perspectives. The contribution of this book is to consider the evolution of the UN collective security system principally from a legal perspective, yet it makes no pretence that the system operates in an idealistic fashion. Law is not always observed favourably. However, it does perform an important normative function within a system of collective security. It provides the framework within which collective security should operate and standards against which the legitimacy of actions can be evaluated. At the same time, while political perspectives on collective security cannot serve such a normative function, they are also necessary as a means of understanding how and why collective security functions as it does in practice.

The case for collective security

Collective Security, as a practice, has important normative value. This book proceeds upon this assumption, regarding collective security to be a worthwhile endeavour. However, collective security has been the subject of a number of criticisms.[69] A detailed discussion of the various criticisms commonly advanced of collective security would consume a separate volume in itself. However, for present purposes, it is important to be aware of the major criticism – and arguably the most powerful – that has been made of collective security. This can generally be summarised in the proposition that collective security is unworkable because the key requirements which need to be satisfied for it to succeed cannot be fulfilled.

68 See, eg., Gauci, J.-P., Jones, K. and Peiris, C., *The Role of Legal Advisers in International Law*, Conference Report (Foreign & Commonwealth Office/BIICL/Brill Nijhoff, 2015), available at https://www.biicl.org/documents/570_the_role_of_legal_advisers_in_international_law_-_conference_report_final26_feb.pdf?showdocument=1#:~:text=The%20principal%20role%20of%20the,to%20shape%20and%20facilitate%20it. See also Cassese, A., 'The Role of Legal Advisers in Ensuring that Foreign Policy Conforms to International Legal Standards,' *Michigan Journal of International Law*, 1992, v.14, n.1, pp.139–170.

69 Carr, E.H., *The Twenty Years Crisis 1919–1939* (2nd ed.) (London: Macmillan, 1981); Mearsheimer, J.J., 'The false promise of international institutions,' *International Security*, 1994–1995, v.19, n.3, pp.5–49, at pp.30–34; Morgenthau, H.J., *Politics Among Nations* (New York: Alfred A. Knopf, 1960), Chapter 34; Thompson, supra n40, pp.757–770; Clark, M.T., 'The trouble with collective security,' *Orbis: A Journal of World Affairs*, 1995, v.39, pp.237–258, at pp.241–245; Betts, R.K., 'Systems for peace or causes of war?,' *International Security*, 1992, v.17, n.1, pp.5–43, at pp.17–20; Joffe, J., 'Collective security and the future of Europe: Failed dreams and dead ends,' *Survival*, 1992, v.34, n.1, pp.36–50, at pp.37–40.

Furthermore, it has been argued that the historical record of attempts to implement collective security supports such a negative view.[70]

It will be recalled that collective security's basis is to be found in the maxim of the 'indivisibility of peace,' and that to function, it is necessary for states to equate their own security with that of every other state, being prepared to engage in collective action against threats posed anywhere whether or not they are perceived as affecting their own immediate interests. The realist school of international relations theory essentially holds that such faith in this ideal is misplaced, as states will not engage in action to tackle threats to the security of other states unless they perceive some important national interest of their own to be at stake. This in turn will mean that the ability to muster the resources necessary to tackle a particular threat cannot be automatically assumed, but will instead depend upon the perception which individual states have of a particular situation's effects upon their important national interests. The importance of the commitment of major powers to a system of collective security has been noted, and often criticisms have stemmed from their inaction in leading collective responses to situations of concern.

Those advocating such a view of collective security's impracticability would certainly seem to be able to cite examples from states' practice in support of their argument. Beginning with the experience of the League of Nations, a number of instances of aggression by one state against another met with no real response from the League's members, notwithstanding their commitment to regard aggression against one as aggression against them all. No military action was taken against Italy after it had invaded Ethiopia, as 'What [the major powers] conceived as their national interests contradicted what collective security required them to do.'[71] Likewise, the Japanese invasion and annexation of the Chinese territory of Manchuria did not meet with any collective military response.[72] In both cases, aggression went unpunished, despite the existence of a collective security system based upon the premise that aggression against one state was to be regarded as aggression against all others. These two examples alone would appear to demonstrate that states' acceptance of the premise that peace is indivisible should not be too readily assumed. The failure of the League is generally reinforced by its inability to prevent the rise of aggressors and the drift towards war that occurred during the 1930s. Within the UN era, collective security enjoys a mixed record. As will be seen, where action has effectively been taken, it is possible to detect motives on the part of participating states which can be based on considerations of perceived national self-interest. For example, as will be seen in Chapter 3, the UN

70 Mearsheimer, ibid, pp.31–33; Morgenthau, ibid, pp.413–422; Thompson, supra n40, pp.762–766; Betts, ibid, pp.19–20; Joffe, ibid, pp.17–20.

71 Morgenthau, supra n69, pp.418–419.

72 Walters, F.P., *A History of the League of Nations* (London: Oxford University Press, 1952), Chapter 40.

action in Korea, in which the US supplied the bulk of the forces involved, can be seen to have served US interests which could be viewed as the underlying motive for the scale of US involvement. Likewise, significant economic interests were at stake when a US-led coalition acted under UN authority to repel Iraq's invasion of Kuwait. It need not be a criticism of a particular collective action that participating states perceive national interests to be at stake in the situation at hand, if collective security's goals are still achieved. However, if the absence of such considerations will make them unwilling to engage in such action, then the potential of collective security is clearly called into question, as it begins to appear selective in its application. The failure of the UN membership to respond robustly to several humanitarian crises, such as the Rwandan genocide and civil war in Somalia during the 1990s, adds weight to the realist critique of collective security's workability.

This criticism of collective security can be seen as the major problem faced by its advocates. It cannot be disputed that the evidence to support such a view appears fairly compelling. However, despite its mixed historical record, it is contended that there are good reasons as to why the pursuit of collective security remains worthwhile.[73] If collective security is regarded as a worthwhile endeavour, the fact that it may not always prove capable of delivering the desired results should not detract from the pursuit of what is regarded as a desirable goal. That collective security's functioning may encounter problems, due to states' unwillingness to put the good of the international community above what they consider to be their national interests, does not provide a sufficient reason to abandon the project. If collective security is abandoned, the end result is a world in which security is left to be achieved through collective defence agreements and the balance of power. The more limited scope of these two mechanisms makes this an unsatisfactory option. In many respects, the UN system of collective security attempts to balance idealist hopes with realist awareness, in that it provides a framework to facilitate collective action in response to a wide range of situations while recognising that this must be utilised in accordance with political realities, hence the conferment of discretionary powers upon the major powers whose perspectives will be central to the viability of effective action in any given situation.

As Kupchan and Kupchan argue, a system of collective security at its worst is likely to be equivalent to a balance of power model under more anarchic conditions at its best.[74] The reason is that 'should non-threatened states opt out of collective action, the remaining coalition would consist of the same directly threatened states as the alliance that would form' in the absence of a collective security system.[75] If

73 See further Downes, G.W. and Iida, K., 'Assessing the theoretical case against collective security,' in Downes, G.W. (ed.), *Collective Security beyond the Cold War* (Ann Arbor: University of Michigan Press, 1994), pp.17–40.

74 Kupchan and Kupchan, supra n34, p.55.

75 Kupchan and Kupchan, supra n34, p.55.

collective security can produce outcomes no worse than its non-existence would do, there is nothing to be lost by pursuing it.

There is a tendency to criticise the failings of the UN based upon unrealistic expectations of what is within its capabilities, overlooking the fact that it has made a positive difference in respect of many situations that have involved threats to international peace and security. The political environment within which it operates means that a collective security system like that established by the UN Charter does not and cannot respond to all threats to the peace which arise.[76] As much was recognised by its founders when crafting its very structure.[77] While ideally a collective response would remove any security threat or defeat any aggressor, the fact that collective security may only be effective in some instances does not mean that its utility is invalidated. Partial success is preferable to no success. The situations in which UN efforts have ameliorated threats to the peace will be demonstrated in subsequent chapters.

The case for collective security from a legal perspective is particularly persuasive. It has been shown that collective security's operation relies upon the existence of some form of institutional and normative framework through which it can be given effect. This has important consequences that add to the value of collective security. First, this framework can improve coordination between those states engaging in collective action, potentially improving its effectiveness. While collective defence arrangements can also offer states the opportunity to coordinate their approach to collective action, within a collective security system, the scale of this coordination is potentially wider due to the more universal scope of the membership and the fact that the ambit of collective security can extend to a much greater sphere of activity than a collective defence agreement. Furthermore, it may well be asked, why states would create and participate in institutions unless they perceived there to be benefits in doing so. That states do utilise the mechanisms of the UN in dealing with security issues would seem to suggest that they perceive there to be benefits in so doing for purposes of international cooperation.[78] The major powers also stand to benefit from taking on additional responsibility for the effective operation of the system.[79] Second, as argued above, through the creation of a normative framework, a collective security system provides standards, based upon shared values of the international community, by which it becomes possible to evaluate the behaviour of states. Hence, a collective security system can

76 Roberts and Zaum, supra n1, p.7.

77 See Chapter 2.

78 Keohane, R.O. and Martin, L.L., 'The promise of institutionalist theory,' *International Security*, 1995, v.20, n.1, pp.39–51.

79 See Krisch, N., 'The Security Council and the great powers,' in Lowe, V., Roberts, A., Welsh, J. and Zaum, D. (eds), *The United Nations Security Council and War* (Oxford: Oxford University Press, 2008), pp.133–153.

confer legitimacy upon the conduct of military action.[80] It is argued that this has enormous value for any collective action. Any action taken in accordance with the norms and procedures laid down in the system is likely to be perceived with greater legitimacy by the international community at large than an action undertaken by a state or a small group of states acting entirely upon their own initiative, because by participating within a collective security system, states are effectively accepting the normative and procedural framework which the system provides for determining when collective action will take place. It is notable that on several occasions states have sought the authorisation of the UN Security Council to undertake military operations, even in situations when it could have been possible to justify action on alternative legal grounds without recourse to the Council, for example to respond to Iraq's invasion of Kuwait even though this could have been justified by reference to the right of collective self-defence. Arguably, the motivating factor for such a course of action has been to maximise the perceived legitimacy of the action in question. Berdal, in his discussion of functions performed by the UN Security Council, places great emphasis on its role as a body capable of conferring legitimacy on international actions, and sees this as one of the dominant causes of the attention given to it by the US.[81]

There are clearly good reasons to pursue collective security. While it is difficult to dismiss the fact that its practice has been somewhat inconsistent, other considerations strongly suggest that it is a goal worth striving for. It has been demonstrated that the concept of collective security is potentially broad and can be given effect to in different ways. Increasingly in the practice of the UN, human security has come to dominate its collective security agenda. Although notions of security evolve, its goal and the basis upon which it rests are both constant. Collective security, to warrant that term, consists of a substantially universal arrangement by states to collectively tackle threats posed to the security of any of their number. The concept rests upon the assumption that 'peace is indivisible.'

Conclusion

The nature of collective security allows it to emerge as a strong means of attaining the maintenance of international security if effectively put into practice. It has been shown that collective security's effective functioning will ultimately depend upon its ability to satisfy certain requirements, which have never been completely fulfilled. The biggest problem for advocates of collective security springs from doubts cast upon the likelihood that states will equate their individual security

80 Claude, I.L., 'Collective legitimization as a political function of the United Nations,' in Kratochwil, F. and Mansfield, E.D. (eds), *International Organization: A Reader* (New York: Harper Collins, 1994), pp.192–201.

81 Berdal, M., 'The UN Security Council: Ineffective but indispensable,' *Survival*, 2003, v.45, n.2, pp.7–30.

with that of all other states and prove fully committed to the collective security enterprise. State practice will be shown to add weight to such a view in the following chapters. However, despite the fact that doubts exist over the utility of a system of collective security, important reasons have been set out as to why it remains a worthwhile goal to pursue. From a legal perspective, a collective security system has clear merits, namely its ability to enhance coordination between states participating in collective action, to provide a normative framework for action and to confer legitimacy upon operations conducted pursuant to the norms and procedures that it lays down. For such reasons, it is believed that the remainder of this book represents a worthwhile endeavour to explore the evolution of collective security as practised within the legal framework established by the UN Charter. The political dynamics of collective security are better left for the main part to scholars of international relations.

2

THE UN CHARTER'S SYSTEM OF COLLECTIVE SECURITY

Introduction

The principal objective of this chapter is to introduce the main features of the collective security system established by the UN Charter, with reference to the factors that influenced the UN's founders to shape the UN system in the manner in which they did, the respective roles of the Security Council and General Assembly within the system, and the dynamics of decision-making within the former body. In so doing, the competing themes running throughout this book are apparent. We see, on the one hand, evidence of a desire to create a flexible model of collective security capable of adaptation in its application. On the other hand, we see that the UN's founders envisaged a discretionary, selective system that would accommodate the interests of the major powers. Both of these perspectives are reinforced by the operation of the UN collective security system in practice.

This chapter does not purport to provide detailed legal analysis of the various collective security mechanisms established by the UN Charter. These are detailed substantively within the subsequent chapters of the book that deal with specific tools of the UN system for responding to threats to international peace and security.[1] Rather, this chapter is concerned with providing essential background to the later chapters' consideration of the tools of the UN collective security system. It is only possible to evaluate the utilisation of collective security measures in practice if there is some appreciation of the intention of the architects of the system that governs the application of such measures, and of the processes through which their utilisation would be possible.

1 See Chapters 4–7 particularly.

DOI: 10.4324/9781003518105-3

The chapter begins by briefly considering the experience of the League of Nations as the world's first attempt at collective security, lessons from which informed the UN's founders when shaping its successor organisation. The key stages in the emergence of the UN are then briefly detailed, before the remainder of the chapter is given over to outlining the key features of the UN collective security system and, more importantly, the factors affecting their inception.

The League of Nations

The creation of the League of Nations formed part of the Peace Settlement that ended World War I and represented the first attempt to establish a global collective security system. The horrors of war led to a consensus among the major international players of the period that nothing on this scale could ever be allowed to occur again, and that to ensure this required states to come together in an international system of collective security.[2] The League's primary purpose, outlined in its preamble, was to 'promote international co-operation and to achieve international peace and security.' Articles 10–17 of the Covenant of the League of Nations formed the core of its collective security system, the thrust of member states' obligations finding expression in Article 10, which provided that:

> The Members of the League undertake to respect and preserve as against external aggression the territorial integrity and existing political independence of all Members...In case of any such aggression or in case of any threat or danger of such aggression the Council shall advise upon the means by which this obligation shall be fulfilled.

The obligation assumed by the League's members evidenced a narrow legal conception of collective security, in contrast to the broader and more flexible approach which would characterise the UN Charter system. Subsequent articles built upon Article 10's core obligation, Article 16 being the most significant, providing for the application of both economic and military sanctions. However, the effectiveness of the League was hampered by both legal and structural defects and political problems. These would provide important lessons for the UN's founders.

The drafting of the Covenant of the League of Nations was far from ideal. No distinction was made between the roles of the Assembly and Council of the League. That both had essentially identical powers gave rise to the potential for conflict to arise between them.[3] Article 5's requirement of unanimous decision-making was

2 On the discussions leading to the creation of the League, see Macmillan, M., *Peacemakers: The Paris Peace Conference of 1919 and its Attempt to End War* (London: John Murray, 2001), pp.92–106.

3 See Articles 3 and 4. Both bodies were empowered to deal 'with any matter within the sphere of action of the League or affecting the peace of the world.'

also a potential hindrance to the League's ability to act, effectively enabling any one state to block action by the League. Ironically, as a consequence of Persia's negative vote, this provision prevented the adoption of a Canadian-sponsored resolution by the Assembly as early as 1923, which purported to leave it to each state individually to decide upon what measures it should take to comply with Article 10's obligation in any given case.[4] The Covenant also failed to outlaw the use of force, instead merely obliging member states to submit their disputes to the League for enquiry or to arbitration or judicial settlement, and to refrain from resorting to war until three months had passed from a report being made or an award being given.[5] The powers open to the League to deal with international disputes were certainly phrased in far more legalistic language than would come to flavour the UN Charter. Arguably, the League also suffered from the failure of the US to join it, despite the significant role played by President Wilson in its creation.[6] This deprived it of the input of a strong emerging power, whose great military potential was evidenced by the role it had played during World War One.

There were clearly weaknesses relating to the form that the League took. While these undoubtedly influenced the drafting of the UN Charter system of collective security, the main causes of the League's downfall were political. Significantly, in spite of its structural flaws the League enjoyed some early successes.[7] Three examples are particularly instructive of the potential that existed for disputes to be resolved under the League's auspices. In 1920, sovereignty over the Åland Islands was disputed by Finland and Sweden. After despatching a commission of enquiry, the Council decided that the Islands rightfully belonged to Finland subject to certain guarantees for the Swedish inhabitants.[8] This decision was accepted by both sides, the League's dispute resolution procedures proving successful.[9] The League also resolved the Corfu incident. Following the assassination of an Italian member of the Conference of Ambassadors on Greek soil, Italy invaded Corfu. Greece made a referral to the Council, which left the matter to the Conference of Ambassadors to resolve due to Italy's unwillingness to have the Council deal

4 See Wilson, P., *Aggression, Crime and International Security: Moral, Political and Legal Dimensions of International Relations* (Oxford: Routledge, 2009), pp.33–34.

5 Article 12.

6 On the US' role in the creation of the League and its subsequent relationship with it, see Fleming, D.F., *The United States and the League of Nations* (New York and London: G.P. Putnam & Sons, 1932). On the failure of the US to accede to League membership, see Ferrell, R.H., *Woodrow Wilson and World War I, 1917–1921* (New York: Harper & Row, 1985), pp.156–177. Ironically, Article 5 of the Covenant provided that the first meeting of the Assembly and Council would be summoned by the US President.

7 See also Lloyd, L., 'The League of Nations and the Settlement of Disputes,' *World Affairs*, 1995, v.157, n.4, pp.160–174.

8 L.N O.J. September 1921, 699. See Brown, P.M., 'The Åland Islands question,' *American Journal of International Law*, 1921, v.15, n.2, pp.268–272; Gregory, C.N., 'The neutralization of the Åland Islands,' *American Journal of International Law*, 1923, v.17, n.1, pp.65–76.

9 See Scott, G., *The Rise and Fall of the League of Nations* (London: Hutchinson, 1973), p.60.

with the matter. Both sides accepted the decision and Italy evacuated Corfu in due course. The League's attitude towards Italy's actions generally was central to its compliance.[10] A final illustration of the League's ability to effectively tackle conflict when it had the requisite degree of political will can be found in the League's response to the Greek–Bulgarian territorial dispute.[11] Following the conclusion of a ceasefire, a commission of enquiry was established to report upon the situation, after which reparations were fixed and suggestions made. Both sides accepted the proposals put to them. Viscount Cecil, a key player in the League, believed that Britain and France were both prepared to use force if the call to end hostilities was not met with,[12] underlining the importance of the attitudes of the major powers to the successful resolution of conflict. In addition, the 1928 Kellogg–Briand Pact suggested a willingness of states to build upon the League's provision, by committing themselves not to resort to war as an instrument of national policy. In a forerunner of the later emergence of UN peacekeeping, the League also showed that it was capable of successfully deploying forces, a 3,300-strong multinational force proving competent in ensuring that the Saar plebiscite ran smoothly in 1935.[13]

The political will necessary to make the League succeed began to decline in the 1930s, with the rise of totalitarian regimes that demonstrated a lack of respect for international law and felt free to violate the League Covenant whenever it provided obstacles to their expansionist foreign policy objectives. Germany, Italy and Japan all withdrew from the League,[14] and by September 1939, only Britain and France remained of the Council's major powers. The exit of these major powers and their increasing opposition to the League weakened its resolve to tackle aggressors in the years leading up to 1939, reinforcing the importance of major power commitment and universality of membership for the successful operation of any system of collective security. Three incidents are particularly illustrative of this. In 1931, Japan invaded the Chinese province of Manchuria, later establishing the puppet state of Manchukuo. Though China called for assistance, the League did no more than call for Japanese withdrawal and recommend negotiations.[15] None of this had any effect, representing a clear failure of the League to apply collective measures against a violator of the Covenant.[16] As Scott bluntly states

10 Scott, ibid, pp.86–88.

11 See Barros, J., *The League of Nations and the Great Powers* (London: Oxford University Press, 1970); Scott, supra n9, pp.126–130.

12 Viscount Cecil, *A Great Experiment* (London: Jonathan Cape, 1941), p.175.

13 See Scott, supra n9, pp.296–300; Walters, F.P., *A History of the League of Nations* (London: Oxford University Press, 1952), pp.586–598; Hill, C.J., 'Great Britain and the Saar Plebiscite of 13 January 1935,' *Journal of Contemporary History*, 1974, v.9, n.2, pp.121–142.

14 Germany and Japan withdrew in 1933, Italy in 1937.

15 See 'League of Nations Assembly report on the Sino-Japanese dispute,' *AJIL Supp*, 1933, v.27, pp.119–154. For discussion see Walters, supra n13, pp.465–499; Scott, supra n9, pp.207–241.

16 See Smith, S.R., *The Manchurian Crisis, 1931–1932: A Tragedy in International Relations* (New York: Greenwood Press, 1970).

the case, 'Japan had committed blatant aggression and she had got away with it.'[17] The League's response to Italy's invasion of Ethiopia in 1935 sent out another wrong message to aggressors. Ethiopia's emperor Haile Selassie made numerous pleas to the League, none of which prevented the country's fall and the occupying power's declaration of an Italian Empire of Ethiopia. Attempts at achieving a peaceful solution having proved fruitless, any suggestion that assistance be given to Ethiopia was never on the cards. France and Britain, the two major League powers, were anxious not to upset Mussolini, seeing him as a potential ally against Hitler in the event of any subsequent war with Germany.[18] This attitude sits at odds with commitment to the 'indivisibility of peace' which requires that all security threats are deemed of concern to the system as a whole, irrespective of their source or the identity of the prima facie most directly affected state. It has been argued that, 'from the moment … that Ethiopia first laid her case before the League, the British and French delegates did their best to find a procedure which should be acceptable to Italy.'[19] Similarly, Beck suggested that the UK and France 'assigned greater importance to the preservation of good relations with Italy than upholding the interest of either Ethiopia or the League.'[20] Though sanctions were applied against Italy under Article 16, these were soon dropped when Ethiopia's defeat became final, providing a perfect example of collective security ideals giving way to perceived national self-interests.[21] The final nail in the League's coffin came with the Munich Agreement of 1938, which was a blatant act of appeasement of a totalitarian regime, and a statement of the unwillingness of the League's major remaining powers to challenge Adolf Hitler's demands. By signing the agreement, Britain and France agreed that Germany should have the Sudetenland area of Czechoslovakia. This represented a significant step back from the collective security ideals that underpinned the League, in that a small power was abandoned in the face of aggression, notwithstanding treaty obligations. The subsequent invasions of Czechoslovakia and Poland were never submitted to the League, which at this point was effectively dead. By the time World War II broke out most members of the League had declared themselves no longer obliged to join in any sanctions or action against aggression should they not want to.[22] Notwithstanding the perceived failure of the League, it is arguably the case that without it, there may never have been a UN. In some respects, it provided a template to be built upon

17 Scott, supra n9, p.241.
18 Scott, supra n9, p.320.
19 Walters, supra n13, p.629.
20 Beck, P.J., 'The League of Nations and the Great Powers, 1936–1940,' *World Affairs*, 1995, v.157, n.4, pp.175–189, at p.176.
21 See Walters, supra n13, pp.623–691; Scott, supra n79 pp.317–368; Barros, J., *Britain, Greece and the Politics of Sanctions: Ethiopia 1935–1936* (London: Royal Historical Society, 1982); Baer, G.W., 'Sanctions and security: The League of Nations and the Italian-Ethiopian war, 1935–1936,' *International Organization*, 1973, v.27, pp.165–179.
22 See Walters, supra n13, pp.777–783.

and improved. As argued by Pedersen, 'the League mattered. In some areas … it midwifed regimes that exist to this day, and in other areas it articulated norms that, very partially observed at the time, have gained in authority.'[23]

The creation of the United Nations

The creation of the UN was the outcome of a series of discussions beginning during World War II and culminating in the San Francisco Conference of 1945, at which the UN Charter was adopted. The origins of the UN have been much detailed elsewhere,[24] but the principal motivation for the creation of a new international collective security system can be attributed to the devastating effects of World War II, and the resulting feeling that a new order was needed to protect against a recurrence of this. As Luck comments, 'Undoubtedly the founders were determined, first and foremost, to devise an international instrument that could help prevent the outbreak of a third interstate war of global proportions in the twentieth century.'[25] This is reflected in the preamble to the UN Charter, the opening lines of which state that, 'We the peoples of the United Nations determined to save succeeding generations from the scourge of war, which twice in our lifetime has brought untold sorrow to mankind.' The planning of a new post-war international order began at an early stage, the role of the US in the early stages of this process being particularly important.[26] The Atlantic Charter of 1941,[27] a joint declaration of principles by US President Roosevelt and British Prime Minister Churchill, can be seen as the first step towards the creation of a new international collective security organisation.[28] Among the principles advanced was the belief that all nations must come to abandon the use of force,[29] ultimately a core principle of the eventual UN Charter.[30] The content of the Atlantic Charter was endorsed

23 Pedersen, S., 'Back to the League of Nations,' *The American Historical Review*, 2007, v.112, n.4, pp.1091–1117, at p.1116. See also Weiss, T.G., 'The United Nations: Before, during and after 1945,' *International Affairs*, 2015, v.91, n.6, pp.1221–1235.

24 See, for example, Ryan, S., *The United Nations and International Politics* (Basingstoke and London: Macmillan, 2000), Chapter 1; Simma, B. et al (eds), *The Charter of the United Nations: A Commentary* (2nd ed.) (Oxford: Oxford University Press, 2002), pp.1–12; Luard, E., *A History of the United Nations Volume 1* (London: Macmillan, 1982), Chapters 2–3.

25 Luck, E.C., 'A Council for all seasons: The creation of the Security Council and its relevance today,' in Lowe, V., Roberts, A., Welsh, J. and Zaum, D. (eds), *The United Nations Security Council and War* (Oxford: Oxford University Press, 2008), pp.61–85, at p.62.

26 See, e.g., Wertheim, S., 'Instrumental Internationalism: The American Origins of the United Nations, 1940–3,' *Journal of Contemporary History*, 2019, v.54, n.2, pp.265–283.

27 For text, see Royal Institute of International Affairs, *United Nations Documents 1941–1945* (London and New York: Oxford University Press, 1946), pp.9–10.

28 Hoopes, T. and Brinkley, D., *FDR and the Creation of the U.N* (New Haven and London: Yale University Press, 1997), pp.36–40.

29 Point 8.

30 Article 2 (4).

in the Declaration of the United Nations, signed by 26 allied states on 1 January 1942, the first time that the term 'United Nations' was used to refer to a group of states acting collectively.[31]

The first serious discussions upon the creation of a new collective security organisation took place in Moscow during 1943. The participants – the USSR, UK, US and China – issued a declaration in which they recognised the need to establish an international organisation charged with the maintenance of international peace and security at the earliest opportunity.[32] The importance of major power commitment to the project was clearly recognised. The provisions that eventually went on to form the content of the UN Charter emerged from the Dumbarton Oaks talks of 1944 and the San Francisco Conference of 1945. At Dumbarton Oaks, discussions first took place between the US, UK and USSR, followed by separate discussions between the former two states and China for political reasons.[33] The aim was to reach agreement between the major allied powers upon a set of proposals for a new collective security organisation, which could then be put to an international conference of states, charged with drawing up the proposed organisation's Charter.[34] For the most part, this was achieved, and the proposals which emanated from the Dumbarton Oaks discussions[35] would go on to form the basis of much of the eventual UN Charter. However, the fact that agreement was not yet possible on the issue of voting procedures within the proposed Security Council illustrated the fact that there remained tensions between the major powers that could threaten the potential of the new organisation.[36]

The San Francisco Conference comprised states that had signed the UN declaration in 1942, had since joined the Allied forces during the war or were otherwise invited at the behest of one of the sponsoring powers. While the final Charter was modelled heavily upon the proposals to have emerged from the Dumbarton Oaks discussions, as will be seen, some amendments were made in response to pressures exerted by smaller states. The UN Charter was approved on 26 June 1945 and came into effect on 10 January 1946.

31 For text, see Simma, B. et al (eds), *The Charter of the United Nations: A Commentary* (Oxford: Oxford University Press, 1994), p.11.
32 For text, see Simma et al, ibid. p. 13.
33 See Ostrower, G.B., *The United Nations and the United States* (New York: Twayne Publishers, 1998), p.19.
34 Unfortunately, there are no official records of the Dumbarton Oaks discussions. See Hilderbrand, R.C., *Dumbarton Oaks* (Chapel Hill and London: University of North Carolina Press, 1990); Campbell, T.M., *Masquerade Peace* (Tallahassee: Florida State University Press, 1973), Chapter 2.
35 On these, see Goodrich, L.M. and Hambro, E., *Charter of the United Nations: Commentary and Documents* (2nd ed.) (London: Stevens & Sons, 1949), pp.6–20.
36 See below.

The UN Charter Framework

Purposes and principles

The purposes of the UN give the first indication of the broad conception of collective security envisaged for it. Notwithstanding its other objectives,[37] that collective security is its principal raison d'être is made clear by Article 1 (1) which states its first purpose as being:

> to maintain international peace and security, and to that end: to take effective collective measures for the prevention and removal of threats to the peace, and for the suppression of acts of aggression or other breaches of the peace, and to bring about by peaceful means, and in conformity with the principles of justice and international law, adjustment or settlement of international disputes or situations which might lead to a breach of the peace.

The very language used in Article 1 (1) in itself advances a conception of collective security which goes beyond merely responding to inter-state aggression to cover other threats to the peace, and which also envisages the use of non-military responses to address these.

Article 2 sets out a series of principles in accordance with which the UN shall act. In apparent contradiction of the special status given to the Security Council's permanent members,[38] the sovereign equality of all members is a core Charter principle.[39] This is best understood in legal terms as indicating a guarantee of formal equality of rights enjoyed by states,[40] as opposed to genuine substantive equality within the most important decision-making processes which take place within the UN system, in the Security Council where political considerations may give rise to inconsistencies within outcomes. The UN Charter nevertheless strives for universality of membership, this being open to 'all peace-loving states' accepting the obligations of membership.[41] While the admission of new members is subject to the approval of the Security Council,[42] facilitating politicisation of this process,[43] no member state has had its rights and privileges suspended or been

37 Broadly speaking, these encompass the development of friendly relations among states, international cooperation in problems of economic, social, cultural and humanitarian characteristics, and encouragement of respect for human rights. See Articles 1 (2), (3) and (4).

38 See below.

39 Article 2 (1).

40 Goodrich and Hambro, supra n35, p.100.

41 Article 4 (1).

42 Article 4 (2).

43 See below in the content of the exercise of the power of veto within the Council.

expelled from the UN even though powers to take such action reside in the UN's principal political organs.[44]

Other key principles within the UN Charter demonstrate an aim to build upon earlier approaches to collective security. In providing that members shall refrain from the threat or use of force against the territorial integrity or political independence of any other state, Article 2 (4) marks the first attempt to outlaw the use of force – as opposed to the vaguer concept of 'war' – in international relations. Although debates continue concerning the extent of Article 2 (4)'s prohibition and the exceptions to it which exist,[45] the underlying objective of the provision is clear: the centralisation of the power to utilise military force in the hands of the Security Council. Except in cases of self-defence, the unilateral use of military force is outlawed. Article 2 (4) has evolved into a principle of customary international law,[46] and its importance is further reinforced by the obligation of states to settle their disputes peacefully.[47] While Article 2 (7) prohibits the UN from intervening 'in matters essentially within the domestic jurisdiction of any state,' it is expressly stated that this 'shall not prejudice the application of enforcement measures under Chapter VII,' in effect providing that if the Security Council chooses to adopt such measures under Chapter VII, the domestic jurisdiction limitation is no longer applicable. As its approach to the question of what constitute threats to the peace under Article 39[48] – the determination of the existence of such threats being a necessary trigger for the possibility of enforcement action – has broadened, the domestic jurisdiction limitation contained in Article 2 (7) has arguably declined in significance. As Nolte argues, it 'has been increasingly eroded and emptied of substance … because more and more matters are no longer recognized as belonging to the domestic jurisdiction of states.'[49] Human rights abuses are the clearest example of this, it increasingly being recognised by the international community that a state is not free to mistreat its own population.[50]

44 Articles 5–6. A possible exception is found in the case of the Republic of China (Taiwan), which was replaced as a member by the People's Republic of China pursuant to GA Res 2758 (1971).

45 See, for example, Henderson, C., *The Use of Force and International Law* (Cambridge: CUP, 2018); Gray, C., *International Law and the Use of Force* (4th ed.) (Oxford and New York: Oxford University Press, 2018); Corten, O., *The Law Against War: The Prohibition on the Use of Force in Contemporary International Law* (2nd ed.) (Oxford: Hart, 2021).

46 *Military and Paramilitary Activities in and against Nicaragua*, Merits, ICJ Rep (1986), p.14.

47 Article 2 (3).

48 See below on the development of the concept of 'threat to the peace' as a means of empowering the Security Council to involve itself in a wider range of situations. See also Manusama, K., *The United Nations Security Council in the Post-Cold War Era* (Leiden: Brill, 2006), pp.51–99.

49 Nolte, G., 'Article 2 (7),' in Simma et al (eds), supra n24, pp.148–171.

50 This is perhaps best evidenced by the General Assembly's endorsement of the *Responsibility to Protect* doctrine at the 2005 World Summit. See GA Res. 60/1, paras.138–139. The doctrine, and its relevance to the UN's collective security practice, is explained further in the next chapter.

The Key Bodies within the UN Collective Security System

There are six principal UN organs, created under the Charter.[51] Of these, the two key political bodies which enjoy specific powers and responsibilities pertaining to the maintenance of international peace and security are the Security Council and the General Assembly. An important contrast can be drawn between the status and functions of these two bodies. The former is designed to be a small, executive-styled body with a membership of just fifteen states at any one time.[52] While ten of these are elected to non-renewable two-year terms,[53] five permanent members were created by the Charter: the US, UK, USSR (subsequently replaced by Russia),[54] China and France.[55] In keeping with the concert-style system of collective security envisaged by the UN's founders, these are afforded privileged status and conferred with the power of veto over proposed action.[56] The Council is conferred with primary, albeit not exclusive, responsibility for the maintenance of international peace and security.[57] It is in support of this purpose that its decisions are considered mandatory and binding upon all UN member states, who are expected to 'accept and carry out' them.[58] Its robust powers extend to the application of economic sanctions and the initiation of military action under provisions found in Chapter VII of the Charter. The conferral of mandatory powers on the Council was a significant development from the situation existing within the League of Nations, whereby member states were not legally required to implement its decisions or recommendations.[59] The intention of the UN's founders in conferring the Security Council with mandatory enforcement powers is evident. They sought a Council for 'all contingencies.'[60] A concert-style system of collective security was clearly envisaged in which threats to the peace were to be tackled by a small executive body, dominated by the world's major powers. A much-criticised problem of the League of Nations had been the absence of several great powers,

51 Article 7.

52 Article 23 (1). Originally, there were only 11 members, increased to 15 in 1963 to account for the surge in the overall size of the UN membership. See GA Res 1991 (XVIII).

53 Article 23 (2).

54 Upon the dissolution of the USSR in late 1991, Russia succeeded to its membership within the United Nations with the support of most other former Soviet constituent republics. This occurred without any formal act being taken to effect this change at the UN level. For a contemporary appraisal of legal controversies arising from this, see Blum, Y., 'Russia Takes Over the Soviet Union's Seat at the United Nations,' *European Journal of International Law*, 1992, v.3, pp.354–361.

55 Article 23 (1).

56 Article 27 (3).

57 Article 24 (1).

58 Article 25.

59 While none of the provisions of the League's Covenant suggest that adopted measures are to have binding effect, the unanimity requirement in decision-making imposed by Article 5 effectively empowers any state to prevent the adoption of measures which it does not wish to enforce.

60 Luck, supra n25, p.63.

most notably the US,[61] and the special role afforded to major powers within the UN is an indication of the extent to which its effectiveness as a collective security organisation was seen as being dependent upon them. The role of the US, USSR and UK – three of the five permanent members – had been critical to allied successes in World War II. As Delbruck notes, to protect against another major war – clearly the primary concern of states in the context of the period – the role played by these states within the UN's collective security system would be crucial.[62] The special position of the major powers originated in the proposals that emerged from the Dumbarton Oaks discussions. Their experience of cooperation in the leadership of the allied campaign during World War II served as the basis for their agreement that the future maintenance of international peace and security by the UN would require them to take a leading role.

Although the main focus of this book is upon activity taken under the auspices of the Security Council, the role of the General Assembly must not be overlooked. It has a universal membership whereby each member state has equivalent status in decision-making processes.[63] However, its powers are only of a recommendatory nature[64] and although the Assembly has specific functions assigned to it under the Charter – for example, to set the UN budget[65] – its role within matters of international peace and security is clearly subsidiary to that of the Council.[66]

The Security Council and the power of veto

A major source of controversy from the inception of the UN project was that of the veto power conferred upon permanent members of the Security Council.[67] While decisions on procedural matters require a qualified majority by virtue of Article 27 (2), Article 27 (3) requires that those concerning non-procedural matters enjoy the concurring votes of all five permanent members, effectively giving each one of them the ability to veto action by the Council. The existence of the veto undoubtedly undermines the ideal of collective security, allowing for action to be blocked even in circumstances in which a significant threat to international peace and security may have arisen, on the basis of just a single state's opposition. However, its inclusion within the Charter can also be taken as recognition that the circumstances required for the operation of ideal collective security were unlikely to be present on all occasions due to a lack of major power consensus on the manner

61 Claude, I.L., *Swords Into Plowshares* (3rd ed.) (London: University of London Press, 1964), pp.80–81.
62 Delbruck, J., 'Article 23,' in Simma et al, supra n31, pp.398–399.
63 Articles 9 (1) and 18 (1).
64 Article 10.
65 Article 17.
66 See Article 12 and discussion below.
67 See Lee, D.E., 'The genesis of the veto,' *International Organization*, 1947, v.1, pp.33–42.

in which the UN system should operate and arguably provides the best example of the extent to which the UN system established in 1945 was shaped by political considerations and intended to be selective in terms of its application.

While the major powers were agreed upon the principle of a veto power, they were unable to agree at Dumbarton Oaks upon the very nature and extent that it should take. As discussed at length elsewhere, the dispute largely centred on the question of whether it should be exercisable by a permanent member in respect of a situation in which it was a party to the dispute in question.[68] Nonetheless, they clearly envisaged a very selective form of collective security being implemented within the UN system, in which it would not be possible for action to be taken in the face of the opposition of a major power. A model for the veto power was eventually agreed upon by the major powers at the Yalta Conference, in which it was agreed that the power would not extend to purely procedural questions or those concerning the pacific settlement of disputes to which the relevant permanent member was a party.[69]

The concerns of smaller states at San Francisco over the scope of the veto power have been the source of much discussion.[70] These concerns evidenced fears that effective UN action may prove impossible where there was insufficient harmony among the major powers. However, attempts to restrict the use of the veto were unsuccessful. For example, an Australian amendment, which sought to define the procedural matters in respect of which the veto would not apply, was rejected,[71] thus effectively meaning that a decision as to whether an issue was procedural or not could be subject to the possibility of veto. The sponsoring powers were adamant in opposing the Australian proposal, the US delegate arguing that unanimity was required 'all along the line,' as any dispute could worsen at a later stage.[72] Other proposed amendments to the power of veto were likewise unsuccessful.[73]

Uncertainty over the scope of the veto power led participants at San Francisco to submit to the sponsoring powers a memorandum containing 23 questions concerning its exercise.[74] In response, the four sponsors issued a joint statement on

68 Goodrich and Hambro, supra n35, p.21; Simma, B., Brunner, S. and Kaul, H.-P., 'Article 27,' in Simma et al (eds), supra n24, pp.476–523, at pp.501–507; Campbell, supra n34, p.38 et seq; Hilderbrand, supra n34, Chapter 8; Hoopes and Brinkley, supra n28, pp.145–155.

69 See Wilcox, F.O., 'The Yalta voting formula,' *American Political Science Review*, 1945, v.39, n.5, pp.943–956.

70 Campbell, supra n34, Chapter 8; Luard, supra n24, pp.45–49; Goodrich and Hambro, supra n35, pp.215–220; Simma, Brunner and Kaul, supra n68, pp.481–482.

71 UNCIO XI, pp.492–495.

72 Ibid.

73 See, for example, UNCIO XI, pp.693–698, 772–778.

74 UNCIO XI, pp.699–709.

the Security Council voting procedure.[75] This statement sought to justify a broad veto power on the grounds that:

> In view of the primary responsibilities of the permanent members, they could not be expected, in the present condition of the world, to assume the obligation to act in so serious a matter as the maintenance of international peace and security in consequence of a decision in which they had not concurred.[76]

That the major powers' insistence upon the veto power won the day is indicative of other states' recognition that this was the price to be paid for ensuring the participation of these powers within the UN. The emphasis placed upon the power of veto by the sponsoring powers at San Francisco is illustrated by Bennett in describing how 'Senator Connally of the United States dramatized the intransigence of the Big Five by tearing to pieces a copy of the proposed Charter and announcing that without the veto there would be no Charter.'[77] This would appear to offer firm evidence of the significance that the major powers attached to the power of veto as a fundamental prerequisite for them to undertake leadership roles within the UN. The system of collective security envisaged was, in the words of the Mexican delegate at San Francisco, one 'in which the mice could be stamped out but one in which the lions would not be restrained.'[78]

Claude writes that:

> The veto was adopted, not because it was believed that it would never be used, but because it was expected that occasions would arise when it should and would be used. It is difficult to believe that the major powers worked as hard as they did to secure acceptance of the veto provision in the conviction that it would be superfluous.[79]

This analysis appears logical, especially in light of the frequency with which the veto came to be exercised during the Cold War period: 121 times by the USSR and 57 times by the US.[80] The very existence of the veto power evidences an apparently limited commitment on the part of the major powers towards collective

75 UNCIO XI, pp.711–714. For discussion, see Gross, L., 'The double veto and the four-power statement on voting in the Security Council,' *Harvard Law Review*, 1953, v.67, n.2, pp.251–280, at pp.259–270.

76 Ibid, Pt.I, para.9.

77 Bennett, A.L., *International Organizations: Principles and Issues* (London: Prentice Hall International, 1991), p.48.

78 Claude, I.L., *Power and International Relations* (New York: Random House, 1962), p.159.

79 Ibid.

80 Bailey, S.D., *The Procedure of the UN Security Council* (2nd ed.) (Oxford: Clarendon Press, 1988), p.209.

security, and the adoption of the veto itself may be seen as an acknowledgement of the fact that the major powers had serious reservations as to their ability to forge unity in the post-war period, and wanted to safeguard against any action being taken which ran contrary to their individual interests. It is, however, possible to overstate the practical significance of the veto power over the longer term. As noted by Gifkins, 'situations where the threat of a veto blocks a resolution in its entirety are rare.'[81] Often the looming existence of the veto power will instead result in resolutions being crafted in language which can be tolerated by all permanent members.[82] Nonetheless, the veto has served to prevent the adoption of resolutions in respect of some important matters or incidents. Although its usage over time has declined, it has been utilised as a tool of a permanent member in the minority on the Council to prevent criticism of itself or an ally, or otherwise block a course of action to which it was strongly opposed.[83] During the Cold War period, the USSR invoked the veto to torpedo applications for admission on the part of several newly emergent states,[84] and to shield itself from international condemnation for its interventions in Hungary and Czechoslovakia.[85] In later years, the US made use of the veto on a number of occasions to prevent criticism of Israel in respect of some of its defence and foreign policy actions taken against neighbouring states or within occupied territory,[86] a policy which has continued up to the present day.[87] Principally exercised by the USSR/Russia and the US,[88] after a decline in usage during the earlier years of the post–Cold War period,[89] the veto has undergone a fresh resurgence in the past decade as tensions between the major

81 Gifkins, J., 'Beyond the veto: Roles in UN Security Council Decision-Making,' *Global Governance*, 2021, v.27, pp.1–24, at p.7.

82 Ibid.

83 That the USSR was the source of most vetoes during the earlier decades of the UN era is attributable to the fact that it was within a minority in a western-dominated Council. The US and other Western permanent members had little need to exercise a veto as they could invariably muster the requisite number of votes to defeat a draft resolution which they opposed. As the political balance within the Council shifted, the US came to exercise more vetoes from the 1970s onwards.

84 The first such vetoes concerned membership applications from Transjordan, Ireland and Portugal in 1946. See UN Doc. S/PV.57. Numerous vetoes followed in respect of applications over the following years, including Vietnam, Laos and Cambodia in 1952. See UN Docs. S/PV.603, S/2758, S/2759, S/2760.

85 On Hungary, see UN Docs. S/PV.754 & S/3730/Rev.1. On Czechoslovakia, see UN Docs. S/PV.1443 & S/8761.

86 See, e.g., UN Docs. S/PV.1662 & S/10784.

87 See, e.g., UN Docs. S/PV.9552 & S/2024/173.

88 As of July 2024, France had only exercised 7 vetoes alone and a further nine in conjunction with the UK and/or US. China had only exercised 3 alone and 16 in conjunction with Russia. The UK had exercised 12 alone, 16 in conjunction with France and/or the US.

89 During the 1990s, for example, only nine vetoes were exercised in total.

powers have generated disagreement over events such as the Syrian Civil War,[90] Russia's invasion of Ukraine[91] and the Israel–Gaza conflict.[92]

The actual practice of the Security Council in terms of the exercise of the veto has seen something of a departure from what might appear to be the strict requirements of Article 27 (3). Although that provision states that decisions of the Council require the 'concurring votes of the permanent members,' suggesting that they must have received the positive vote of all five permanent members, the practice of the Council has been not to treat abstentions as amounting to negative votes. This has not been particularly controversial. Arguably it represents a sensible approach, as to treat an abstention as a negative vote would be effectively to force permanent members to take an affirmative decision to support or block a specific decision when they may wish to do neither. Such a rigid approach would also produce more situations in which Security Council decision-making is impossible,[93] and the more sensible approach taken evidences an instance of the flexible development of key provisions of the UN collective security apparatus in a manner that enables it to be applied with a greater degree of success.

Decision-making by the Security Council under Chapter VII: The importance of Article 39

The enforcement powers conferred upon the Security Council by Chapter VII, to respond to threats to international peace and security, are extensive. While under Article 2 (4) UN member states undertake to 'refrain from the threat or use of force against the territorial integrity or political independence of any state, or in any manner inconsistent with the purposes of the United Nations,' the enforcement powers afforded to the Security Council permit it to initiate military action in response to a range of situations which go beyond simply responding to one state's use of force against another. Article 39 has been described as the 'gateway provision'[94] to these enforcement powers. It empowers the Security Council to

90 Russia and China exercised a series of vetoes on draft resolutions concerning the Syrian Civil War. See, e.g., UN Docs. S/PV.6627, S/2011/612, S/PV.6711, S/2012/77, S/PV.6810, S/2012/538, S/PV.7180, S/2014/348.

91 As would be expected, Russia vetoed an attempt by the Security Council to pass comment on its invasion of Ukraine. See UN Docs. S/PV.8879 & S/2022/155.

92 Draft resolutions pertaining to the situation in respect of Israel/Gaza following the Hamas attack on Israel of 7 October 2023 have been vetoed by the US, Russia and China on account of the wording contained. Draft resolutions S/2023/773, S/2023/970, and S/2024/173 were all vetoed by the US. Russia and China in turn vetoed draft resolutions S/2023/792 and S/2024/239.

93 Of all the permanent members, China has availed itself of its right of abstention the most often. See Holland, C., 'Chinese attitudes to international law: China, the Security Council, sovereignty, and intervention,' *New York University Journal of International Law and Politics Online Forum*, July 2012, v.51, pp.1–44.

94 White, N.D., *Keeping the Peace: The United Nations and the Maintenance of International Peace and Security* (2nd ed.) (Manchester and New York: Manchester University Press, 1997), p.173.

determine the existence of a 'threat to the peace, breach of the peace, or act of aggression,' following which it may respond to the existence of such a situation by adopting non-military sanctions or, if these are considered inadequate, by choosing to apply military enforcement measures. The language contained in Article 39 provides for a broader approach to collective security than that provided for under the League of Nations Covenant – where members were obliged to offer a collective response only in cases of aggression against one of their number[95] – allowing the Council flexibility in bringing a potentially wide range of situations within its remit for the possible application of enforcement measures. However, it also builds in an element of discretion to the operation of collective security within the UN system. This warrants the conclusion of one study of the Security Council, that it constitutes a

> selective security system … in which it is not objective criteria that determine whether, or how meaningfully the Council will get involved in a conflict, but rather the interplay of interest-based calculations of Council members, their allies, countries potentially contributing troops to peacekeeping operations, and often the conflict states themselves.[96]

This, of course, challenges a core assumption of ideal collective security: that all threats anywhere will meet with the common concern and action of the international community.

The conceptualisation of security threats within the national policy strategies individually adopted by the P5 was considered in the previous chapter, and these may have some bearing upon their attitudes to situations which appear on the Security Council's agenda. China, for example, has a long-standing practice of placing emphasis upon principles of non-intervention and state sovereignty in evaluating potential responses to matters brought within the Council's remit.[97] While its position has evolved somewhat in this respect,[98] it has served as the basis for abstentions in respect of a number of resolutions tabled in the Council, China having abstained on votes with greater frequency than any other permanent member.[99] While a degree of principle may be detected in such an approach, divisions within the Council's decision-making processes invariably arise from political tensions. The examples alluded to above within the context of discussion of the

95 Article 10.

96 Von Einsiedel, S., Malone, D.M. and Ugarte, B.S., *The United Nations Security Council in an Age of Great Power Rivalry* (Tokyo: United Nations University Working Paper Series, 2015), p.7.

97 See, e.g., Holland, supra n93; MacLeod, L., 'China's Security Council engagement: The Impact of Normative and Causal Beliefs,' *Global Governance*, 2017, v.23, n.3, pp.383–401.

98 See ibid.

99 See Wuthnow, J., *Chinese Diplomacy and the UN Security Council: Beyond the Veto* (London: Routledge, 2012), pp.12–37.

veto power serve as illustrative cases in point, permanent members' relationships with the states or actors forming the focus of debate in given cases being central to the positions which they choose to adopt. Of course, no decisions can be taken by the P5 acting alone, a qualified majority of the Council's full membership being required to act. Thus, the non-permanent membership should not be omitted in discussions of the decisions which the Council is able to reach or failures to act on its part. The P5 go to some lengths to secure the support of non-permanent members for resolutions they intend to table, unanimity being a highly valued commodity.[100] Non-permanent members may be particularly influential where they have special understanding of or interest in a given situation which they are able to lead the Council's deliberation of.[101] However, notwithstanding this potential capacity, the unique ability of the P5 to individually block action means that the non-permanent members cannot override the wishes or objections of them, but must rather cooperate with them if they wish to further any particular cause.

In practice, the Security Council has opted to categorise most situations in respect of which it has considered the application of Chapter VII measures as 'threats to the peace.' While the determination that there has been an 'act of aggression' has not featured in the practice of the Council,[102] more serious situations involving inter-state armed conflict have been categorised by it as 'breaches of the peace.' However, this term has only rarely been used, reserved for such serious instances of inter-state conflict as the Korean War,[103] the Falklands conflict,[104] Iraq's invasion of Kuwait[105] and the Iran–Iraq War.[106] For legal purposes, it is not particularly important which of the terms included in Article 39 is used by the Council, as all open up the possibility of enforcement measures being adopted under Chapter VII. As noted in the previous chapter, the Security Council has over time broadened the notion of what can constitute a threat to the peace to the point where a wide range of situations are potentially amenable to action under Chapter VII.[107] Indeed, it can be argued that 'most of the matters on which the Council

100 Gifkins, supra n81, pp.9–14.

101 For illustrative examples of such non-permanent member influence, see Farrall, J., Loiselle, M.-E., Michaelsen, C., Prantl, J. and Whalan, J., 'Elected member influence in the United Nations Security Council,' *Leiden Journal of International Law*, 2020, v.33, n.1, pp.101–115; Pay, V.N. and Postolski, R., 'Power and Diplomacy in the United Nations Security Council: The Influence of Elected Members,' *The International Spectator: Italian Journal of International Affairs*, 2022, v.57, n.2, pp.1–17.

102 See Frowein, J.A. and Krisch, N., 'Article 39,' in Simma et al (eds) supra n24, pp.717–729, at p.722.

103 SC Res 82 (1950).

104 SC Res 502 (1982).

105 SC Res 660 (1990).

106 A breach of the peace was also found to arise as a result of the Iran-Iraq war; SC Res 598 (1987).

107 See Franck, T.M., 'The Security Council and "Threats to the Peace": Some remarks on remarkable recent developments,' in Dupuy, R.J. (ed.), *The Development of the Role of the Security Council* (Dordrecht, Boston and London: Martinus Nijhoff, 1993), pp.83–110. For a more recent,

spends its time these days ... were not even mentioned in the Charter.'[108] For example, humanitarian crises,[109] the removal of democratically elected regimes[110] and the failure to hand over suspects wanted in connection with terrorist charges[111] are just some of the situations to have triggered the determination of the existence of threats to the peace within the meaning of Article 39. As early as its 1992 summit, the Council explicitly recognised that, 'The non-military sources of instability in the economic, social, humanitarian and ecological fields have become threats to peace and security.'[112] The evolution of understandings of the scope of threats to the peace has only continued to grow. For example, although tensions within the P5 have prevented a formal determination under Article 39 being adopted, there is growing support for the contention that climate change per se represents a threat to international peace and security.[113] At the same time, the Council has proven more willing to conceptualise public health epidemics and pandemics in security terms. Building on its earlier characterisation of the Ebola epidemic as giving rise to a threat to international peace and security,[114] in the wake of the global pandemic which took hold in 2020, it determined COVID-19 to similarly fall within the scope of Article 39.[115] Clearly, collective security under the UN Charter has been conceived in broader terms than the League of Nations model's concern with joining together to aid a state that has been the victim of aggression. Of course, one consequence of a broad conception of collective security is that

more comprehensive investigation of the P5's approach to the determination of threats to the peace, see Paige, T.P., *Petulant and Contrary: Approaches by the Permanent Five Members of the UN Security Council to the Concept of 'threat to the Peace' Under Article 39 of the UN Charter* (Leiden: Brill, 2019).

108 Luck, supra n25, p.62.

109 Arguably, the first determination that a humanitarian crisis posed a threat to the peace came in the form of resolution 688 (1991), which deemed the consequences of Iraq's repression of its northern Kurdish population to threaten international peace and security. The first determination of the occurrence of a threat to the peace arising from the consequences of internal conflict is found in resolution 733 (1992) relative to Somalia.

110 For example, in Haiti; see SC Res 841 (1993).

111 For example, in the case of Libya's failure to hand over the suspected Lockerbie bombers; see SC Res 748 (1992).

112 UN Doc S/PV.3046, at p.124.

113 See, e.g., Wilson, G., 'Climate Change as a "Threat to the Peace": Responding to Climate Change through the UN Collective Security System,' *International Journal of Climate Change: Impacts and Responses*, 2020, v.12, n.3, pp.33–44; Nevitt, M., 'Is Climate Change a Threat to International Peace and Security?' *Michigan Journal of International Law*, 2021, v.42, n.3, pp.527–579.

114 SC Res 2177 (2014). See Wilson, G., 'Collective Security, 'Threats to the Peace,' and the Ebola Outbreak,' *Journal of the Philosophy of International Law*, 2015, v.6, n.1, pp.1–23.

115 SC Res 2532 (2020). See Pobje, E., 'COVID-19 and the Scope of the UN Security Council's Mandate to Address Non-Traditional Threats to International Peace and Security,' *ZaoRV*, 2021, v.81, pp.117–146.

the expectations of the system are greater, giving rise to increased likelihood that accusations of failure will be levelled when these are not met.

The peaceful settlement of disputes

The consideration of the Security Council's powers to effect the peaceful settlement of disputes takes place in Chapter 4. However, we note their existence here to reinforce the fact that the comprehensive system of collective security established by the UN Charter embraces a variety of responses to threats to the peace, from measures involving diplomacy at the lower end of the scale of intensity to coercive military measures at the upper end. Unlike Chapter VII powers highlighted below, the six articles that comprise Chapter VI are not dependent for their invocation upon a prior determination having been made under Article 39. These contain similar provisions to those found within the League of Nations Covenant,[116] although they are more detailed and extensive. Phrased in broad, general terms, they empower the Security Council to discuss and make recommendations on disputes which may not have yet escalated to the point where a more serious threat to the peace exists and more forcible measures under Chapter VII are contemplated. States are obliged to seek to resolve their disputes through peaceful modes,[117] underlining the primary responsibility of states to resolve their disputes themselves. Parties failing to resolve their disputes peacefully are obliged to refer them to the Council.[118] The more robust mechanisms of the collective security system are certainly not envisaged as coming into play unless pacific resolution of a situation giving rise to concern has proven futile. The Security Council enjoys a general power to investigate any dispute that might give rise to international friction in order to determine whether it is likely to endanger international peace and security,[119] and to make recommendations for the settlement of disputes.[120] This underlines the central role of the Council, which is able to involve itself in any situation in order to promote its peaceful resolution. Significantly, a role for the UN Secretary-General is envisaged in efforts taken towards settling disputes through peaceful or diplomatic means, thus transforming the role from being simply that of an administrative official as it had been within the League of Nations system.[121]

116 See, for example, Articles 12–13 and 15 of the Covenant of the League of Nations 1919.
117 Article 33.
118 Article 37.
119 Article 34.
120 Article 36.
121 See Chapter 4. Although this is the commonly held view of the role of the Secretary-General within the League, some commentators have suggested that the first holder of the position, Sir Eric Drummond, actually performed a political role behind the scenes. See, for example, Barros, J., *Office Without Power: Secretary-General Sir Eric Drummond 1919–1933* (Oxford: Clarendon Press, 1979); Rovine, A.W., *The First Fifty Years: The Secretary-General in World Affairs 1920–1970* (Leiden: Sitjhoff, 1970), Chapter 1.

Chapter VII collective security powers of the Security Council

Following a determination under Article 39, the Security Council may choose to apply non-military or military measures in response. Article 41 governs non-military sanctions imposed by the Council and provides that:

> The Security Council may decide what measures not involving the use of armed force are to be employed to give effect to its decisions, and it may call upon the Members of the United Nations to apply such measures. These may include complete or partial interruption of economic relations and of rail, sea, air, postal, telegraphic, radio, and other means of communication, and the severance of diplomatic relations.

The range of sanctions made possible by Article 41 is broad and covers any conceivable non-military measures which the Council may wish to impose upon states as a means of attempting to alleviate security threats, encompassing both economic and diplomatic sanctions. That non-military sanctions appear before military measures in Chapter VII implies that they should be considered in response to security threats before military action is contemplated, a view supported by the wording of Article 42, pertaining to military enforcement action, which allows the Council to commence such action 'should the … Council consider that measures provided for in Article 41 would be inadequate or have proved to be inadequate.' The role of non-military sanctions as one of the tools of the UN collective security system is explored in detail in Chapter 5.

Military enforcement action is provided for by Article 42, which empowers the Security Council to

> take such action by air, sea or land forces as may be necessary to maintain or restore international peace and security. Such action may include demonstrations, blockade, and other operations by air, sea, or land forces of Members of the United Nations.

This arguably represents collective security in its most conventional form. A shared belief of the UN's founders was that the organisation must be provided with the means to enable it to undertake military action to respond to outbreaks of aggression or disturbances of the peace, the League of Nations having been unable to muster an effective military response to acts of aggression when member states declined to commit their armed forces in defence of the League's collective security guarantee. Article 42 was theoretically strengthened by subsequent provisions of Chapter VII, which sought to confer upon the Security Council an effective military enforcement capability.

Under Article 43 (1), member states 'undertake to make available to the Security Council forces, on its call and in accordance with a special agreement … armed forces, assistance, and facilities ... ' Similar provision is made in Article 45 for air force contingents to be made available to the Council. In addition, a Military Staff Committee (MSC) is established by Article 47, consisting of the chiefs of staff of the Security Council's permanent members, and charged with taking responsibility for the strategic direction of forces placed at the Council's disposal. As Bryde comments, 'the proposed composition [of the MSC] has to be seen in light of the idea of the Great Powers' special responsibility for world peace.'[122] In contrast to the League of Nations system, a centralised, coordinated, collective force was envisaged.[123] The military enforcement capacity of the League had extended no further than the power conferred upon the Council to recommend what contributions members should make towards a force taking action to uphold the Covenant's provisions,[124] and so was far more of an ad hoc nature.

The provisions contained in Chapter VII concerning the arrangements for the application of military enforcement measures were based largely upon the proposals that emerged from the Dumbarton Oaks discussions. While the participants at Dumbarton Oaks found it relatively easy to agree that forces would be supplied to the Council by virtue of standby arrangements, as opposed to the creation of a permanent international force, the debate over the form of air power to be made available to the Security Council evidenced crucial differences of opinion among the major powers. Debate centred on the question of whether a permanent international air force should be established for use by the UN, or whether instead member states should undertake to provide air force contingents in a way similar to that by which they undertook to make standby forces available to the Security Council. The Soviet Union was particularly disposed towards the idea of creating a permanent international air force for use by the Security Council. The idea came to find less enthusiasm with the other participants, notably the US, who ultimately preferred national air force contingents to be made available to the Security Council along similar lines to the way in which standby forces would be supplied to it.[125] It has been suggested that a key motive behind the US attitude on this issue was the fact that it enjoyed the most equipped air force at the time, and by opposing an international air force would keep more control in this respect in its own hands.[126] In any event, the debate over air power demonstrates some underlying disagreements over the framework that should govern enforcement action, and the potential for political considerations to dictate the stance states would choose to take upon issues of collective security. Another source of contention worth noting arose from the Soviet Union's support for a provision whereby those states unable to provide

122 Bryde, D., 'Article 47,' in Simma et al (eds), supra n31, at p.646.
123 Frowein, J.A., 'Article 43,' in Simma et al (eds), supra n31, at pp.629–630.
124 Article 16.
125 Hildebrand, supra n34, pp.142–156; Hoopes and Brinkley, supra n28, pp.143–144.
126 Luard, supra n24, p.28.

forces to the Council in accordance with Article 43 would instead make military bases available. This did not find favour with the US, who apparently viewed it as a device by which the USSR may seek to control bases in neighbouring states.[127] Again, this serves to demonstrate the extent to which the major powers' approach to the practice of collective security within the UN system was influenced by political considerations – particularly, mutual suspicion of each other – from the outset. For such reasons, the provisions for conferring the Security Council with its own military capability were never implemented, fundamental disagreements existing between the major powers over the principles which would govern the supply of standby forces to the Council.[128] Thus, the Security Council has never been able to 'take' military action in the strict sense implied by Article 42, adopting instead a practice of authorising other actors to do so under its authority.[129]

The demarcation of collective security functions between the Security Council and regional bodies

No overview of the major collective security provisions of the UN Charter would be complete without mention of the role afforded to regional arrangements. The UN Charter provides for, and indeed actively encourages, a general role for regional arrangements in efforts concerned with the maintenance of international peace and security, especially through pacific modes of settlement. We consider in depth the role of regional arrangements within the UN system in Chapter 8, but briefly outline core Charter provisions here to demonstrate the intentions of the UN's founders in respect of the pre-eminence of the Security Council in matters affecting international peace and security. Article 52 (2) provides that member states shall make every effort to achieve pacific settlement of local disputes through regional arrangements before referring them to the Security Council, evidently affording regional arrangements the primary responsibility for resolving disputes peacefully. However, where more serious measures are concerned, regional arrangements clearly take on a subsidiary role to that of the Council. Although Article 53 (1) envisages that 'the Security Council shall, where appropriate, utilise regional arrangements for enforcement action under its authority,' this is subject to the proviso that they may not engage in enforcement action without the authorisation of the Security Council, clearly envisaging the enforcement role of regional arrangements as being that of agents of the Council, taking action only under its overall direction and authority. This view is strengthened by Article 54's

127 Frowein, supra n123, p.637.
128 See Chapter 3.
129 See Chapter 7.

requirement that regional arrangements keep the Council informed of activities they are undertaking or contemplating.[130]

The early planning of the UN system saw differences of opinion surface between the major powers upon the role that regional bodies would play in enforcement action. British Prime Minister Winston Churchill, in particular, was in favour of considerable responsibility being conferred upon such bodies for the maintenance of international peace and security, famously remarking that, 'There should be several regional councils, august but subordinate, [and] that these should form the massive pillars upon which the world organisation would be founded in majesty and calm.'[131] While recognising the potential value of regional collective security mechanisms, other major powers had greater reservations about conferring regional arrangements with a degree of autonomy that would remove them from the ultimate control of the Security Council. The US was particularly concerned with ensuring that very clear limits were placed upon the responsibilities of regional arrangements.[132] In the event, the Dumbarton Oaks discussions reached a compromise upon the role of regional bodies, permitting their utilisation for enforcement action, but only with the authorisation of the Security Council.

At the San Francisco Conference, smaller powers primarily consisting of Latin American states pushed strongly for the strengthening of provisions governing enforcement action undertaken by regional bodies, the most radical suggestions seeking to remove regional action from UN oversight.[133] Latin American states in particular were keen to achieve some form of special recognition for their own recently developed regional security system and sought to develop the provisions that eventually formed Chapter VIII to strengthen the recognition afforded to regional arrangements.[134] The sponsoring powers were unwilling to concede enforcement powers to regional bodies without these being dependent upon a Security Council mandate. A motivating factor was surely the risk that such a decision would encourage a proliferation of regional arrangements over which the major powers would collectively have little control, weakening the UN Charter's system of collective security. Perhaps an even more significant consideration was the fact that by affording too much autonomy to regional arrangements, the major powers would risk allowing one another to establish powerful spheres of influence within their respective regions. This view is supported by a statement of John Foster Dulles, one of the US contingent at San Francisco, that a regional excep-

130 Despite the apparent Charter requirement that regional arrangements taking enforcement action do so under Security Council authority, in practice, some have acted on their own initiative without any meaningful UN oversight. See Chapter 8.

131 Claude, supra n61, p.113.

132 Hildebrand, supra n34, pp.163–170.

133 Franck, T., 'Who killed Article 2 (4)?,' *American Journal of International Law*, 1970, v.64, pp.809–837, at p.823.

134 See UNCIO XII, pp.771–784.

tion for the Inter-American system from UN control would 'invite a European regional arrangement … which the Soviet Union will dominate and where we will through the Security Council have no voice.' Hence, there were good reasons why the major powers would be inclined to maintain Security Council control over enforcement action undertaken by regional arrangements, as this would ensure each of them a guarantee that no action could be taken which they did not support. The only concession made to the smaller powers at San Francisco was the insertion into the Charter of Article 51, permitting collective self-defence and receiving unanimous support from the assembled states.[135] The pressure leading to its adoption can be seen as recognition of the potential difficulties the Security Council may face in taking effective measures against aggression in situations where a permanent member had an interest at stake that would lead it to veto such action. Notably, by embracing collective self-defence, Article 51's effect is to ensure that action taken under the auspices of regional arrangements in response to an attack upon one of their number is not precluded by the absence of a Security Council mandate. However, the fact that Article 51 provides only a qualified right of self-defence – conceived as existing only until the Council had taken 'measures necessary' for the maintenance of international peace and security – is also notable, highlighting the determination of the permanent members to retain overall control of all military actions.

The legitimacy of the Security Council: Reform debates

The perceived legitimacy of the Security Council as the body tasked with the primary responsibility for the maintenance of international peace and security has been called into question on several fronts, serving in turn as the basis for reform debates centred on its composition and voting procedure.[136] As argued by the present author previously, three interrelated assertions can be made by way of challenging the Council's legitimacy.[137] Firstly, the special status of its permanent members – and the identity of those afforded such status – is based on a series of geopolitical realities existing in 1945 and which do not reflect contemporary global

135 UNCIO XII, p.680 et seq.

136 There exists a vast literature on Security Council reform debates. See, e.g., Bourantonis, D., *The History and Politics of UN Security Council Reform* (London: Routledge, 2005); Fassbender, B., 'All Illusions Shattered? Looking Back on a Decade of Failed Attempts to Reform the UN Security Council,' *Max Planck Yearbook of United Nations Law*, 2003, v.7, pp.183–218; Fitzgerald, A., 'Security Council Reform: Creating a More Representative Body of the Entire U.N. Membership,' *Pace International Law Review*, 2000, v.12, n.2, pp.319–365; Hassler, S., *Reforming the UN Security Council Membership: The Illusion of Representativeness* (London: Routledge, 2013); Weiss, T.G. and Young, K.E., 'Compromise and Credibility: Security Council Reform?' *Security Dialogue*, 2003, v.36, n.2, pp.131–154.

137 Wilson, G., 'Enhancing diversity and representation within the United Nations Security Council: The dilemmas of reform,' *International Politics*, 2019, v.56, n.4, pp.495–513, at pp.498–499.

power balances. The status afforded the P5 by the UN Charter reflected a belief that the victorious allied powers would be central to the Council's effectiveness in acting, grounded in collective security's ideal requirement of the commitment to the system of the major powers. However, while new major powers have emerged over the course of the post-war era, such as Germany and Japan, the likes of the UK and France have seen their status as world powers questioned. Writing in 2004, the UN's own *High-Level Panel on Threats, Challenges and Change* suggested that, 'the financial and military contributions … of some … permanent members are modest compared to their special status.'[138] Secondly, the related argument can be made that the Council is insufficiently representative of the UN membership at large. Notwithstanding the fact that membership has progressively increased to 193 states currently, the size of the Council has not increased since 1963 and still sits at 15.[139] Although the election of the non-permanent membership takes place in accordance with a formula to ensure that all regions are represented,[140] these are far from homogenous, while the privileged permanent membership remains imbalanced in favour of Western states and contains no representation from the Global South in particular. Finally, in consequence of the aforementioned factors, the Council is subject to criticism on account of its perceived inconsistent or partial approach to situations posing threats to international peace and security. This conflicts with the collective security ideal of states' commitment to the 'indivisibility of peace,' whereby all security threats are regarded to be the concern of all irrespective of their source or whom they affect.[141] The ability of the P5 to utilise the veto to protect their interests has been detailed already above, but more generally the political priorities of the Council's members may inform the level of attention afforded towards any given situation of concern or the extent to which robust measures are taken to address it. The Council's minimal efforts to address the Rwandan genocide have been cast in such terms, for example, when contrasted with its more significant response to the events of 9/11,[142] which directly affected a permanent member in the form of the US. More generally, it has been felt that Africa has been neglected by the Council, due in no small part to the absence of any permanent member from that continent.[143]

Driven by the aforementioned concerns, long-running reform debates have centred on enhancing the representative credentials of the Security Council, with

138 *High-Level Panel on Threats, Challenges and Change, A More Secure World: Our Shared Responsibility*, 2004, UN Doc. A/59/565, para.246.

139 Originally the Security Council consisted of just eleven members, six being non-permanent. A further four non-permanent seats were added in 1963 pursuant to GA Res 1991A (XVIII).

140 GA Res 1991 (XVIII).

141 See Chapter 1.

142 High-Level Panel report, supa n138, para.41.

143 See, e.g., the comments of the representative of St Kitts and Nevis in a UN General Assembly debate on reform: UN Doc. GA/11450.

an open-ended UN working group having been tasked with considering reform proposals since 1993.[144] Its periodic discussions have, however, demonstrated that while there is a broad consensus on the need for reform, there is a much greater divergence of opinion regarding the form which it should take.[145] Effectiveness is also a criterion of legitimacy, and a key tension to manage within reform proposals has been to 'maintain … a fragile balance between representation, legitimacy and efficiency,'[146] ensuring that in enhancing the Council's representativeness it does not become so unwieldy as to undermine its capacity to act. Importantly, any reform to the composition or procedure of the Security Council would require amendment of the UN Charter, a process governed by Article 108. Critically, any amendment in turn requires the assent of the P5.[147] This arguably shuts off the most radical reform options, such as curtailment of the P5 veto power, with the result being that most reform proposals have essentially confined themselves to looking at how the Council's membership can be expanded to broaden representation of the diverse strands of the UN's membership. The greatest barrier to reform arises from lack of agreement on who should be the beneficiaries of expanded membership, particularly any new permanent seats that might be created.

Assessments of the merits of potential new permanent members typically place emphasis upon the contributions which they might make towards the maintenance of international peace and security, alongside the extent to which they broaden the geographic balance of the permanent membership.[148] This would seem entirely logical given that it is by reference to these criteria that non-permanent members are to be elected to the Council,[149] while the body's core business is discharging primary responsibility for the maintenance of international peace and security.[150] However, the application of both of these sets of considerations is fraught with difficulty. States' capacity to contribute towards the maintenance of international peace and security may be assessed by reference to various factors: for example, military expenditure, financial contributions towards the UN budget and participation in peacekeeping operations.[151] Each generates a different set of deserving

144 The formally 'Open-Ended Working group on the Question of Equitable Representation on and Increase in the Membership of the Security Council and Other Matters Related to the Security Council' was created pursuant to GA Res 48/26 (1993).

145 See, e.g., the Working group's 2015 discussion document: https://www.un.org/en/ga/screform/77/pdf/2015-07-31-screform-ign.pdf.

146 Bourantonis, supra n136, p.10.

147 This is in addition to a two-thirds majority in support of the proposed amendment within the General Assembly.

148 See, e.g., the works cited above, supra n136.

149 Article 23 (1) provides that in electing the ten non-permanent members, 'due regard' should be paid to 'the contribution of Members of the United Nations to the maintenance of international peace and security … and also to equitable geographical distribution.'

150 Article 24 (1).

151 Wilson, supra n137, pp.504–505.

candidates for permanent membership, each with its own drawbacks. While Japan and Germany are the biggest contributors to the UN budget outside of the current P5,[152] they would not perhaps be regarded as greatly diversifying the character of the permanent membership, while many of the biggest contributors to UN peacekeeping seldom, if ever, feature among those touted as potential new permanent members.[153] The diversification of representation is also problematic as an objective in identifying the most appropriate candidates for permanent membership. While a number of major powers in the world's under-represented regions are often cited as worthy of this status,[154] the question arises as to whether they are necessarily representative of their regions given the diversity of religious, cultural, linguistic and political identities present in each of them.[155] This is complicated yet further by the existence of significant political rivalries between two or more major powers in most of the regions concerned,[156] giving rise to competing claims to enhanced status within the UN's decision-making apparatus.

That there are no obvious answers to the dilemmas of Security Council reform has led some to consider more pragmatic, modest means of improving its procedures for decision-making as a means of enhancing its perceived legitimacy.[157] It is undoubtedly the case that major reform to the body is unlikely to occur in the foreseeable future. It might also be noted that significant change is not without its dangers, not least the prospect that just as a model adopted in 1945 has come to be seen as outdated in some respects, any reforms adopted in the here and now may similarly not stand the test of time as geopolitical circumstances change and renewed calls for fresh reforms emerge yet again.[158]

The role of the General Assembly within the collective security system

Although this book is primarily concerned with the use of the collective security powers entrusted to the Security Council, given the pre-eminent status

152 On the basis of the most recent assessed contributions, Japan and Germany are the third and fourth biggest contributors to the UN budget respectively, contributing larger sums than three current permanent members. See GA Res 76/238.

153 As of 30 June 2024, the three largest individual contributors of personnel to UN peacekeeping operations were Nepal, Rwanda and Bangladesh, none of whom are touted as potential future permanent members. See *Contribution of Uniformed Personnel to UN by Country and Personnel Type*, available at https://peacekeeping.un.org/sites/default/files/01_contributions_to_un_peacekeeping_operations_by_country_and_post_75_june_2024.pdf. Ghana, Morocco and Ethiopia also featured among the top ten contributors.

154 For example, Brazil, India, and Nigeria, amongst others.

155 See Wilson, supra n137, pp.505–506.

156 See Wilson, supra n137, pp.506–507.

157 See, e.g., Weiss and Young, supra n136; Schrijver, N., 'Reforming the UN Security Council in Pursuance of Collective Security,' *Journal of Conflict and Security Law*, 2007, v.12, n.1, pp.127–138.

158 See Wilson, supra n137, pp.507–508.

afforded it by the UN Charter in this arena of activity, it would be remiss to omit to have regard to the role assigned by the Charter within this realm to the General Assembly. To a large extent, its junior position in this area reinforces the selective, concert-style form of collective security envisaged by the UN's founders. Nonetheless, the General Assembly is granted some powers in the security sphere, albeit not of a mandatory nature and more general in character. The recommendatory powers enjoyed by the Assembly are contained within Articles 10–14 of the UN Charter. Article 10 entitles the Assembly to 'discuss any questions or any matters within the scope of the present Charter' and 'make recommendations to the Members of the United Nations or to the Security Council or to both on any such questions or matters.' That the Assembly does have a competence to involve itself in matters pertaining to international peace and security is made clear by Article 11 (1), which empowers it to consider the general principles of cooperation in the maintenance of international peace and security and to make recommendations in this area. Furthermore, it 'may discuss any questions relating to the maintenance of international peace and security brought before it … and … make recommendations with regard to any such questions.'[159] The dominant role of the Security Council is made apparent, however, by Article 11 (2)'s proviso that 'any question on which action is necessary shall be referred to the Security Council.' This has been taken to refer to enforcement action which only the Council has mandatory powers to initiate,[160] although the judgement of the International Court of Justice (ICJ) in the *Expenses* case might be read as lending some support for the view that this does not preclude the Assembly *recommending* that states apply enforcement measures.[161] The pre-eminence of the Council is further reinforced by the combined effect of Articles 14 and 12 (1). While Article 14 empowers the Assembly to 'recommend measures for the peaceful adjustment of any situation …,' which prima facie constitutes a broad recommendatory power, this is subject to the caveat contained in Article 12 (1) that the Assembly may not make any recommendations with regard to a situation in respect of which the Security Council is exercising the functions conferred upon it by the Charter. Although this provision could be clearer, as no guidance is provided by it upon when the Council will be taken to be 'exercising' its functions,[162] the implication of Article 12 (1) is evident. The Security Council enjoys precedence in matters concerning international

159 Article 11 (2).

160 Hailbronner, K. and Klein, E., 'Article 11,' in Simma et al (eds), supra n24, pp.276–287, at pp.281–284.

161 *Certain Expenses of the United Nations*, ICJ Rep, 1962, p.151, at pp.164–165. See White, supra n94, pp.151–152; Hailbronner, K. and Klein, E., 'Article 10,' in Simma et al (eds), supra n24 pp.257–275, at pp.264–266.

162 However, Article 12 (2) provides that the secretary-general (with the Security Council's consent) will inform the General Assembly at each session of any matters related to the maintenance of international peace and security which are being dealt with by the Council and when the Council ceases to be dealing with them.

peace and security, and the General Assembly is not to usurp the Council's primary responsibility in this regard by becoming involved in matters that the Council is already dealing with. By distinguishing between the respective roles of the two bodies and giving pre-eminence to one, the Charter seeks to avoid the potential for disputes to arise between them through a duplication of roles as existed within the League of Nations.

At San Francisco, several proposals emanating from smaller states sought to enhance the powers of the General Assembly vis-à-vis those of the Security Council, the most wide-ranging of which were proposals by New Zealand that Council decisions concerning enforcement action should be subject to the approval of the Assembly.[163] However, given that the powers ultimately conferred upon the General Assembly went no further than enabling it to make recommendations with regard to situations which the Security Council was not exercising its powers in respect of, the major powers were successful in preserving the Security Council's superior role. At the same time, the fact that the smaller states sought to enhance the powers of the General Assembly at San Francisco is testament to the serious reservations which they had as to the likelihood that the major powers would be able to act with sufficient unity to make collective security a reality, especially in light of the veto power afforded to the Security Council's permanent members. These concerns may be seen as the impetus for the attempts of smaller states to strengthen other provisions of the UN Charter, including the powers afforded to the General Assembly, but also to regional arrangements.[164]

Although Article 12 (1) states that the Assembly shall not make recommendations in respect of a situation in which the Security Council is exercising its Charter functions, in practice this provision appears to have been interpreted liberally and been of little practical hindrance to its adoption of recommendations. As propounded by Hailbronner and Klein, one theory would hold that the effect of Article 12 (1) is to deny the Assembly the right to issue recommendations on any matter which at the time is on the agenda of the Security Council, early practice appearing to follow this view, with the Assembly refraining from issuing recommendations on situations that formally remained on the agenda of the Council.[165] However, as they note, the General Assembly has ultimately come to decide for itself if the Security Council is exercising its 'functions' in respect of a situation of concern, the mere existence of an item on the Council's agenda being insufficient to determine that the Council is 'functioning' if no action is taken by it.[166] Inaction by the Council, because of political divisions or the power of veto, has led on

163 UNCIO III, p.488.
164 See above.
165 Hailbronner, K. and Klein, E., 'Article 12,' in Simma et al (eds), supra n24, pp.287–298, at pp.289–292.
166 See also White, supra n94, pp.161–169.

occasion from its earlier years to the Assembly stepping in to call for the adoption of particular measures, for example over the apartheid regime in South Africa.[167]

Prima facie, the adoption of recommendations by the General Assembly is a more straightforward process than is decision-making within the Security Council, each UN member state having one vote within that forum and none being endowed with a veto power.[168] However, recommendations pertaining to the maintenance of international peace and security require a two-thirds qualified majority,[169] underlining the importance of the building of coalitions to support or oppose proposals under debate. Various blocs of states are represented within the General Assembly, some regional in character, others formed around common interests.[170] The larger a bloc is, the more likely it is able to further the shared interests of its membership within General Assembly debates. Of particular significance are the Non-Aligned Movement (NAM) and Group of 77 (G77), both containing a majority of UN member states. Originally established in 1961 to further the interests of developing countries within the context of the Cold War,[171] the 120-state strong NAM is not formally aligned with any of the UN's major powers. Its key contemporary concerns have included disarmament, UN reform and enhancing the General Assembly's oversight of the Security Council.[172] Formed at a similar time, the G77 represented states seeking to engage the UN in development-related issues,[173] and is currently the largest interest bloc within the UN, consisting of 134 members. The sheer size of blocs such as the NAM and G77 enables them to exert significant influence over the General Assembly's agenda where they remain united, there being clear incentives for the UN's major powers to accommodate their perspectives when seeking to further action through the Assembly,[174] although it should not be assumed that any bloc remains static in its outlook.[175]

Although the UN Charter clearly envisaged a subsidiary role for the General Assembly in matters pertaining to international peace and security, in the

167 GA Res 1761 (XVII).

168 Article 18 (1).

169 Article 18 (2).

170 For example, the Alliance of Small Island States (AOSIS) represents the interests of 39 small island and low-lying coastal states, particularly in respect of the effects of climate change.

171 See Luthi, L.M., 'The Non-Aligned Movement and the Cold War, 1961–1973,' *Journal of Cold War Studies*, 2016, v.18, n.4, pp.98–147.

172 See Strydom, H., 'The Non-Aligned Movement and the Reform of International Relations,' *Max Planck Yearbook of United Nations Law*, 2007, v.11, pp.1–46.

173 See Lees, N., 'The endurance of the G77 in international relations: South-south ideology and voting at the United Nations 1970–2015,' *Japanese Journal of Political Science*, 2023, v.24, pp.310–330.

174 See Nurullayev, D. and Papa, M., 'Bloc politics at the UN: How Oher States Behave When the United States and China-Russia Disagree,' *Global Studies Quarterly*, 2023, v.3, pp.1–11.

175 See, e.g., Brazys, S. and Panke, D., 'Why do states change positions in the United Nations General Assembly?' *International Political Science Review*, 2017, v.38, n.1, pp.70–84.

aftermath of the outbreak of the Korean War an attempt was made by Western states to enhance the Assembly's status in this regard. The Security Council had only been able to sanction military action to be undertaken by a US-led coalition due to the fact that the Soviet Union was boycotting the Council at the time on account of the UN's failure to seat the new Chinese communist regime in place of the nationalist regime which it had recently toppled. Had it been present it would likely have vetoed UN support for such action against another communist state in the form of North Korea. Mindful of the likelihood that the Council would be unable to act in a similar future instance after the USSR had returned to participating in its deliberations, the then Western majority within the General Assembly sought to confer it with the capacity to recommend military enforcement measures in circumstances where the Security Council was prevented from doing so due to the exercise of the veto. The overwhelmingly supported Uniting for Peace resolution[176] provided that:

> if the Security Council, because of lack of unanimity of the permanent members, fails to exercise its primary responsibility for the maintenance of international peace and security in any case where there appears to be a threat to the peace, breach of the peace, or act of aggression, the General Assembly shall consider the matter immediately with a view to making recommendations to Members for collective measures, including in the case of a breach of the peace or act of aggression the use of armed force when necessary, to maintain or restore international peace and security.[177]

The intention of Uniting for Peace is clear, envisaging the General Assembly stepping in to recommend Chapter VII military enforcement measures if the Security Council is unable to reach agreement on the adoption of such measures. It does raise the question as to whether the General Assembly is legally entitled to issue recommendations for measures to be taken that extend to the use of military force. Initial Soviet opposition to the legality of Uniting for Peace was based upon the argument that such a role for the General Assembly ran counter to the content of Articles 10–14, which prioritised the role of the Security Council in the maintenance of international peace and security. Where the use of the veto occurred within the Council, this was part of the exercise of the Council's functions as set out within the Charter, and thus not sufficient cause to claim that the Council had failed to consider the matter and permitting the Assembly to issue recommendations in the

176 GA Res 377 (V) (1950). The resolution was adopted with 52 positive votes, 5 opposed and 2 abstentions.

177 For some background to the adoption of the resolution, see Woolsey, L.H., 'The "Uniting for Peace" resolution of the United Nations,' *American Journal of International Law*, 1951, v.45, n.1, pp.129–137.

area of military enforcement. Furthermore, coercive action was within the sole remit of the Council.[178]

Some international lawyers have attempted to provide a legal basis for the powers envisaged for the General Assembly by Uniting for Peace on the grounds that only *mandatory* measures are within the sole ambit of the Council, and that this should not preclude the adoption of *recommendations* by the Assembly if it forms the view that the exercise of the power of veto within the Council means that it is not exercising its functions in the sense of Article 12.[179] Such a view may find some support in the ICJ's judgement in the *Expenses* case,[180] in which there was some suggestion that 'action' in the sense of Article 11 (2) – the provision which requires the General Assembly to refer matters on which 'action' is necessary to the Security Council – refers to mandatory, coercive action which the Council orders,[181] leaving open the possibility that coercive action recommended by the Assembly is not precluded. Arguably of greatest significance, however, is the fact that the resolution has been utilised by states subsequently, including the USSR, which initially opposed its legal validity, suggesting possible acceptance within state practice of its lawfulness.[182] New light was shed upon the issue by the ICJ in its advisory opinion concerning the legality of the construction by Israel of a wall in the occupied Palestinian territory.[183] The advisory opinion had been requested by the General Assembly,[184] following the Security Council's failure to declare the wall's construction illegal due to the exercise of the veto by a permanent member.[185] Israel's argument that the General Assembly was precluded from acting by Article 12 (1) of the UN Charter in respect of the issue in light of its continued existence on the Security Council's agenda was rejected by the Court, which took the view that the inability of the Council to reach a decision due to the opposition of a permanent member was exactly the kind of situation envisaged by Uniting for Peace for the General Assembly to consider.[186] In reaching its conclusion on the matter, the Court made reference to the way in which states' interpretations of Uniting for Peace had evolved over time to enable the General Assembly to adopt recommendations in respect of situations still on the Council's agenda.[187]

178 See White, supra n94, p.174.

179 See White, supra n94, p.174. See also Andrassy, J., 'Uniting for Peace,' *American Journal of International Law*, 1956, v.50, pp.563–582.

180 Supra n161.

181 Supra n161, p.162 et seq.

182 Sands, P. and Klein, P., *Bowett's Law of International Institutions* (5th ed.) (London: Sweet & Maxwell, 2001), pp.33–34.

183 Legal Consequences of the Construction of a Wall in the Occupied Palestinian Territory, (2004) 43 *I.L.M* 1009.

184 GA Res/ES-10/14 (2003).

185 UN Doc. S/PV.4841, 4842.

186 Supra n36, paras.24–31.

187 Supra n36, para.27.

In practice, the Uniting for Peace resolution has been of limited significance. It has only been invoked on a handful of occasions in order to convene the General Assembly in an emergency special session, the most recent of which followed Russia's invasion of Ukraine in February 2022.[188] None of the invocations of Uniting for Peace have actually resulted in a recommendation by the General Assembly that coercive military measures be applied by states in response to a situation,[189] although it was, however, under the terms of Uniting for Peace that the Assembly created the first UN peacekeeping operation, the United Nations Emergency Force (UNEF) I.[190] Zaum suggests that while 'envisaged as the main pathway for the General Assembly to address issues of war and conflict ... [Uniting for Peace] turned increasingly into an instrument used to raise issues of political importance to the Non-Aligned Movement in the General Assembly ...,'[191] arguing that the fact that it 'contributed little to strengthening the UN's capacity for collective security ... reflects the growing marginalization of the General Assembly by the Security Council.'[192] In practice, Uniting for Peacc served to provide a forum within which the General Assembly might debate matters upon which the Council was simply unable to take any action, albeit confining itself to the adoption of resolutions recommendatory or condemnatory in nature, yet unaccompanied by any calls for the deployment of military forces. For example, it was during sessions convened under the Uniting for Peace procedure that the Assembly recommended admission to the UN of Palestine,[193] the adoption of measures for the protection of Palestinian residents,[194] and demanded that Russia cease its use of force against Ukraine.[195] None of these calls could have found their way into resolutions adopted by the Security Council due to the veto power of the US and Russia in particular, given the subject matter concerned.

On a positive level, the adoption of Uniting for Peace demonstrated a willingness on the part of member states to develop a flexible approach to the interpretation of UN Charter provisions. It was 'undoubtedly a step in the evolution of the

188 Pursuant to SC Res 2623 (2022).

189 On its usage, see Sands and Klein, supra n182; White, supra n94, pp.175–178; Kenny, C., 'Responsibility to recommend: The role of the UN General Assembly in the maintenance of international peace and security,' *Journal on the Use of Force and International Law*, 2016, v.3, n.1, pp.3–36. On its earliest uses, see Petersen, K.S., 'The uses of the Uniting for Peace resolution since 1950,' *International Organization*, 1959, v.13, pp.219–232.

190 GA Res 1000 (ES-1) (1956). See Pearson, L.B., 'Force for U.N,' *Foreign Affairs*, 1957, v.35, n.3, pp.395–404.

191 Zaum, D., 'The Security Council, the General Assembly, and war: The Uniting for Peace resolution,' in Lowe, Roberts, Welsh and Zaum, supra n25, pp.154–174, at p.155.

192 Zaum, ibid, p.156.

193 GA Res ES-10/23 (2024).

194 GA Res ES-10/L.25 (2023).

195 GA Res ES-11/1 (2022). A series of subsequent resolutions adopted during the same session addressed the ongoing conflict in Ukraine, including condemnation of the Russian-held referendums in several oblasts as a precursor to their annexation. See GA Res ES-11/4 (2022).

law of the United Nations,'[196] which would allow the Charter framework to be used in a manner that may enable it to overcome political obstacles to further the core aims and objectives with which the UN had been established. On the other hand, albeit free of the political constraints of the Security Council, the General Assembly's potential capacity to adopt condemnatory or recommendatory resolutions with prima facie greater ease fails to build in recognition of the geopolitical realities which must be taken into account as part of any course of action in the manner that the Council is forced to. For this reason, it is unlikely to come to challenge the pre-eminent decision-making authority of the Security Council in the collective security arena.

Notwithstanding its comparatively limited role in the maintenance of international peace and security, a key contribution of the General Assembly on a more general level has been to use its broad powers of discussion and recommendation to contribute to some notable developments via the adoption of statements of shared legal norms and principles. These have included, for example, its landmark resolutions on the 'Declaration on Principles of International Law Concerning Friendly Relations and Co-operation among States in Accordance with the Charter of the United Nations'[197] and on the 'Definition of Aggression.'[198] These have come to serve as essential points of reference in legal discourse pertaining to issues such as the use of force and non-intervention,[199] matters going to the core of the principle of collective security. The role of the Assembly in norm evolution has been such as to lead White to suggest that in light of its practice 'in certain areas of recommendation, for example on disarmament and on general principles of international peace, the General Assembly is undoubtedly the primary organ.'[200] It should also be noted that the Assembly has been willing to take up matters where the Security Council has proven unable or unwilling to do so. For example, the situation arising from the white minority's unilateral declaration of independence in Southern Rhodesia during the 1960s was determined to constitute a threat to the peace by the General Assembly[201] some time before the Security Council took any steps in response.[202] It has also on its own initiative adopted resolutions critical of North Korea's human rights record,[203] called for Israel to comply with the

196 Andrassy, supra n179, p.581.
197 GA Res 2625 (XXV) (1970).
198 GA Res 3314 (XXIX) (1974).
199 See, e.g., Vinuales, J. (ed.), *The UN Friendly Relations Declaration at 50: An Assessment of the Fundamental Principles of International Law* (Cambridge: CUP, 2020), in particular chs. 3 & 5; Bruha, T., 'The General Assembly's Definition of the Act of Aggression,' in KreB, C. and Barriga, S. (eds), *The Crime of Aggression: A Commentary* (Cambridge: CUP, 2016), pp.142–177.
200 White, supra n94, p.183.
201 GA Res 1889 (XVIII).
202 See White, supra n94, p.165.
203 GA Res 62/167 (2007).

Geneva Conventions within the occupied territories[204] and affirmed its commitment to the territorial integrity of Ukraine at the time of the Crimean crisis.[205] On each occasion, the Assembly was able to at least place on record the widely shared position of the international community where such inclination was not present within the Council.[206]

Subsidiary organs

The UN Charter permits both the General Assembly and the Security Council to establish subsidiary organs as they deem necessary for the performance of their functions.[207] While the plethora of subsidiary organs created to date is beyond the parameters of this book, it should be noted that these can – and are – established to support the UN's political organs in the discharge of their responsibilities relating to the maintenance of international peace and security. Peacekeeping operations and sanctions committees established by the Security Council are generally regarded as subsidiary organs,[208] for example, while the General Assembly has also established bodies whose work supports the wider peace and security objectives of the organisation in a more practical setting. A case in point is the Office for the Coordination of Humanitarian Affairs (OCHA), established in 1991 to strengthen coordination of humanitarian emergency assistance.[209] Headed by the Under Secretary-General for Humanitarian Affairs, much of OCHA's work is focused on alleviating the humanitarian consequences of conflict situations.[210] The long-standing Office of the High Commissioner for Refugees has a similar focus, providing assistance to those in flight from their homes.[211] Over time, the scope of its activities has expanded, including to encompass internally displaced persons within its reach. Like the OCHA, much of the UNHCR's work takes place in regions afflicted by conflict, this being the source of population movements.[212]

204 GA Res 67/119 (2012).
205 GA Res 68/262 (2014).
206 This is apparent from the fact that China and Russia voted against the first of these resolutions, the US the second, and Russia the third.
207 In addition to the general power contained in Article 8, specific powers in this respect are conferred upon the General Assembly and Security Council by virtue of Articles 22 and 29.
208 See Chapters 6 and 5.
209 GA Res 46/182 (1991).
210 See, e.g., OCHA, *OCHA Annual Report 2023* (Geneva: OCHA, 2024).
211 The Statute of the Office was set out in GA Res 428 (V). See Loescher, G., 'UNHCR's Origins and Early History: Agency, Influence, and Power in Global Refugee Policy,' *Refuge*, 2017, v.33, n.1, pp.77–86.
212 See UNHCR, *Global Report 2023* (Geneva: UNHCR, 2024).

Conclusion

This chapter has outlined the most important features of the collective security system created by the UN Charter with reference to some of the key considerations that shaped their creation. The overview provided herein demonstrates the presence of the two competing impulses that have dominated the operation of the UN collective security system from its very inception. Undoubtedly, the UN's founders drew on lessons from the League of Nations experience in creating a collective security apparatus that adopted a broader conception of security threats, but which also contained more robust mechanisms for responding to these, evidenced particularly by the military enforcement provisions contained in Chapter VII. In this respect, the willingness to develop collective security mechanisms to facilitate effective responses to security threats and take account of new needs is apparent. However, the UN Charter system was shaped primarily by the major powers of the day, and they were very cautious in ensuring that a discretionary, and potentially selective, system of collective security was implemented in which their agreement to any given course of action would be essential. The creation of their power of veto within the Security Council served as the strongest evidence of this intention. To this day, the very legitimacy of the Council continues to be called into question on account of its composition and decision-making processes, while efforts to strengthen the capacity of the General Assembly in the collective security arena can be seen in this same light. However, while the Assembly has demonstrated a fair degree of creativity in performing its subsidiary role with respect to the maintenance of international peace and security, the Security Council remains the undisputed primary actor within this field. It is very important that this is borne in mind when the limitations of the various tools of the UN collective security system become clearer in subsequent chapters.

3

A BRIEF OVERVIEW OF THE UN ERA

Introduction

This chapter builds upon the previous two chapters' discussion of the concept of collective security and its implementation in the UN Charter system by providing a brief overview of some of the key stages in the evolution of the practice of collective security within the UN Charter framework from its inception to the present day. In so doing, the chapter aims to provide contextual background to the discussion which takes place in subsequent chapters of the principal tools of the UN collective security system. It does not purport to provide any significant legal analysis of aspects of the UN Charter framework, which is provided where appropriate in subsequent chapters. Nor does it seek to provide a detailed history of the UN as a collective security actor. Rather, its overview is structured around four overlapping periods in the organisation's evolution, these being the Cold War period; the initial optimism of the early post–Cold War era; the more challenging period which soon followed thereafter; and the current period within which we find the UN. Through tracing some of the key events and stages in the evolution of the UN collective security framework, this chapter seeks to reinforce the extent to which the two contradictory impulses evidenced by the UN's founders in the previous chapter – to create a broad and flexible framework through which collective security could be implemented, while maintaining political discretion and selectivity over its operation in practice – have persisted in the development of the UN collective security function, sometimes operating hand in hand. The historical background provided against which the tools of the collective security system have been utilised also enhances attempts to subject them to meaningful evaluation, culminating as it does in presenting a picture of where the UN is today.

DOI: 10.4324/9781003518105-4

The Cold War

Although the UN Charter had provided a detailed legal framework through which robust measures were available to the Security Council with which to respond to threats to international peace and security, political disagreements among the permanent members at the beginning of the Cold War period meant that it was not possible to actually give effect to such measures on any meaningful level for four decades. However, while this is perhaps the theme which forms the basis for most narratives of the UN's collective security system during the Cold War, a second theme must not be overlooked. This can be found in terms of the UN system's demonstrable capacity to evolve flexibly and adopt creative techniques during this period in other respects, in order to facilitate important contributions towards the maintenance of international peace and security.

Paralysis within the Security Council

It will be recalled from Chapter 1 that one of the requirements for the successful operation of a system of collective security is the existence of a sufficient degree of major power commitment and cooperation. From the early days of the UN's existence, this was lacking as the onset of the Cold War served to inject a significant degree of paralysis into the Security Council's capacity to deliberate and act. Two examples illustrate the lack of major power cooperation particularly effectively: the early failure to create the standby forces envisaged by the UN Charter to facilitate military enforcement action under Chapter VII, and the emergence of superpower spheres of influence combined with the frequent exercise of the veto power by the US and USSR, especially.

Failure to create standby forces

The failure of the Security Council to implement arrangements for the standby forces envisaged by Article 43 of the UN Charter was documented in the previous chapter. In order to bring into force special agreements with member states which would provide it with the forces needed for it to undertake military enforcement operations, the Security Council charged the Military Staff Committee with considering and reporting upon the principles which should govern the conclusion of such agreements. However, the report to emerge from this exercise revealed marked differences of opinion among the permanent members,[1] in particular between the Soviet Union and the others, over the appropriate way to proceed. Of the 41 articles which comprised the report, agreement was only possible on 25 of

1 UN Doc. S/336.

them.[2] The major disagreements included a difference of opinion over the size of the forces to be made available to the Council, the US envisaging far larger numbers than the other powers, in particular the Soviet Union.[3] There was also disagreement over the question of the nature of contributions to be made towards the forces by the permanent members. The Soviet Union believed that these should be strictly equal in respect of numbers contributed to the different components of the forces, whereas the others preferred to require merely that the contributions of the permanent members be comparable, allowing for differences in the size of contributions towards the force's different components.[4] Other disagreements included the issue of the location of forces made available to the Security Council. The USSR held the view that contingents should remain located within the territory of the state to which they belonged. Others envisaged a system of bases at which contingents could be stationed.[5]

The source of much of the disagreement between the permanent members was inherently political. That the major disagreements were between the USSR and thc other members can be attributed in large part to a Soviet desire to restrict Western domination of the UN, at a time during which the USSR found itself potentially politically marginalised. As Bowett states, 'the Soviet Union was, in political terms in a minority of one and evidently feared the advantages which might have accrued to the West under the Western proposals.'[6] Ultimately, agreement was not possible upon the principles to govern the conclusion of special arrangements to confer upon the Security Council a military enforcement capacity largely because of a lack of political harmony among the permanent members. However, the inability of the Council to put into place arrangements to enable it to undertake military enforcement measures did not prove in itself to be the stumbling block to the Council taking military enforcement action during the Cold War. The political circumstances of the period were such that it was largely impossible to reach agreement among the permanent members upon the use of appropriate measures in the first place, meaning that the absence of forces at the Council's disposal, while indicative of the political tensions by which the UN was beset, did not matter a great deal on a practical level.

2 See Bowett, D.W., *United Nations Forces* (London: Stevens & Sons, 1964), pp.12–18; Grove, E., 'UN armed forces and the Military Staff Committee,' *International Security*, 1993, v.17, n.4, pp.172–182; Luard, E., *A History of the United Nations, Volume 1* (London: Macmillan, 1982), pp.93–105.
3 Bowett, ibid, p.15; Luard, ibid, p.101.
4 Supra n1, Article 11.
5 Supra n1, Article 32.
6 Bowett, supra n2, p.18.

The veto and superpower spheres of influence

We noted in the previous chapter the importance attached to the power of veto by the UN's major founders. The extent to which this power would come to hamper the UN in effectively discharging its primary responsibility for the maintenance of international peace and security, however, would depend upon the state of relations between those same powers. Unfortunately, with the early onset of the Cold War, the motivation for the insertion of this power within the UN Charter became all too apparent. For four decades, the world was essentially divided into two blocs which were respectively dominated by the two superpowers, the US and USSR,[7] in turn effectively paralysing the Security Council's capacity to meaningfully respond to threats to and breaches of the peace. The discretionary nature of the collective security system established by the UN Charter meant that each superpower would be disposed to veto any attempt by other members of the Council to respond to any situation that it considered fell within its sphere of influence. This was the case in respect of a series of interventions by both of the superpowers within states falling in their spheres of influence.[8] On the Soviet side, two such examples were military interventions undertaken in Hungary and Czechoslovakia, during 1956 and 1968, to ensure that these states remained firmly within the Soviet sphere of influence at a time when there were indications that they were in the process of pursuing more liberal policies than the USSR was prepared to tolerate.[9] While it would be easy to characterise these interventions as violations of Article 2(4) of the UN Charter, and threats to or breaches of the peace under Article 39, the Soviet veto precluded any response from the Security Council.[10] Likewise, the 1979 Soviet intervention in Afghanistan was not subject to a response by the Council, and attempts at condemnation met with the Soviet veto once again.[11] US interventions within the American continent were also immune from Security Council action. While in early episodes, such as the intervention in the Dominican Republic during 1965,[12] the US did not need to exercise the veto to defend its position due to Western domination of the Council,[13] the veto was exercised to prevent criticism of two of its military incursions during the 1980s. The first of these was the invasion

7 See, e.g., Dukes, P., *The Superpowers: A Short History* (London: Routledge, 2001), pp.85–142.

8 See White, N.D., *Keeping the Peace: The United Nations and the Maintenance of International Peace and Security* (2nd ed.) (Manchester and New York: Manchester University Press, 1997), pp.11–20.

9 See Vadney, T.E., *The World Since 1945* (2nd ed.) (London: Penguin, 1992), pp.198–201; Lundestad G., *East, West, North, South: Major Developments in International Politics 1945–1996* (2nd ed.) (Oslo: Scandinavian University Press, 1997), pp.230–232, 250–252.

10 See UN Docs S/3730/Rev.1; S/PV.754 (Hungary), S/8761; S/PV.1443 (Czechoslovakia).

11 UN Docs S/13729; S/PV.2190.

12 See Vadney, supra n9, pp.299–300.

13 See White, supra n8, pp.13–14.

of Grenada during 1983,[14] an operation which only avoided condemnation by the Security Council due to the US's exercise of the veto.[15] Likewise, its veto was used to block any pronouncement by the Council upon its 1989 intervention in Panama.[16] Thus, on both sides of the superpower divide, Security Council responses to events which could justifiably have been brought within the remit of its primary responsibility for the maintenance of international peace and security were thwarted by the veto power. The statistics on the use of the veto power within the Security Council demonstrate succinctly the extent to which its collective security capacity was stalled. Although all permanent members made some use of the veto during the Cold War period,[17] the overwhelming majority of vetoes were exercised by the two superpowers. Between 1946 and 1986, the USSR used its veto power 121 times, while the US had done so on 57 occasions.[18]

While we have highlighted the inability of the Security Council to tackle intra-bloc situations during the Cold War, inter-bloc disputes – in which the superpowers were involved in some capacity on opposite sides – were also difficult for it to respond to. The classic example is the Vietnam War, arguably the most serious armed conflict of the period, which barely featured on the Council's agenda throughout its duration. As White notes, the war was only given consideration by the Council on four occasions. No measures were ever adopted in response.[19] During the Cold War, collective security cannot prima facie be said to have operated on anything other than a very limited level, and to a large extent appeared to give way to a balance of power system. States sought to protect their security interests through more traditional mechanisms, such as the conclusion of collective defence arrangements, no doubt influenced by the fact that little potential was seen in relying upon the Security Council to guarantee their security. The two most notable examples of collective defence alliances formed in the early days of the Cold War are those of NATO and the Warsaw Pact, established fundamentally to oppose potential threats from the states within the bloc comprising the other alliance.[20] The paralysis of the Security Council is, arguably, evidenced well by the fact that despite there being by some estimates close to 200 armed conflicts or

14 For discussion of the incident, see Davidson, S., *Grenada: A Study in Politics and the Limits of International Law* (Aldershot: Avebury, 1987).
15 UN Docs S/16077/Rev.1; S/PV.2491.
16 UN Docs S/21048; S/PV.2902.
17 China, however, only exercised its power of veto once during the entire Cold War period, in respect of the admission to UN membership of Bangladesh. See UN Doc. S/PV.1660.
18 Bailey, S.D., *The Procedure of the UN Security Council* (2nd ed.) (Oxford: Clarendon Press, 1988), p.209.
19 White, supra n8, pp.17–20.
20 For an overview of perspectives of the Cold War rivalry between the two alliances, see Mastny, V., 'The new history of cold war alliances,' *Journal of Cold War Studies*, 2002, v.4, n.2, pp.55–84.

crises occurring in the UN's first 40 years,[21] there were very few determinations by the Council under Article 39 that there existed a threat to the peace, breach of the peace or act of aggression. In the same period, the Council only authorised military enforcement measures[22] and non-military sanctions[23] twice respectively.

The creative development of the UN Charter framework

Notwithstanding the general paralysis experienced by the Security Council during the Cold War period, in some important respects, the UN Charter's collective security framework was creatively developed in order to permit the organisation to make a meaningful contribution to the maintenance of international peace and security, albeit on a far more limited scale than might have been the case had the major powers been prepared to cooperate more readily. The adoption of the Uniting for Peace resolution has already been detailed in the previous chapter as a mechanism through which efforts were made to permit the General Assembly to step into a void created by Security Council deadlock, while the response to aggression against the Republic of Korea and the emergence of UN peacekeeping represent other significant examples of creativity against a backdrop of limitations arising from the kinds of constraints detailed above.

Korea

While the Security Council authorised the use of force by the UK for the limited purpose of enforcing a trade embargo imposed upon Southern Rhodesia in 1966,[24] the only notable instance of military enforcement action taken under its authority in the Cold War period came following North Korea's invasion of the Republic of Korea in 1950. The ability of the Council to give its approval to military action to repel the aggression was only possible due to the absence of the Soviet Union from the Security Council at the time in protest at the non-admission of communist China to the UN in place of the nationalist Chinese regime it had recently displaced. The Council responded to North Korea's aggression by adopting three resolutions in quick succession. First, it determined that the attack upon the Republic of Korea amounted to a breach of the peace,[25] thus providing the necessary precondition for the later adoption of Chapter VII enforcement measures. This was soon followed up by a recommendation that, 'Members of the United Nations

21 Lowe, V., Roberts, A., Welsh, J. and Zaum, D (eds), *The United Nations Security Council and War* (Oxford: Oxford University Press, 2008), p.709 et seq.

22 SC Res 83 (1950); SC Res 221 (1966).

23 In relation to Southern Rhodesia, see SC Res 221 (1966), later added to by SC Res 253 (1968); SC Res 277 (1970); SC Res 409 (1977). In relation to South Africa, see SC Res 418 (1977).

24 SC Res 221 (1966).

25 SC Res 82 (1950).

furnish such assistance to the Republic of Korea as may be necessary to repel the armed attack and to restore international peace and security in the area.'[26] Finally, the Council recommended that member states providing forces or assistance on the basis of Resolution 83 make such resources available to a unified command under the US. It requested the US to designate a commander of the forces, and to provide the Council with reports on action taken by the forces. Use of the UN flag by the forces was also authorised.[27] The action succeeded in reversing North Korea's invasion and ended when an armistice was eventually agreed between UN forces and North Korea in 1953.

The legal issues arising from military action in Korea are addressed in Chapter 7, but a number of important observations can be drawn from the event in terms of the evolution of the UN as a collective security actor.[28] Lacking its own forces, the action was essentially left to a coalition of willing states under US command. Though 16 states participated in the operation, the US provided the bulk of the forces.[29] There was very little by way of Security Council oversight of the operation, other than a request in Resolution 84 that reports be submitted to the Council on action taken, while the forces' commander, Douglas MacArthur, is on record as testifying that the forces he led had little contact with the UN.[30] Nonetheless, the Council's pronouncements upon Korea in its resolutions – in particular through its call for states to offer military assistance to the Republic of Korea in order to reverse the North Korean aggression – transformed the action into a UN military enforcement action.

The approach taken by the Security Council in the Korean incident was a consequence of the failure to implement the standby arrangements envisaged by Article 43. Without its own forces, *it* could not *take* action. It could, however, confer legitimising authority on actors able and willing to take such action. This approach to its military enforcement powers arguably marked an early incarnation of the model which would come to govern military enforcement measures in later years when the Council became able to concur upon their adoption more readily. However, two key factors combined to make Korea an isolated instance of military enforcement action being possible under UN authority. First, the USSR's absence from the Council was crucial. Had it been present, it would certainly have vetoed the relevant resolutions adopted by the Council.[31] Second, the foreign policy goals of the US were also central. It supplied the bulk of the forces and ran the

26 SC Res 83 (1950).

27 SC Res 84 (1950).

28 On the action as an exercise in collective security, see Wright, Q., 'Collective security in the light of the Korean experience,' *ASIL Proceedings*, 1951, v.45, pp.165–181.

29 Bowett, supra n2, pp.39–40.

30 Bowett, supra n2, p.42.

31 This would not, of course, have precluded action being taken in collective self-defence of the Republic of Korea pursuant to Article 51.

operation, clearly considering itself to have national interests at stake in protecting against the spread of communism which underpinned its approach to the Korean situation. The Republic of Korea was an important state to the US in the Cold War context, having fallen into the Western camp in the aftermath of World War II, whereas its North Korean neighbour had fallen under Soviet influence.[32] Thus, the action which took place in Korea was the product of unique circumstances which would not be present at any other point during the Cold War period and serves to reinforce the limitations of the collective security system, in particular the extent to which it is reliant on the interests and unity of the major powers. It was against this backdrop that Western powers moved to introduce the Uniting for Peace resolution within the General Assembly.

The creation of peacekeeping

Arguably, the greatest example of the capacity of the UN collective security system to evolve flexibly to make a valuable contribution to the maintenance of international peace and security during the politically tense Cold War period is found in the development of peacekeeping,[33] a process through which non-combatant forces were deployed under a UN command to literally keep the peace between previously warring factions. Beginning with the creation of UNEF I by the General Assembly to monitor the ceasefire agreement reached by Israel and Egypt in 1956 following the Suez crisis, the earliest peacekeeping operations were deployed to areas of tension where a fragile peace was in place, to keep that peace by monitoring ceasefires and performing similar functions. The mandates of the United Nations Force in Cyprus (UNFICYP),[34] the United Nations India–Pakistan Observer Mission (UNIPOM) along the India–Pakistan border,[35] and UNEF II in the Middle East all followed UNEF I's template in this respect.[36] As the Cold War waned, peacekeeping operations began to take on wider functions, such as election monitoring and responsibility for transitional administration, a role undertaken by the United Nations Transitional Authority in Cambodia (UNTAC).[37] Early peacekeeping operations were deployed in accordance with a series of

32 See Wolfers, A., 'Collective security and the war in Korea,' *Yale Review*, 1954, v.43, pp.481–502, at pp.489–492; Stueck, W., 'The United Nations, the Security Council, and the Korean War,' in Lowe et al, supra n21, pp.265–279.

33 A detailed discussion of the development of peacekeeping is provided in Chapter 6. The brief reference made to its emergence here is simply to illustrate the ability of the UN collective security system to develop new techniques to respond to security threats even while its capabilities were restricted in other respects as a consequence of the absence of major power cooperation within the Security Council.

34 SC Res 186 (1964).

35 SC Res 209 (1965).

36 SC Res 340 (1973).

37 SC Res 745 (1992).

principles necessitated by the political circumstances of the period.[38] Not being military enforcement operations, peacekeeping forces did not enjoy mandates permitting them to adopt coercive measures in the performance of their mandates, being empowered to use force only in self-defence. Furthermore, they were only deployed with the consent of the states upon whose territory they would be stationed. While the first peacekeeping operation, UNEF I, was established by the General Assembly, subsequent operations were created by the Security Council. A guiding principle for early operations was that forces deployed for peacekeeping would not include units supplied by permanent members of the Council, making their authorisation and functioning possible within the context of the superpower rivalry which characterised the Cold War era.

Although not expressly provided for within the UN Charter, the deployment of peacekeeping forces has generally been accepted as a lawful activity. The ICJ has ruled that the creation of UNEF I was legally permissible,[39] and that furthermore the General Assembly may establish such operations, only mandatory enforcement action being within the sole remit of the Security Council. Peacekeeping has often been dubbed 'chapter six and a half action,' involving measures which go beyond the pacific settlement procedures provided in Chapter VI of the UN Charter but do not constitute the coercive application of military force envisaged by Chapter VII. The development of peacekeeping, arguably, provides a prime example of member states using the legal framework of the UN Charter in a sufficiently flexible manner to allow new mechanisms to be developed in response to conflict situations when the prevailing political climate prevents the Charter's collective security apparatus from functioning in the way originally envisaged.

The Early post–Cold War: New opportunities and an activist Security Council

As the Cold War drew to its conclusion at the end of the 1980s, newfound cooperation between the superpowers created new opportunities for the contribution which the UN could make towards the maintenance of international peace and security. Particularly important was the accession to power of the reform-minded Mikhail Gorbachev in the USSR, and a resulting improvement of relations between it and the US, making a number of important breakthroughs possible.[40] One of collective security's core requirements – major power commitment and cooperation – appeared to have been substantially achieved, a perspective underscored by a steep decline in the exercise of the veto power within the Security

38 These are briefly summarised by Weiss, T.G., Forsythe, D.P. and Coate, R.A., *The United Nations and Changing World Politics* (2nd ed.) (Boulder: Westview, 1997), pp.52–58.

39 *Certain Expenses of the United Nations*, ICJ Rep 1962, p.151.

40 See Berridge, G.R., *Return to the UN: UN Diplomacy in Regional Conflicts* (London: Macmillan, 1991).

Council.[41] The newly active Security Council, underpinned by P5 cooperation, was central to diplomatic efforts which brought about the end of several long-running disputes, something which had been hindered in some contexts during the Cold War by virtue of the superpowers being indirectly on opposite sides to the disputes in question. One such example was the long-running Iran–Iraq war, brought to an end in 1988 in accordance with ceasefire terms contained in a unanimous Security Council resolution.[42] The late 1980s also saw the Central American peace process take place under UN supervision as states in the region coming out of conflict sought to make the transition to peaceful and democratic rule. As part of this process, UN peacekeeping operations were deployed to the region. The United Nations Observer Group in Central America (ONUCA) was tasked with verifying states' compliance with their undertakings to cease support for irregular forces and not to allow their territory to be used to launch attacks on neighbouring states,[43] and the later United Nations Observer Mission in El Salvador (ONUSAL) was deployed to supervise the implementation of the peace agreement reached by the El Salvadoran government and opposition forces designed to end their long-running civil war.[44] There was also a UN role in Namibia, where South African withdrawal and a peaceful transition to independence followed on from a diplomatic process supported by both the US and USSR and the deployment of the United Nations Transition Assistance Group (UNTAG) peacekeeping operation to monitor the implementation of the peace agreement and supervise elections.[45] The resolution of the Namibian situation was particularly significant given the considerable number of vetoes that had been exercised on the issue over the previous decade and beyond.[46]

While some examples of expanded peacekeeping functions in the early post–Cold War era are illustrated above, UN peacekeeping more generally underwent a transformation during this time. Approximately, 20 peacekeeping operations or observer missions were created in the period 1987–1992 alone, which exceeded the number established in the previous 40 years. Peacekeeping operations increasingly undertook mandates which went beyond the initially limited functions of peacekeeping, involving them in wider transitional roles. UNTAC in Cambodia was particularly impressive in this respect, effectively taking on the administration

41 During an unprecedented three-year period, no vetoes were exercised between May 1990 and May 1993.

42 SC Res 598 (1988). For discussion of UN involvement, see Tripp, C., 'The Security Council and the Iran-Iraq War,' in Lowe et al, supra n21, pp.368–383, especially at pp.379–381.

43 SC Res 644 (1989).

44 SC Res 693 (1991).

45 SC Res 632 (1989).

46 Beginning with a US/UK/France veto in 1975 (UN Doc. S/PV.1829), eight draft resolutions pertaining to the situation in Namibia were vetoed by two or more of the Western permanent members.

of the state and supervision of free elections.[47] From the early 1990s onwards, the Security Council also began to finally exercise its Charter powers to impose non-military sanctions and authorise military enforcement measures with a degree of frequency.[48] The extent to which a new wave of optimism had emerged about the potential role of the UN as a collective security actor became apparent following Iraq's invasion of Kuwait in 1990. A united Security Council moved to label the invasion a 'breach of the peace,'[49] quickly following this up with the imposition of non-military sanctions,[50] and eventually moving to authorise a US-led coalition of states to use 'all measures necessary' to liberate Kuwait.[51] While flaws in the wording of the resolution would give rise to later problems,[52] the action which it was adopted to sanction proved effective in bringing about Kuwait's liberation. The successful resolution of the Gulf conflict led President Bush to hail the emergence of a 'new world order,'[53] and in his prominent *Agenda for Peace*, the new UN Secretary-General Boutros Boutros-Ghali envisaged an ambitious and positive role for the UN in the new political climate.[54]

Reality dawns: New challenges, taking stock and renewed tensions

The initial optimism which accompanied the end of the Cold War period was relatively short-lived as the UN quickly became beset by new challenges, amid changing circumstances. Three key themes might be discerned within developments during the first decade or so of the post–Cold War era after the highs illustrated above. The limitations of the UN collective security system were exposed amid a surge in conflict situations finding themselves on the Security Council's agenda for which the requisite commitment to take concerted action proved lacking; a series of efforts were made to 'take stock' of the new global security environment and improve the capacity of the UN system; and in the post-millennium years particularly, renewed tensions between the P5 were seen in the responses afforded to a series of high-profile situations.

47 See, e.g., Keller, L., 'UNTAC in Cambodia – from Occupation, Civil War and Genocide to Peace,' *Max Planck Yearbook of United Nations Law*, 2005, v.9, n.1, pp.127–178.
48 See further Chapters 5 and 7.
49 SC Res 660 (1990).
50 SC Res 661 (1990).
51 SC Res 678 (1990).
52 This is considered later. See Chapter 7.
53 Speech to US Congress, 6 March 1991.
54 UN Doc. A/47/277-S/24111. Boutros-Ghali later revisited his initially optimistic proposals three years later in *Supplement to an Agenda for Peace* in light of subsequent developments. See UN Doc. A/50/60-S/1995/1.

The 1990s, new challenges and the 'commitment gap'

The greater wave of activity attempted by the Security Council in the early post–Cold War era ultimately meant that it became overburdened against a backdrop of waning political commitment on the part of its members to apply the measures and provide the resources necessary for effectively responding to a number of the situations deemed to threaten international peace and security. Unfortunately, the new wave of optimism which had begun to inform discourse on the possibilities for the UN in the post–Cold War era, following the Gulf conflict, soon began to recede as it became embroiled in a series of challenging crises which cast a shadow over its capacity to function effectively as a collective security actor. No sooner was the Gulf conflict resolved, there emerged a series of new conflict situations – most prominently those in former Yugoslavia, Somalia and Rwanda[55] which would plague the UN for the first half of the 1990s. At the same time, the concept of collective security itself was in a process of evolution whereby it was increasingly coming to encompass threats within states, particularly those posed to human security as the humanitarian effects of conflict began to attract increased international attention. Most determinations by the Security Council of the existence of a threat to the peace under Article 39 from the 1990s onwards in one way or another concerned situations producing harmful humanitarian consequences. The problem of adopting a broad approach to collective security is that inevitably the expectations of the UN are increased.

The 1990s alone saw a dozen instances in which the Council authorised military enforcement measures,[56] and non-military sanctions were applied in respect of a similar number of situations.[57] However, despite a much greater willingness on the part of the Council to make use of its powers under the Charter, there remained a degree of reluctance among the UN membership to act under the authority conferred by the Council acting under those powers, the so-called 'commitment gap.' Unlike during the Cold War, the biggest obstacle to action lay not in the exercise of the veto power, which had declined in usage, but the unwillingness of states to commit the resources required to realise mandates conferred by the Council. Although military intervention in former Yugoslavia,[58] Somalia[59] and Rwanda[60] was authorised by the Council for broadly humanitarian purposes, the perceived failure of states to act effectively and provide the resources required to

55 On the peacekeeping and military enforcement responses to these situations, see Chapters 6 and 7.
56 Lowe et al, supra n21, p.672 et seq.
57 Lowe et al, supra n21, p.678 et seq.
58 See, for example, SC Res 816 (1993).
59 SC Res 794 (1992).
60 SC Res 929 (1994).

respond to these crises provoked much criticism of the UN's shortcomings.[61] In particular, the failure to prevent genocide in Rwanda during 1994 was for many a low point in the organisation's history.[62] UN peacekeeping also became discredited during the 1990s as operations were conferred with unrealistic mandates that were not matched by the appropriate provision of resources, and peacekeeping became blurred with military enforcement. In a number of situations, supposedly peacekeeping operations were deployed in environments where there was simply no peace to keep and tasked with mandates to use military force under Chapter VII, leading supposedly impartial peacekeepers to become parties to conflicts which they were simultaneously supposed to be involved in defusing.[63]

Taking stock

Notwithstanding its perceived shortcomings during the 1990s, in a number of key policy initiatives the UN advanced a broad conception of its role as a collective security actor and demonstrated a willingness to give consideration to strategies for enhancing the organisation's capabilities in this regard. While the optimistic outlook found in Secretary-General Boutros Boutros-Ghali's *Agenda for Peace*[64] – which considered the post–Cold War opportunities for the UN – was soon overtaken by events, a follow-up report sought to temper this with a greater degree of realistic reflection which took account of the newfound state of geopolitics.[65] However, it was from around the millennium that a serious focus was placed upon improving the UN's capacity to undertake effective peacekeeping operations, protect civilians during humanitarian crises, improve sanctions regimes, and more generally function as a collective security actor. Against perceptions of peacekeeping failures during the 1990s, the Brahimi report considered the future direction of UN peacekeeping,[66] highlighting the key challenges it faced and making recommendations to be actioned to improve the prospects of future peacekeeping operations being able to succeed.[67] The extent to which human security lay at the very heart of the contemporary collective security agenda was reinforced by the

61 See generally Ramsbotham, O. and Woodhouse, T., *Humanitarian Intervention in Contemporary Conflict: A Reconceptualization* (London: Polity Press, 1996), Chapters 6–7; Economides, S. and Berdal, M., *United Nations Interventionism, 1991–2004* (Cambridge: Cambridge University Press, 2007), Chapters 3–5; Ryan, S., *The United Nations and International Politics* (Basingstoke and London: Macmillan, 2000), pp.114–121, 123–133.

62 See *Report of the Independent Inquiry into the Actions of the United Nations during the 1994 Genocide in Rwanda*, UN Doc. S/1999/1257.

63 See Chapter 6.

64 UN Doc. A/47/277-S/24111.

65 *Supplement to an Agenda for Peace*, supra n54.

66 UN Doc. A/55/305-S/2000/809.

67 See Chapter 6. Post-Brahimi, there has also been a UN working group tasked with consideration of issues pertaining to peacekeeping operations. See UN Doc. S/PRST/2001/3.

UN's endorsement of the Responsibility to Protect doctrine.[68] Developed by the International Commission on Intervention and State Sovereignty,[69] the doctrine essentially holds that states have a responsibility to protect their populations from serious human rights abuses, and that where they are unable or unwilling to do so, the international community assumes a responsibility to provide such protection. Various initiatives were undertaken outside of the UN from the late 1990s onwards to consider means of improving the effectiveness of sanctions while minimising their harmful humanitarian effects, an issue brought to the fore by the experience of sanctions on Iraq. However, since 2000, there has been a UN working group on sanctions with the remit 'to develop general recommendations on how to improve [their] effectiveness ...'[70] One of the broadest reviews of the UN's collective security function emerged in 2004's *High-Level Panel Report on Threats, Challenges and Change* which gave comprehensive consideration to the full range of security threats and challenges facing the UN,[71] evidencing a broad conception of collective security,[72] and made proposals for strategies to address these.

Tensions among the P5 and 'bypassing' of the Security Council

From around the turn of the century, the Security Council for the most part began to make use of its powers to initiate military enforcement measures, non-military sanctions and the deployment of peacekeeping operations without the degree of criticism encountered for their perceived shortcomings during the 1990s. However, some key incidents from this time served to expose the extent to which divisions between the permanent members once again undermined the Council's capacity to act, resulting in turn in it being bypassed in order to serve objectives supported by one or more of the P5. Events in respect of Kosovo and Iraq were particularly illustrative of a potential for the twenty-first century Security Council to be beset by divisions comparable to those experienced during the Cold War.

Kosovo

The first major post–Cold War division among the P5 within the Security Council appeared in respect of the situation in Kosovo, a province of the Federal Republic of Yugoslavia (FRY) where approximately 90% of the population was

68 GA Res. 60/1, paras.138–140.

69 *The Responsibility to Protect: Report of the International Commission on Intervention and State Sovereignty*, available at http://responsibilitytoprotect.org/ICISS%20Report.pdf.

70 UN Doc. S/2000/319.

71 UN Doc. A/59/565. For discussion, see Odello, M., 'Commentary on the United Nations High-level Panel on Threats, Challenges and Change,' *Journal of Conflict and Security Law*, 2005, v.10, n.1, pp.231–262.

72 Ibid, paras.17–43.

of Albanian ethnicity. Tensions between the federal authorities and the Kosovar Albanian population had been building up for some time and by 1998, there was full-scale conflict as a series of oppressive measures, including serious human rights abuses, were perpetrated against the population of Kosovo.[73] The Security Council responded by imposing an arms embargo and calling for a peaceful resolution of the situation,[74] as well as determining that its subsequent deterioration constituted a threat to international peace and security in the region.[75] Following the failure of the FRY to comply with agreements signed with representatives of the warring factions, pressure from Western states began to mount for some form of military intervention to put an end to the atrocities being perpetrated by federal forces and restore peace to Kosovo. However, it was apparent that any attempt to confer authority for such action through a Security Council resolution would be vetoed at the very least by Russia which had enjoyed close ties to Serbia, the dominant constituent state within the FRY. In the event, NATO commenced an air campaign against the FRY which ultimately brought about a fresh agreement between the FRY and the Kosovar Albanian leadership and ended the hostilities. While the military action was never expressly authorised by the Council, suggesting that it constituted a violation of Article 2 (4) of the UN Charter,[76] a draft resolution condemning NATO's actions introduced in the Council by Russia and China was rejected by a vote of 12 to 3,[77] arguably placing it in a legal 'no-man's land' whereby it had neither been authorised nor condemned as unlawful. It is important to note, however, that following the NATO action which effectively bypassed the Council's role as the sole authority legally able to sanction the use of force other than that exercised in self-defence, the role of the UN became critical in enhancing the legitimacy of subsequent initiatives taken to further the restoration of peace and security to Kosovo. By Resolution 1244, the Security Council established an interim United Nations Mission in Kosovo (UNMIK) that assumed responsibility for the civil administration of Kosovo pending a final settlement of its status. This step received the support of 14 of the Council's members, including Russia, underlining the importance attached to UN involvement in the process by states that had opposed the initial NATO action and evidencing the legitimating role that the UN is uniquely capable of performing.

73 See O'Neill, W.G., *Kosovo: An Unfinished Peace* (Boulder: Lynne Rienner, 2002), pp.21–35; Independent International Commission on Kosovo, *The Kosovo Report* (Oxford: Oxford University Press, 2000), pp.33–83.

74 SC Res 1160 (1998).

75 SC Res 1199 (1998).

76 On the legality of the NATO action, see Kritsiotis, D., 'The Kosovo crisis and NATO's application of armed force against the Federal Republic of Yugoslavia,' *International and Comparative Law Quarterly*, 2000, v.39, pp.330–359.

77 UN Doc S/1999/328.

9/11, Afghanistan and Iraq

The terrorist attacks on US soil of 11 September 2001 had a considerable impact upon the foreign and defence policy objectives of a number of states as the US and its allies launched a so-called 'war on terror,' a term loosely applied to actions designed to root out and destroy terrorist networks. Two major US-led military operations followed on from 9/11, neither of which the UN had any meaningful role in. The legal issues which these have given rise to have been considered elsewhere.[78] Within weeks of 9/11, the US-led Operation Enduring Freedom commenced action against Afghanistan, ultimately bringing about the removal from power of the Taleban regime, a perceived harbourer of Al-Qaeda, the perpetrators of 9/11. Although never sanctioned by the Security Council, the action enjoyed wide international support and was formally based upon the right of states to use force in self-defence in the event of an armed attack.[79] It is, however, significant that following the overthrow of the Taleban, the important legitimating function of the UN was once again recognised as Security Council authority was sought and awarded for the deployment of the International Security Assistance Force (ISAF) operation to stabilise the country during its transitional phase towards democracy.[80] Unlike action against Afghanistan, however, the 2003 US-led invasion of Iraq would be the cause of deep divisions at the UN.

Iraq had featured on the Security Council's agenda for over a decade following its invasion of Kuwait when a US/UK-led operation was launched in 2003 to overthrow the government of Saddam Hussein. The history of the UN's involvement with Iraq has been subject to much more detailed discussion elsewhere,[81] and we only briefly touch upon the issue here in order to highlight the international divisions which it gave rise to. The ceasefire which ended the 1990–1991 Gulf conflict, contained in Resolution 687, imposed disarmament obligations upon Iraq and subjected it to wide-ranging economic sanctions. Iraq's alleged non-compliance with these brought it into dispute with the Council on several occasions in the years that followed, and on some occasions resulted in air strikes being conducted against targets in Iraq by the US and UK, purportedly on the basis of authority contained

78 See, for example, Moir, L., *Reappraising the Resort to Force: International Law, Jus ad Bellum and the War on Terror* (Oxford: Hart, 2010); Duffy, H., *The 'War on Terror' and the Framework of International Law* (Cambridge: Cambridge University Press, 2005); Gazzini, T., *The Changing Rules on the Use of Force in International Law* (Manchester: Manchester University Press, 2006); Conte, A., *Security in the 21st Century* (Aldershot: Ashgate, 2005).

79 This is not to say that there are no legal difficulties with holding Afghanistan responsible for the 9/11 attacks by Al-Qaeda. See, for example, Williamson, M., *Terrorism, War and International Law* (Dartmouth: Ashgate, 2009); Wilson, G., 'The impact of 9/11 on the use of force in international law: Ten years on,' in Utley, R. (ed.), *9/11: Ten Years After* (Farnham: Ashgate, 2012), pp.179–195, at pp.184–186.

80 SC Res 1396 (2001).

81 See, for example, Malone, D., *The International Struggle over Iraq: Politics in the UN Security Council, 1980–2005* (Oxford: Oxford University Press, 2006).

in the earlier Resolution 678 which was adopted to sanction military action to liberate Kuwait, although opposed by much of the UN's membership.[82] The issue of Iraq came to a head in 2003 when, following its alleged failure to cooperate satisfactorily with UN weapons inspectors, a US/UK-led operation invaded the country and removed Saddam Hussein from power. There was widespread international opposition to the action, including from the other three permanent members, Russia, China and France. There had been no express Security Council authorisation for the action and the legal arguments of the intervening states were dubious at best, a point to which we will return in Chapter 7. UN Secretary-General Kofi Annan pronounced the action unlawful,[83] and its occurrence left the UN looking heavily marginalised, it having had no meaningful role in the decision to take action. Significantly, however, in a similar vein to post-intervention actions in Kosovo and Afghanistan, following the removal of Saddam Hussein from power the intervening states again showed themselves eager to gain UN support for the process of reconstructing the state and overseeing its transition towards democratic structures. In Resolution 1483, adopted with 14 positive votes, the Security Council lifted the economic sanctions that had endured against Iraq for so long and conferred a Chapter VII mandate upon the occupying powers in support of the reconstruction of Iraq. Again, this underlined the importance of the UN's legitimating function.

The UN Collective Security System Today

The first quarter of the twenty-first century has seen the UN faced with a series of major international developments carrying profound implications for the maintenance of international peace and security. During this period, states such as Libya, Syria, Sudan and South Sudan have been gripped by internal conflict, while interstate conflict ensued following Russia's invasion of Ukraine. The long-running Israeli–Palestinian conflict entered a new phase when Hamas' attack on Israel in October 2023 sparked renewed hostilities between Israel and Gaza. The UN has also sought to contend with the emergence of new security challenges, ranging from the effects of climate change to those of public health emergencies such as the COVID-19 pandemic. The foregoing is just a snapshot of this period. In keeping with a pattern seen through much of the UN era, recent years have seen

82 For discussion of the legality of some of the air strikes against Iraq during the 1990s, see Gray, C., 'After the ceasefire: Iraq, the Security Council and the use of force,' *British Year Book of International Law*, 1994, v.65, pp.135–174; Lobel, J. and Ratner, M., 'Bypassing the Security Council: Ambiguous authorizations to use force, ceasefires and the Iraqi inspection regime,' *American Journal of International Law*, 1999, v.93, pp.124–154; White, N.D., 'The legality of the threat of force against Iraq,' *Security Dialogue*, 1999, v.30, n.1, pp.75–86.

83 'Iraq war illegal, says Annan,' *BBC News*, 16 September 2004, at http://news.bbc.co.uk/1/hi/3661134.stm.

dividing lines emerge in respect of a number of situations amid growing political tensions between the P5, resulting in inaction (or heavily limited action) on the part of the Security Council. However, before leaping to assertions that a new Cold War has begun, it should also be noted that twenty-first century developments have simultaneously seen ongoing engagement by the Council in respect of a larger number of situations and active utilisation of peacekeeping operations and sanctions regimes.

Business as usual: Chapter VII resolutions, sanctions and peacekeeping regimes

Over the course of the decade and a half up to 2024, the Security Council continued to adopt a relatively consistent number of resolutions,[84] a substantial proportion of which were adopted with express reference to Chapter VII of the UN Charter,[85] where the teeth of the collective security system are located. Very few issues entered the Council's agenda for the first time during this period, and these tended to take the form of significant new developments such as the commencement of the Libyan civil war,[86] the aftermath of the coup d'etat in Mali,[87] the breakout of conflict in South Sudan[88] and the consequences in turn of Russia's annexation of Crimea[89] and invasion of Ukraine.[90] The matters which have attracted the lion's share of the Council's time over the period in question have concerned events within the African continent and the Middle East, the former accounting for over 50% of items discussed.[91] It is important to note that most resolutions adopted by the Security Council have been unanimous,[92] those pertaining to the

84 The most active year in this period was 2016 when 77 resolutions were adopted, the quietest being 2023 when just 50 were.

85 For example, 42 of the 77 resolutions adopted in 2016 fell under Chapter VII, while 25 of the 50 adopted in 2023 did.

86 First placed on the Council's agenda on 22 February 2011. See *Table of First Appearance of Agenda Items 1946–2022*, available at https://main.un.org/securitycouncil/sites/default/files/first_appearance_of_agenda_item.pdf.

87 First placed on the Council's agenda on 20 December 2012. See *Table of First Appearance*, ibid.

88 First placed on the Council's agenda on 11 November 2013. See *Table of First Appearance*, supra n86.

89 First placed on the Council's agenda on 28 February 2014. See *Table of First Appearance*, supra n86.

90 First placed on the Council's agenda on 11 April 2022. See *Table of First Appearance*, supra n86.

91 This is documented in successive *Annual Highlights* publications of the Security Council. See, e.g., *Highlights of Security Council Practice 2017*, p.12, where it is noted that during that year 62.9% of the Council's decisions concerned Africa.

92 Documented in various *Annual Highlights* publications. For example, in 2023, 70% of resolutions were adopted unanimously (*Highlights of Security Council Practice 2023*, p.46). However, back in 2015, unanimous decisions accounted for 88% of all resolutions (*Highlights of Security Council Practice 2015*, p.9).

African continent being a good case in point. However, responding to events in the Middle East has been more contentious and the source of most exercises of the veto power.[93]

That the Security Council has been able to find consensus on a substantial body of issues with which it has been faced has enabled it to continue to oversee the imposition of a number of sanctions regimes and deployment of a wave of peacekeeping operations in response to identified threats to the peace. Although only one new sanctions regime has been established in the past decade,[94] the Council has been able to extend and vary longer established regimes.[95] Similarly, while a number of peacekeeping operations have completed their mandates in the decade and a half up to 2024,[96] support existed for the creation of several others in the same period,[97] most of which were tasked with a mandate which included functions pertaining to the protection of civilians. At the same time, a series of long-running operations remained deployed.[98] It is important to bear this continuing wave of activism on the Council's part in mind when pondering some of the dividing lines which have emerged on specific situations considered below.

Dividing lines

The Arab Spring: Libya and Syria

The Arab Spring, a term applied to a series of uprisings which broke out in the Arab World from 2011 onwards, resulted in the removal of long-standing authoritarian regimes in Tunisia, Egypt and Libya, and the descent of Syria into a long-running civil war. In the UN's response to the conflicts which engulfed Libya and Syria, clear dividing lines emerged between the Security Council's permanent members as to what would be deemed appropriate action on its part. In response to conflict in Libya between the Gaddafi regime and opposition forces, the Security Council authorised states to take military enforcement measures 'to protect civilians and civilian populated areas under threat of attack,'[99] while also imposing sanctions

93 In the period from 2015 to 2024, 22 of 33 vetoed resolutions concerned the Middle East.

94 In respect of Haiti, established by SC Res 2653 (2022).

95 See, e.g., *Repertoire of the Practice of the Security Council*, 25th Supplement, 2022, Part VII, pp.25–47.

96 These included MINURCAT, UNMIS and UNMIT, all of which ended their mandate in 2011; UNMIL in 2015; UNOCI in 2017; MINUSTAH in 2017; and UNAMID in 2020.

97 For example, MONUSCO (SC Res 1925 (2010)), UNISFA (SC Res 1990 (2011)), UNMISS (SC Res 1996 (2011)), MINUSMA (SC Res 2100 (2013)) and MINUSCA (SC Res 2149 (2014)) were all created during this period.

98 As of 1 September 2024, 7 of 11 operations deployed had been created pre-millennium. Some, such as UNFICYP in Cyprus and UNTSO in the Middle East, could be traced back as far as 1964 and 1948, respectively.

99 SC Res 1973 (2011).

on figures within the Gaddafi regime.[100] Although Russia and China permitted the relevant resolutions to pass by not exercising their power of veto, that they and three other Council members abstained on Resolution 1973 demonstrated uneasiness over the initiation of military enforcement measures. In the event, action taken by NATO on the basis of that resolution included wide-ranging air strikes against the military infrastructure of the Gaddafi regime and undoubtedly aided the eventual toppling of the regime by opposition forces.[101] The nature of military action taken met with opposition from a number of states, including Russia, who felt that this represented too broad an interpretation of the authority conferred by Resolution 1973.[102] The result was that when faced with decisions over responding to the Syrian Civil War, Russia and China would be even more reluctant to countenance the adoption of any measures by the Security Council. As put by Chariza, 'NATO's action against Libya went far beyond their expectation … [Russia and China] were not prepared to be misled again by the West into supporting UNSC sanctions or military intervention against Syria.'[103] Arguably influenced by the Libyan episode, combined with ties to the country,[104] Russia and China vetoed a series of draft resolutions pertaining to the Syrian conflict over a number of years, including those condemnatory of acts of the Assad regime against sections of the civilian population during the civil war in that country including the use of chemical weapons.[105] This effectively sidelined the Security Council from the conflict. As a result, the US and other Western states proceeded to bypass the Council in launching air strikes against targets in Syria in the aftermath of chemical weapons attacks,[106] which in turn appeared to receive considerable political support even

100 SC Res 1970 (2011).

101 See Wilson, G., 'The United Nations Security Council, Libya and resolution 1973: Protection of civilians or tool for regime change?,' in Panara, C. and Wilson, G. (eds), *The Arab Spring: New Patterns for International Law and Democracy* (Boston/Leiden: Brill, 2013), pp.101–122, at pp.105–106.

102 Ibid, pp.110–113.

103 Chariza, M., 'Soft Balancing Strategy in the Middle East: Chinese and Russian Vetoes in the United Nations Security Council in the Syrian Crisis,' *China Report*, 2014, v.50, n.3, pp.243–258, at p.252.

104 Chariza, ibid, pp.249–50.

105 See, e.g., UN Docs S/2012/77; S/2012/538; S/2014/348; S/2016/846;* S/2016/1026; S/2017/172; S/2017/315;* S/2017/962;* S/2018/321;* S/2019/756; S/2019/961; S/2020/661; S/2020/693; S/2022/538;* S/2023/507* (* indicates vetoed by Russia alone). For the Security Council debates, see UN Docs S/PV.6711; S/PV.6810; S/PV.7180; S/PV.7785; S/PV.7825; S/PV.7893; S/PV.7922; S/PV.8105; S/PV.8228; S/PV.8623; S/PV.8697; S/2020/657; S/2020/681; S/PV.9087; S/PV.9371.

106 See, e.g., Westbrook, C., 'Legality and morality in International Law: The Syria Air Strikes,' *New York University Journal of International Law & Politics*, 2019, v.51, pp.953–964; Scharf, M.P., 'Striking a Groatian Moment: How the Syria Airstrikes Changed International Law Relating to Humanitarian Intervention,' *Chicago Journal of International Law*, 2018, v.19, n.2, pp.586–614, at pp.590–593.

if lacking the legitimacy that is conferred by the legal authority of the Security Council.[107]

Ukraine

Russia's invasion of Ukraine in February 2022 came less than a decade after it had earlier intervened in that state and annexed the bordering regions of Crimea, Donetsk and Luhansk.[108] In a precursor to the events of 2022, the Security Council was unable to address this situation due to Russia exercising its power of veto in respect of attempts within the Council to pass comment on it.[109] The situation arising from Russia's invasion of Ukraine was arguably much graver and represents a most recent instance of the Security Council being precluded from tackling a significant conflict owing to the direct involvement of one of its permanent members, exercising its veto to prevent any response on the Council's part in a manner reminiscent of its use during the Cold War to place the conduct of the superpowers beyond the purview of the Council.[110] The first instance of the invasion of a sovereign state within Europe since World War II, the challenges posed for the maintenance of international peace and security were immense. However, the Council was confined to transferring the matter to the General Assembly,[111] which roundly condemned the Russian invasion,[112] although any meaningful action such as the imposition of sanctions only took place under the auspices of regional bodies and individual states.[113]

Israel/Palestine

The final example of recent dividing lines between the permanent members of the Security Council can be found with the outbreak of the Israel–Gaza conflict

107 See ibid.

108 For discussion of the legal issues raised, see Wilson, G., 'Secession and Intervention in the Former Soviet Space: The Crimean Incident and Russian Interference in Its 'Near Abroad,' *Liverpool Law Review*, 2016, v.37, n.3, pp.153–175.

109 See UN Docs. S/2014/189; S/2015/562. For the accompanying Council debates on the vetoed resolutions, see UN Docs. S/PV.7138; S/PV.7498.

110 See UN Doc. S/2022/155. For discussion of the legal issues raised by the invasion, see Cavandoli, S. and Wilson, G., 'Distorting Fundamental Norms of International Law to Resurrect the Soviet Union: The International Law Context of Russia's Invasion of Ukraine,' *Netherlands International Law Review*, 2022, v.69, n.3, pp.383–410; Hilpold, P., 'Justifying the Unjustifiable: Russia's Aggression against Ukraine, International Law, and Carl Schmitt's "Theory of the Greater Space" ("GroBraumtheorie"),' *Chinese Journal of International Law*, 2023, v.22, pp.409–433; Kelly, M., 'The Role of iInternational Law in the Russia-Ukraine War,' *Case Western Reserve Journal of International Law*, 2023, v.55, n.1, pp.61–92.

111 By SC Res 2623 (2022).

112 GA Res ES-11/1.

113 See Cavandoli and Wilson, supra n110, pp.387–88.

in October 2023. This represents only the latest stage in the long-running Israeli–Palestinian conflict, during which the US has been prepared to exercise its veto frequently to shield Israel from criticism for actions directed against Palestinian populations and occupied territories, leaving such criticism to be laid out instead in resolutions adopted by the General Assembly.[114] Following the Hamas incursion into Israel and seizure of hostages on 7 October 2023, Israel responded with heavy-scale military action against targets within Gaza, generating widespread concerns as to the humanitarian consequences of such action and potentially compatibility with international humanitarian law. Although some modest Council pronouncements on the matter have been possible,[115] the US has vetoed several draft resolutions which it has considered insufficiently balanced, [116] while its own proposals have met with Russian and Chinese vetoes on a similar basis.[117]

Conclusion

The overview provided within this chapter of some of the key stages in the history of the UN reinforces the extent to which the development of the UN collective security system has simultaneously functioned in accordance with restraints imposed by the political priorities of the major powers and their relationships with one another, while at the same time proving responsive to changing circumstances and being capable of flexible development to meet new challenges.

One could be forgiven for drawing negative conclusions upon the contribution of the UN as a collective security actor from an overview of its history to date. The Cold War saw the Security Council paralysed, hindering its ability to function in the manner envisaged by the UN Charter, and while the early post–Cold War period saw fresh optimism as the major powers began to cooperate in responding to some of the major international crises of the time, the limited commitment displayed by states to use UN mechanisms to effectively tackle some of the crises which emerged throughout the 1990s further undermined its authority. The divisions which emerged following the military actions taken without UN authority against the FRY in 1999 and Iraq in 2003 reinforced the limitations of the UN system, as have more recent tensions between the Security Council's permanent members in respect of Syria, Ukraine and Israel–Gaza. Thus, a requisite degree of major power consensus upon the appropriate functioning of the UN collective security system cannot be assumed.

114 For example, in 2015 alone see GA Resolutions 70/16, 70/17, 70/83, 70/89 and 70/90.
115 See SC Res 2728 (2024), which called for a ceasefire during the month of Ramadan, the release of hostages and access for humanitarian aid.
116 See UN Docs. S/2023/773; S/2023/970; S/2024/173. For the Council's debates on these draft resolutions, see UN Docs. S/PV.9442; S/PV.9499; S/PV.9552.
117 See UN Docs. S/2023/792; S/2024/239. For the Council's debates over the proposed resolutions, see UN Docs. S/PV.9453; S/PV.9584.

However, although this book accepts some of the traditional realist criticisms of the operability of collective security,[118] it is easy to overlook the extent to which the UN collective security system has proven itself to be adaptable to changing needs. Although the Cold War is generally regarded as a dark period in which the UN was incapable of making any meaningful contribution to the maintenance of international peace and security, in reality, the organisation proved itself sufficiently adaptable to the environment within which it found itself to be able to make some significant advances, notwithstanding difficult circumstances. Several notable developments are evidenced during this time. Lacking a military enforcement capacity of its own, the Korean incident saw the Security Council interpret its powers in the realm of military enforcement flexibly in order to effectively contract its military enforcement function to other actors under its authority, an approach which it would continue in the post–Cold War era. Similarly, the passage of Uniting for Peace evidenced a desire on the part of many states to confer the UN with an alternative mechanism for commencing action when paralysis of the Security Council prevented it from performing the role envisaged for it by the UN Charter. Finally, the creation of peacekeeping represented an attempt to create an additional collective security tool which might be utilised in lower intensity situations unhindered by the obstacles associated with the more robust collective security measures provided for by Chapter VII of the Charter. The subsequent chapters, in which four specific tools of the UN collective security system are considered in detail, will illustrate further the flexibility of the Charter framework and the ability of this system to evolve in response to changing circumstances. While the post–Cold War era witnessed various setbacks for the UN, these were in part a consequence of the UN's own success and willingness to broaden its approach to collective security. Following on from early post–Cold War successes and set against an enhanced conception of security which encompassed action to relieve humanitarian suffering, expectations of the UN had grown. While it had become more active than it had ever been in addressing threats to international peace and security, greater expectations meant that notwithstanding some relative successes, its shortcomings would always form the focus of much attention. Even though the Security Council has been effectively bypassed on some occasions when states have launched unilateral military action, that it has quickly been involved in post-conflict reconstruction and peace-building efforts in locations such as Kosovo and Iraq evidences the unique legitimacy that states consider it to have. Notwithstanding the emergence of a series of divisions between the P5 on situations which still represent global 'hot spots' today, it can also be noted that the Council continues to take an active role vis-à-vis the utilisation of measures such as sanctions and peacekeeping operations in several contingencies for which broad support exists.

118 See Chapter 1.

4

DIPLOMATIC RESPONSES TO SECURITY THREATS

Introduction

Traditional discussions of collective security have tended to focus upon the utilisation of military means, or at the very least measures of a coercive or mandatory nature, to respond to security threats. However, the UN Charter system envisages that a broad range of responses will be available for responding to a threat to the peace in any given situation. Before proceeding to consider those measures generally perceived as the most robust – non-military sanctions and military enforcement action – it is appropriate to, firstly, appraise the UN system's utilisation of diplomatic responses in attempting to resolve situations considered to threaten international peace and security. Successful resolution of disputes through such means removes the need for more robust measures to be applied, which are generally accompanied by greater human and economic costs, making diplomatic solutions the preferred mode for removing threats to international peace and security. Indeed, Article 2 (3) obliges UN member states to settle their disputes peacefully, although this may be regarded as a more practical step at an earlier stage of a dispute given that it further states the purpose of this obligation being to ensure 'that international peace and security, and justice, are not endangered.' While diplomacy may continue where a dispute escalates into full-blown conflict, it may also be the case that more robust measures also receive consideration.

Diplomacy has been helpfully defined as 'the conduct of international relations by negotiation and other peaceful means (such as clarifying intentions and gathering information) which are either directly or indirectly, immediately or eventually,

DOI: 10.4324/9781003518105-5

designed to promote negotiation.'[1] The nature of diplomacy is such that it is capable of being employed largely free of legal regulation. States and other international actors are obviously able to engage in dialogue concerning disputes arising between themselves, possibly assisted by third parties acceptable to both sides, and may do so with a view to the resolution of such disputes at any time. As long as such discussions remain free of attempted coercion through the application of sanctions, military or otherwise,[2] international law offers little by way of regulation of such interactions. A wide range of measures initiated by various actors potentially fall within the scope of diplomatic responses to security threats, but considerations of space restrict our focus to some of the more prominent aspects of diplomatic or non-coercive responses that take place broadly under UN auspices. First, we consider the extent to which the Security Council is able to effectively make use of provisions of Chapter VI of the UN Charter in promoting the peaceful resolution of disputes giving rise to real or potential threats to international peace and security. After briefly noting the role of the General Assembly in the promotion of the peaceful settlement of disputes, the central part of the chapter is then given to the role played by the UN Secretary-General in diplomatic efforts to respond to situations threatening international peace and security. The Secretary-General has become the most prominent actor associated with diplomacy under UN auspices. Indeed, it may be contended that in the diplomatic arena 'the true centre of action lies with the Secretary-General and his agents.'[3] Finally, we briefly consider the role of other actors in brokering the peaceful resolution of disputes in support of the primary UN objective of the maintenance of international peace and security.

Measures under Chapter VI

The nature of Chapter VI measures

The provisions contained in Chapter VI of the UN Charter are phrased in relatively general language. Rather than conferring the Security Council with very specific powers, they constitute a framework under which states are obliged to attempt to resolve their disputes peacefully, and the Council is effectively afforded a supervisory role in assisting them to do so. Three general points can be made about the nature of Chapter VI provisions. First, the Security Council cannot act under its Chapter VI powers in order to compel the settlement of any dispute.

1 Berridge, G., 'The UN and the world diplomatic system: Lessons from the Cyprus and US–North Korea talks,' in Bourantonis, D. and Evriviades, M. (eds), *A United Nations for the Twenty-First Century* (The Hague, London and Boston: Kluwer, 1996), pp.105–126, at p.105.

2 In such cases, the legal frameworks deriving from Articles 41 and 42 of the UN Charter will obviously have some bearing upon the relevant course of action.

3 Ratner, S.R., 'Image and reality in the UN's peaceful settlement of disputes,' *European Journal of International Law*, 1995, v.6, pp.426–444, at p.427.

'When acting under Chapter VI … [it] is generally confined to measures of a non-coercive nature which possess no legally binding character for the parties to a dispute.'[4] If the Council wishes to coerce states through the application of mandatory measures, it should act under Chapter VII where its enforcement powers are to be found.[5] No obligation is placed upon states by the provisions of Chapter VI beyond a general requirement that they are prepared to avail themselves of pacific methods of settlement with a view to the resolution of their disputes,[6] and that if they cannot resolve these themselves they will submit them to the Security Council, as provided for by Article 37. In this sense, obligations under Chapter VI are essentially procedural. Second, the fact that the Council may have already taken action under Chapter VII in relation to a recognised threat to international peace and security does not preclude its continuation of efforts to resolve the situation through peaceful means. In practice, the mere existence of an Article 39 determination in relation to a situation, and the adoption of measures under Article 41 or 42, have not usually resulted in the ending of all attempts to achieve satisfactory resolution through peaceful means. Indeed, measures under Chapters VI and VII will often be related to one another. The coercive nature of Chapter VII measures can serve as part of a programme of initiatives designed to bring about eventual peaceful resolution through the exertion of pressure upon the disputing parties. A good case in point is that of the response to the conflict which accompanied the break-up of Yugoslavia during the early to mid-1990s. Even following the imposition of non-military sanctions and the authorisation of military measures under Chapter VII,[7] efforts under UN auspices to facilitate a diplomatic solution continued unabated.[8] While sanctions and NATO's military action may have been central in bringing the conflict to an end, the settlement officially delivering peace to Bosnia-Herzegovina could only be produced by the parties themselves coming to peace talks in Dayton.[9] The Council has also deployed diplomatic missions comprising its own members to support peace processes in states which remained

4 Tomuschat, C., 'Article 33,' in Simma, B. et al (eds), *The Charter of the United Nations: A Commentary* (2nd ed.) (Oxford and New York, 2002), pp.583–594, at p.584.

5 Although these most obviously include non-military sanctions and military enforcement measures under Articles 41 and 42, the Security Council can also order states to abide by provisional measures adopted under Article 40.

6 See further Tomuschat, supra n4, at p.584.

7 Although an arms embargo was imposed by SC Res 713 (1991), comprehensive economic sanctions were first imposed by SC Res 757 (1992). Air strikes by NATO were authorised by SC Res 816 (1993).

8 For discussion of these efforts see Woodward, S.L., 'The Security Council and the wars in the Former Yugoslavia,' in Lowe, V., Roberts, A., Welsh, J. and Zaum, D. (eds), *The United Nations Security Council and War* (Oxford: Oxford University Press, 2008), pp.406–441. For an insight from a key player within peace negotiations, see, among other accounts, Bildt, C., *Peace Journey: The Struggle for Peace in Bosnia* (London: Weidenfeld & Nicolson, 1998).

9 See, for example, Gaeta, P., 'The Dayton agreements and international law,' *European Journal of International Law*, 1996, v.7, n.2, pp.147–163.

subject to UN sanctions at the time, for example to the Democratic Republic of the Congo,[10] South Sudan[11] and Guinea-Bissau[12] in 2018 and 2019, respectively. Third, unlike the measures provided for in Chapter VII, when acting under Chapter VI, the Security Council does not need to have made any determination that there exists a threat to the peace, breach of the peace or act of aggression. Instead, the various provisions of Chapter VI refer to 'situations' or 'disputes' which the Council can take up, arguably permitting its consideration of situations of a lower level of intensity.[13]

The relatively general powers conferred upon the Security Council by Chapter VI can be summarised in two fundamental propositions. The first of these is that the Security Council enjoys the general power to make recommendations for the peaceful settlement of disputes. This fact is made clear by several of the provisions of Chapter VI. Article 33 (2) states that the Council 'shall, when it deems necessary, call upon the parties to settle their disputes by [peaceful] means,' as set out in Article 33 (1), which lists these as entailing 'negotiation, enquiry, mediation, conciliation, arbitration, judicial settlement, resort to regional agencies or arrangements, or other peaceful means ...'[14] Notwithstanding the fact that the Council is here empowered to 'call upon' states to resolve their disputes through the aforementioned means, the power is effectively recommendatory in the sense that states cannot be obliged to reach any particular settlement. The Council's general power of recommendation is reinforced further by Article 36 (1)'s empowerment of it to 'recommend appropriate procedures or methods of adjustment' at any stage of a dispute, and Article 37's proviso that where parties fail to settle a dispute in accordance with measures set out in Article 33 (1), the Council shall decide whether to act under Article 36 if the continuance of the dispute is likely to endanger the maintenance of international peace and security.

A second fundamental proposition to be made in relation to Chapter VI is that in support of its general recommendatory powers, the Security Council may under Article 34 'investigate any dispute, or any situation which might lead to international friction or give rise to a dispute, in order to determine whether [its] continuance ... is likely to endanger the maintenance of international peace and security.' This is effectively a means of providing the Council with the opportunity to avail itself of further information that it deems necessary if it is to be able

10 UN Doc. S/2018/1030.

11 UN Doc. S/2019/825.

12 UN Doc. S/2019/303. This mission also visited the Cote d'Ivoire.

13 Indeed, Article 34 permits the Council's investigations of situations 'which *might* lead to international friction or give rise to a dispute.' The implication is clear: situations yet to reach the status of 'threat to the peace' are within the remit of Chapter VI measures.

14 On such methods of settlement, see further Brownlie, I., 'The peaceful settlement of international disputes,' *Chinese Journal of International Law*, 2009, v.8, n.2, pp.267–283; Merrills, J.G. and De Brabandere, E., *International Dispute Settlement* (7th ed.) (Cambridge: Cambridge University Press, 2022), Chapters 1–7.

to make meaningful recommendations for the settlement of disputes, or potential disputes. It may also benefit the Council's exercise of its Chapter VII powers, as should an investigation conclude that a threat to international peace and security is present, the Council can move to make a determination under Article 39 and possibly follow this up with the application of specific Chapter VII measures. There are different modes through which the Council's investigatory power may be exercised, including, for example, the deployment of fact-finding missions or investigatory commissions to trouble spots. Article 34's power of investigation is expressly strengthened by the power which the Council enjoys under Article 29 to create subsidiary organs as it deems necessary for it to perform its functions, thus permitting it to create such bodies.[15] Although there is some suggestion that the power contained in Article 34 is limited to investigations to consider whether the continuation of the situation in question is likely to endanger the maintenance of international peace and security,[16] the Council can be regarded as having a wider general competence of investigation in support of its primary responsibility for the maintenance of international peace and security.[17]

Detailed treatment of the substantive nature of Chapter VI's provisions has been adequately provided elsewhere.[18] For present purposes, the primary objective is to consider the extent to which the Council has effectively been able to make use of its principal Chapter VI powers in practice.

The Council's Practice

It has been suggested that 'the legal literature on Chapter VI remains sparse,'[19] which probably reflects the fact that undertaking investigations and making recommendations for the peaceful settlement of disputes – which broadly speaking

15 See Saul, M.W. and White, N.D., 'Legal means of dispute settlement in the field of collective security: The quasi-judicial powers of the Security Council,' in French, D., Saul, M.W. and White, N.D. (eds), *International Law and Dispute Settlement: New Problems and Techniques* (Oxford: Hart, 2010), pp.191–214, at p.198. There is no definition in the Charter of what will constitute subsidiary organs, but the Repertory of United Nations Practice outlines some common characteristics, detailed in Goodrich, L.M., Hambro, E. and Simons, A.P., *Charter of the United Nations: Commentary and Documents* (3rd ed.) (New York and London: Columbia University Press, 1969), pp.102–104. See also Sarooshi, D., 'The legal framework governing United Nations subsidiary organs,' *British Year Book of International Law*, 1996, v.LXVII, pp.413–478. Some examples of subsidiary organs are provided by Sands, P. and Klein, P., *Bowett's Law of International Institutions* (5th ed.) (London: Sweet & Maxwell, 2001), p.70 et seq.

16 Schweisfurth, T., 'Article 34,' in Simma et al, supra n4, pp.594–608, p.600.

17 Schweisfurth, ibid, p.595.

18 See, for example, Tomuschat, supra n4; Schweisfurth, T., 'Article 34' and 'Article 35' in Simma et al, supra n4, pp.594–608, 608–615; Giegerich, T., 'Article 36,' 'Article 37' and 'Article 38,' in Simma, B. et al (eds), *The Charter of the United Nations: A Commentary* (3rd ed.) (Oxford and New York, 2012), pp.1119–1145, 1146–1160, 1160–1170.

19 Ratner, supra n3, p.427.

are the very powers provided for the Security Council by that chapter – are matters which are largely free of legal regulation. Furthermore, the Council's diplomatic profile has been labelled 'low-key and obscure,'[20] reflecting the fact that activity in this arena invariably takes place behind closed doors. Although it may be observed that 'over time delegates to Council meetings [have] cited [Chapter VI] articles less frequently,'[21] there is nonetheless a body of practice which has been built up by the Council in making use of its investigatory and recommendatory powers under Chapter VI.

Investigation by the Council

In order to investigate disputes or situations which might lead to international friction or give rise to a dispute, the Security Council enjoys a considerable degree of discretion in deciding how it will undertake this function, Article 34 providing no stipulation in this respect.[22] In practice, the UN Secretary-General and his special representatives have come to play a significant role in the performance of fact-finding or investigatory functions,[23] something which has been actively encouraged by the UN membership at large.[24] Their efforts aside, the Council has relied upon the establishment and deployment of a number of bodies in order to obtain a closer appreciation of situations of concern. Although such bodies have been afforded various different labels – for example, fact-finding missions, commissions of inquiry and investigatory commissions – for the most part, there has been little to distinguish them in terms of their functions. While the Council has seldom expressly invoked Article 34 as a basis for its investigations,[25] there are some obvious examples of it having sanctioned such processes. Schweisfurth catalogued 17 instances on which the Council had ordered investigations under Chapter VI during the Cold War period.[26] On some occasions, the Council requested that the

20 Iji, T., 'The UN as an International Mediator: From the Post-Cold War Era to the Twenty-First Century,' *Global Governance*, 2017, v.23, pp.83–100, at p.83.

21 Ratner, supra n3, p.435.

22 For a perspective on the legal parameters of the Security Council's investigatory powers, see Kerley, E.L., 'The powers of investigation of the United Nations Security Council,' *American Journal of International Law*, 1961, v.55, pp.892–918.

23 See below.

24 In its *Declaration on Fact-Finding by the United Nations in the Field of the Maintenance of International Peace and Security*, the General Assembly suggested that preference should be given to the utilisation of the secretary-general for fact-finding tasks; GA Res 46/59, para.15. See further Berg, A., 'The 1991 declaration on fact-finding by the United Nations,' *European Journal of International Law*, 1993, v.4, pp.107–114, at pp.109–110.

25 A point noted recently in the Security Council's Repertoire for 2022. Indeed, Schweisfurth notes that in only two Cold War incidents in which the Council ordered investigations into particular situations did it expressly refer to Article 34; Schweisfurth, supra n16, pp.596–598.

26 Schweisfurth, supra n16, pp.596–598. On the Council's practice, see also Kolb, R., *An Introduction to the Law of the United Nations* (Portland: Hart, 2010), pp.50–62. On early Article 34 investigations by the Council, see Kerley, supra n22, pp.907–918.

secretary-general despatch a special representative to investigate a situation of concern, for example in response to the existence of a frontier dispute between Iraq and Iran,[27] and to assess the situation on the ground in East Timor following its annexation by Indonesia.[28] However, the Council has also created its own bodies for the purpose of conducting investigations.

In only the fourth resolution adopted by the Security Council, a subcommittee of five of its members was created to examine the situation existing in Spain under the regime of General Franco, in order to determine whether it threatened international peace and security.[29] This was soon followed by the creation of commissions of investigation to investigate border disputes between Greece and neighbouring states,[30] and between India and Pakistan.[31] The former comprised all members of the Council, the latter three members, and both investigatory bodies were formally created with express reference to Article 34. Although not formally based on Article 34, similar techniques were subsequently employed in relation to the Corfu Channel dispute[32] and situations of concern involving Laos,[33] Cambodia–Vietnam,[34] Guinea,[35] Senegal,[36] Zambia,[37] Benin,[38] the Seychelles,[39] Iran–Iraq[40] and Angola.[41] The Council termed the bodies it created in these cases as 'subcommittees,' 'special missions' or 'commissions of investigation,' but all involved a small subgroup of the Council's membership being tasked with investigating and reporting upon the situations concerned.[42] The Council's limited use of its investigatory powers during the Cold War can be explained by reference to the political stalemate that severely restricted its ability to discharge its functions during that period, the examples referred to herein largely concerning matters outside the centre stage of the superpower struggle. Although helpful in improving the quality of information available to the Council, their true value would be

27 UN Doc. S/11229 (1974).
28 SC Res 384 (1975).
29 SC Res 4 (1946).
30 SC Res 15 (1946).
31 SC Res 39 (1948).
32 SC Res 19 (1947).
33 SC Res 132 (1959).
34 SC Res 189 (1964).
35 SC Res 289 (1970), 295 (1971).
36 SC Res 294 (1971).
37 SC Res 326 (1973).
38 SC Res 404 (1977).
39 SC Res 496 (1981).
40 SC Res 514 (1982).
41 SC Res 571 (1985).
42 In an exception, while calling for an immediate and impartial investigation into the circumstances surrounding the death of the Congolese Prime Minister Patrice Lumumba, the Council specified no body to perform this function. See SC Res 161 (1961).

illustrated by resulting actions or recommendations emanating from the Council in response, something that came in short supply during the Cold War.[43]

It might have been expected that the end of the Cold War would lead to an increased use by the Security Council of its Chapter VI investigatory powers. However, as Schweisfurth notes, the 1990s saw the Council increasingly adopt its resolutions under Chapter VII,[44] making use of the greater degree of political consensus between the permanent members to endow its resolutions with mandatory force. Nonetheless, the Council continued to create investigatory bodies in the post–Cold War era.[45] Examples include the commission of inquiry established to investigate arms flows to Rwanda,[46] and later the international independent investigatory commission despatched to Lebanon to assist the domestic authorities to investigate the circumstances surrounding the assassination of the former Lebanese Prime Minister Rafic Hariri, in 2005.[47] Following a report pointing to Syrian involvement,[48] endorsed by the Security Council,[49] a tribunal was established by agreement between the Council and Lebanon to try those responsible for the assassination, albeit this constituted action under Chapter VII and not Chapter VI.[50] The Security Council continues to despatch general visiting missions in support of its efforts to enhance its understanding of situations within its remit. 25 such missions were established in the period 2014–2023,[51] with the DRC and Ethiopia being the location of the latter two missions despatched in this time.[52] While the use of investigatory techniques has undoubtedly improved the information available to the Council when deciding upon the recommendation of appropriate responses to situations of concern, one of the drawbacks of Chapter VI action – and hence a cause of greater recourse to action under Chapter VII – lies in its non-mandatory nature. A fact-finding/investigatory mission authorised under Chapter VI cannot be enforced upon the territory of the affected states but must operate strictly with their consent.[53] The limitations that this gives rise to are illustrated by the case involving border disputes between Eritrea and Djibouti,

43 See below.
44 Schweisfurth, supra n16, pp.607–608.
45 For examples of fact-finding missions established by the Security Council, see, e.g., Ramcharan, B.G., *Preventive Diplomacy at the UN* (Bloomington: Indiana University Press, 2008), pp.73–74.
46 SC Res 1013 (1995).
47 SC Res 1595 (2005).
48 UN Doc. S/2005/662.
49 SC Res 1636 (2005).
50 SC Res 1757 (2007).
51 See *Highlights of Security Council Practice 2023*, Chart 7, available at https://main.un.org/securitycouncil/en/content/highlights-2023-D10.
52 See UN Doc. S/PV.9297. For details of earlier Security Council missions despatched in the 1990s and 2000s, see Schweisfurth, T., 'Article 34,' in Simma et al, supra n18, pp.1086–1107, at pp.1093–1094.
53 This was reinforced in the *Declaration on Fact-finding*, supra n24, para.6.

where Eritrea refused to accept the deployment of a UN fact-finding mission.[54] Even where utilised smoothly, the benefits of fact-finding exercises are undermined where the prevailing political circumstances are not conducive to bringing moral force to bear upon disputant states' willingness to implement any recommendations which the Council may choose to issue.

Recommendations by the Council

Numerous examples abound of recommendations by the Council under Chapter VI. In exercising its power to make recommendations for the resolution of disputes, the Security Council has most frequently restricted itself to recommending that the states concerned submit themselves to negotiations.[55] Among the more prominent examples of this are its calls for the UK and Argentina to seek a diplomatic solution to the Falklands conflict[56] and for Iraq and Kuwait to enter negotiations to resolve the issues which had led Iraq to invade Kuwait in 1990.[57] In both cases, however, military action ultimately brought about resolution of the situation. Arguably, the popularity of the recommendation of negotiations between the parties lies in the fact that this is the least politically intrusive of the options open to the Council and in an atmosphere charged with the political agendas of several states, especially during the Cold War era, it invariably represents the option upon which consensus is most easily obtainable. More specific recommendations are prone to the exercise of the power of veto, particularly where a permanent member considers its interests as being affected, as happened for example in the case of the Greek border incident when the adoption of recommendations made by the commission of investigation established by the Council was vetoed by the USSR.[58] Occasionally, however, the Council has recommended a more specific course of action. In some of the earliest situations to be discussed by the Council, it recommended that the Corfu Channel dispute between the UK and Albania be resolved by referral to the ICJ,[59] while recommending that the disputing parties resolve their disputes with the assistance of a UN-appointed medium or body in respect of the Indian–Pakistani dispute over Kashmir,[60] Arab–Israeli disagreements[61] and the dispute between Indonesia and the Netherlands.[62]

54 UN Doc. SC/9570.
55 Tomuschat, supra n4, p.593.
56 SC Res 502 (1982).
57 SC Res 660 (1990). For other examples, see Tomuschat, supra n4, p.593.
58 UN Doc. S/360/Rev. 1 (1947). See White, N.D., *Keeping the Peace: The United Nations and the Maintenance of International Peace and Security* (2nd ed.) (Manchester and New York: Manchester University Press, 1997), p.84.
59 SC Res 22 (1947).
60 SC Res 47 (1948).
61 SC Res 50 (1948); SC Res 93 (1951).
62 SC Res 67 (1949).

On some occasions, the Council has actually recommended terms for settlement of a dispute, as it is empowered to do by Article 37 (2). This provision has been expressly invoked in a number of the Council's resolutions.[63] In one of the best-known examples, Resolution 242 suggested a series of principles to govern the resolution of the Arab–Israeli conflict following the 1967 Six-Day War.[64] These have, however, yet to be implemented although they are widely regarded as continuing to provide the appropriate starting point for bringing peace to the Middle East. The recommendation or endorsement of terms of settlement became more commonplace in the early post–Cold War era, as the Council's approach to the Central American[65] and Cambodian[66] peace processes evidenced.[67]

Clearly of central importance is not so much the fact that recommendations for the peaceful resolution of disputes can be made by the Council, but the extent to which these are acted upon by those to whom they are directed to effectively bring about the peaceful resolution of the dispute in question.[68] It is undoubtedly the case, however, that in the absence of the greater pressure which comes with the adoption of measures under Chapter VII, for disputes to be resolved peacefully in accordance with the provisions of Chapter VI requires that the parties concerned are committed to resolving their disputes in such a manner.[69] Practice has shown that in a number of low-intensity conflicts or disputes this has been achievable,[70] while long-running disputes where the parties concerned have come to adopt intransigent positions may be less amenable to the tools of diplomacy. Offers of UN mediation have been declined in some prominent cases – for example, by Israel at the time of the Six-Day War in 1967, by Iran during the hostage crisis and by Vietnam following its invasion of Cambodia[71] – highlighting the limitations of recommendatory measures grounded in Chapter VI. Even where undertaken, efforts to assist the disputant parties peacefully settle their disagreements hinge upon various factors. For example, in considering the lack of success within early UN efforts to resolve the Kashmir issue Hilall points to 'lack of trust

63 See, for example, SC Res 47 (1948), SC Res 80 (1950), SC Res 91 (1951), SC Res 122 (1957), SC Res 138 (1960), SC Res 242 (1967), SC Res 637 (1989), SC Res 731 (1992), cited by Kolb, supra n26, pp.50–62.
64 See further Ratner, supra n3, p.432–433.
65 See SC Res 637 (1989).
66 See SC Res 668 (1990).
67 See Ratner, supra n3, pp.437–438.
68 A survey of the relative merits of the various modes of peaceful settlement which the Council may recommend lies outside our present remit. For an overview, see Brownlie, supra n14; Merrills and De Brabandere, supra n14.
69 The Council can of course endow its recommendations with mandatory force by adopting them under Chapter VII.
70 See Kolb, supra n26, p.62.
71 Ratner, supra n3, p.436.

and mutual suspicion on the part of both Pakistan and India.'[72] Meanwhile, the lack of progress seen in more recent UN mediation efforts to resolve the Syrian conflict has been attributed to a lack of unity among the Security Council's permanent membership.[73] Those situations in which the Council has proceeded to apply measures under Chapter VII lacked the necessary ingredient of the disputant parties' amenability towards dialogue with a view to a peaceful outcome. It is arguable, however, that irrespective of their practical effect, recommendations adopted by the Council can in the appropriate circumstances have considerable 'legitimising' value by throwing the weight of the UN behind particular states, causes or desired outcomes.[74]

A note on the General Assembly

While this book focuses principally upon the role of the UN Security Council as a collective security actor, it has already been noted that the General Assembly enjoys competence in issuing recommendations in the area of international peace and security.[75] In respect of recommendations for the peaceful settlement of disputes, it is notable that Article 35 (1) entitles states to bring disputes, or situations which may lead to international friction or give rise to a dispute, to the attention of the Security Council *or* the General Assembly. Where such matters are brought to the attention of the General Assembly, its consideration of them is subject to the terms of Articles 11 and 12.[76] Broadly speaking, this entitles the Assembly to make recommendations in respect of such a dispute or situation,[77] so long as the Council is not exercising its functions in relation to it.[78] The General Assembly has also provided support for UN fact-finding missions in a more general sense through its adoption of its *Declaration on Fact-finding by the United Nations in the Field of the Maintenance of International Peace and Security*,[79] which sets out guidance to govern their use.

Being unrestrained by the political factors which can hinder Security Council decision-making, especially the power of veto, the General Assembly may theoretically serve as a better forum for initiating recommendations for the peaceful settlement of disputes. One possible drawback of the Assembly performing a greater

72 Hilall, A.Z., 'Kashmir dispute and UN Mediation efforts: An historical perspective,' *Small Wars and Insurgencies*, 1997, v.8, n.2, pp.61–86.
73 See Hellmuller, S., 'Peacemaking in a shifting world order: A macro-level analysis of UN mediation in Syria,' *Review of International Studies*, 2022, v.48, n.3, pp.543–559.
74 On the UN's legitimising role, see Claude, I.L., 'Collective legitimization as a political function of the United Nations,' *International Organization*, 1966, v.20, n.3, pp.367–379.
75 See Chapter 2.
76 Article 35 (3).
77 Article 11 (2).
78 Article 12 (1).
79 GA Res 46/59 (1991).

role in this respect, however, may lie in what has been noted as its tendency to adopt resolutions built on voting majorities in comparison to the delicate political compromises which underpin the adoption of Security Council recommendations,[80] arguably making the latter more realistic as means of achieving their objectives. Furthermore, given that like Chapter VI resolutions of the Council, recommendations issued by the General Assembly have no binding force, there is no reason why the role performed by it in this respect is likely to be any more successful than that undertaken by the Security Council.

Diplomacy by the UN Secretary-General

The Charter framework

Undoubtedly, the most public face of UN diplomacy has been that of the secretary-general. More than any other body within the UN system, his office has visibly been used in pursuit of efforts to promote the peaceful settlement of international disputes, and for this reason forms the central part of this chapter's discussion of diplomatic responses to security threats. The starting point for consideration of the role of the secretary-general in this respect must be those UN Charter provisions that pertain to the office. Articles 97–100 are rather broadly phrased and provide relatively limited guidance upon the scope of his authority. This has led Newman to comment that they form a procedural base that a secretary-general can maximise according to his personal skills, but always within parameters set by a political environment essentially beyond his control.[81] The post holder is appointed by the General Assembly on the advice of the Security Council[82] and is essentially the compromise candidate of the permanent members.[83] However, the independent character of the office of secretary-general is emphasised by Article 100 (1)'s proviso that he and his officials shall not seek or receive instructions from any government or external body.[84]

80 White, supra n58, pp.193–198.

81 Newman, E., 'Secretary-general,' in Weiss, T.G. and Daws, S. (eds), *The Oxford Handbook on the United Nations* (Oxford: Oxford University Press, 2007), pp.175–192, at p.176.

82 For an overview of the appointment process, see Keating, C., 'Selecting the world's diplomat,' in Chesterman, S. (ed.), *Secretary or General?* (Cambridge: Cambridge University Press, 2008), pp.47–66; Szsaz, P.C., 'The role of the UN secretary-general: Some legal aspects,' *New York University Journal of International Law and Politics*, 1991–1992, v.24, pp.161–198, at pp.161–170; Gordenker, L., *The UN Secretary-General and the Maintenance of Peace* (New York: Columbia University Press, 1967), Chapter 3.

83 See Parker, J.E., 'Electing the UN secretary-general after the cold war,' *Hastings Law Journal*, 1992–1993, v.44, n.1, pp.161–184, at pp.172–175.

84 Furthermore, Article 100 (2) obliges states to respect the independent character of the office and not to seek to influence the secretary-general or his staff in the performance of his responsibilities.

Notwithstanding the express administrative functions entrusted to the Secretary-General,[85] a solid legal basis for his performance of a diplomatic role can be found in Articles 98 and 99. Article 98 states that the office-holder 'shall perform other functions as are entrusted to him by [the UN's] organs,' thus enabling diplomatic tasks to be assigned, in particular by the Security Council. It is, however, Article 99 that has been of the greatest significance in conferring the secretary-general with an independent role in the diplomatic arena, entitling him to 'bring to the attention of the Security Council any matter which in his opinion may threaten the maintenance of international peace and security.' It was recognised at the outset of the UN era that this gave the secretary-general a far-reaching power to take political initiatives.[86] Dag Hammarskjold described Article 99 as the provision which, more than any other, transformed the role from being that of a mere administrative official to one enjoying explicit political responsibility. By implication he felt that it necessarily gave the secretary-general 'a broad discretion to conduct inquiries and to engage in informal diplomatic activity.'[87] In a detailed study of the role, Schwebel argues that seven interlocking powers flow from Article 99: (i) the authority to bring matters of international peace and security to the attention of the Security Council; (ii) individual political personality; (iii) the power to report any developments; (iv) the power to undertake inquiries and investigations in order to decide whether to act; (v) the choice of the most appropriate means of implementing Article 99; (vi) making declarations and offering proposals for the resolution of disputes; (vii) a springboard to appeal to world public opinion.[88] In essence, Article 99 has enabled the secretary-general to assert a broad right of independent action in diplomatic terms.

Although it may be argued that to interpret Article 99 as conferring the secretary-general with the power to promote the pacific settlement of disputes through his own good offices is to stretch its terms too far, such a contention has received no notable support and there is broad agreement upon the adoption of a wide interpretation of the role afforded to the secretary-general by Article 99. The importance attached to the diplomatic role of the office is arguably evidenced by the fact

85 Article 97 provides that the secretary-general shall be the UN's chief administrative officer, while Article 98 provides that he shall act in that capacity in all meetings of the various UN organs and will make an annual report on the UN's work to the General Assembly. On the UN secretary-general's administrative functions, see Rivlin, B., 'The UN secretary-generalship at fifty,' in Bourantonis, D. and Wiener, J. (eds), *The United Nations in the New World Order: The World Organization at Fifty* (London: Palgrave Macmillan, 1996), p.85 et seq.

86 See, for example, Kunz, J.L., 'The legal position of the secretary-general of the United Nations,' *American Journal of International Law*, 1946, v.40, pp.786–792.

87 Hammarskjold, D., 'The international civil servant in law and in fact,' in Foote, W. (ed.), *Servant of Peace: A Selection of the Speeches and Statements of Dag Hammarskjold, Secretary-General of the United Nations 1953–1961* (New York: Harper and Row, 1962), p.335.

88 Schwebel, S.M., *The Secretary-General of the United Nations: His Political Powers and Practice* (Cambridge: Harvard University Press, 1952), pp.17–48.

that invariably those appointed to the position have entered the office having had considerable previous diplomatic experience.[89]

That the secretary-general is entitled to undertake an independent diplomatic role is further reinforced by reference to the doctrine of implied powers. Firmly established in the *Reparations* case, the ICJ ruled that the UN 'must be deemed to have those powers which, though not expressly provided in the Charter, are conferred upon it by necessary implication as being essential to the performance of its duties.'[90] A broad approach to implied powers was reaffirmed in the *Expenses* case where the ICJ determined that 'when [the UN] takes action which warrants the assertion that it was appropriate for the fulfilment of one of the stated purposes of the United Nations, the presumption is that [it is not] ultra vires.'[91] Effectively, UN organs are thus able to exercise those powers not expressly conferred by the Charter, but which further the purposes advanced by the Charter, so long as the powers implied do not entail the performance of acts that are expressly prohibited by the Charter. That the primary purpose of the UN is the maintenance of international peace and security has enabled holders of the office of secretary-general to interpret their powers flexibly in order to advance the office in pursuit of this objective.[92] So long as the secretary-general does not seek to usurp powers reserved for the Security Council or act in a manner which conflicts with its actions or decisions, he has considerable freedom of independent action. As Cordovez has argued, successive secretaries-general have shown that they are not restricted by a narrow interpretation of the scope of UN Charter provisions. The diplomatic role performed by the secretary-general during the Cold War is illustrative of this.[93] As will be seen, numerous examples abound of holders of the office of secretary-general having provided their good offices to assist with the negotiation, mediation or investigation of disputes, and the formation of fact-finding missions has been regularly undertaken by the secretary-general in support of diplomatic initiatives.[94] In many cases, the role performed by the secretary-general can be regarded as very much complementing Article 33 (1)'s requirement

89 Trygve Lie, Dag Hammarskjold, Kurt Waldheim, Boutros Boutros-Ghali and Ban Ki-moon all held office as their country's foreign minister at some point, while Antonio Guterres was the first former head of government appointed to the post. Hammarskjold, U Thant, Waldheim, Javier Pérez de Cuéllar and Moon had all served in the diplomatic service of their country, whereas Kofi Annan had a long diplomatic career at the UN.

90 *Reparation for Injuries Suffered in the Service of the United Nations*, ICJ Rep 1949, p.174, at p.182.

91 *Certain Expenses of the United Nations*, ICJ Rep 1962, p.151, at p.168.

92 See Lavalle, R., 'The "inherent" powers of the UN secretary-general in the political sphere: A legal analysis,' *Netherlands International Law Review*, 1990, v.37, n.1, pp.22–36.

93 Cordovez, D., 'Strengthening United Nations diplomacy for peace: The role of the secretary-general,' in UNITAR, *The United Nations and the Maintenance of International Peace and Security* (Leiden: Brill, 1987), pp.161–175.

94 See Bourloyannis, M.C., 'Fact-finding by the secretary-general of the United Nations,' *New York University Journal of International Law and Politics*, 1989–1990, v.22, pp.641–669; Pasternack,

that parties to a dispute seek to resolve their differences peacefully by resort to measures that include negotiation, enquiry, mediation and conciliation, all techniques with which the secretary-general has been associated in practice.

Influences on the diplomatic role of the UN secretary-general

Given the flexible legal framework applicable to the diplomatic role performed by the secretary-general, understanding the possibilities and limitations of the office in respect of the perceived success or failure of any individual to have served in the position is best understood by reference to three key factors. These can broadly be categorised as the political environment existing during a secretary-general's term in office, his personal qualities and his relationship with the UN membership at large, but in particular with the permanent members of the Security Council.[95]

Political environment

The international political climate is not static, and in the context of international diplomacy, some periods are more challenging than others as situations involving tension or conflict emerge or recede, and the attitudes of the key players within the international community towards these shift. The prevailing political environment has impacted upon the perceived diplomatic performance of the secretary-general. Throughout much of the Cold War, conditioned by the effects of détente, decolonisation and North–South friction, successive secretaries-general developed a tradition of mediation, the direction of peacekeeping operations, early warning and conflict prevention functions and diplomatic face-saving.[96] However, the lack of unified major power support for their efforts at times inevitably limited what was achievable through such efforts. By contrast, the newfound cooperation among the major powers which characterised the end of the Cold War period created the impetus for a series of initiatives in which the then Secretary-General Javier Pérez de Cuéllar was able to play a meaningful role.[97] Generally, the state of the world at any one moment in time may present the secretary-general with greater challenges or alleviate his workload. Arguably, the deadlock within the Security Council that pervaded the Cold War meant that relatively limited expectations

S., 'The role of the secretary-general in helping to prevent civil war,' *New York University Journal of International Law and Politics*, 1992–1993, v.26, pp.701–760, at pp.713–718.

95 Various commentators have recognised the importance of these factors. See, for example, Goodrich, L.M., 'The political role of the secretary-general,' *International Organization*, 1962, v.16, n.4, pp.720–735. Brian Urquhart argues that the main factors in the development of the office have been the personality of the incumbent and the political climate in which he had to operate; Urquhart, B., 'Selecting the world's CEO,' *Foreign Affairs*, 1995, v.74, n.3, pp.21–26, at p.23.

96 Newman, supra n81, pp.179–180.

97 See, for example, Lankevich, G.J., *The United Nations under Javier Perez De Cuellar, 1982–1991* (Lanham: Scarecrow Press, 2001), pp.55–83.

existed in respect of the role that could be performed by the secretary-general in the peace and security context. By contrast, in the early post–Cold War era, against a backdrop of optimism that accompanied some of the UN's early successes in this new era, the various spiralling conflict situations appearing upon the UN's radar increased expectations that the secretary-general could effectively utilise his good offices by way of response. The resurfacing of P5 divisions in recent years has, however, imposed renewed potential limitations, as highlighted, for example, by the inability of diplomatic initiatives under the direction of the secretary-general to tackle the Syrian Civil War.[98]

Personal qualities

Notwithstanding the political environment in which the secretary-general must operate, his individual personal qualities can make a difference to his perceived diplomatic successes or failings. As Finger and Saltzman write, 'a secretary-general who is respected by governments and the media for his competence, judgment, and integrity can have substantial impact.'[99] Essentially, a difficult challenge for any secretary-general is to employ his personal qualities in a manner that enables him to make an effective contribution to peace and security initiatives, while not antagonising any of the major international players to the extent that his office's capabilities become paralysed. This challenge is perhaps best summarised by Thakur, who comments that a secretary-general must be a 'politician, diplomat and international civil servant all rolled into one.'[100] A number of personal qualities are likely to be especially relevant to the performance of the secretary-general.[101] Of particular importance to the perceived success of any office-holder is, arguably, the degree of leadership which he is seen to exercise in the discharge of his functions.[102] Trinh, for example, discusses the idea of the 'bully pulpit' in referring to the ability of the secretary-general to use his position to encourage states to take, or refrain from taking, certain actions in pursuit of the UN's objectives and values and highlights Kofi Annan's use of his position to make several important pronouncements, expressing his views on matters such as the US-led

98 See below with reference to the deployment of special representatives of the secretary-general.

99 Finger, S.M. and Saltzman, A.A., *Bending with the Winds: Kurt Waldheim and the United Nations* (New York: Greenwood, 1990), p.42.

100 Thakur, R., *The United Nations, Peace and Security* (Cambridge: Cambridge University Press, 2006), p.321.

101 These have been detailed elsewhere. See, for example, Thakur, ibid, pp.330–333; Skjelsbaek, K., 'The UN secretary-general and the mediation of international disputes,' *Journal of Peace Research*, 1991, v.28, n.1, pp.99–115, at pp.107–108.

102 See Thakur, supra n100, pp.333–339.

invasion of Iraq.[103] Similarly, Antonio Guterres has used his office to push for international cooperation in tackling the COVID-19 pandemic,[104] including a call for a global ceasefire in support of this goal.[105]

Relationship with the UN membership

Each secretary-general owes his position to the UN membership, in particular the permanent members of the Security Council, each of whom has a power of veto over his appointment or reappointment.[106] Any office-holder must ensure that he retains the support and confidence of the wider UN membership, in particular the permanent members, for his diplomatic efforts to enjoy the maximum prospect of success. Barros argues that 'the bench-mark which differentiates some secretaries-general as more important than others is to be found in their tact and discretion, and particularly in their ability to maintain the trust and confidence of the great powers.'[107] The secretary-general's need to maintain good relations with the major powers has been the subject of considerable discussion.[108] Luck makes the point effectively when commenting upon the extent to which Boutros Boutros-Ghali and Kofi Annan came to lose the confidence of the US during their terms in office, in no small part due to the fact that they found themselves at odds with the US over important policy matters.[109] While a potential quality, displays of strong leadership by the secretary-general can equally be counterproductive. As Gordenker writes in respect of the first two office holders and their interventions in respect of the Korean and Congo crises, 'on two important occasions when the secretary-general attempted to exert an unaccustomed degree of leadership, he incurred the savage enmity of the Soviet Union.'[110]

103 Trinh, Q., 'The bully pulpit,' in Chesterman, supra n82, pp.102–120. See also Adebajo, A., 'Pope, pharaoh, or prophet? The secretary general after the cold war,' in Chesterman, supra n82, pp.139–157.

104 See, e.g., 'Remarks to the Security Council on the COVID-19 Pandemic,' 9 April 2020, available at https://www.un.org/sg/en/content/sg/speeches/2020-04-09/remarks-security-council-covid-19-pandemic.

105 See, e.g., 'Secretary-General's Appeal for Global Ceasefire,' 23 March 2020, available at https://www.un.org/sg/en/content/sg/statement/2020-03-23/secretary-generals-appeal-for-global-ceasefire.

106 See Keating, supra n82, pp.47–66.

107 Barros, J., 'The importance of secretaries-general of the United Nations,' in Jordan, R.S. (ed.), *Dag Hammarskjold Revisited: The UN Secretary-General as a Force in World Politics* (Durham: Carolina Academic Press, 1983), at p.33.

108 See Rivlin, supra n85; Schwebel, supra n88, pp.63–173; Cockayne, J. and Malone, D., 'Relations with the Security Council,' in Chesterman, supra n82, pp.69–85.

109 Luck, E.C., 'The secretary-general in a unipolar world,' in Chesterman, supra n82, pp.202–231.

110 Gordenker, L., 'The secretary-general,' in Barros, J. (ed.), *The United Nations: Past, Present and Future* (New York: The Free Press, 1972), pp.104–142, at pp.127–128.

Diplomacy by the UN secretary-general in practice

Although Article 99 of the UN Charter is generally regarded as the umbrella provision which implicitly empowers the secretary-general to undertake diplomatic initiatives to respond to situations which threaten, or may come to threaten, international peace and security, in practice holders of the office have not tended to expressly cite the legal basis for their actions in this regard. Fiedler notes that Article 99 has only been formally applied twice,[111] by Dag Hammarskjold in respect of the Congo conflict[112] and by Kurt Waldheim in respect of the occupation of the US embassy in Tehran.[113] However, Article 99 has been implicitly relied upon in a substantial number of cases where the secretary-general has acted on his own initiative with a view to the resolution of a dispute or conflict situation.[114] On other occasions, the Security Council has tasked the secretary-general with a diplomatic role, which can be grounded in Article 98.

The diplomatic techniques employed by the secretary-general in practice have encompassed the deployment of fact-finding missions in order to ascertain the circumstances surrounding situations giving cause for concern,[115] and the provision of his 'good offices' in order to promote dialogue between the parties in dispute with a view to a peaceful settlement,[116] or to prevent or contain it.[117] Indeed, it has been suggested by one commentator that the secretary-general has primarily become the UN's 'good officer.'[118] The provision of his good offices can be regarded as encompassing those modes of peaceful settlement referred to in Article 33 (1), and which parties in dispute are encouraged to make use of.[119] Certainly, various examples of the provision of 'good offices' by the secretary-general can be found.[120] A detailed discussion of the various diplomatic initiatives undertaken by the secretary-general would extend to numerous volumes and is beyond our present remit.[121] Thus, we confine ourselves here to highlighting some of the key

111 Fiedler, 'Article 99,' in Simma, supra n4, pp.1217–1230, at pp.1220–1223.

112 UN Doc. S/4381.

113 UN Doc. S/13646.

114 Fiedler, supra n111, pp.1223–1230.

115 On fact-finding by the UNSG, see Bourloyannis, supra n94.

116 On the use of good offices, see Franck, T.M., 'The secretary-general's role in conflict resolution: Past, present and pure conjecture,' *European Journal of International Law*, 1995, v.6, pp.360–387.

117 See Ramcharan, supra n45, pp.81–102.

118 Franck, supra n116, p.360.

119 Whitfield, T., 'Good offices and "groups of friends,"' in Chesterman, supra n82, pp.86–101, at p.87.

120 For an overview, see, for example, Franck, supra n116, pp.362–375; Franck, T.M. and Nolte, G., 'The good offices function of the UN secretary-general,' in Roberts, A. and Kingsbury, B. (eds), *United Nations, Divided World* (2nd ed.) (Oxford: Oxford University Press, 1993), pp.143–182; Gordenker, supra n82, pp.159–202.

121 In addition to the memoirs and biographies of the individuals who have served as secretary-general, there are numerous overviews of the various diplomatic initiatives for which they have

diplomatic initiatives within which individual post holders have been involved, set against the influences upon the role of the secretary-general outlined above, in order to demonstrate the possibilities and limitations of the office in providing a mechanism for meaningful responses to situations threatening international peace and security.

That the secretary-general could perform an independent diplomatic role was established early in the term of the first holder of the office, Trygve Lie, who considered that Article 99 gave him a broad role in matters of international peace and security.[122] Although Lie attempted to undertake a number of diplomatic initiatives in respect of situations of tension, the prevailing political climate of the Cold War hampered many of these efforts.[123] For example, his attempts to mediate a resolution of the blockade of Berlin were superseded by direct discussions between the superpowers.[124] The political capital enjoyed by Lie was undermined further by the strong stances he adopted on the Korean War, which earned him the enmity of a major power in the shape of the USSR.[125] Dag Hammarskjold, Lie's successor, has been dubbed the 'most remarkable' secretary-general,[126] and primarily conceived of his office in terms of diplomacy.[127] Prominent examples of diplomatic successes can be found in his term in office, although these were arguably helped by the presence of favourable political circumstances. For example, Hammarskjold undertook a successful independent mission to China to negotiate the release of US airmen captured during the Korean War.[128] Significantly, however, his mission had the implicit approval of the superpowers[129] and there was General Assembly support for his efforts.[130] Following the Suez crisis and the resulting military conflict between Egypt and Israel, the UK and France, Hammarskjold played a key role in negotiating a peaceful resolution which gave rise to the creation of the first UN peacekeeping operation, to supervise the cessation of hostilities.[131]

---

been responsible. See, for example, Gordenker, supra n82, pp.159–234, on the role played by the secretary-general in the negotiation and mediation, investigation and observation of disputes.

122 See Lie, T., *In the Cause of Peace* (London: Macmillan, 1954), pp.41–42.

123 See Rovine, A., *The First Fifty Years: The Secretary-General in World Politics, 1920–1970* (Leiden: Sijthoff, 1970), pp.201–269.

124 See Barros, J., *Trygve Lie and the Cold War* (Chicago: Northern Illinois University Press, 1989), pp.135–156; Lie, supra n109, Chapter 12.

125 For discussion, see Lie, supra n122, Chapter 18; Barros, ibid, Chapter 8.

126 Urquhart, B., 'The evolution of the secretary-general,' in Chesterman, supra n82, pp.15–32, at p.19.

127 Schachter, O., 'The international civil servant: Neutrality and responsibility,' in Jordan, supra n107, pp.39–63.

128 See Urquhart, supra n126, pp.94–131.

129 See Trachtenberg, L.S., 'Dag Hammarskjold as leader: A problem of definition,' *International Journal*, 1982, v.37, n.4, pp.13–35, at pp.616–622.

130 GA Res 90 (IX).

131 See Urquhart, supra n126, pp.159–195; Rikhye, I.J., 'Hammarskjold and peacekeeping,' in Jordan, supra n107, pp.77–109.

While peacekeeping receives treatment in its own right later in this book,[132] the role of Hammarskjold in establishing the first operation and developing the principles which would govern peacekeeping operations was considerable and demonstrated that new peaceful solutions could be devised in the right circumstances. Notwithstanding Hammarskjold's obvious strengths and successes, he recognised that his ability to succeed was contingent upon having broad UN support for his efforts and that the parties concerned were amenable to a peaceful solution.[133] As Schachter notes, only rarely did Hammarskjold offer the provision of his good offices in the absence of a Security Council or General Assembly mandate,[134] and when he did, for example when visiting Laos in 1959,[135] it was at the request of the parties to the dispute. Although Hammarskjold was given considerable scope over responding to civil war in the Congo in 1960, the intransigence of the parties and tensions with some of the major powers undermined his efforts.[136] Although his tragic death in 1961 during the midst of this conflict arguably prevented fuller assessments of his efforts in the Congo, it is to be noted that relations with the USSR had deteriorated over the position which he had taken.

The terms in office of U Thant and Kurt Waldheim saw no major diplomatic successes achieved by either secretary-general, although the potential of the office during the 1960s–1970s was largely conditioned by the political dynamics of the Cold War environment. Thant offered or provided his good offices in respect of numerous disputes or situations giving rise to international tension, sometimes at the request of the Security Council or General Assembly, sometimes on the basis of invitation by the parties.[137] However, the major crises of the period, which effectively pitted the US and USSR against one another, were not amenable to his diplomatic intervention. His efforts to promote negotiations over the Vietnam War never really took off the ground,[138] and despite the fact that his efforts to intervene in the Cuban Missile Crisis were praised in an unprecedented joint letter from the US and USSR,[139] the situation was effectively resolved by direct discussions between

132 See Chapter 6.

133 Goodrich, L.M., 'Hammarskjold, the UN, and the office of the secretary-general,' *International Organization*, 1974, v.28, n.3, pp.467–483, at pp.478–479.

134 Schachter, O., 'Dag Hammarskjold and the relation of law to politics,' *American Journal of International Law*, 1962, v.56, pp.1–8, at p.6.

135 See Elarby, N., 'The office of the secretary-general and the maintenance of international peace and security,' in UNITAR, supra n93, pp.177–209, at pp.190–196.

136 The Congo crisis is far too complicated to be given any meaningful treatment here. For a more detailed exposition, see Urquhart, supra n126, pp.389–456.

137 See Jackson, W.D., 'The political role of the secretary-general under U Thant and Kurt Waldheim: Development or decline?,' *World Affairs*, 1978, v.140, n.3, pp.230–244, at p.232 et seq on those situations where Thant intervened as a mediator at the request of the parties. On the diplomatic efforts of Thant more generally, see Nassif R., *U Thant in New York 1961–1971* (New York: Hurst, 1988), Chapter 7.

138 See Nassif, ibid, Chapter 4.

139 See Nassif, supra n137, p.37.

the protagonists themselves.[140] Successful outcomes facilitated by Thant came where the superpower interests at stake were limited or non-existent and where his intervention had been encouraged by the parties. For example, the dispute over the status of Bahrain was resolved when his recommendations were accepted by the UK and Iran.[141] Like Thant, Kurt Waldheim was not responsible for any major diplomatic successes during his tenure as secretary-general, notwithstanding the provision of his good offices in a number of situations.[142] Like Thant, he had to operate against a backdrop of superpower tensions which restricted the prospects of the office. Diplomatic achievements occurred where political circumstances facilitated this. For example, Jackson argues that his most important involvement was in respect of the situation in Cyprus where the US interest in achieving a settlement and a generally neutral General Assembly attitude worked in Waldheim's favour.[143] Waldheim was also able to secure the release of French hostages held by POLISARIO, the Western Saharan independence movement. However, the public damage which can be done when high-profile diplomacy fails was made apparent when Waldheim's visit to Tehran following the seizure of hostages in the US embassy failed to secure their release. This prompted Waldheim himself to note that, 'if there was one experience which proved the limits and frustrations of this job, it was that trip to Teheran.'[144]

As the Cold War drew towards an end and superpower cooperation significantly increased, the role which could effectively be undertaken by the secretary-general in diplomatic efforts to resolve conflict likewise increased considerably. Although it is arguably true that 'to an extent he was at the right place at the right time,'[145] Javier Pérez de Cuellar's good offices were put to effective use in respect of a wide range of situations involving parties in dispute.[146] These included his mediation in the Iran–Iraq war, Afghanistan and the Gulf conflict,[147] the resolution of the Central American peace process[148] and conflict in Namibia.[149] While

140 See Thant, U, *View from the UN* (New York: Doubleday, 1978), Chapter 8.

141 UN Doc. S/9772.

142 See Waldheim, K., *In the Eye of the Storm* (London: Weidenfeld & Nicolson, 1985). For a briefer overview, see Finger and Saltzman, supra n99, pp.41–70.

143 Jackson, supra n137, pp.237–238.

144 Waldheim, supra n142, p.11.

145 Newman, E., *The UN Secretary-general from the Cold War to the New Era* (London: Macmillan, 1998), p.60.

146 For a detailed account of the main uses of Pérez de Cuéllar's good offices, see Newman, ibid, pp.62–109; Lankevich, supra n97, pp.55–123; Franck and Nolte, supra n120, pp.143–182.

147 On which, see Arakov, V., 'The secretary-general in the Afghanistan conflict, the Iran–Iraq War, and the Gulf crisis,' in Rivlin, B. and Gordenker, L. (eds), *The Challenging Role of the UN Secretary-General* (New York: Greenwood, 1993), pp.152–175.

148 See Pellicer, O., 'The United Nations in Central America: The role of the secretary-general,' in Rivlin and Gordenker, ibid, pp.76–89.

149 Ofuatey-Kodjoe, W., 'The role of the UN secretary-general in the decolonization of Namibia,' in Rivlin and Gordenker, supra n147, pp.133–151.

such contributions were made possible by the newfound cooperation among the major powers within the Security Council, Pérez de Cuéllar's individual abilities may be evidenced by successes such as persuading Libya and Malta to take their continental shelf dispute to the ICJ, and his effective resolution of the dispute between New Zealand and France over the Rainbow Warrior incident.[150]

The greater prospects that existed for the diplomatic role of the secretary-general following the end of the Cold War were implicitly acknowledged by the Security Council when it formally invited the greater use of the secretary-general's good offices in responding to situations of international concern.[151] The continued significance of these good offices was exemplified by the fact that in his first year in office alone, Boutros Boutros-Ghali undertook 75 missions of a fact-finding or good offices nature, visiting 23 states.[152] Unfortunately, despite initial optimism over the capabilities of his office, in diplomatic terms Boutros-Ghali's single term in post proved disappointing as serious disagreements with major powers, particularly the US, and his perceived lack of diplomatic tact undermined efforts aimed at the resolution of conflict.[153] Although his later years in office would be troubled by a fallout with the US over the 'oil for food' scandal at the UN and disagreement over the US-led invasion of Iraq, for much of his time in office Kofi Annan was regarded as a considerable success, evidenced by his receipt of the Nobel Peace Prize in 2001. However, while Annan is regarded as having restored the UN's prestige, combining modest charm and moral gravity, and establishing himself as a world leader with broad freedom of action,[154] his contribution to the peace and security agenda went beyond his diplomatic efforts to involvement in important policy debates.[155] Most prominently these included the emergence of the doctrine of the *Responsibility to Protect* and the *High-Level Panel Report on Threats, Challenges and Change*.[156] Annan's successor, Ban Ki-Moon, undertook numerous diplomatic missives, one assessment towards the end of his first term in office suggesting that he had 'spent more than one-third of his time on the road …

150 For the secretary-general's ruling, see *American Journal of International Law*, 1987, v.81, p.325.

151 UN Doc. S/23500.

152 Murthy, C.S.R., 'The role of the UN secretary-general since the end of the cold war,' *Indiana Journal of International Law*, 1995, v.35, pp.181–196.

153 See Newman, supra n145, pp.110–126. Boutros-Ghali's various disagreements with the US are detailed in his memoirs. See Boutros-Ghali, B., *Unvanquished* (New York: Random House, 1999).

154 Traub, J., *The Best Intentions: Kofi Annan and the UN in the Era of American Power* (London: Bloomsbury, 2006), p.6. A similar assessment was provided by Meisler, who commented that, 'the times required a leader of diplomatic skill, openness, and moral strength, and Annan fit these needs in a remarkable way'; Meisler, S., *Kofi Annan: A Man of Peace in a World of War* (Hoboken, NJ: John Wiley & Sons, 2007), p.4.

155 On some of his main diplomatic initiatives, see Traub, ibid, Chapters 5–6.

156 Such developments are beyond the remit of the present chapter, which focuses on diplomatic responses to security threats.

organizing a number of unobtrusive UN efforts.'[157] His earlier diplomatic missions included trips to Sri Lanka, to urge access for humanitarian aid to refugee camps as the country's civil war came to an end, as well as brokering the intervention of African Union peacekeepers in Sudan's Darfur region.[158] However, the longer-term effects of both efforts would be undermined by the intransigence of the parties concerned,[159] underlining the limitations of the office.[160]

As the diplomatic practice accumulated by the various holders of the office of secretary-general illustrates, the role has been developed to allow on occasions for an important contribution to be made to diplomatic efforts to promote the peaceful settlement of disputes, primarily through the secretary-general's provision of his good offices. As has been noted, a number of factors will bear upon the contribution which any individual can make in any given situation and the centrality of the wider political environment and relations with the major powers to what may be achieved is apparent. Where the parties are unwilling to cooperate or the UN membership's key players are unwilling to provide the necessary resources to support such efforts,[161] the potential of the good offices technique is limited. When cooperation is forthcoming and diplomatic efforts have the support of the key international players, much is possible.

Special Representatives of the Secretary-General

In support of their diplomatic efforts, successive secretaries-general have appointed special representatives to act on their behalf in providing good offices to assist disputing or warring parties in reaching a peaceful settlement. Numerous individuals have been conferred with this status.[162] While some have been little-known figures, others have enjoyed a prominent profile, for example former US Secretary of State Cyrus Vance – tasked to broker peace talks between the parties to conflict within the former Yugoslavia – or former UN Secretary-General Kofi Annan, appointed as his successor's special representative to pursue a diplomatic breakthrough in the Syrian Civil War. Given the various responsibilities of the secretary-general, the role of his special representative is effectively to represent him in a specific situation in order to provide a more focused presence in efforts

157 Schlesinger, S. and Glez, D., 'Bosom Buddies? Ban and Obama's Curious Relations,' *World Policy Journal*, 2010, v.27, n.1, pp.87–95, at p.88.

158 See Ki-Moon, Ban., *Resolved: Uniting Nations in a Divided World* (New York: Columbia University Press, 2021), chs.9 & 14.

159 See Schlesinger and Glez, supra n157, pp.88–89.

160 Schlesinger and Glez, supra n157, p.91. See also generally Ki-Moon, supra n158, for his account of various diplomatic initiatives undertaken during his term in office.

161 Franck, supra n116, p.373.

162 For examples, see Ramcharan, supra n145, pp.117–126. See also Barber, R., 'The case for UN-supported, ASEAN-led negotiations on Myanmar,' *Australian Journal of International Affairs*, 2023, v.77, n.3, pp.325–332, at pp.327–329.

directed towards peaceful settlement. The success of the efforts of special representatives has varied in accordance with the same factors that have determined the relative success of diplomatic efforts of individual secretaries-general, being effectively extensions of his personage. Thus, their role does not receive any extensive consideration here. Where circumstances have been favourable, the contributions of special representatives have been significant. For example, Bell highlights the important roles performed by Jean Arnault and Alvaro de Soto respectively in the mediation of peace settlements in Guatemala and El Salvador,[163] undertaken at a time of increased P5 cooperation. By contrast, while three successive special representatives sought to broker mediation of the Syrian Civil War, the existence of P5 disunity over the situation and the clustering of key regional and international actors on different sides of the conflict meant that they lacked the requisite prevailing political circumstances necessary for success.[164]

Reforming the process of appointing the UN Secretary-General: Legitimising the Role

Since around the time of Ban Ki-Moon's appointment as secretary-general, there has been renewed pressure for reform to the appointment process to bolster the perceived legitimacy of the office-holder. The UN Charter provides little guidance on the process beyond stating that appointment is made by the General Assembly on the recommendation of the Security Council.[165] In accordance with an early stated preference of the General Assembly,[166] a practice emerged whereby the Council would settle on one candidate in private discussions, with this individual being confirmed in post by the Assembly.[167] The Assembly had no real input into the process, being presented with a fait accompli which represented a compromise the Council – and especially its veto-wielding permanent members – could agree upon. This process was followed for seventy years. However, ahead of the 2016 process to appoint Ban's successor, a series of reform pressures emanating from various civil society groups had been growing.[168] Common themes included calls for a more transparent and inclusive process in which the General Assembly would be presented with a greater opportunity to influence the outcome, while

163 Bell, C., *On the Law of Peace* (Oxford: Oxford University Press, 2008), pp.67–68.
164 Hellmuller, supra n73.
165 Article 97.
166 GA Res 11 (I).
167 For an overview of the appointment process, see Keating, supra n82.
168 These included from the ACT and NAM groups of states, the reforming group *1 for 8 Billion*, and the *Elders* group of leading statesmen and women. For discussion, see Terlingen, Y., 'A Better Process, a Stronger UN Secretary-General: How Historic Change was forged and What Comes Next,' *Ethics & International Affairs*, 2017, v.31, n.2, pp.115–127, at pp.118–122; Weiss, T.G. and Carayannis, T., 'Windows of opportunity for UN reform: Historical insights for the next Secretary-General,' *International Affairs*, 2017, v.93, n.2, pp.309–326, p.309 et seq.

there was also a widely shared belief that the appointment of a female secretary-general was overdue. In 2016, for the first time, applications were effectively invited for the position,[169] with candidates invited to present vision statements and engage with the General Assembly membership. Of the thirteen candidates under consideration, nine were Eastern European, seven female and four satisfied both of these criteria. However, notwithstanding this new level of transparency, the eventual nominee, Antonio Guterres, was determined in private by the Security Council, being the only candidate to be neither Eastern European nor female. In this sense, little had actually changed. As a result, calls for reform have not abated. While a common theme has been a desire to curb the P5's control of the process in favour of a more democratic process,[170] proposals have also included restricting a secretary-general to a single, albeit longer term in office as a means of strengthening his independence of action.[171]

Ad hoc diplomatic initiatives by other actors in support of UN objectives

In addition to the UN's own organs, external actors have on occasion emerged to undertake or support diplomatic initiatives in response to situations of concern which have engaged the UN. Although regional bodies have an explicit mandate within the UN Charter to assist their members to peacefully resolve their disputes,[172] this aspect of their role is considered in Chapter 8.[173] Here we make brief reference to some of the more prominent ad hoc diplomatic efforts of other actors in support of UN objectives. Occasionally, individual states have proven capable of performing a key role in the mediation of disputes between other states. Merrills and De Brabandere offer some illustrative examples of situations where this has occurred, citing the Soviet role in the mediation of the Indian–Pakistani dispute over Kashmir in 1965, which was 'instrumental in securing a cease-fire when war had already broken out,' and Algeria's intervention in the hostages dispute between the US and Iran.[174] In the post–Cold War era, some states came to perform mediatory functions over a period of time in respect of particular long-running disputes, for example Norway in brokering the Israeli–Palestinian Oslo Accords, or Qatar in seeking to mediate the Lebanese and Yemeni civil war situations.[175] The possibility and value of diplomatic intervention by individual third

169 See GA Res 69/321 (2015).

170 See Thakur, R., 'Choosing the Ninth United Nations Secretary-General: Looking Back, Looking Ahead,' *Global Governance*, 2017, v.23, n.1, pp.1–13, at pp.8–9.

171 See, e.g., 1 for 8 Billion proposals, available at https://1for8billion.org/ten-urgent-reforms.

172 Article 52 (2).

173 See, however, for a brief treatment of the role of regional organisations in the peaceful settlement of disputes, Merrills and De Brabandere, supra n14, ch.13; Bell, supra n163, pp.69–72.

174 Merrills and De Brabandere, supra n14, pp.67–69. See also Brownlie, supra n14, p.168 et seq.

175 See, eg., Iji, supra n20, pp.89–96.

states will hinge on a number of political factors: the willingness of a third state to intervene, which may depend upon its perception of political benefits to be gained from so doing; the amenability of the parties in dispute to a peaceful resolution; and the state of relations between the third state and the parties to the dispute.

More common has been the formation of loose ad hoc groups of states for the purpose of providing diplomatic assistance with the mediation of peaceful solutions to situations involving conflict or dispute between or within other states. These groupings have sometimes been labelled 'groups of friends,'[176] and have been particularly prominent in efforts to facilitate the peaceful settlement of long-running conflicts through the creation of detailed peace agreements and post-conflict structures.[177] Although perhaps more significant in the post–Cold War era, there were some important ad hoc multilateral diplomatic initiatives during the Cold War period designed to further the cause of peaceful settlement. For example, the 'Contact Group' for Namibia sought to negotiate an agreement for its independence from the late 1970s to early 1980s.[178] While unsuccessful at the time, the group has been credited with having nonetheless contributed to some important advances.[179] As the Cold War came to a close, UN efforts to broker peace in Central America and Cambodia benefitted from the role played by a number of states working together in support of these objectives. In support of the Central American peace process, the Contadora group was formed by the foreign ministers of a number of Central and Latin American states during the early 1980s to mediate the related conflicts in the region and is credited with having laid down the groundwork for the eventual peace agreements within the region.[180] A considerable number of states participated in the Paris peace talks which ultimately led to a peace agreement between the parties in conflict in Cambodia, paving the way for interim UN administration of the country pending free elections.[181] The 'Contact Group' consisting of France, Germany, the UK and US, together with the EU, was at the heart of initiatives to broker a peaceful solution to the conflict which accompanied the break-up of Yugoslavia during the 1990s. Similarly, the later 'Contact Group,' enjoying a similar membership,[182] was central to the Rambouillet accords reached with the FRY which sought to end conflict in the province of Kosovo.[183]

176 Whitfield, supra n119, pp.86–101.
177 For discussion of instances of the utilisation of 'groups of friends,' see Iji, supra n20.
178 The Contact Group consisted of the US, UK, France, Canada and West Germany.
179 See Karns, M.P., 'Ad hoc multilateral diplomacy: The United States, the Contact Group, and Namibia,' *International Organization*, 1987, v.41, n.1, pp.93–123.
180 See generally Wehr, P. and Lederach, J.P., 'Mediating conflict in Central America,' *Journal of Peace Research*, 1991, v.28, n.1, pp.85–98.
181 The states concerned are listed in the Final Act of the Paris Peace Conference on Cambodia of 23 October 1991, para.3.
182 The US, UK, France, Germany, Italy and Russia.
183 See Weller, M., 'The Rambouillet conference on Kosovo,' *International Affairs*, 1999, v.75, n.2, pp.211–251. Although some have suggested that the EU has proven more effective than

Since 2002, the 'Quartet' group of the US, Russia, EU and UN has sought to mediate – so far unsuccessfully – a resolution of the long-running Middle East conflict. A word of caution is, however, necessary where multiple actors become involved in diplomatic efforts to resolve a situation of international concern. Progress can be complicated by various actors pursuing competing objectives, a problem identified in respect of initiatives to resolve the Libyan and Syrian civil wars.[184]

Conclusion

Peaceful efforts to resolve situations threatening international peace and security under UN auspices have a mixed record. The fact that in a considerable number of conflicts the Security Council proceeds to adopt measures under Chapter VII, even in circumstances in which diplomatic efforts continue to be ongoing, underlines the limitations of the diplomatic mechanism for tackling threats to the peace. The two competing themes which pervade this book are clearly present when we have regard to diplomacy in support of UN objectives within the realm of international peace and security. The success of diplomatic efforts in any given situation has very much been contingent upon whether these have taken place within the context of existing political circumstances that are conducive to facilitating the settlement of the dispute in question. The willingness of the concerned parties to submit themselves to the possibility of peaceful settlement is key among these in the absence of the modes of coercion that the Security Council is empowered to use in order to effect the restoration of international peace and security under Chapter VII. As a tool of the UN collective security system, peaceful settlement is clearly limited and for the Security Council to effectively respond to many situations threatening international peace and security requires resort to more robust measures. However, at the same time, it is possible to identify a creative evolution of the UN's diplomatic machinery and the legal framework governing it. This is particularly the case in respect of the diplomatic functions performed by the secretary-general. While the UN Charter provisions pertaining to the role are relatively brief, vague and general, successive holders of the office have interpreted their duties in a creative manner in order to enable them to make a meaningful diplomatic contribution through their performance of investigatory exercises, the provision of their good offices and the deployment of special representatives to spearhead diplomatic missions on their behalf.

the UN in mediating progress in settling Kosovo's final status. See, e.g., Bergman, J., 'Same Table, Different Menus? A Comparison of UN and EU Mediation Practice in the Kosovo-Serbia Conflict,' *International Negotiation*, 2018, v.23, pp.238–257.

184 See Hellmuller, S. and Salaymeh, B., 'Multiparty mediation in a challenging world: The emergence and impact of parallel processes to UN peacemaking in Syria and Libya,' *International Journal of Conflict Management*, 2024, v.35, n.1, pp.129–149.

5

THE USE OF NON-MILITARY SANCTIONS

Introduction

Following a determination by the UN Security Council under Article 39 of the UN Charter that there exists a threat to the peace, breach of the peace or act of aggression, it is empowered to give consideration to the application of measures provided for by Articles 41 and 42. Article 41 provides for the application of non-military measures by the Council. Although a wide range of measures potentially falls under Article 41, in practice, it is largely associated with the application of sanctions. Traditionally, these were imposed against states whose actions in some respect threatened international peace and security, but in the post–Cold War era, non-state actors and individuals have increasingly also been subject to sanctions.

Non-military sanctions might be regarded as a mid-level response to situations that threaten international peace and security, consisting of measures exceeding diplomatic pressure but not extending to the application of military force. Their 'political logic,' according to Cortright et al, 'lies in the desire of policymakers to have options other than war for applying pressure on targeted states, entities, and individuals accused of violating international norms.'[1] Arguably, sanctions have long been regarded as politically 'cheap' by those who decide upon their adoption. Unlike military measures, they 'do not generate sombre processions of body bags bringing home the mortal remains of the sons and daughters of the[ir]

1 Cortright, D., Lopez, G.A. and Gerber-Stellingwerf, L., 'The sanctions era: Themes and trends in UN Security Council sanctions since 1990,' in Lowe, V., Roberts, A., Welsh, J. and Zaum, D. (eds), *The United Nations Security Council and War* (Oxford: Oxford University Press, 2008), pp.205–25, at p.206.

DOI: 10.4324/9781003518105-6

constituents.'[2] However, the conventional wisdom that held non-military sanctions to carry less devastating humanitarian consequences has been challenged, not least by the experience of Iraq during the 1990s.[3] Their utilisation also rests upon the assumption that those against whom they are directed are rational actors likely to be moved to adjust their behaviour as a result of their effects.[4] This assumption has also been challenged by the lessons of recent history, as shall be seen.

This chapter begins by considering the legal framework applicable to the imposition of non-military sanctions by the Security Council. This is then followed by consideration of the Council's practice of applying sanctions and its move towards a greater focus upon the adoption of targeted measures in the twenty-first century. The various problems associated with sanctions regimes are then considered, before attention is given to steps that may be taken to improve their effectiveness and perceived legitimacy.

The legal framework applicable to Article 41

The scope of Article 41

Non-military sanctions as a tool with which the UN Security Council can respond to situations that it has determined constitute a threat to the peace, breach of the peace or act of aggression are provided for in Article 41 of the UN Charter. However, it should be noted that Article 41 provides no exhaustive definition of the range of sanctions available to the Council and does not actually make reference to 'sanctions' by name. In the context of the UN collective security system, the term 'sanction' implies a measure which broadly takes the form of a punishment or restriction imposed upon a targeted state, entity or individual as a consequence of its breach of international norms.[5] They represent 'collective measures imposed by organs representing the international community, in response to perceived unlawful or unacceptable conduct by one of its members and meant to uphold standards of behaviour required by international law.'[6] While all UN sanctions are inherently punitive to some degree, their intended objective is to have the effect of coercing their targets to change their behaviour and comply with the demands of the Security Council. Article 41 specifically states that the Council 'may decide

2 Reisman, W.M. and Stewick, D.L., 'The applicability of international law standards to United Nations economic sanctions programmes,' *European Journal of International Law*, 1998, v.9, pp.84–141, at pp.93–94.

3 See below.

4 See further Reisman and Stewick, supra n2, pp.90–92.

5 See further Abi-Saab, G., 'The concept of sanction in international law,' in Gowlland-Debbas, V. (ed.), *United Nations Sanctions and International Law* (The Hague: Kluwer, 2001), pp.29–41.

6 Schrijver, N., 'The use of economic sanctions by the UN Security Council: An international law perspective,' in Post, H.G. (ed.), *International Economic Law and Armed Conflict* (Leiden: Brill, 1994), pp.123–162, at p.125.

what measures not involving the use of armed force are to be employed to give effect to its decisions,' and gives examples of such measures, providing that they 'may include complete or partial interruption of economic relations and of rail, sea, air, postal, telegraphic, radio, and other means of communication, and the severance of diplomatic relations.' Although not an exhaustive list, the inclusion of such examples makes it clear that Article 41 was designed specifically with the application of such non-military sanctions in mind.[7] In practice, the Security Council has acted under Article 41 to impose sanctions taking the form of arms embargoes, trade embargoes, financial sanctions and travel, aviation and diplomatic restrictions. It has not traditionally referred to Article 41 when deciding upon the imposition of non-military sanctions,[8] tending instead to simply state that it is acting under Chapter VII in adopting the relevant resolutions. That the actual basis for such measures is Article 41 is generally undisputed. However, the Council did specifically invoke Article 41 in a number of sanctions-creating resolutions over a period of time from the mid-2000s onwards.[9]

While Article 41 is most closely associated with the application of non-military sanctions of the kind referred to, it has also been clearly established that it can provide a legal basis for a fuller range of measures not involving the use of armed force. In the *Tadic* case, the International Criminal Tribunal for Yugoslavia (ICTY) came to the conclusion that the legal basis for its creation by the Council – which had simply been done by reference to Chapter VII[10] – could be found in Article 41.[11] In establishing the ICTY, the Council had adopted a measure which did not extend to the use of armed force, and which was adopted in response to a recognised threat to the peace (armed conflict and the perpetration of international crimes in former Yugoslavia) as provided for by Article 41. The creation of UN territorial administration in territories such as Kosovo and East Timor can also be based upon Article 41,[12] while some commentators have also considered UN peacekeeping operations to have their legal basis in Article 41.[13] Within this chapter, our attention is confined to UN sanctions as they are most usually understood:

7 Although the UN's founders evidently decided against an exhaustive elaboration of measures covered by Article 41 so as not to restrict the Security Council's freedom of action, a proposal to add to the examples contained in Article 41 was rejected at the San Francisco Conference; UNCIO III, pp.189–231, p.221, Doc.2 G/7 (d) (1).

8 For a notable exception, see SC Res 232 (1966) pertaining to Southern Rhodesia.

9 See, for example, SC Res 1718 (2006); SC Res 1737 (2006); SC Res 1970 (2011); SC Res 2048 (2012).

10 SC Res 827 (1993).

11 *Prosecutor v. Tadic*, Case No.IT-94-1AR72, Decision on the Defence Motion for Interlocutory Appeal on Jurisdiction (Oct. 2, 1995), *ILM* 32 (1996).

12 See Frowein, J.A. and Krisch, N., 'Article 41,' in Simma et al (eds), *The Charter of the United Nations: A Commentary* (2nd ed.) (Oxford: Oxford University Press, 2002), pp.735–749, at pp.743–745.

13 See Chapter 6.

measures involving the application of some form of restriction upon states or other targeted entities, in furtherance of the objective of maintaining or restoring international peace and security.

Although it is possible for the Security Council to merely recommend the imposition of non-military sanctions, where it *decides* upon their utilisation under Article 41, member states are obliged to observe them and give effect to their implementation.[14] The terms used in Articles 39 and 41 make this clear. Article 39 refers to the Council's ability to 'decide' upon measures in accordance with Articles 41 and 42. A decision of the Council differs from a recommendation by virtue of its obligatory nature, Article 25 categorically stating that members 'agree to accept and carry out the decisions of the Security Council.'[15] Article 41 reinforces the obligation of members to apply non-military sanctions by providing that it can 'decide' upon what measures are to be employed to effect its 'decisions,' and that it 'may call upon ... Members to apply such measures.'[16] The obligation to give effect to decisions of the Council to impose sanctions is reinforced by the often-overlooked Charter stipulation that 'The Members of the United Nations shall join in affording mutual assistance in carrying out the measures decided upon by the Security Council.'[17] Where giving effect to sanctions requires states to depart from obligations under other international agreements, Article 103 is quite emphatic in stating that obligations under the UN Charter are to take precedence.

Limitations on the application of non-military sanctions

General limitations

Although the Security Council has a considerable degree of discretion when deciding upon the application of Chapter VII measures, this is not absolute and it must act in accordance with limitations imposed by the UN Charter and general international law.[18] Charter provisions impose some express limitations upon the

14 This was made clear by the Security Council itself in resolution 232 in relation to Southern Rhodesia. While in its earlier resolutions, the Council had called on member states to refrain from trade and diplomatic relations with Southern Rhodesia, in resolution 232 it 'decided' that they should desist from a series of listed relations with it. Significantly, the Council reminded members 'that the failure or refusal ... to implement the present resolution shall constitute a violation of Article 25 of the [UN] Charter.'

15 Delbruck, J., 'Article 25,' in Simma et al, supra n12, pp.452–464, pp.455–458.

16 See Frowein and Krisch, supra n12, pp.735–749, p.739.

17 Article 49.

18 See further Dapo, A., 'The International Court of Justice and the Security Council: Is there room for judicial control of decisions of the political organs of the United Nations?,' *International and Comparative Law Quarterly*, 1997, v.46, n.2, pp.309–343, at pp.316–327; Hinjosa Martinez, L.M., 'The legislative role of the Security Council in its fight against terrorism: Legal, political and practical limits,' *International and Comparative Law Quarterly*, 2008, v.57, n.2, pp.333–359.

Council's ability to apply non-military sanctions.[19] First, it may only impose non-military sanctions if it has determined that there exists a threat to the peace, breach of the peace or act of aggression pursuant to Article 39, which specifically links the imposition of both military and non-military enforcement measures to such a determination, by providing that it is following this determination that the Council shall 'decide what measures shall be taken in accordance with Articles 41 and 42, to maintain or restore international peace and security.'[20] Second, the Security Council is also explicitly required to act in accordance with the purposes and principles of the UN by virtue of Article 24(2).[21] These are broadly phrased and, arguably, 'give little sense of tangible constraint.'[22] In his detailed treatment of the legal framework applicable to sanctions, Farrall suggests that they are too vague and general to provide meaningful limitations.[23] While the fact that the first listed purpose of the UN is the maintenance of international peace and security gives the Council considerable flexibility in justifying actions taken for this objective, sight should not be lost of the fact that Article 1 (3) also directs the UN to achieve international cooperation in solving problems of a humanitarian character and in the promotion and encouragement of respect for human rights. While subsidiary to the objective of maintaining international peace and security, the Security Council nonetheless ought arguably to have regard to human rights/humanitarian considerations when taking decisions. The extent to which this restricts its ability to impose non-military sanctions is considered further below.

Several commentators have made reference to the need for the Council to respect the limits of proportionality when acting under Chapter VII,[24] there being wide support for the view that there must be some correlation between the sanctions measures which are adopted by the Council and the objectives which they are intended to further. In particular, as measures adopted under Chapter VII must be in support of the maintenance or restoration of international peace and security,

19 See Dam de Jong, D., 'Who is Targeted by the Council's Sanctions? The UN Security Council and the Principle of Proportionality,' *Nordic Journal of International Law*, 2020, v.89, pp.383–398, p.386; Farrall, J.M., *United Nations Sanctions and the Rule of Law* (Cambridge: Cambridge University Press, 2007), pp.68–76.

20 On a small number of occasions, however, there has been no Article 39 determination, for example in relation to sanctions imposed by SC Res 820 (1993), SC Res 1160 (1998), SC Res 1737 (2006). As Farrall argues, however, the best legal interpretation is that the relevant resolutions contained an implicit finding that an Article 39 type situation existed. See Farrall, ibid, pp.82–85.

21 This is reinforced by Article 25's provision that member states agree to accept and carry out decisions 'in accordance with the present charter.'

22 Craven, M., 'Humanitarianism and the quest for smarter sanctions,' *European Journal of International Law*, 2002, v.13, n.1, pp.43–61.

23 Farrall, supra n19, p.68.

24 See, for example, Dam de Jong, supra n19; Farrall, supra n19, pp.223–229; Reisman and Stewick, supra n2, pp.128–131; Manusama, K., *The United Nations Security Council in the Post-Cold War Era* (Leiden: Brill, 2006), pp.128–131; Angelet, N., 'International law limits to the Security Council,' in Gowlland-Debbas, supra n5, pp.71–82, at pp.72–74.

they must be demonstrably directed at this objective. The need for proportionality within Security Council decision-making is further underlined by the formulation of some key UN Charter provisions which require that action taken by the Council is 'necessary' to achieve this specified purpose.[25] The concept of proportionality is central to the law of countermeasures and can reasonably be expected to inform decision-making in relation to sanctions.[26] It is particularly relevant within the context of sanctions which generate significant humanitarian consequences, undermining their perceived legitimacy where any tangible gain from their imposition appears minimal when set against possibly wider devastating consequences. To some extent, the principle of proportionality has informed the UN's sanctions policy, with the creation of humanitarian exemptions within sanctions regimes and the shift over time to the adoption of more targeted sanctions measures indicators of this.[27] However, criticisms continue to be levelled in respect of some aspects of UN sanctions regimes. The comprehensive sanctions imposed upon North Korea, for example, have been criticised by some commentators as lacking in terms of proportionality.[28] The application of sanctions to individuals has also been increasingly challenged on the basis of concerns rooted in a combination of their alleged disproportionate nature and infringement of individual human rights.[29]

Under general international law, the Security Council cannot act in a manner that involves it violating jus cogens, those peremptory international legal norms from which no derogation is permissible.[30] The most obvious application of sanctions which may have some bearing upon such norms is likely to be found in those situations where sanctions are alleged to be responsible for serious humanitarian

25 Although Article 41 does not use the term 'necessary' in relation to the measures that it envisages, Articles 40 and 42 do in relation to the adoption of provisional measures and military enforcement measures respectively. However, the role of proportionality in the sanctions context is nonetheless apparent from Article 41's proviso that these are to be adopted to give effect to its decisions: there must, thus, be some correlation between the objective of a Council resolution and the means adopted to further this. See Hinjosa Martinez, supra n18, at p.349; Angelet, supra n21, at pp.72–74.

26 See further Crawford, J., 'The relationship between sanctions and countermeasures,' in Gowlland-Debbas, supra n5, pp.57–68.

27 See, e.g., Dam de Jong, supra n19, pp.387–389.

28 See, e.g., Smith, H., 'The ethics of United Nations sanctions on North Korea: effectiveness, necessity and proportionality,' *Critical Asian Studies*, 2020, v.52, n.2, pp.182–203.

29 See below.

30 Article 53 of the Vienna Convention on the Law of Treaties makes all treaty provisions which conflict with jus cogens void. See further Orakhelashvili, A., 'The impact of peremptory norms on the interpretation and application of United Nations Security Council resolutions,' *European Journal of International Law*, 2005, v.16, n.1, pp.59–88; Hossain, K., 'The concept of jus cogens and the obligation under the U.N. Charter,' *Santa Clara Journal of International Law*, 2005, v.3, n.1, pp.72–98; Gill, T.D., 'Legal and some political limitations on the power of the UN Security Council to exercise its enforcement powers under Chapter VII of the Charter,' *Netherlands Yearbook of International Law*, 1995, v.26, pp.33–138, at p.79 et seq.

consequences which potentially involve fundamental norms of international human rights or humanitarian law being compromised. There have also been a series of challenges brought in domestic or regional courts which call into question the validity of UN sanctions on account of their perceived incompatibility with individual rights. We turn to such issues below. However, in the absence of jus cogens violations, it should be recalled that states' obligations arising under the UN Charter should prima facie take precedence over obligations arising under any other international treaties.[31] The importance of adherence to core values of the rule of law principle in Security Council decision-making has also led to the advancement of various criteria which ought to govern its approach to issues such as the application of sanctions.[32]

Limitations arising from international humanitarian/human rights norms

Arguably, the strongest arguments for a need to subject the imposition of non-military sanctions to some form of restraint arise from concerns surrounding their potential to give rise to serious humanitarian consequences affecting civilian populations. In such cases, the question to be asked is whether international standards contained in core provisions of international human rights law (IHRL) and international humanitarian law (IHL) can be applied to Security Council decision-making over the adoption and implementation of sanctions. However, although some effects of UN sanctions regimes may appear prima facie to violate norms contained within these branches of international law, it is difficult to apply their provisions directly to the application of non-military sanctions.

IHL only applies during times of armed conflict[33] and is concerned with the treatment of wounded combatants, prisoners of war and civilians during warfare, as well as attempting to regulate the methods and means of warfare that can legitimately be employed. Whereas military sanctions under Article 42 of the UN Charter generate, or contribute towards, the existence of armed conflicts, measures under Article 41 do not.[34] However, the relevance of IHL to the application of sanctions resulting in humanitarian suffering appears understandable, at least by

31 Article 103, UN Charter.

32 Farrall, supra n19, pp.40–42, suggests that the principles of transparency, consistency, equality, due process and proportionality should guide the Council in taking decisions over the application of sanctions. As he goes on to discuss (pp.135–229), there have historically been major shortfalls in the Council's satisfaction of such principles.

33 Article 2 common to the four Geneva Conventions of 1949: (I) Convention for the Amelioration of the Condition of the Wounded and Sick in Armed Forces in the Field; (II) Convention for the Amelioration of the Condition of the Wounded and Sick and Shipwrecked Members of Armed Forces at Sea; (III) Convention Relative to the Treatment of Prisoners of War; (IV) Convention Relative to the Protection of Civilian Persons in Time of War.

34 Sassoli, M., 'Sanctions and international humanitarian law,' in Gowlland-Debbas, supra n5, pp.241–248, at p.241.

way of analogy, when some pertinent provisions of the Geneva Conventions are considered.[35] For example, Article 23 of the 4th Geneva Convention obliges parties to an armed conflict not to place restrictions upon the provision of humanitarian relief; Article 89 of the same convention imposes strict minimum requirements to govern the provision of food to those who have been interned during an armed conflict; and Article 91 requires every place of internment to have adequate medical facilities. Prima facie, a situation can be envisaged whereby Article 41 sanctions have the effect of compromising the realisation of the values that such provisions of IHL evidently seek to uphold. Wide-ranging sanctions could certainly have the effect of interfering with the effective delivery of humanitarian relief to those requiring it, in turn hindering the provision of adequate food and medical supplies or services. The experience of Iraq is an often-cited case in point.[36] However, to argue that the UN Security Council is bound directly by norms of international humanitarian law when imposing sanctions remains problematic.

Although it has long been recognised that the UN enjoys international legal personality,[37] it is not a signatory to any of the instruments of international humanitarian law such as the Geneva Conventions, these being only open to membership for states. While the UN has explicitly acknowledged that it is restrained by general principles of international humanitarian law when undertaking military operations,[38] it is somewhat different to apply international humanitarian law to military action – which is the very field of activity which it was conceived to govern – and to apply it to the imposition of non-military sanctions, which it quite obviously was not.[39] This lies at the heart of the problem of attempting to use IHL to place limitations upon the Security Council's power to impose sanctions where these have humanitarian implications. Consideration of the relationship between UN sanctions and IHL can be traced back over a period of time.[40] It has been acknowledged that it is difficult to establish a direct relationship where the former measures are legally conditioned by the latter. IHL is concerned with the manner in which warfare may be legitimately conducted and it is a tenuous argument to

35 See Kondoch, B., 'The limits of economic sanctions under international law: The case of Iraq,' *International Peacekeeping: The Yearbook of International Peace Operations*, 2001, v.7, pp.267–294, at pp.284–287.

36 See below.

37 *Reparations for Injuries Suffered in the Service of the United Nations*, Advisory Opinion, ICJ Rep 1949, p.174.

38 UN Doc. ST/SGB/1999/13.

39 Some do argue that sanctions imposed during a state of armed conflict are governed by IHL. See, for example, Joyner, C., 'United Nations sanctions after Iraq: Looking back to see ahead,' *Chicago Journal of International Law*, v.4, n.2, 2003, pp.329–354, at p.348.

40 See Craven, supra n22; O'Connell, E., 'Debating the law of sanctions,' *European Journal of International Law*, v.13, n.1, 2002, pp.63–79; Joyner, ibid; Sassoli, supra n31.

suggest that sanctions constitute a form of warfare.[41] Sanctions which may have a negative humanitarian impact – essentially comprehensive trade embargoes – are not imposed as part of a military campaign. Whereas IHL has rules pertaining to access to food and medical supplies on the part of civilians, it has no rules relating to trade and exports.[42] Although in some circumstances, sanctions may produce the kind of negative humanitarian consequences which IHL contains provisions to guard against, it is difficult to categorise sanctions regimes in such cases as violations of it. Orakhelashvili has made a case for the applicability of IHL to UN sanctions by drawing upon some of its core provisions which sanctions have the capacity to impact upon,[43] for example the prohibition on the starvation of civilians.[44] However, while fundamental norms of international humanitarian law are widely accepted as constituting jus cogens,[45] it is through the manner in which warfare is waged that these norms are violated. As an actor that is not generally a party to conflict when imposing sanctions, and which does not always impose sanctions during situations involving the existence of armed conflict, the Security Council cannot easily be regulated by IHL when imposing non-military sanctions. This has led to the charge that, 'populations adversely affected by sanctions have fewer legal rights than those involved in war.'[46] Although it would appear extremely difficult to attempt to apply IHL to UN sanctions policy as a legal constraint, a strong case can be made for IHL to nonetheless inform the approach of the Security Council towards the imposition and continuation of sanctions regimes where they may give rise to serious humanitarian implications. As Joyner convincingly argues, 'one might logically conclude that actions prohibited during armed conflict ought to be prohibited during peacetime as well.'[47] There is no reason why IHL could not be applied by analogy to sanctions as a minimum standard which ought to guide decision-making in this area.[48] In fact, there are indications that this is a consideration drawn upon by the Council, it having emphasised itself that its measures are not intended to have adverse humanitarian consequences for civilians.[49]

41 The concept of 'economic warfare' is essentially a political slogan rather than a term with any legal content.
42 Sassoli, supra n34, pp.242–243.
43 Oakhelashvili, A., *Collective Security* (Oxford: Oxford University Press, 2011), pp.127–128.
44 Article 54, Protocol Additional to the Geneva Conventions Relating to the Protection of Victims of International Armed Conflicts 1977.
45 See, for example, Nieto-Navia, R., 'International peremptory norms (jus cogens) and international humanitarian law' (The Hague, 2001), available at http://www.iccnow.org/documents/WritingColombiaEng.pdf.
46 Smith, supra n28, p.183.
47 Joyner, supra n39, p.349.
48 Sassoli, supra n34, p.244.
49 SC Res 2610 (2021).

Unlike IHL, which is only applicable during instances of armed conflict, IHRL enjoys more general application, being relevant also in peacetime. It is possible to identify fundamental norms contained within IHRL which are compromised when sanctions severely impact upon the well-being of the civilian population.[50] Extensive suffering might be regarded as inconsistent with such fundamental civil and political rights such as the right to life,[51] or such core economic, social and cultural rights as the right to an adequate standard of living, which includes the right to food[52] and the right to the highest attainable standard of health.[53] The International Covenant on Economic, Social and Cultural Rights (ICESCR) committee itself suggested that sanctions might violate basic economic, social and cultural rights, at a time when comprehensive economic sanctions were in place against Iraq and generating humanitarian consequences.[54] Certain rights contained in international and regional human rights instruments enjoy qualifications or limitations, however, and make provision for states parties to derogate from their obligations under them in appropriate circumstances,[55] the thrust of their obligations being to protect these rights to the extent reasonable in the circumstances broadly in accordance with the concept of proportionality. However, the most fundamental of human rights are absolute in nature, must be protected in full and enjoy the status of jus cogens.[56] While the violation of such rights would be likely to be unlawful if perpetrated through a deliberate policy on the part of the Security Council, which involved, say, the starvation of a people or the commission of war crimes,[57] there are again difficulties in applying human rights norms to the Security Council's imposition of sanctions in all but the most extreme of circumstances. Most human rights instruments define them in jurisdictional or territorial terms: states are responsible for protecting the rights of individuals within

50 For a brief discussion of potential consequences for a series of human rights norms, see Dupont, P.-E., 'Human rights implications of sanctions,' in Asada, M. (ed.), *Economic Sanctions in International Law and Practice* (London & New York: Routledge, 2020), pp.39–61, at pp.43–47.
51 Protected by, for example, Article 3, Universal Declaration of Human Rights 1948; Article 2, European Convention on Human Rights 1950; Article 6, International Covenant on Civil and Political Rights 1966.
52 Article 11, International Covenant on Economic, Social and Cultural Rights 1966.
53 Article 13, ibid. See also Heupel, M., 'With power comes responsibility: Human rights protection in United Nations sanctions policy,' *European Journal of International Relations*, 2011, v.19, n.4, pp.773–796, at pp.778–783.
54 UN Committee on Economic, Social and Cultural Rights, *The Relationship between Sanctions and Respect for Economic, Social and Cultural Rights*, UN Doc. E/C.12/1997/8.
55 See, for example, Articles 5–6 and 8–11, European Convention on Human Rights 1950.
56 Orakhelashvili, supra n43, p.125. See Bianchi, A., 'Human rights and the magic of jus cogens,' *European Journal of International Law*, 2008, v.19, n.3, pp.491–508; de Wet, E., 'The prohibition of torture as an international norm of jus cogens and its implications for national customary law,' *European Journal of International Law*, 2004, v.15, n.1, pp.97–121.
57 See Dapo, supra n18, at p.324; Clapham, A., 'Sanctions and economic, social and cultural rights,' in Gowlland-Debbas, supra n5, pp.131–141, at p.134.

their territory and subject to their jurisdiction.[58] Only the ICESCR places a more general obligation to protect rights which omits reference to territorial or jurisdictional factors.[59] Obviously, the UN generally lacks jurisdiction over any particular territory or individuals definable in territorial terms.[60] Nor is it a signatory to any of the many human rights treaties. Nonetheless, a strong case can be made in support of the view that the UN must adhere to international human rights standards. Given that an overwhelming majority of its members are parties to the most significant human rights treaties,[61] it is arguable that by extension the UN is obliged to act in accordance with widely accepted human rights norms.[62] As an organisation, the UN is simply the collective voice of its membership and acts upon the basis of decisions taken by the states which comprise it. It would be undesirable if the various human rights norms that govern their conduct in all other respects were not equally applicable to their actions taken through the forum of the UN.

However, it will generally be difficult to demonstrate that in imposing non-military sanctions in a given situation the Security Council has set out on a policy designed to have a negative effect on respect for core human rights norms.[63] It is also the case, as Orakhelashvili emphasises, that some degree of hardship for the civilian population is a constituent element of the concept of sanctions.[64] As one commentator has argued, 'senders of sanctions cannot be held responsible unless they intentionally seek to violate' fundamental humanitarian or human rights norms. 'Definitions of genocide, torture, racism or other violations of human rights require an intention to commit the violation.'[65] Sanctions naturally have the ability to infringe on the general well-being of civilian populations to some extent in most cases, but to suggest that this in itself prevents their imposition would seriously undermine the collective security function of the Security Council, perhaps leading one to concur with Craven, who suggests that 'given the broad discretion assumed by the Security Council ... the role of humanitarian arguments will invariably be confined to one of ameliorating adverse consequences, rather

58 See, for example, Article 2, International Covenant on Civil and Political Rights 1966; Article 1, European Convention on Human Rights 1950.

59 Article 2 (2).

60 The exception is where the UN has assumed responsibility for the administration of a territory. On the UN's performance of territorial administrative functions generally, see Wilde, R., *International Territorial Administration* (Oxford: Oxford University Press, 2008).

61 For example, 167 states are parties to the International Covenant on Civil and Political Rights (ICCPR).

62 See the references contained in n50–51 supra.

63 While the concept of bad faith can be identified as a factor which may invalidate decisions of the Council, demonstrating its existence is notoriously difficult. See Cryer, R., 'The Security Council and Article 39: A threat to coherence?,' *Journal of Armed Conflict Law*, 1996, v.1, pp.161–195, at p.169.

64 Orakhelashvili, supra n43, p.124.

65 O'Connell, supra n40.

than of limiting the capacity to impose those measures in the first place.'[66] As Orakhelashvili notes, whereas 'certain core rights relating to the direct protection of the individual must be protected to the fullest extent possible, a principle of proportionality must guide the infringement of other derogable human rights.'[67] Arguably, it is the proportionality requirement which will be central in ensuring sanctions regimes are compatible with fundamental humanitarian and human rights norms. As Reisman and Stewick argue, 'Non-military instruments should be tested rigorously against the criteria of the International Law of Armed Conflict and other relevant norms of contemporary international law before a decision is made to initiate or to continue to apply them.'[68] As shall be seen, the Council has increasingly utilised targeted sanctions under Article 41 as a means of protecting against unnecessary negative humanitarian consequences of sanctions regimes, reinforcing the view that it recognises the importance of acting in accordance with limitations made desirable by reference to standards contained in IHL and IHRL.

Domestic or regional legal limitations upon the application of non-military sanctions arising from individual human rights concerns

The potential legal limitations to the Security Council's power to impose non-military sanctions arising from humanitarian concerns considered above to some extent represent restrictions that are more theoretical or hypothetical in nature. While the subject of debate among international lawyers, they have not served to pose a direct legal challenge to the scope of the Council's power under Article 41. However, the Council's shift towards the utilisation of targeted sanctions which include the imposition of restrictions upon individuals has led to challenges to specific measures insofar as they pertain to named individuals. As explained by Tzanakopoulos with reference to challenges brought in national courts, 'Faced with the lack of any judicial remedies against Security Council decisions … affected persons are resorting to domestic courts, attacking the domestic acts adopted in implementation of the relevant resolutions.'[69] However, similar challenges have also arisen under international and regional human rights frameworks, sometimes resulting in the effective curtailment of the application of the sanctions concerned. The source of most of the prominent legal challenges has been the sanctions regime established pursuant to Resolution 1267,[70] which provided for the application of targeted sanctions against listed individuals associated

66 Craven, supra n22, p.43.
67 Orakhelashvili, supra n43, p.125.
68 Reisman and Stewick, supra n2, p.95.
69 Tzanakopoulos, A., 'United Nations Sanctions in Domestic Courts,' *Journal of International Criminal Justice*, 2010, v.8, pp.249–267, at p.250.
70 SC Res 1267 (1999).

with Al-Qaida and the Taleban,[71] and has been developed and modified through subsequent resolutions.[72]

The most prominent early instance of a successful challenge to the implementation of targeted UN sanctions is found in the *Kadi* case.[73] Kadi was one of the individuals subject to sanctions imposed by the Security Council pursuant to Resolution 1267 on the basis of their association with Al-Qaida and the Taleban. Kadi's challenge was, however, brought under the auspices of the European Union's legal machinery and directed against the validity of the EU regulation which had been adopted to impose EU measures to give effect on a regional basis to the restrictions set out in Resolution 1267. The European Court of Justice, in finding in Kadi's favour, ruled that the EU regulation in question contravened a series of fundamental rights recognised in EU law – including the rights to judicial review, to a hearing and to privacy – and annulled it.[74] While it has been noted that the Court was technically not reviewing the UN resolution, but rather an EU act,[75] the outcome is nonetheless to undermine the scope of the Security Council's capacity to act without restraint.

Similar issues have been considered elsewhere. For example, the compatibility of travel bans imposed upon individuals under authority conferred by the Resolution 1267 sanctions regime with the European Convention on Human Rights has been considered by the European Court of Human Rights in cases brought concerning Switzerland's implementation of these measures,[76] with particular emphasis being placed upon the application of a proportionality test to evaluate potential infringement of the rights to privacy and an effective remedy under Articles 8 and 13 of the ECHR. The UN's own Human Rights Committee found against Belgium in a similar case arising from its addition of individuals to a list subject to restrictions determined to constitute violations of Articles 12 and

71 For discussion of the 1267 sanctions regime's origins and evolution, see Duffy, H. and van den Herik, L., 'Terrorism and the Security Council,' in GeiB, R. and Melzer, N. (eds), *The Oxford Handbook of the International Law of Global Security* (Oxford: OUP, 2021), pp.193–212.

72 Including recently, e.g., SC Res 2734 (2024).

73 *Yassin Abdullah Kadi and Al Barakaat International Foundation v. Council of the European Union and Commission of the European Communities*, Cases C-402/05 P and C-415/05 P.

74 For discussion, see Posch, A., 'The Kadi case: Rethinking the relationship between EU law and international law,' *Columbia Journal of European Law*, 2009, v.15, pp.1–5; Jayakody, N., 'Refining United Nations Security Council Targeted Sanctions,' *Security and Human Rights*, 2018, v.29, pp.90–119, at pp.102–105; Happold, M., 'Targeted Sanctions and Human Rights,' in Happold, M. and Eden, P. (eds), *Economic Sanctions and International Law: Law and Practice* (London: Bloomsbury, 2016), pp.87–112, at pp.99–109.

75 Happold, ibid, p.92.

76 *Nada v Switzerland*, Application No 10593/08, Merits, 12 September 2012; *Al Duilmi and Montana Management Inc v Switzerland*, Application No 5809/08, Judgement, 21 June 2016. For discussion, see Jayakody, supra n74, pp.105–107.

17 of the ICCPR.[77] Challenges to a state's implementation of UN sanctions have also arisen in domestic courts, an example in point being *Abdelrazik v Canada*,[78] where a sanctioned individual successfully challenged Canada's implementation of a travel ban mandated by Resolution 1267 on the basis of its alleged incompatibility with Canada's domestic *Charter of Rights and Freedoms*.[79] The effect was essentially to force Canada into a breach of its international obligations in order to comply with a domestic ruling.[80]

Clearly, the imposition of targeted sanctions upon individuals has given rise to a series of challenges which effectively take the form of conflicts between states' duties stemming from their UN membership and individual rights protected under their domestic constitutional frameworks and/or human rights mechanisms to which they are parties. As far back as October 2009, it had been noted that over 30 legal challenges had been presented to the application of sanctions against named individuals stemming from the regime established by Resolution 1267.[81] Importantly, it should be noted that in the kinds of situations referred to there is no direct challenge to the legal authority of the Security Council per se. Rather, it has been measures adopted by states or regional organisations to give effect to UN sanctions that the legal validity of which has been questioned, rather than the actual UN acts themselves. Theoretically, thus, Article 103 – which directs states to prioritise obligations arising under the UN Charter from those arising under other treaties – is not violated, as it has been the very fact that states have sought to give effect to their obligations under the UN Charter that has served as the basis for the ensuing legal challenges. Nevertheless, the effectiveness of targeted sanctions is called into question if attempts to implement them are sabotaged by legal processes external to the UN system. This underlines the importance of the Security Council taking into account the concerns underpinning the legal challenges brought against measures implementing UN sanctions as part of their approach to sanctions design, enforcement and monitoring. We return to this point below.

77 *Sayadi and Vinck v Belgium* (1472/2006), Views, CCPR/C/94/D/1472/2006. For discussion, see Jayakody, supra n74, pp.101–102.

78 *Abousifan Abdelrazik v Minister of Foreign Affairs and Attorney General of Canada*, 2009. FC 580, 4 June 2009.

79 For discussion, see Tzanakopoulos, supra n69.

80 Tzanakopoulos, supra n69, p.261.

81 Portela, C., 'National implementation of United Nations sanctions,' *International Journal*, 2009–10, Winter, pp.13–30, at pp.21–26. For a series of examples of legal challenges brought against sanctions implementing measures, see Tzanakopoulos, supra n69, pp.250–251.

The Security Council's practice of applying non-military sanctions

This section is not intended to provide a detailed analysis of the various sanctions regimes to have been imposed by the Security Council. An overview of UN sanctions regimes can be found elsewhere.[82] Rather, we set out some of the main features of the Council's practice in respect of the imposition of non-military sanctions and show how this has changed over time. We begin by briefly considering the purposes for which non-military sanctions have been utilised and the targets against which they have been directed, before proceeding to afford a brief overview of their utilisation to date and the degree to which they were perceived as having satisfied their objectives. Consideration is finally given to the Council's approach to the administration and monitoring of sanctions. This then leads naturally into the evaluation of the problems associated with the imposition of sanctions in the practice of the Council, which takes place in the subsequent section.

The purposes and targets of non-military sanctions

Purposes

In legal terms, the overriding purpose of any sanctions regime applied by the Security Council under Article 41 must be the maintenance or restoration of international peace and security. That is not to say that they may not also serve additional purposes which complement or at least do not detract from this objective. Ordinarily, sanctions are imposed following a determination under Article 39 that there exists a threat to the peace, breach of the peace or act of aggression, this provision further stating that it is following such a determination that the Council may decide to apply measures under either Article 41 or 42. Sanctions 'aim to induce a state or non-state entities to change behaviour that is in violation of international standards and possibly … in order to remove the threat to or restore international peace and security.'[83] The key to understanding the purposes of sanctions lies in appreciating the broad conception of 'threats to the peace' developed by the Security Council, as considered in Chapter 2. This has meant that a wide range of situations are potentially amenable to the application of sanctions. Biersteker et al consider sanctions to serve one or more of three broad purposes: to coerce a target, to constrain it, or to stigmatise it.[84] While the former two

82 Details of existing sanctions regimes can be found in the Sanctions committees section of the UN website, http://www.un.org/sc/committees/. Overviews of sanctions imposed up to the early twenty-first century can be found in, for example, Farrall, supra n19, Appendix 2; Lowe et al, supra n1, Appendix 4.

83 Orakhelashvili, supra n43, p.121.

84 Biersteker, T.J., Tourinho, M. and Eckert, S.E., 'Thinking about United Nations targeted sanctions,' in Biersteker, T.J., Eckert, S.E. and Tourinho, M. (eds), *Targeted Sanctions: The Impacts and Effectiveness of United Nations Action* (Cambridge: CUP, 2016), pp.11–37, at p.21.

aims appear directed to effect practical impacts which increase the likelihood of an actor ceasing from or not starting to engage in behaviour which threatens or breaches international peace and security, the third purpose can nonetheless be seen as intended to weaken its international reputation and provide incentives for similarly so doing. Breaking down the purposes of sanctions yet further, Farrall identifies seven more specific objectives which have driven the imposition of sanctions: ending rebellion, invasion or external aggression; restoring legitimate government; protecting human rights; encouraging disarmament; establishing peace; addressing international terrorism; and promoting good governance.[85] A survey of UN sanctions regimes will reveal that one or more of these objectives have been at stake on each occasion when sanctions have been applied. In accordance with the shift towards a more human-centric model of collective security practised by the UN, it has increasingly become the norm for non-military sanctions to be applied in response to situations characterised by features or consequences of a broadly humanitarian nature, be this via measures to weaken the ability of warring parties to continue to wage warfare; restore ousted democratically elected governments; combat international terrorism; or encourage the disarmament of regimes deemed a wider international threat.[86] Sometimes the narrower specific objectives of particular measures have been designed to serve a wider purpose, for example the adoption of measures to tackle the illegal exploitation of natural resources in West Africa as a means of depriving warring factions of a major source of revenue.[87]

Targets

Traditionally, collective security was regarded in state-centric terms and consequently states were traditionally regarded as the main target of sanctions. Indeed, the earliest instances of sanctions being imposed by the UN Security Council both during the Cold War and in the early post–Cold War era took the form of measures imposed against states. However, as the Council has over time adopted a broadened conception of what can amount to a 'threat to the peace,' it has increasingly been prepared to apply sanctions against non-state actors.[88] Non-state actors subject to sanctions have generally fallen into two categories. First, factions that have been parties to armed conflicts determined to pose a threat to international peace and security by the Security Council have been targeted with sanctions since the

85 See Farrall, supra n19, Chapter 7. See also Farrall, supra n19, pp.86–102 for a more specific breakdown of situations resulting in the imposition of sanctions.

86 For a summary of the objectives of UN sanctions, see Giumelli, F., 'Understanding United Nations targeted sanctions: An empirical analysis,' *International Affairs*, 2015, v.91, n.6, pp.1351–1368, p.1357.

87 See Dam de Jong, supra n19, pp.390–393.

88 On targets of UN sanctions, see Giumelli, supra n86, pp.1359–1360; Farrall, supra n19, ch.6.

early 1990s,[89] principally taking the form of arms embargoes. The first instance of sanctions being imposed upon a non-state entity came in the form of resolution 820's measures against the Bosnian Serbs during the Yugoslav conflict, which was soon followed by the imposition of sanctions upon the National Union for the Total Independence of Angola (UNITA) faction to Angola's civil war by resolutions 833 and 864. The significance of measures adopted against non-state entities is underlined by the fact that over a 25-year period from the early post–Cold War era onwards, 28 rebel groups had been sanctioned via a range of measures extending to 13 civil war situations.[90] Second, in a process accelerated by the move towards the greater use of targeted measures, financial and travel sanctions have been directed against individuals. A major development in this respect was the establishment of the targeted sanctions regime consisting of measures against individuals associated with Al-Qaida and the Taleban pursuant to Resolution 1267.[91] Several prominent individuals have also been subject to targeted sanctions, including figures within the Libyan regime of Colonel Gaddafi who were sanctioned both following the Lockerbie bombing[92] and the 2011 uprisings in Libya,[93] as well as members of the Liberian government of Charles Taylor,[94] members of the junta and Revolutionary United Front (RUF) during Sierra Leone's civil war,[95] and members of leadership elites within Sudan[96] and Iran.[97]

The application of sanctions during the Cold War

During the Cold War era, non-military sanctions were only imposed by the Security Council on two occasions. The general political climate of the time made it difficult to achieve any consensus within the Council upon the adoption of such measures, and the two instances of their utilisation fell outside of the main arena of superpower rivalry. Following the unilateral declaration of independence by the minority white regime in Southern Rhodesia in 1965, the Council called for a voluntary oil embargo upon the country,[98] later making this mandatory and adding an arms embargo and extensive trade sanctions,[99] as well as travel, diplomatic

89 See Farrall, supra n19, pp.129–132.
90 Radtke, M. and Jo, H., 'Fighting the hydra: United Nations sanctions and rebel groups,' *Journal of Peace Research*, 2018, v.55, n.6, pp.759–773, p.760.
91 See also, e.g., SC Res 1333 (2000); 1390 (2002).
92 SC Res 748 (1992); SC Res 883 (1993).
93 SC Res 1970 (2011).
94 SC Res 1343 (2001); SC Res 1532 (2004).
95 SC Res 1171 (2000).
96 SC Res 1591 (2006).
97 SC Res 1737 (2006).
98 SC Res 221 (1966).
99 SC Res 232 (1966).

and financial measures.[100] Sanctions were only finally lifted following the end of minority rule in 1979.[101] Clearly motivated by its policy of apartheid, the acquisition of arms by South Africa was determined to constitute a threat to the maintenance of international peace and security.[102] In response, a mandatory arms embargo was imposed against the country,[103] remaining in force until free multiracial elections were held some 17 years later.[104] The effectiveness of sanctions in both cases is highly questionable given the extent of their violation and the fact that they remained in place for such a long period of time. At an early stage in the application of sanctions against Southern Rhodesia, the Security Council itself acknowledged that a number of states were failing in their obligations to implement them.[105] While Crawford identified some domestic impact resulting from sanctions within South Africa,[106] the exact extent to which they contributed to the eventual demise of apartheid is difficult to assess as a consequence of other factors also at play, or what has been labelled as the phenomena of 'multi-causality.'[107] This makes it difficult to regard the sanctions imposed as having been undeniably successful in achieving their objectives.[108]

The 1990s: The sanctions decade

The end of the Cold War and the newfound cooperation between the permanent members within the Security Council gave rise to unprecedented activity on its part, most notably in respect of the adoption of measures under Chapter VII. This

100 SC Res 253 (1968); SC Res 277 (1970); SC Res 409 (1977).

101 SC Res 460 (1979).

102 SC Res 418 (1977), para.1. This followed the long-standing existence of a voluntary arms embargo called for by SC Res 181 (1963). The centrality of South Africa's apartheid policy to the Council's approach is made apparent by the preamble to resolution 418 which 'strongly condemn[ed] the South African Government for its acts of repression, its defiant continuance of the system of apartheid and its attacks against neighbouring independent States' and 'consider[ed] that the policies and acts of the South African Government are fraught with danger to international peace and security.'

103 Ibid, paras.2–4.

104 SC Res 919 (1994). On sanctions against Southern Rhodesia, see Zacklin, R., *The United Nations and Rhodesia* (New York: Praeger Publishers, 1974).

105 SC Res 253 (1968). See also Reisman and Stewick, supra n2, pp.96–101; Stephenson, G.V., 'The impact of international economic sanctions on the internal viability of Rhodesia,' *Geographical Review*, 1975, v.65, n.3, pp.377–389.

106 Crawford, N.C., 'The humanitarian consequences of sanctioning South Africa: A preliminary assessment,' in Weiss, T.G., Cortright, D., Lopez, G.A. and Minear, L., *Political Gain and Civilian Pain* (Lanham: Rowan & Littlefield, 1997), pp.57–89.

107 Cortright, D. and Lopez, G.A., 'Economic sanctions and human rights: Part of the problem or part of the solution?,' *International Journal of Human Rights*, 1997, v.1, n.2, pp.1–25, at pp.13–14.

108 See also Levy, P.I., *Sanctions on South Africa: What Did They Do?*, Economic Growth Center Discussion Paper No.796, Yale University, 1999, available at http://aida.wss.yale.edu/growth_pdf/cdp796.pdf.

included the imposition of non-military sanctions in response to a range of situations that had been determined to threaten international peace and security during the 1990s, leading to the period being labelled as 'the sanctions decade.' Here we provide a brief overview and identify some of the key themes of some of the main sanctions regimes of the 1990s.

Iraq

Comprehensive economic sanctions were imposed upon Iraq by Resolution 661 following its invasion of Kuwait in 1990, their objective being straightforward: generating pressure which would bring about Iraq's departure from Kuwait.[109] Although Kuwait was subsequently liberated by military action, these sanctions remained in place as their purposes were adjusted and they became linked to Iraq's compliance with disarmament obligations contained in the ceasefire reached between it and the Security Council, contained in Resolution 687,[110] which ended the military conflict. These wide-ranging sanctions, labelled the 'longest, most comprehensive, and most controversial in the history of the [UN],'[111] remained in place until the regime of Saddam Hussein had been overthrown in 2003,[112] and are acknowledged as having been responsible for considerable humanitarian suffering in Iraq, including increased mortality and malnutrition rates.[113] Even in the earliest days of sanctions, a report by the Athisaari mission noted that sanctions 'had already adversely affected the country's ability to feed its people.'[114] Particular criticism has been directed at the inadequacy of provisions made for humanitarian exemptions to the sanctions. Resolution 661 exempted from sanctions 'supplies intended strictly for medical purposes, and, in humanitarian circumstances, foodstuffs,'[115] and Resolution 687 provided that sanctions would not extend to the export of foodstuffs and items for essential civilian needs. In practice, however,

109 In its previous Resolution 660, the Security Council had determined that Iraq's invasion of Kuwait amounted to a breach of the peace. Resolution 661, adopted just four days later, referred back to Resolution 660, noting that Iraq had failed to comply with the demands contained therein (para.1) and that 'as a consequence' the Council had decided to impose the sanctions detailed 'to secure compliance of Iraq' with those demands (para.2.).

110 SC Res 687 (1991), paras.9–13.

111 Cortright, Lopez and Gerber-Stellingwerf, supra n1, p.207.

112 SC Res 1483 (2003).

113 See Ali, M.M. and Shah, I.H., 'Sanctions and childhood mortality in Iraq,' *The Lancet*, Issue 9218, 2000, p.1851; Hoskins, E., 'The humanitarian impacts of economic sanctions and war in Iraq,' in Weiss, Cortright, Lopez and Minear, supra n106, pp.91–147; Joyner, supra n36, pp.334–343; Craven, supra n22, p.44 et seq; Heine-Ellison, S., 'The impact and effectiveness of multilateral economic sanctions: A comparative study,' *International Journal of Human Rights*, 2001, v.5, n.1, pp.81–112, pp.93–96; Kondoch, supra n32, pp.279–280.

114 UN Doc. S/22366.

115 Paras.3 (c), 4.

the determination of 'humanitarian circumstances' was left to the sanctions committee.[116]

Although an 'oil for food' initiative was designed to allow Iraq to trade a certain amount of oil in exchange for foodstuffs and medical supplies,[117] as well as to pay compensation in relation to Iraq's invasion of Kuwait as required by Resolution 687, various obstacles resulting from political disagreement among the permanent membership of the Security Council hindered its operation.[118] Furthermore, the US made it very clear that it was not inclined to support the lifting of sanctions while Saddam Hussein remained in power, even though his removal was not a formally stated objective of the sanctions.[119] Cortright and Lopez identify eight conditions that at some point were required to be satisfied if sanctions against Iraq were to be lifted.[120] This underlines the scope which exists for a sanctions regime to be politicised to the extent that it ceases to function in accordance with the very purposes for which it was established in the first place.

It is difficult to consider sanctions upon Iraq as having contributed towards any positive outcome,[121] although some commentators have credited them with having aided the success of UN weapons inspections, which were able to make huge progress with the identification and dismantling of Iraq's weapons infrastructure, as required by Resolution 687.[122] The actual impact of sanctions on Iraq led to them being labelled in one study 'the most effective of all twentieth century economic sanctions.'[123] However, effectiveness in terms of enforcement and impact does not necessarily equate with success in achieving their objectives.[124] Certainly, it must be doubted as to whether the US and its allies considered the sanctions successful given their decision to invade Iraq in 2003 on the basis of their purported non-compliance with UN weapons decommissioning demands.[125]

116 SC Res 666 (1990).
117 SC Res 986 (1995).
118 See Cortright, D. and Lopez, G.A., *The Sanctions Decade: Assessing UN Strategies in the 1990s* (Boulder: Lynne Rienner, 2000), Chapter 3; Orakhelashvili, supra n43, pp.141–148; Kondoch, supra n35, p.278.
119 See Cortright, Lopez and Gerber-Stellingwerf, supra n1, pp.207–210.
120 Cortright and Lopez, supra n107, p.43 et seq.
121 See, however, Suzuki, K., 'Iraq,' in Asada, supra n60, pp.178–199. Suzuki suggests that measures against Iraq represented the most successful case of UN sanctions (p.178).
122 See Cortright, Lopez and Gerber-Stellingwerf, supra n1, pp.207–210; Lopez, G.A. and Cortright, D., 'Containing Iraq: Sanctions worked,' *Foreign Affairs*, v.83, n.4, 2004, pp.90–103.
123 Shehabaldin, A. and Laughlin, W.M., 'Economic sanctions against Iraq: Human and economic costs,' *International Journal of Human Rights*, 1999, v.3, n.4, pp.1–18, at p.1.
124 Indeed, that the US and UK felt it necessary to invade Iraq in 2003 on the pretext of dismantling their weapons of mass destruction capacity suggests very strongly that these permanent members of the Council were dissatisfied with the success of sanctions.
125 See Chapter 6.

Other non-military sanctions during the 1990s

Although the sanctions regime imposed upon Iraq has been the biggest source of controversy among early post–Cold War era measures, the 1990s also saw comprehensive economic or trade embargoes imposed in other instances. Comprehensive sanctions were applied in response to both the conflict which accompanied the break-up of Yugoslavia from 1992 onwards,[126] in conjunction with an arms embargo,[127] and following the seizure of power in Haiti by a military junta in 1993–1994.[128] The objective of the sanctions in the case of Yugoslavia was to exert pressure for the cessation of hostilities.[129] The comprehensive economic sanctions imposed by Resolution 757 remained in force for three and a half years until the conclusion of the Dayton peace agreement, at which point they were suspended indefinitely.[130] Although not attracting as much attention as those imposed upon Iraq, sanctions nevertheless had some humanitarian impact,[131] and a report compiled under OSCE auspices concluded that they achieved the objectives pursued by the Security Council, the economic sanctions in particular being remarkably effective.[132] Their success in contributing towards the resolution of the conflict, however, is a matter of some debate.[133] While by some assessments they were an important factor in bringing the parties to peace talks,[134] for others it was the application of NATO airpower under UN Security Council authority that was central to achieving this goal. As with the experience of Iraq, this reinforces the fact that it cannot be assumed that there will be any correlation between the actual material impact of sanctions and their success in achieving their desired outcomes.

The seizure of power in Haiti by a military junta, labelled a threat to international peace and security,[135] also resulted in the imposition of comprehensive sanctions.[136] However, although a fuel embargo had already been in place for about a year at the time of their adoption,[137] the comprehensive measures

126 SC Res 757 (1992).

127 SC Res 713 (1991).

128 SC Res 917 (1994).

129 SC Res 757 (1992), para.3 stated that the measures would remain in place until the Council's demands contained in SC Res 752 (1992) were complied with. The primary demand of resolution 752 was that the parties cease fighting (para.1).

130 SC Res 1022 (1995). Suspension of the sanctions' application to the Bosnian Serbs did not, however, occur for another year: SC Res 1074 (1996).

131 See Heine-Ellison, supra n113, pp.96–99.

132 UN Doc. S/1996/776, p.13.

133 See, for example, Reisman and Stewick, supra n2, pp.112–117.

134 See Cortright and Lopez, supra n107, Chapter 4; Devlin, J. and Dashti-Gibson, S., 'Sanctions in the former Yugoslavia: Convoluted goals and complicated consequences,' in Weiss, Cortright, Lopez, and Minear, supra n106, pp.149–187, at pp.171–175.

135 SC Res 841 (1993).

136 SC Res 917 (1994). Para.16 stated clearly that the measures imposed would be kept under continuous review until the return of the democratically elected president.

137 Imposed by SC Res 841 (1993).

were only in force for four months when the democratically elected government of President Jean-Bertrand Aristide was returned to power following a US-led military intervention,[138] and sanctions were lifted.[139] These undoubtedly contributed towards human suffering, although the scale of this has been disputed.[140] The plight of the civilian population received little attention from the Security Council and the failure of sanctions is possibly evidenced by the fact that the junta only relinquished power in the face of an imminent US-led military intervention authorised by the Council in Resolution 940, again demonstrating that regardless of their impact, economic sanctions have proven poor at coercing their targets to adjust their behaviour to satisfy the Council's demands.

Although the 'smart sanctions' agenda is often seen as a product of various initiatives held around the millennium, the Security Council was already beginning to adopt some more targeted sanctions measures during the 1990s. In addition to embargoes on the sale of petroleum or fuel,[141] the Council moved to restrict the trade in diamonds from African regions where they provided warring parties with a lucrative source of income which enabled them to continue their military campaigns. Targeted at the rebel UNITA movement, the first such sanctions were imposed to prohibit the export of diamonds from Angola which had not been certified by the government.[142] They were lifted following resolution of the Angolan conflict.[143] Although their monitoring and enforcement proved difficult,[144] similar measures were later applied to Sierra Leone[145] and Liberia.[146]

In a precursor to more common usage in the twenty-first century, the 1990s also saw the first instances of UN sanctions applied against individuals targeted by the Security Council on account of their status as leaders or decision-makers whom it sought to pressurise to comply with its demands. These took the form principally of financial asset freezes and travel bans. Libya's leadership initially faced diplomatic and travel restrictions following its failure to hand over suspects wanted for trial in connection with the Lockerbie bombing,[147] later supplemented with the imposition of a freeze on Libyan assets.[148] A similar freeze was

138 Authorised by SC Res 940 (1994).

139 SC Res 944 (1994).

140 See Reisman, W.M., 'Haiti and the validity of international action,' *American Journal of International Law*, 1995, v.89, n.1, pp.82–84; Cortright and Lopez, supra n107, Chapter 5; Zaidi, S., 'Humanitarian effects of the coup and sanctions in Haiti,' in Weiss, Cortright, Lopez and Minear, supra n106, pp.189–212.

141 In relation to Libya (SC Res 883 (1993)), Angola (UNITA) (SC Res 864 (1993)) and Sierra Leone (SC Res 1132 (1997)).

142 SC Res 1173 (1998).

143 SC Res 1448 (2002).

144 Heine-Ellison, supra n113, pp.99–103.

145 SC Res 1306 (2000).

146 SC Res 1343 (2001).

147 SC Res 748 (1992).

148 SC Res 883 (1993).

placed upon Haitian assets following the seizure of power there by the military junta.[149] Combinations of targeted measures were also applied against UNITA,[150] the Sudanese government[151] and the Taleban regime in Afghanistan.[152] The success of these various sanctions regimes has been mixed at best. For example, post-Lockerbie sanctions against Libya were generally effectively enforced and credited with having had some impact, through their political isolation of Libya, in bringing about its eventual compliance with UN Security Council demands. However, Cortright and Lopez, in a detailed study of the impact of targeted sanctions, have concluded that their effects in respect of Libya, Sudan and the Taleban were minimal.[153] The value of travel sanctions in particular was called into question by Conroy, who found that these measures when imposed upon the leadership of UNITA, Sudan and the Taleban were either widely violated or failed to impact upon their conduct.[154]

The most commonly applied form of sanction during the 1990s was that of the arms embargo, imposed as a means of attempting to minimise the capacity of warring parties to continue their military campaigns in former Yugoslavia,[155] Somalia,[156] Liberia,[157] Angola,[158] Rwanda,[159] Sierra Leone[160] and the FRY.[161] In addition, arms embargoes also formed part of the measures imposed against Libya[162] and Haiti.[163] Although several of these measures were eventually terminated,[164] the impact of arms embargoes in removing the threats to the peace which they were established to address appears to have been minimal at best.[165] In practice, they were poorly enforced and monitored, and it is questionable whether

149 SC Res 841 (1993).
150 SC Res 1127 (1997); SC Res 1173 (1998).
151 SC Res 1054 (1996).
152 SC Res 1267 (1999).
153 Cortright and Lopez, supra n107, pp.107–127.
154 See Conroy, R.W., 'The UN experience with travel sanctions: Selected cases and conclusions,' in Cortright and Lopez, supra n1118, pp.145–169.
155 SC Res 713 (1992).
156 SC Res 733 (1992).
157 SC Res 788 (1992).
158 SC Res 864 (1993).
159 SC Res 918 (1994).
160 SC Res 1132 (1997).
161 SC Res 1160 (1998).
162 SC Res 748 (1992).
163 SC Res 841 (1993).
164 In respect of former Yugoslavia (SC Res 1021 (1995)), Libya (SC Res 1506 (2003)), Haiti (SC Res 944 (1994)), UNITA (SC Res 1448 (2002)) and FRY (SC Res 1367 (2001)).
165 See Vines, A., 'Can UN arms embargoes in Africa be effective?,' *International Affairs*, 2007, v.83, n.6, pp.1107–1122; Cortright and Lopez, supra n118, Chapters 9–10; Bondi, L., 'Arms embargoes: In name only?,' in Cortright, D. and Lopez, G.A. (eds), *Smart Sanctions: Targeting Economic Statecraft* (Lanham: Rowman & Littlefield, 2002), pp.109–123; Brzoska, M., 'Putting more teeth into UN arms embargoes,' in Cortright and Lopez, infra, pp.125–143.

they contributed towards any significant amelioration of conflict or circumstances representing threats to the peace.[166]

Making sanctions smarter

The various problems associated with sanctions, and in particular the controversial experience of Iraq, led to various investigations from the late 1990s onwards into methods through which their effectiveness could be improved and their harmful consequences minimised. Discourse involving the UN, various states, public sector bodies, non-governmental organisations (NGOs) and academics began to focus upon ways in which the UN could move towards the greater use of 'smart sanctions,' a term coined to refer to sanctions regimes devised in such a manner that on one hand their effectiveness would be improved through better enforcement and the direct targeting of those whose actions they were designed to influence, while simultaneously minimising the risk of negative effects for civilian populations or other states. As articulated by the executive summary of the Bonn seminar, which considered improvements to arms embargoes and travel sanctions, 'The value of smart sanctions lies in the fact that they … [are] … sharply focused on the targeted leadership or group, with little if any negative impact on civilian populations and third States.'[167] A series of studies and initiatives generated various recommendations for improving the design and implementation of sanctions, including the Interlaken, Bonn-Berlin and Stockholm processes, as well as discussions within the Security Council and its specially created informal working group on sanctions.

From 1997, the Swiss government began to facilitate dialogue on targeted financial sanctions through the Interlaken process, through which seminars held in 1998–1999, gave participants the opportunity to consider problems associated with the implementation of financial sanctions and make recommendations for their improved effectiveness.[168] These included suggestions to tackle the potential politicisation of sanctions regimes containing financial measures by ensuring that the resolutions establishing them were sufficiently clear so as to leave no uncertainty over their intended scope or target.[169] The possible desirability of 'sunset' clauses to be inserted into sanctions-creating resolutions – thus preventing permanent members from vetoing any attempt to end sanctions where they had outlived

166 Ibid.

167 *Smart Sanctions, The Next Step: Arms Embargoes and Travel Sanctions, First Expert Seminar, Bonn, November 21–23, 1999 – A Brief Overview of Security Council Applied Sanctions*, p.2.

168 See *Expert Seminar on Targeting UN Financial Sanctions, March 17–19, 1998;* 2nd *Interlaken Seminar on Targeting United Nations Financial Sanctions*, 29–31 March, 1999, both available at http://www.seco.admin.ch/themen/00513/00620/00639/00641/index.html?lang=en.

169 *Expert Seminar on Targeting UN Financial Sanctions*, ibid, p.43.

their purpose – was also touched upon.[170] Preconditions for the successful implementation of sanctions measures within states' domestic laws were identified and draft model law provisions formulated,[171] while the need for regular monitoring of sanctions regimes was noted for not only measuring their effectiveness but to take account of their humanitarian effects and make provision for exemptions where appropriate.[172] The Bonn-Berlin process, consisting of two seminars held in Germany in 1999–2000 focused specifically on the design and implementation of arms embargoes and travel sanctions. It resulted in the creation of model Security Council resolutions to govern the creation of new arms embargoes and travel sanctions, among other recommendations for improvements to the implementation of travel bans and arms embargoes.[173]

With a more comprehensive focus than the Interlaken and Bonn-Berlin initiatives, the Stockholm process explored the successful implementation of targeted sanctions in all their forms: arms embargoes, financial sanctions, travel bans and targeted trade sanctions.[174] Three specialist working groups were established to explore respectively means for improving the UN's creation and administration of targeted sanctions; their implementation by member states; and improving the accuracy of sanctions measures and managing their evasion. Many of the recommendations to emerge from the Stockholm process echoed the outcomes of earlier investigations into targeted sanctions. Clarity in sanctions-creating resolutions with early assessment of their likely impact was advocated,[175] as was the need to improve monitoring of sanctions regimes through the provision of greater support for expert panels and specialist monitoring bodies established to investigate the practical implementation of sanctions.[176] It was recommended that member states' implementation of sanctions could be improved by the provision of guidance on model legislation to enforce them,[177] as well as through practical guidance and the conduct of periodic reviews of their administration. To counter the evasion of sanctions, the importance of pre-assessments of the feasibility of sanctions and contingency planning was advocated.[178]

170 *Expert Seminar on Targeting UN Financial Sanctions*, supra n150, p.44. A similar argument can be applied to military enforcement authority conferred by the Security Council. See Chapter 7.

171 2nd *Interlaken Seminar*, supra n168, pp.59–62 and Annexes 1–2.

172 2nd *Interlaken Seminar*, supra n168, pp.43–4, p.46.

173 See *Design and Implementation of Arms Embargoes and Travel and Aviation Related Sanctions: Results of the 'Bonn-Berlin Process,'* available at http://www.watsoninstitute.org/tfs/CD/booklet_sanctions.pdf.

174 See Wallensteen, P., Staibano, C. and Eriksson M. (eds), *Making Targeted Sanctions Effective: Guidelines for the Implementation of UN Policy Options* (Department of Peace and Conflict Research, Uppsala University, 2003), available at http://pcr.uu.se/digitalAssets/99/99313_Final_report_complete.pdf.

175 Wallensteen et al, ibid, p.IV.

176 Wallensteen et al, supra n174, p.V.

177 Wallensteen et al, supra n174, p.VI.

178 Wallensteen et al, supra n174, pp.IV–VI.

By the time of the aforementioned initiatives, consideration of means for improving the effectiveness and minimising negative impacts of sanctions had been taking place at the Security Council level for a number of years. As early as 1995, the P5 expressed their support for having regard to minimising the humanitarian effects of sanctions when sanctions regimes are designed and implemented.[179] Expert studies commissioned by the Department for Humanitarian Affairs in 1995 and 1997 had resulted in the development of methodologies for assessing the humanitarian impact of sanctions regimes,[180] while in 1998, the Council endorsed a number of proposals, advanced by the secretary-general,[181] for improving the effectiveness of arms embargoes.[182] The following year, the Council's membership universally agreed to follow a number of 'practical proposals' to improve the work of sanctions committees, including the periodic assessment of the effectiveness of sanctions regimes, periodic meetings to discuss their humanitarian and economic impact, and visits by the chairs of sanctions committees to regions affected by them.[183] The Council met periodically to discuss general issues relating to sanctions,[184] and listened to the views of active participants within the Bonn-Berlin, Interlaken and Stockholm processes.[185] An informal working group of the Council on general issues related to sanctions was created in 2000,[186] with a mandate to 'develop general recommendations on how to improve the effectiveness of [UN] sanctions.'[187] The working group considered issues including the monitoring of sanctions regimes, their duration and lifting, the assessment of their unintended impact and improving implementation, ending its work in 2006.[188] Building upon earlier pronouncements by the Council's membership, in a 2002 non-paper, the working group pronounced its agreement upon a number of recommendations which should inform the Council's sanctions policy.[189]

The Twenty-First century: Targeted sanctions

Influenced by the legacy of the widely condemned sanctions regime visited upon Iraq and discourse upon the adoption of 'smart' sanctions, in the twenty-first

179 UN Doc. S/1995/300.
180 See Doxey, M.P., *United Nations Sanctions: Current Policy Issues* (Dalhousie: Centre for Political Studies, 1999), pp.20–23.
181 UN Doc. A/52/871.
182 SC Res 1196 (1998).
183 UN Doc. S/1999/92.
184 For example, UN Docs S/PV.4128; S/PV.4394; S/PV.4713.
185 For example, UN Docs S/PV.4394; S/PV.4713.
186 UN Doc. S/2000/319.
187 UN Doc. S/2005/841.
188 Terminated by SC Res 1732 (2006).
189 *Informal Working Group of the Security Council on General Issues of Sanctions Group of the Security Council on General Issues of Sanctions*, Non-paper/Rev 10, 26 September 2002.

century, the Security Council has moved towards the adoption of a much more targeted policy towards the imposition of non-military sanctions than was seen during the 1990s. In 2000, then Under-Secretary-General for Political Affairs, Kieran Prendergast, noted that 'the Council is now more inclined towards adopting "smart" sanctions which impose coercive measures on specific decision-making groups while avoiding direct impact on the vulnerable.'[190] An overview of sanctions regimes in place during the first quarter of the twenty-first century bears this out. A predominantly two-pronged approach has been taken by the Council whereby on one hand arms embargoes continue to be imposed in respect of those situations where armed conflict is present, in an attempt to stem the flow of the means of waging warfare to the factions concerned, and on the other, sanctions of a financial, diplomatic or travel-related nature have been applied against specific individuals or groups which the Council wishes to influence.[191] As of December 2024, 14 UN sanctions regimes were in place.[192] Arms embargoes and restrictions placed upon individuals were commonplace within thc overwhelming majority of these. It is perhaps notable that more UN sanctions regimes have been terminated than created since the millennium.[193]

With its move towards a more targeted sanctions policy, to a large extent, the Security Council has abandoned the use of comprehensive economic sanctions, the principal source of criticism in respect of their catastrophic humanitarian effects in the case of Iraq, particularly during the 1990s. As of December 2024, only North Korea is subject to a wide-ranging trade embargo,[194] although this nonetheless targets particular items such as luxury goods[195] – more likely to be destined for leadership figures – rather than general foodstuffs or humanitarian supplies. Economic sanctions are generally much more narrowly targeted and focused on specific items linked to their overriding purpose. For example, the current measures imposed against Al-Shabaab incorporate an embargo on the trade of charcoal and explosive device components,[196] while measures imposed upon Libya extend to trade in petroleum.[197] Similarly, targeted trade restrictions were

190 UN Doc. S/PV.4128, p.4.

191 See, eg., *Repertoire of the Practice of the Security Council*, 26th Supplement, 2023, Part VII, p.30.

192 For detailed accounts of these, see https://main.un.org/securitycouncil/en/sanctions/information.

193 On terminated regimes, see https://main.un.org/securitycouncil/en/sanctions/terminated-sanctions.

194 Established by SC Res 1718 (2006), the sanctions have subsequently been modified and expanded. See, e.g., SC Res 2270 (2016). For discussion of the North Korean sanctions regime, see Berger, A., 'North Korea: Design, implementation and evasion,' in Asada, supra n50, pp.157–177; Habib, B., 'The enforcement problem in Resolution 2094 and the United Nations Security Council sanctions regimes: Sanctioning North Korea,' *Australian Journal of International Affairs*, 2016, v.70, n.1, pp.50–68.

195 See, e.g., UN Doc. S/2009/364; SC Res 2094 (2013).

196 SC Res 2713 (2023).

197 SC Res 1970 (2011).

also found in the Council's imposition of an embargo upon the sale of diamonds originating in Liberia and Sierra Leone,[198] on account of the fact that control of the region's diamond trade by factions in the conflicts in those states generated a vital source of income strengthening their capacity to continue the conflict. In pursuit of the Council's principal concern in respect of the perceived threat posed by Iran's development of nuclear military capabilities, sanctions against that state contained restrictions upon the trade of materials that could be used to aid Iran in pursuing this aim.[199]

Arms embargoes formed part of almost all sanctions regimes in place as of December 2024.[200] The region which has been the greatest target of arms embargoes has been the African continent, with measures of this nature since the millennium having been applied in response to conflict situations affecting Ethiopia and Eritrea,[201] Liberia,[202] the Democratic Republic of the Congo,[203] the Côte d'Ivoire,[204] Sudan,[205] South Sudan,[206] Somalia,[207] and the Central African Republic.[208] The effect of these embargoes might be questioned given that they continue to remain in place in respect of most of these situations,[209] in some cases, a number of years after first imposed. Measures targeted against individuals have also featured in every sanctions regime in place as of December 2024. These have been so extensively used that only one of these regimes did not contain any travel bans,[210] and only one did not impose freezes on individuals' financial assets.[211] Targeted individual sanctions have been utilised against a series of high-profile political figures with the decision-making authority to change a state's course of conduct in order to comply with the requirements of the Security Council resolutions which served as the basis for the imposition of sanctions. In the early post-millennium period

198 SC Res 1306 (2000); SC Res 1343 (2001).
199 SC Res 1737 (2006).
200 Arms embargoes were only absent from the measures imposed pursuant to SC Res 1636 (2005), directed specifically at individuals suspected of involvement in the terrorist act responsible for the assassination of former Lebanese prime minister Rafiq Hariri, and measures concerning Guinea-Bissau (SC Res 2048 (2012)) which were limited to the imposition of a travel ban.
201 SC Res 1298 (2000).
202 SC Res 1343 (2001).
203 SC Res 1533 (2004).
204 SC Res 1572 (2004).
205 SC Res 1591 (2005).
206 SC Res 2206 (2015).
207 SC Res 2713 (2023).
208 SC Res 2745 (2024).
209 The sanctions regime in place in respect of Ethiopia/Eritrea was brief, lasting from 2000–2001 (See UN Doc S/PRST/2001/14), while measures in respect of Liberia and the Cote d'Ivoire were terminated after being in place for over a decade. See respectively SC Res 2283 (2016), 2288 (2016).
210 The sanctions regime imposed in respect of Iraq pursuant to SC Res 1518 (2003).
211 The sanctions regime imposed in respect of Guinea-Bissau pursuant to SC Res 2048 (2012).

these included leading members of the Taleban regime in Afghanistan,[212] Charles Taylor of Liberia[213] and senior figures within the government of Sudan.[214] Colonel Gaddafi of Libya was later subjected to targeted sanctions,[215] while a travel ban was also imposed upon a number of individuals responsible for seizing power in a military coup in Guinea-Bissau.[216] There is little evidence to suggest that such forms of individually targeted measures have been tools of significant influence.[217]

The administration and monitoring of sanctions

The role of the Security Council within the application of sanctions has essentially been that of an initiator and overseer. While it is responsible for deciding upon their imposition and the broad form which they will take, set out in its relevant resolutions, their day-to-day administration has been routinely placed in the hands of sanctions committees created by the Council whenever new sanctions regimes have been introduced.[218] These are effectively special subcommittees of the Council on which all of its members are represented and are usually the key body at the UN level in terms of being tasked with the responsibility for giving effect to sanctions. The legal basis for the Council's creation of sanctions committees can be found in Article 29 of the Charter, which empowers it to create subsidiary organs. While the specific mandate of each sanctions committee will depend upon the terms of the resolution which creates it, a number of key functions have been common across sanctions committees. These have involved determining the specific extent of sanctions and making provision where relevant for exemptions to be made to their application on humanitarian grounds, a function first conferred upon a sanctions committee in the Council's very first sanctions venture, concerning Southern Rhodesia.[219] Sanctions committees also monitor the implementation of sanctions and keep under review their actual impact and the extent to which they are being enforced by states. By obtaining such information, sanctions committees are theoretically able to provide the Council with a picture of individual sanctions regimes in operation from which it can make further decisions in respect of their possible continuation, strengthening, revision or suspension. However, that sanctions committees operate by consensus can prove problematic

212 SC Res 1333 (2000); SC Res 1390 (2002).
213 SC Res 1532 (2004).
214 SC Res 1591 (2005).
215 SC Res 1970 (2011).
216 SC Res 2048 (2012).
217 See Conroy, supra n154; Elliott, K.A., 'Analyzing the effects of targeted sanctions,' in Cortright and Lopez, supra n154, pp.171–182.
218 On the role of sanctions committees, see Farrell, supra n19, pp.147–157; Frowein and Krisch, supra n12, at p.748.
219 See Burci, G.L., 'Interpreting the humanitarian exceptions through the sanctions committees,' in Gowlland-Debbas, supra n5, pp.143–154, at p.143.

where political motivations serve as a barrier to their revision or termination when they are failing to achieve their objectives, generating undesirable, harmful effects, or have effectively outlived their utility where the objectives for which they were created have been satisfied.[220] Sanctions committees have been further supported through the work of specialist bodies established to perform monitoring and investigatory functions in order to improve the level of information available to the Council on their implementation and make recommendations for their more effective administration. Taking the form of commissions of inquiry and bodies of experts,[221] these originated with the creation of UNICOI,[222] which was tasked with investigating violations of an arms embargo imposed against Rwanda and Zaire.[223] Shortly thereafter came the creation of a panel of experts to monitor compliance with sanctions imposed against Angola,[224] since when this technique for monitoring sanctions has become commonplace.[225]

Whereas criticisms of the administration of non-military sanctions during the 1990s focused to a large extent on their humanitarian effects, since the end of that decade and the accompanying shift towards the adoption of targeted measures against individuals, concerns increasingly came to centre on the implications for the human rights of such affected individuals and the availability of means for challenging their inclusion within lists of those subject to specified restrictions. The resulting 'undoing' of sanctions measures indirectly via rulings of domestic and regional courts on human rights or constitutional grounds was highlighted above, while it was noted that by 2009, over 50 UN member states had expressed concerns regarding the satisfaction of due process and transparency standards within the UN's approach to the administration of sanctions.[226] Such concerns must be understood within the context of the scale upon which UN sanctions are now targeted against individuals, for example, there being 676 individuals and 193 entities subject to measures contained in sanctions regimes during 2023.[227]

Developments have, however, taken place since the late 2000s which have sought to address some of the criticisms of the process by which sanctions measures are imposed upon individuals. An important action was the Security Council's creation of an ombudsperson responsible for reviewing requests from individuals and entities to be removed from the list of those sanctioned pursuant to

220 See below.
221 On the functions of these bodies, see Farrall, supra n19, pp.157–180.
222 United Nations Commission of Inquiry.
223 SC Res 1013 (1995).
224 SC Res 1237 (1999). For some of the earlier reports which resulted, see, for example, UN Docs S/2000/203; S/2000/1026; S/2000/1225.
225 See Cortright et al, supra n1, pp.220–221.
226 Portela, supra n81, pp.26–27.
227 See Highlights of Security Council Practice 2023, available at https://main.un.org/securitycouncil/en/content/highlights-2023#:~:text=In%202023%2C%20Council%20members%20held,Palestinian%20question%2C%20Yemen%20and%20Syria.

the sanctions regimes pertaining to ISIL and Al-Qaida.[228] Established in 2009, the Ombudsperson's mandate has been extended and revised on multiple occasions,[229] and its most recent mandate extends until 2027.[230] The Ombudsperson reports regularly to the Security Council on the delisting cases considered under the remit of the office. The significance of the office in terms of remedying the subjection of individuals to targeted sanctions in circumstances where this was either based on inaccurate information or gave rise to difficulties in procedural/human rights terms is perhaps underlined by the fact that it had accepted 111 delisting petitions as of September 2024.[231] Delisting requests pertaining to measures applied under other sanctions regimes are governed by a different system. First established in 2006,[232] this is now governed by a delisting procedure established in 2024.[233] A Focal Point is tasked with adjudicating on delisting petitions submitted under the process, while also responsible for giving consideration to granting humanitarian exemptions. Ultimately, however, decisions of the Ombudsperson or Focal Point are recommendatory in nature and require the confirmation of the relevant sanctions committee in order for the measures in question to be varied or terminated in respect of the individuals concerned.

Problems associated with non-military sanctions

The application of non-military sanctions by the Security Council has been subject to criticism on several grounds, but there are arguably four main problems that have been associated with them. First, it is contended that sanctions have generally proven ineffective in achieving their objectives. Thakur has gone so far as to argue that 'there is still not a major comparative study which establishes their efficacy.'[234] A study of 115 cases of sanctions regimes in the period 1914–1990 suggested that sanctions failed to achieve even partial success in 66% of cases, reinforcing this contention.[235] Even former UN Secretary-General Boutros

228 SC Res 1904 (2009). For discussion of the role and functions of the Ombudsperson, see Eden, P., 'United Nations Targeted Sanctions, Human Rights and the Office of the Ombudsperson,' in Happold and Eden, supra n74, pp.135–170.

229 See, eg., SC Res 1989 (2011), SC Res 2083 (2012), SC Res 2161 (2014), SC Res 2253 (2015), SC Res 2368 (2017), SC Res 2610 (2021).

230 SC Res 2734 (2024).

231 UN Doc. S/2024/696, para.5.

232 SC Res 1730 (2006).

233 SC Res 2744 (2024).

234 Thakur, R., *The United Nations, Peace and Security* (Cambridge: Cambridge University Press, 2006), p.136.

235 Hufbauer, G.C., Schott, J.J. and Elliott, K.A., *Economic Sanctions Reconsidered* (Washington DC: Peterson Institute for International Economics, 1991), pp.93–94, cited by Mack, A. and Khan, A., 'UN sanctions: A glass half full?,' in Price, R.M. and Zacher, M.W. (eds), *The United Nations and Global Security* (Basingstoke: Palgrave Macmillan, 2004), pp.109–121, at p.110.

Boutros-Ghali dubbed sanctions a 'blunt instrument.'[236] Second, notwithstanding their ability to achieve their objectives, sanctions have proven problematic on grounds of principle as a consequence of some of the undesirable effects for which they have been responsible, particularly their humanitarian effects, which we have already established compromise core values of international humanitarian and human rights law. These negative consequences of sanctions have in turn undermined their perceived legitimacy, as have the effects of measures targeted against individuals, which have been challenged numerous times on human rights grounds. The negative effects of sanctions upon third states might also be noted. Third, sanctions regimes have on occasion become politicised. Finally, their success is notoriously difficult to measure, giving rise to further problems of its own.

Problems of effectiveness

Failure to influence or weaken targets

To succeed, sanctions must be capable, through their effects, of coercing their targets into adjusting the particular course of behaviour that the Security Council has determined poses a threat to international peace and security. However, this assumes that the targets of sanctions will be vulnerable to the measures imposed, and that the actors whom sanctions seek to influence will respond to their impact rationally. As Cortright and Lopez note, in practice sanctions 'are limited tools of influence.'[237] Apart from their dependence upon effective enforcement,[238] to have any impact, sanctions must be designed in such a manner that they are imposed against a state or targeted entity that is vulnerable to their impact. Earlier UN sanctions regimes placed significant reliance upon the imposition of embargoes upon the trade in essential products for which the state concerned is heavily reliant upon imports of or revenue from export of, or arms embargoes to restrict the capacity of warring parties to continue their struggle. The capacity of such measures to exert influence over targeted regimes has been questioned. Even assuming that sanctions had a significant economic impact in a given case, that this in turn led key decision-makers to adjust their course of behaviour relied upon them acting rationally in response to such effects. Experience has demonstrated that often this has not been the case. Iraq provides us with arguably the best example, the catastrophic effects of sanctions upon the civilian population at large proving incapable of moving Saddam Hussein to adjust his behaviour to the satisfaction of the Security Council.[239] The assumption that economic hardship is

236 UN Doc. A/Res/51/242, para.70.

237 Cortright and Lopez, supra n165, p.15.

238 See below.

239 The effects of sanctions upon Iraq's civilian population have been well documented. See the references contained in supra n97. That sanctions remained in place for over 12 years until the

directly proportional to political change has rarely proven to be the case. Sanctions regimes can in fact serve to strengthen existing support for their targets among local constituencies as they exploit the very imposition of sanctions to create a 'rally round the flag' movement in which the international community as represented by the UN becomes perceived locally as the villain, as opposed to the entity the sanctions were supposed to weaken.[240] One study has found that sanctions regimes have served to strengthen a regime upon which they were imposed in 35% of cases.[241] Sanctions may also give rise to the emergence of black markets for the trade in scarce goods, which may in turn be controlled by a targeted regime and foster greater levels of corruption or criminality, something the aforementioned study has found as occurring in 58% of instances of sanctions being imposed.[242] More generally, there is demonstrable evidence of targeted regimes employing a range of creative evasion strategies to avoid or minimise the effects of sanctions.[243] A case in point has been North Korea, subject to wide-ranging sanctions measures for a significant period of time, whose evasive activity has been highlighted by a number of commentators.[244] Although some of the aforementioned issues have perhaps been prima facie addressed by the move towards a focus on the imposition of sanctions targeted against individuals, evasive strategies undermining their use have also been identified, a recent example being the ISIL/Al-Qaeda sanctions monitoring team's report noting the use of technological means of evading restrictions contained within the relevant sanctions measures.[245]

Poor enforcement

A more significant practical limitation of sanctions derives from a lack of adequate enforcement. Sanctions can only ever be effective if implemented and enforced by the international community at large. While the Security Council determines the scope of sanctions to be imposed in a given situation, their practical implementation becomes the responsibility of member states who are expected to give effect to these under the terms of their own domestic legal frameworks. These can vary

removal of the regime of Saddam Hussein by the US/UK-led invasion adds weight to the view that despite their severe impact upon Iraq's society and economy, sanctions failed to move the Iraqi leadership to meet UN demands. A contrary view, however, would emphasise the very limited international support for the US/UK invasion and suggest that sanctions at the very least contained any more serious threat to international peace and security which might be posed by Iraq. See, for example, Lopez and Cortwright, supra n122.

240 Mack and Khan, supra n235.

241 Eriksson, M., 'The unintended consequences of United Nations targeted sanctions,' in Biersteker et al, supra n84, pp.190–219, at pp.202 et seq.

242 Eriksson, ibid.

243 See, e.g., Biersteker et al, supra n84, p.29; Smith, supra n28, pp.185–188.

244 See, e.g., Habib, supra n194, pp.61–64; Berger, supra n194, pp.169–172.

245 UN Doc. S/2024/556, paras.94–118.

considerably.[246] As noted earlier, the actual enforcement of sanctions by individual states has proven problematic in cases where legal challenges on human rights or constitutional grounds have led to the disapplication of sanctions against named individuals,[247] underscoring the need for UN administrative and monitoring mechanisms to address such concerns within their processes to avoid these conflicts arising in the first place.[248] The need for a holistic approach to the implementation of sanctions, in which close co-operation takes place between the UN, other organisations and member states, has been noted by the Security Council itself.[249] If a sufficient number of states are unable or unwilling to enforce them, their potential utility is undermined immediately. According to one analyst, that the major problem for sanctions is their monitoring is 'glaringly obvious.'[250] Various reports have highlighted poor enforcement of a number of sanctions regimes. However, while some weaknesses in enforcement have stemmed from legal challenges at a domestic level, the effectiveness of sanctions is also undermined where states choose not to comply with UN sanctions regimes in the first place. This problem has been particularly noticeable in respect of arms embargoes,[251] with the South African experience providing an early example,[252] and the violation of the arms embargo imposed upon Sudan a later illustration,[253] its severity being highlighted by its breach by states including two permanent members of the Security Council, Russia and China.[254]

Problems of undesirable consequences

Humanitarian effects and individual human rights

It is widely acknowledged that UN sanctions are capable of generating unintended consequences in a significant proportion of cases.[255] The major principled criticism of sanctions has concerned the humanitarian consequences to which they have, on occasion, given rise. As Mack and Khan argue, 'The most damaging

246 See generally Gowlland-Debbas, V. (ed.), *National Implementation of UN Sanctions* (Leiden: Brill, 2004).
247 See Portela, supra n81.
248 See further below.
249 See, eg., SC Res 2617 (2021).
250 Stremlau, J., *Sharpening International Sanctions: Towards a Stronger Role for the United Nations* (New York: Carnegie Commission on Preventing Deadly Conflict, 1996).
251 See, for example, Vines, supra n165, at pp.117–118; Bondi, supra n165; Brzoska, supra n165; Cortright and Lopez, supra n118, Chapter 10. See also *Smart Sanctions, the Next Step*, supra n167.
252 *Smart Sanctions, the Next Step*, supra n167, paras.16–17.
253 SC Res 1556 (2006).
254 Vines, supra n165, p.117.
255 One study has in fact concluded that sanctions generally give rise to unintended consequences in 94% of cases. See Biersteker et al, supra n84, pp.27–28.

charge against sanctions ... is that they impose widespread suffering on ordinary people.'[256] Former UN Secretary-General Kofi Annan, in his 1998 Annual Report, stated that '... humanitarian and human rights policy goals cannot easily be reconciled with those of a sanctions regime.'[257] The classic case cited has been that of Iraq, noted above, where sanctions were widely accepted as being responsible in large part for such effects as increased malnutrition and mortality levels. The extent to which economic sanctions have caused humanitarian hardship in some cases has been hotly debated, particularly as 'conditions of multi-causality' operate in each case,[258] but they undoubtedly have the potential to hit hard the civilian populations of target states. The more comprehensive economic sanctions are, the greater the risk of this is. The incompatibility of negative effects on civilian populations with norms of international humanitarian and human rights law makes this undesirable. While the Council's move towards a more targeted sanctions policy may have gone some way towards reducing the humanitarian effects of sanctions for civilian populations, a proclaimed objective of the Council,[259] the problem has not disappeared. This is borne out by criticisms of the sanctions regime imposed against North Korea, labelled by former UN Secretary-General Ban Ki-Moon as 'the toughest and most comprehensive ... ever imposed by the Council.' [260] A long-standing criticism of humanitarian exemptions applied to sanctions has been that too often restrictive approaches have been adopted towards what constitute items required for humanitarian purposes,[261] with one major UN report alleging that 'humanitarian exemptions tend to be ambiguous and are interpreted arbitrarily and inconsistently. Delays, confusion and the denial of requests to import essential humanitarian goods cause resource shortages.'[262] More recently, then Under-Secretary-General for Humanitarian Affairs Martin Griffiths urged that more action be taken to protect civilians against the humanitarian effects of sanctions, one suggestion offered being to build in more comprehensive humanitarian exemptions within measures adopted by the Council.[263]

While the move towards targeted individual sanctions has gone some way towards ameliorating their harshest humanitarian consequences, concerns have shifted towards the adequacy of the safeguards afforded by the mechanisms

256 Mack, A. and Khan, A., 'The efficacy of UN sanctions,' *Security Dialogue*, 2000, v.31, n.3, pp.279–292, p.280.

257 UN Doc. A/53/1.

258 Weiss, Cortright, Lopez and Minear, supra n106, pp.35–53.

259 See, eg., SC Res 2610 (2021).

260 Quoted in Smith, supra n28, p.183.

261 See, for example, Van Brabant, K., *Can Sanctions Be Smarter? The Current Debate: Report of a Conference Held in London, 16–17 December 1998* (London: The Humanitarian Policy Group and the Relief and Rehabilitation Network at the Overseas Development Institute, 1999), p.30.

262 *Promotion and Protection of the Rights of Children/Impact of Armed Conflict on Children*, UN Doc. A/51/306, para.128.

263 UN Doc. SC/14788, 7 February 2022.

through which individuals are subjected to Council-imposed restrictions.[264] The implications for their human rights have been considered above, with the ensuing domestic legal challenges only serving to undermine the integrity and effectiveness of the UN's sanctions. However, as has also been noted, developments have taken place which enhance opportunities for individual listings to be challenged and reviewed within the UN's own machinery.

Effects on third states

While often overlooked, wide-ranging economic sanctions can also have a potentially devastating effect on third states by depriving them of vital sources of income. While Article 50 of the UN Charter allows states which suffer from special economic problems as a result of sanctions to consult the Security Council with a view to resolving those problems, in practice, this measure has been of little real value.[265] Twenty-one states addressed the Council in relation to the negative effects which they alleged that sanctions imposed upon Iraq had upon them, but the only response took the form of a sanctions committee recommendation that the international community provide assistance to such states and a request by the Security Council that the secretary-general despatch a special representative to assess the effects upon such states.[266] An informal grouping arranged for the provision of some compensatory funds, albeit leaving many feeling that their needs had been inadequately addressed.[267] Representations were also made following the imposition of economic sanctions upon former Yugoslavia, again resulting in requests for other states to provide assistance to those affected.[268] No serious measures were taken to alleviate the harm suffered by third states with the Security Council simply appealing to relevant organisations and states to provide what assistance that they could.[269] In the case of sanctions against Haiti, representations by the Dominican Republic were never even considered. Then Secretary-General Boutros Boutros-Ghali himself acknowledged an urgent need to respond to the needs of third states,[270] as did his successor Kofi Annan in his 1998 annual

264 See, eg., Heupel, supra n53, pp.783–789; Jayakody, supra n74, pp.112–116.

265 See *Smart Sanctions, The Next Step,* supra n167, pp.45–48.

266 UN Doc. S/21938.

267 See Al-Khasawneh, B.H., 'Consultation under Article 50 of the United Nations Charter: The experience of the Middle East,' in Gowlland-Debbas, supra n5, pp.325–333; Doxey, supra n180; Conlon, P., *United Nations Sanctions Management: A Case Study of the Iraq Sanctions Committee, 1990–1994* (New York: Transnational Publishers, 2000), pp.98–110.

268 See some of the various Sanctions committees reports, for example, UN Docs S/26040, 26040/Add.1, 26040/Add.2, and recommendations of the Security Council, for example, UN Docs S/6056, 26282, 26905. See also reports on the subject to the General Assembly, UN Docs A/51/317, A/52/308.

269 See Doxey, supra n180.

270 UN Doc. A/53/1, Supra n257, para.70.

report.[271] To some extent, the adoption of a more targeted sanctions policy by the Security Council should serve to minimise the economic consequences of sanctions measures upon third states, although it is also apparent that the mechanisms provided for within the UN Charter for dealing with such scenarios have not resulted in the development of any significant initiatives to support third states disproportionately affected by sanctions.

Politicisation of sanctions regimes

From a legal perspective, a sanctions regime is imposed to respond to a threat to the peace and should be terminated once that threat has ceased to exist.[272] However, the Iraq experience demonstrated the scope for a sanctions regime to evolve in terms of the political objectives attached to it by members of the Security Council, not necessarily directly linked to its legal basis. In the case of Iraq, for example, a small number of major powers led by the US and UK proved rigidly unwilling to consider a relaxation of some of the measures in place in response to Iraq's compliance with obligations under UN Security Council resolutions, even where there was a growing body of international support for such a move.[273] Technically, in what is termed the use of the 'reverse veto,' a sanctions regime which carries no time limit can exist in perpetuity as long as a permanent member opposes its termination.[274] The inadequate articulation of the objectives underlying sanctions in Security Council resolutions has also been critiqued. Where phrased in general terms – for example, establishing peace and stability, securing the future and ongoing verification of disarmament, or ensuring the target state stops supporting terrorism – considerable scope is left for Council members to disagree upon their achievement,[275] making reaching consensus upon their termination problematic.

Measuring success

A more general difficulty with sanctions concerns the measurement of their success. While Article 41 imposes no requirement that sanctions be utilised as a necessary precursor to any military action, it also provides no restriction or guidance upon the duration for which they may be applied in any given case. Although full

271 UN Doc. A/53/1, supra n257, para.63.

272 Article 41's power to impose sanctions follows from a determination that there exists a threat to the peace under Article 39. Where the threat to the peace ceases to be present, there can be no resulting power to impose or continue to impose sanctions.

273 See Kondoch, supra n35, pp.274–278.

274 Oette, L., 'A decade of sanctions against Iraq: Never again! The end of unlimited sanctions in the recent practice of the UN security council,' *European Journal of International Law*, 2002, v.13, n.1, pp.93–103.

275 This was also commented upon in the Interlaken process. See *Expert Seminar on Targeting UN Financial Sanctions,* supra n168, at p.18.

or substantial compliance with the demands of the Security Council can be taken to indicate a successful outcome to the imposition of sanctions,[276] the real problem lies in determining how long sanctions ought to be persevered with in circumstances in which they are having no noticeable impact upon the policies of the targeted states, individuals or entities, especially where they have simultaneously resulted in significant undesirable consequences. Furthermore, it is difficult to measure the success of sanctions, given that they seldom, if ever, produce immediate compliance with the demands of the Security Council. This is not to say that they have no impact. For example, there is a degree of consensus in support of the view that sanctions had some impact in eventually leading to Libya's handover of suspects wanted for trial in connection with the Lockerbie bombing as a result of the international isolation of Libya.[277] That other sanctions regimes have been lifted, sometimes after relatively short periods of time, may be indicative of some perceived success on their part.[278] The impact of sanctions is however the source of contention. For example, while some have argued that sanctions imposed on Yugoslavia during the 1990s helped to bring the Serbs to the Dayton peace talks, others put this down principally to the effects of military action undertaken by NATO.[279] Measuring the success of sanctions is complicated by the phenomena of multi-causality,[280] whereby significant developments may have their origins in a number of causes, the relative impact of each individually being difficult to quantify.

Has the Security Council's approach to non-military sanctions improved?

It is apparent that as a tool for responding to situations which pose a threat to international peace and security, non-military sanctions are far from perfect and are subject to their limitations. The problems with which they are often associated, discussed above, stand as testament to this. The harshest critics of non-military sanctions would argue that they are a futile tool and may go so far as to call for their abolition as a tool of the UN collective security system. However, for all of their limitations, they clearly remain a central plank within the UN collective security strategy. Their role in effecting positive change in particular

276 Heine-Ellison, supra n113, suggests success is demonstrated when (1) the target state concedes to a significant part of the demands, (2) following the threat or application of sanctions and (3) there is no more credible explanation for the change of behaviour (at pp.87–88).

277 Cortright, Lopez and Gerber-Stellingwerf, supra n1, pp.211–213.

278 For example, the sanctions regime imposed in respect of Mali by SC Res 2374 (2017) came to an end after just six years. Similarly, sanctions on Iran (established by SC Res 1737 (2006)) were wound up in 2015 (SC Res 2231) pursuant to the Joint Comprehensive Plan of Action reached by a number of major powers with Iran.

279 See, for example, Mack and Khan supra n256, pp.280–281.

280 Cortright and Lopez, supra n107, at pp.13–14.

circumstances may be difficult to quantify, certainly given the operation of the phenomena of multi-causality, but there is some cause to believe that they have a part to play in this respect. The termination of various sanctions regimes would suggest that their objectives have been satisfied at least to some extent. In this vein, the emphasis within sanctions discourse has centred on means of improving their effectiveness and minimising their unintended consequences. UN sanctions policy has demonstrated a capacity to adapt in order to address its perceived shortcomings. Arguably, this was first seen towards the end of the 1990s as the Security Council moved away from the utilisation of comprehensive economic sanctions in large part to respond to the widespread criticisms of their considerable humanitarian effects. While the shift to a more targeted sanctions policy went some way towards tackling this problem, however, the imposition of sanctions on designated individuals gave rise to its own challenges on human rights grounds, with legal outcomes in domestic and regional courts serving to undermine their effective application. Again, developments ensued within the process by which sanctions are administered and reviewed at the UN level in order to minimise the scope for their challenge.

The biggest ongoing practical challenges for UN non-military sanctions arguably concern their scope for politicisation and the manner of their enforcement. Proposals were advanced over two decades ago for the adoption of measures which carried the potential to minimise the risk of sanctions regimes being politicised by major powers for purposes exceeding the objectives for which they were created, which may extend to the prevention of their termination after these were served.[281] Those proposals included the use of precise, clear standard language in resolutions creating sanctions; time limits attached to sanctions regimes; the clear articulation within sanctions-creating resolutions of the conditions that would need to be met for their lifting; and the immediate suspension of sanctions when such specified conditions had been satisfied. There is evidence to suggest that progress has been made in giving partial effect to such proposals. It was noted shortly after their advancement that objectives contained within sanctions-creating resolutions were starting to be defined in clearer terms,[282] but it remains the case that sanctions regimes are not typically established with a fixed end date. While sanctions regimes are subject to ongoing review and modification, the ability of a permanent member to veto any changes permits it to effectively keep in place indefinitely measures which may have outlived their original purpose. The introduction of time limits would protect against this, while allowing for the continuation of widely supported measures to be authorised by a positive vote of

281 Informal Working Group of the Security Council, supra n189.

282 Knight, W.A., 'Improving the effectiveness of UN arms embargoes,' in Price, R.M. and Zacher, M.W. (eds), *The United Nations and Global Security* (New York: Palgrave Macmillan, 2004), pp.39–55, at p.44.

the Security Council. Similarly, although the objectives of particular sanctions measures may have become clearer in the resolutions creating them, there has not been much development in respect of a clearer articulation of the conditions which would warrant the termination of sanctions and the creation of any mechanism to facilitate this to take place.

The effective implementation of sanctions depends in large part on measures taken by individual member states to apply them, both in legislative and practical terms. Challenges in respect of the former aspect have arisen where individual human rights protections have been invoked as a barrier to their implementation, although steps at the UN level have gone some way towards enhancing means of challenging and reviewing the listing of sanctioned individuals.[283] However, on a practical level, greater cooperation between the UN and other organisations and individual states would arguably be helpful. The effectiveness of sanctions measures can also be well served by the regular assessment of measures in force with a view to modification where necessary, something which has developed considerably since the establishment of specialist bodies to assist in sanctions monitoring and advising the relevant sanctions committees on their operation.

Conclusion

The experience of sanctions imposed by the UN Security Council demonstrates well the ability of the UN Charter framework to evolve in response to new needs and perceptions of what collective security requires by way of responses to situations threatening international peace and security taking the form of non-military sanctions. Although debates will undoubtedly continue on the merits of non-military sanctions as an effective means of responding to threats to the peace, it appears clear that at best they are of limited utility. Although on occasions this may be, at least in part, a consequence of the poor enforcement of sanctions by states for political motivations, it would appear that often it is simply a consequence of inherent flaws within the very concept of sanctions as a tool of coercive influence. At the same time, where military action may be regarded as a drastic step or lacks sufficient political support to make it a viable option, sanctions at least represent a mechanism by which the UN is able to send out a clear signal of its displeasure at particular situations and may, in appropriate circumstances, act as a lever with which to further political dialogue towards a satisfactory resolution of situations which pose a threat to the peace. The legitimacy of the sanctions weapon was called into question during the 1990s, particularly as a result of the experience of Iraq, which suggested that there was, at the time, insufficient regard for core values enshrined in international humanitarian and human rights norms.

283 The importance of sanctions review where appropriate has been noted by the Security Council itself. See SC Res 2611 (2021).

The sanctions regime's legitimacy was also seriously undermined by the politicisation of decision-making within the Security Council over the continuation of sanctions and humanitarian exemptions permitted. Informed by this experience, the Council demonstrated its capacity for innovation in moving towards a more targeted approach to sanctions. This in turn gave rise to new challenges, which again the Council has sought to address through further actions in terms of the administration and monitoring of UN sanctions.

Criticisms of sanctions have not gone away. While the merits of sanctions in general remain heavily debated, and their imposition and design will inevitably continue to be influenced by political considerations among the P5, it is fair to say that the Council at the very least has demonstrated its ability to develop its use of the sanctions tool in response to changing pressures as the post–Cold War era has progressed.

6

PEACEKEEPING

Introduction

The creation and development of the institution of peacekeeping under UN auspices represents a remarkable instance of the evolution of the UN collective security system. Unlike other tools of the system discussed within the present book, at no point is 'peacekeeping' mentioned within the UN Charter. Although the term is difficult to define with any degree of precision, as will become apparent below, the concept of peacekeeping broadly understood represents an attempt by the UN to develop a mechanism through which it is able to support efforts aimed at the creation or maintenance of peace, or at the very least conflict avoidance, through the deployment of (traditionally) non-combatant forces on the ground to undertake a variety of functions. UN peacekeeping began as an 'improvised response' to the Suez crisis in 1956[1] and has evolved ever since as operations have gradually undertaken a wider range of functions and the legal principles by which they have been governed have been called into question or reinterpreted.[2] While earlier operations were essentially deployed to keep parties in conflict apart, primarily through ceasefire patrolling tasks, as the UN's conception of collective security increasingly came to embrace human security the nature of peacekeeping – and

1 Abi-Saab, G., 'United Nations Peacekeeping old and new: An overview of the issues,' in Warner, D. (ed.), *New Dimensions of Peacekeeping* (Dordrecht, Boston and London: Martinus Nijhoff, 1995), pp.1–9, at p.1.

2 For an overview of the development of UN peacekeeping up to the early Post–Cold War era, see Goulding, M., 'The evolution of United Nations peacekeeping,' *International Affairs*, 1993, v.69, n.3, pp.451–464; Lee, R.S., 'United Nations peacekeeping: Development and prospects,' *Cornell International Law Journal*, 1995, v.28, pp.619–629.

DOI: 10.4324/9781003518105-7

the legal principles by which it operated – evolved accordingly, becoming concerned with assisting conflict-affected societies through transitional phases and later affording protection to civilians at risk of harm. This enlarged conception of peacekeeping was not without its problems. During the 1990s in particular, ambitious mandates conferred upon operations in very difficult circumstances led to debates taking place upon the very purpose of peacekeeping and the principles by which it should operate. Although peacekeeping has arguably stabilised as an institution during the twenty-first century, debates continue in respect of its central purposes, the principles which guide its functioning and the adequacy of resources provided for the deployment of UN operations.

This chapter begins by making some observations on the difficulties of defining peacekeeping, before drawing some initial conclusions upon possible legal bases for the establishment of UN peacekeeping operations, encompassing both the earliest UN peacekeeping deployments and more complex operations to have been created in the post–Cold War era. We then move on to consider how peacekeeping has evolved conceptually through what can be identified as a series of generations within the development of its functions and guiding principles, and the key consequences thereof. The chapter concludes by considering the nature of modern-day peacekeeping operations and the main challenges which they continue to face, while offering some thoughts on the mechanism's future role as a tool of the UN collective security system.

The meaning and legal basis of peacekeeping

The problem of definition

The difficulty of defining peacekeeping lies in the fact that it is a concept which has evolved in both political and legal terms in response to changing circumstances, rather than finding its creation in an express provision of a legal document such as the UN Charter. As a result, there is no universally agreed definition of what it actually encompasses, and at different stages in its evolution, it has arguably meant different things.[3] There is no single template of what a peacekeeping operation looks like or does, although different themes and functions have been prevalent at different times.[4] Frederking's definition of peacekeeping as 'the use of troops to ensure the implementation of peace agreements' may well broadly

3 See further Sloan, J., *The Militarisation of Peacekeeping in the Twenty-First Century* (Oxford and Portland: Hart, 2011), pp.12–16.

4 Even during the early development of UN peacekeeping, Bowett set out a number of categories of peacekeeping operation. See Bowett, D.W., *United Nations Forces* (London: Stevens & Sons, 1964), pp.268–274. Goulding identifies six kinds of peacekeeping operation. See Goulding, supra n2, pp.456–460. See also Schachter, O., 'Authorized uses of force by the United Nations and regional organizations,' in Damrosch, L.F. and Scheffer, D.J. (eds), *Law and Force in the New International Order* (Boulder: Westview Press, 1991), p.65, at p.80.

describe earlier UN peacekeeping operations which were deployed with functions centred on the monitoring of ceasefire agreements or the withdrawal of troops to established boundaries,[5] but does not account for the realities of later peacekeeping operations which came to perform a wider range of functions including the assumption of responsibility for the protection of the delivery of humanitarian assistance and civilian populations at risk of attack. Following the expansion of UN peacekeeping in the 1990s, then Secretary-General Boutros Boutros-Ghali noted that the concept of peacekeeping is not static and that there are as many types of operations as there are types of conflict.[6] In 1992, he defined UN peacekeeping in rather general terms as entailing 'a United Nations presence in the field, hitherto with the consent of all the parties concerned, normally involving United Nations military and/or police personnel and frequently civilians as well.'[7] However, while this definition can be applied to many operations, it tells us nothing of the purposes of peacekeeping. Furthermore, as will be seen, that peacekeeping operations operate only with the consent of all concerned parties is a principle to have been challenged by some post–Cold War deployments.

Doyle and Sambaris attempt to encapsulate the more comprehensive nature of some of the peacekeeping operations created from the 1990s up to the modern day, suggesting that, 'Today peacekeeping is the multidimensional management of a complex peace operation, usually in a post-civil war context, designed to provide interim security and assist parties to make those … transformations that are essential to make a peace sustainable.'[8] However, while this definition can be applied to several operations and recognises the potentially broad ambit of 'peacekeeping,' it tells us relatively little about what peacekeeping operations do and cannot be applied to every mission that has been labelled a peacekeeping operation.

Understanding the nature and functions of peacekeeping can only be achieved through a historical overview of its development. As will be seen below, UN peacekeeping has evolved through a series of generations, each characterised by particular features in relation to the role which operations have performed and/or the principles by which they have been governed. Although the emergence of each new generation of peacekeeping operations did not mean operations deployed in accordance with the features of earlier generations ceased to exist, each new generation marked a conceptual development in the status of peacekeeping and posed new legal and/or political challenges for the UN. Before considering these developments, however, it is necessary to give some attention to possible bases for the derivation of legal authority for the creation of peacekeeping operations.

5 Frederking, B., *The United States and the Security Council* (Oxford: Routledge, 2007), p.41.

6 1993 *UNYB* 3.

7 *An Agenda for Peace*, UN Doc. A/47/277-S/24111, para.20.

8 Doyle, M.W. and Sambaris, N., 'Peacekeeping operations,' in Weiss, T.G. and Daws, S. (eds), *Oxford Handbook on the United Nations* (Oxford & New York: Oxford University Press, 2008), p.23.

The legal basis for peacekeeping

Drawing any firm conclusions on the legal basis for UN peacekeeping is problematic for two main reasons. First, as noted above, there is no uniform template that can be applied to each and every instance of UN peacekeeping. The varied mandates enjoyed by peacekeeping forces mean that it is difficult to locate their legal bases in a common provision. Second, in creating peacekeeping operations, the Security Council (and the General Assembly when creating UNEF I,[9] generally regarded as the first peacekeeping operation) has tended not to refer to any specific legal basis under which it is acting. Although from the 1990s onwards, it has been increasingly common for resolutions of the Council that create peacekeeping operations to invoke Chapter VII of the UN Charter,[10] which reflects the extent to which they have been endowed with powers to use coercive military force, the Council has failed to make any reference to specific Charter articles. This is true of all UN peacekeeping operations currently in existence, albeit the more recently created of these were all established under Chapter VII of the Charter.[11]

The first generally recognised peacekeeping operation, UNEF I,[12] was created by the General Assembly in 1956 to supervise a ceasefire between Israel and Egypt and the withdrawal of forces to their own territory, although subsequent operations have all been created by the Security Council. Although the legal basis of UNEF I was never made explicit,[13] it was deployed with the consent of the states upon whose territory it would be based, was to remain strictly neutral between the parties and could only resort to force in self-defence.[14] These principles would

9 GA Res 1000 (ES-1) (1956).

10 See further below.

11 See respectively the mandates conferred upon UNMIK (SC Res 1244 (1999)), MONUSCO (SC Res 1925 (2010)), UNISFA (SC Res 1990 (2011)), UNMISS (SC Res 1996 (2011)), MINUSCA (SC Res 2149 (2014)).

12 Although UNEF I is widely regarded as the first UN peacekeeping operation, there were earlier UN observer missions deployed to the Balkans (United Nations Special Committee on the Balkans (UNSCOB), established by GA Res 109 (II)), India-Pakistan (United Nations Military Observer Group in India and Pakistan (UNMOGIP) established by SC Res 47 (1948)) and the Middle East (United Nations Treaty Supervision Organization (UNTSO), established by SC Res 50 (1948)). For brief details, see Bothe, M., 'Peacekeeping,' in Simma, B. et al (eds), *The Charter of the United Nations: A Commentary* (2nd ed.) (Oxford: Oxford University Press, 2002), pp.648–700, at p.665. There were also initiatives undertaken under the auspices of the League of Nations which might be regarded as a precursor of what would become UN peacekeeping; see Bothe, infra, pp.664–665; Nasu, H., *International Law on Peacekeeping: A Study of Article 40 of the UN Charter* (Leiden: Martinus Nijhoff, 2009), pp.37–69.

13 That it had been lawfully created was, however, established by the ICJ decision in the *Expenses* case; *Certain Expenses of the United Nations*, ICJ Rep 1962, p.151, pp.166–168.

14 These principles were outlined by Hammarskjold in his *Summary Study of the Experience Derived from the Establishment and Operation of the Force: Report of the Secretary-General*, UN Doc. A/3943, 9 October 1958.

be at the heart of virtually all subsequent operations up until at least the 1990s.[15] Commentators, however, disagree to some extent as to the legal basis for these traditional peacekeeping operations. Although some have sought to locate the legal basis for traditional peacekeeping in 'chapter six and a half' of the UN Charter,[16] on the grounds that it went beyond the diplomatic measures provided for by Chapter VI but did not amount to the employment of coercive military force envisaged by Chapter VII, this logic is unsatisfactory. There is no 'chapter six and a half,' and there can be no legal authority derived from a non-existent part of the UN Charter.[17]

As will become apparent in the discussion which follows, the traditional principles by which UN peacekeeping operations operate became called into question in a number of post–Cold War operations – in particular, through the conferment of authority to use force going beyond self-defence upon a number of operations and the uncertainty over the existence of consent to their deployment from concerned parties – thus reinforcing the possibility that they cannot be founded upon the same legal base as operations which adhere strictly to the principles of traditional peacekeeping. Prima facie, a military operation authorised to use force for purposes beyond self-defence and which does not enjoy the consent of the sovereign authority upon whose territory it is deployed would seem to fall within the ambit of Article 42's power of the Security Council to initiate the application of coercive military measures. Core international legal norms, such as the principle of non-intervention,[18] and Article 2 (4)'s prohibition on the use of force against a state's territorial integrity and political independence arguably necessitate this.[19] However, the Security Council has never been more specific when creating peacekeeping operations with such robust mandates than to proclaim that it was acting under Chapter VII. At the same time, much emphasis in official discourse has

15 An exception was arguably that of the United Nations Operation in the Congo (ONUC), discussed below.

16 Indeed, Dag Hammarskjold himself referred to such a basis. For discussion, see Hillen, J.F., 'UN collective security: Chapter six and a half,' *Parameters,* 1994, v.24, pp.27–37.

17 That does not, of course, mean that such legal authority cannot be established on the basis of the doctrine of implied powers. See below.

18 This is enshrined within a number of key instruments. These include most prominently Article 2 (7) of the UN Charter, which provides that 'Nothing … shall authorize the United Nations to intervene in matters which are essentially within the domestic jurisdiction of any state ….' See also the *Declaration on the Inadmissibility of Intervention in the Domestic Affairs of States and the Protection of their Independence and Sovereignty,* which provides that, 'No State has the right to intervene, directly or indirectly, for any reason whatever, in the internal or external affairs of any other State' (GA Res 2131 (XX), para.1).

19 Article 42 operates as an exception to Article 2 (4)'s prohibition upon the use of force. Article 2(7) explicitly states that the prohibition of intervention in matters within the domestic jurisdiction of a state does not apply to enforcement measures adopted under Chapter VII, which include military measures under Article 42. Therefore, deployment of forces without the consent of the host state would be lawful if done on the basis of Article 42.

been placed upon the compliance of such operations with the traditional principles of peacekeeping, thus leaving some ambiguity as to their exact legal basis.[20] As Sloan notes, the problem has been confounded by the fact that 'the Security Council routinely invokes Chapter VII when establishing peace-keeping operations … [yet] has somewhat disingenuously contrived to maintain that host state consent, non-use of force and impartiality are basic principles of peacekeeping operations.'[21] Where peacekeeping mandates are consented to by states whose territory they are to be performed upon, the need for any authority under Chapter VII can be called into question. However, the invocation of Chapter VII arguably leaves little doubt as to the existence of mandatory powers to resort to force on the part of peacekeeping operations, which may be particularly helpful from a legal perspective in the event that the continued existence of consent becomes uncertain, as occurred for example in respect of peacekeeping in former Yugoslavia and Somalia.[22]

Although the legal basis of UN peacekeeping is perhaps best understood by considering the development of peacekeeping in practice, taking into account changes in its functions and powers over time, we first give some initial consideration to possible legal bases for peacekeeping operations and in so doing demonstrate the considerable conceptual confusion which exists in this area.

Authority from express UN Charter provisions

Being able to locate a power enjoyed by an international organisation in an express provision of its constituent instrument has a certain degree of convenience to it, making the power's parameters clearer and its existence less open to dispute. Although the UN Charter contains no reference to peacekeeping, several commentators have sought to identify authority for the creation and deployment of UN peacekeeping operations in some of its provisions. A number of Chapter VI provisions might be taken to lend implicit support for the use of peacekeeping as a technique aimed at supporting the pacific settlement of disputes. For example, parties to a dispute the continuation of which is likely to endanger the maintenance of international peace and security are directed to firstly seek a solution through peaceful means of their own choice,[23] and the Security Council may call upon them to settle their dispute using such means.[24] While Article 33 (1) provides

20 Terms such as the authorisation of 'all necessary measures' or similar are generally regarded as the Council's code for the conferment of a military enforcement mandate. However, while such terms have appeared in some resolutions creating peacekeeping mandates under Chapter VII, they have been absent from others. This only adds to the confusion.

21 Sloan, supra n3, p.3.

22 See below.

23 Article 33 (1).

24 Article 33 (2).

examples of peaceful modes of settlement, these do not include any reference to the deployment of forces in any form. However, the list of examples contained therein is not exhaustive and does not exclude other modes of peaceful settlement being utilised. A clear role for peacekeeping forces in the process of dispute resolution can be identified.[25] It is plausible that the deployment of a peacekeeping force can aid the maintenance of a fragile peace between two parties in dispute. As will be seen, this was the very raison d'être of the earliest UN peacekeeping operations. Furthermore, the deployment of peacekeeping forces could serve to support some of the modes of settlement expressly referred to by Article 33 (1), for example mediation, Tomuschat noting that, 'The establishment of a peace-keeping force can also serve to mediate in a power struggle between adversary factions within a nation.'[26] The Council itself may also at any stage of a dispute recommend appropriate procedures or methods of adjustment.[27] This again could be taken to provide a legal base upon which the deployment of peacekeeping forces could be justified as there is no reason why the Council could not recommend such a step as part of an overall strategy for the peaceful adjustment of a dispute. Article 36 (1) has been acknowledged by some commentators as a suitable legal basis for some peacekeeping operations.[28]

Although the Security Council has never referred to any specific Chapter VI provisions as the basis for its creation of peacekeeping forces, the fact that it never asserted it was acting under Chapter VII until the 1990s (while a number of operations continue to function without any reference to Chapter VII in their mandates) might be taken to suggest that it has traditionally considered itself to be acting under Chapter VI, although the failure to cite any particular provisions prevents such a conclusion from being clearly drawn. Some scepticism must, however, be noted over the suitability of Chapter VI provisions as a legal base for peacekeeping operations. As Sloan notes,[29] no Chapter VI powers envisage peacekeeping, and the provisions of that chapter are best seen as relating to traditional diplomatic measures, which do not extend to the kinds of activities undertaken by peacekeeping operations. Furthermore, at best, Chapter VI provisions could only provide authority for the deployment of operations that acted in accordance with the principles of traditional peacekeeping. Chapter VI only envisages peaceful measures and later operations which have been empowered to use force beyond self-

25 See, for example, Merrills, J.G. and De Brabandere, E., *International Dispute Settlement* (7th ed.) (Cambridge: Cambridge University Press, 2022), pp.355–360.

26 Tomuschat, C., 'Article 33,' in Simma et al, supra n12, pp.583–594, at p.589.

27 Article 36. See also Articles 37(2) and 38, which confer the Council with similar powers.

28 See, for example, Orakhelashvili, A., 'The legal basis of the United Nations peacekeeping operations,' *Virginia Journal of International Law*, 2002–2003, v.43, pp.485–524, at p.491; White, N.D., 'The UN Charter and peacekeeping forces: Constitutional issues,' *International Peacekeeping*, 1996, v.3, pp.43–63, at p.60.

29 Sloan, supra n3, pp.78–80.

defence could only be legally justified by reference to the enforcement provisions of Chapter VII. Cox takes a narrower view of the ambit of activity encapsulated by Chapter VI, arguing that even 'insofar as UN peacekeeping forces are entitled to use force in self-defence they cannot be regarded as purely pacific means of dispute settlement under Chapter VI.'[30] Clearly, there are doubts over the validity of Chapter VI provisions as a legal base for at least most UN peacekeeping operations that have been created.

Although the Security Council has increasingly asserted that it is acting under Chapter VII when establishing peacekeeping operations,[31] it has not cited any specific provision of that chapter as its legal basis for action either. Given that the Council sometimes refers to Chapter VII and sometimes doesn't, it is questionable whether it is appropriate to base any operation on a Chapter VII provision when the relevant resolutions make no reference to that chapter. Although when imposing non-military sanctions or authorising military enforcement measures, the Council likewise does not tend to refer specifically to Articles 41 and 42 which permit it to take such action, it does nonetheless tend to refer to Chapter VII within which they are contained. Articles 39–42 are all sufficiently construed that they lend themselves open to being cited as possible legal bases for the creation of peacekeeping operations. Although best known for empowering the Council to determine the existence of a threat to the peace, breach of the peace or act of aggression, Article 39 also allows it to make recommendations to maintain or restore international peace and security. Prima facie, the deployment of a peacekeeping operation might constitute such a recommendation,[32] just as it may under some Chapter VI provisions discussed above. However, there is only limited support for Article 39 serving such a role. Furthermore, as it only covers 'recommendations,' it could not provide legal justification for more robust operations mandated to use non-defensive force in the absence of the consent of the concerned parties. Article 40 allows the Council to call upon parties in dispute to comply with provisional measures it deems necessary or desirable. Occasionally, the Council appears to have used peacekeeping operations in the enforcement of provisional measures.[33] As Nasu suggests, 'given the purpose of Article 40 is to prevent an aggravation of armed conflicts,' the deployment of peacekeeping operations can be seen to further the objectives of that provision.[34] In a similar vein, McCoubrey and White note that, 'peacekeeping is not the same as peaceful settlement; it is simply a

30 Cox, K.E., 'Beyond self-defence: United Nations peace-keeping operations and the use of force,' *Denver Journal of International Law and Policy*, 1998–1999, vol.27, pp.239–273, at p.248.

31 This began with the mandates conferred upon operations deployed to former Yugoslavia and Somalia. See below.

32 Sloan, supra n3, pp.81–87; Orakhelashvili, supra n28, p.492.

33 For example, ONUC's role in the Congo. See White, supra n28, at pp.54–55.

34 Nasu, supra n12, p.86.

provisional measure aimed at stopping the fighting,'[35] leading Orakhelashvili to comment that the prevailing view is that Article 40 is the 'most proper legal basis' for peacekeeping.[36] There is some logic in the invocation of Article 40 in relation to peacekeeping operations which comply with the traditional principles of peacekeeping, but when their observance is lacking or in question, as Frowein and Krisch comment, 'it appears, however, doubtful whether [deployment] can be based entirely on Art.40 ... this approach would constitute an evasion of Art.42 which exclusively regulates compulsory military operations.'[37] Although a commonly cited basis for some operations,[38] it might be questioned whether it is appropriate to view all peacekeeping operations as merely provisional measures, given that often they have been deployed as part of a peace settlement;[39] in this sense, they may be regarded as part of the ultimate solution.

Article 42 is the express power which permits coercive military action to be taken by the Council, although in practice the Council confers authority to apply military measures on willing states and organisations acting upon its behalf.[40] Its attraction as a legal base for the creation of peacekeeping operations arguably lies in the fact that it permits the exercise of coercive military force, a power that increasingly came to be conferred upon peacekeeping operations in the post–Cold War era. Where else could such authority be derived from? The problem lies in the fact that Article 42 is very much concerned with coercive military force employed against a non-consenting target, whereas in most peacekeeping operations, there is no such authority to use force and/or the force is officially deployed only with the consent of the parties against whom force might conceivably be applied under the operation's mandate. The ICJ drew a distinction between peacekeeping and military enforcement in the *Expenses* case,[41] although significantly at that moment in time peacekeeping operations had not come to perform functions that involved the application of coercive military force. post–Cold War practice, as will be seen, would appear to strengthen the case to ground a number of operations in the kind of authority envisaged by Article 42.

Although primarily associated with non-military sanctions, Article 41 empowers the Council more generally to decide upon the imposition of measures not involving the use of armed force. This led to the ICTY in the *Tadic* case deciding that it could provide the basis for the tribunal's creation.[42] The creation of any operation

35 McCoubrey, H. and White, N.D., *The Blue Helmets: Legal Regulation of United Nations Military Operations* (Aldershot: Dartmouth, 1996), p.5.
36 Orakhelashvili, supra n28, p.495.
37 Frowein, J.A. and Krisch, N., 'Article 40,' in Simma et al, supra n12, pp.729–735, at p.732.
38 See Sloan, supra n3, pp.87–95. See also Nasu, supra n12, pp.71–106.
39 See further below.
40 See Chapter 7.
41 *Expenses* case, supra n13, p.171.
42 *Prosecutor v. Tadic*, Case No.IT-94-1AR72, Decision on the Defence Motion for Interlocutory Appeal on Jurisdiction (Oct. 2, 1995), *ILM* 32 (1996).

sanctioned to employ armed force would arguably be categorically prohibited by the terms of Article 41, which provides authority for 'measures not involving the use of armed force.' Although traditional peacekeeping forces have not generally been deployed with mandates to use offensive force, they nonetheless comprise armed forces, making it debatable whether a reasonable interpretation of Article 41 extends to their creation. However, some have suggested that Article 41 only excludes military enforcement measures under Article 42 and can therefore provide a possible base for peacekeeping operations which do not involve the use of force beyond measures taken in self-defence.[43] However, Article 41 is concerned with decisions – diktats of the Council which member states are obliged to accept and effect. By contrast, traditional peacekeeping operations only deploy with the consent of the parties to the dispute. The withdrawal of consent to such operations has been regarded as having the effect of removing a key prerequisite for their presence, as occurred when UNEF I was withdrawn from Egyptian territory following the revocation of Egyptian consent to its presence.[44]

While a number of Charter provisions have some merit as possible legal bases for at least some kinds of peacekeeping operations, they all come with their problems, and it is difficult to identify any single provision that might serve as an unchallenged legal basis for the full spectrum of operations that have been deployed since 1956. This leads us to consider the relevance of implied powers to the practice of peacekeeping.

The doctrine of implied powers

The doctrine of implied powers has already been touched upon.[45] That UN organs enjoy implied powers was accepted by the ICJ in the *Reparations* case when it stated that the organisation 'must be deemed to have those powers which, though not expressly provided in the Charter, are conferred upon it by necessary implication as being essential to the performance of its duties.'[46] In practice, a broad approach to the doctrine of implied powers has been taken, the ICJ subsequently ruling on the legality of the creation of UNEF I in the *Expense*s case, where it ruled that 'when [the UN] takes action which warrants the assertion that it was appropriate for the fulfilment of one of the stated purposes of the United Nations,

43 See, for example, Tsagourias, N., 'Consent, neutrality/impartiality and the use of force in peacekeeping,' *Journal of Conflict and Security Law*, 2006, v.11, n.3, pp.465–482, at p.471; Orakhelashvili, supra n28, pp.493–494. Kondoch suggests the UNTAET operation in East Timor can be based on Article 41. See Kondoch, B., 'The United Nations administration of East Timor,' *Journal of Conflict and Security Law*, 2001, v.6, pp.245–265, at p.256.

44 See below.

45 See Chapter 4.

46 *Reparation for Injuries Suffered in the Service of the United Nations*, ICJ Rep 1949, p.174, at p.182.

the presumption is that [it is not] ultra vires.'[47] Effectively, if an action serves purposes or functions contained within the Charter, it will not be unlawful unless there is an express provision prohibiting such an action. This potentially provides a broad scope for action on the UN's part which can extend to the creation and deployment of peacekeeping forces.

The UN may create peacekeeping forces if they can be seen to further any of the organisation's purposes and there is no express prohibition of this form of action by any Charter provision.[48] Although the ICJ did not expressly state from which Charter provision an implied power to create peacekeeping operations stemmed, Article 1 has been cited as providing an appropriate constitutional basis.[49] The first listed purpose of the UN is the maintenance of international peace and security,[50] and peacekeeping operations are clearly created and deployed in furtherance of that broad objective. Any peacekeeping mandate which respects the principles applicable to the earliest operations – impartiality, consent to deployment on the part of those whose territory forces would be stationed on, and the use of force only in self-defence – is not expressly prohibited by the UN Charter. However, where a peacekeeping mandate contains a conferment of authority to use force in circumstances other than self-defence, this prima facie violates the Charter prohibition on the use of force[51] in the absence of the Charter-provided exceptions. Except when military force is applied in self-defence,[52] Article 42 provides a power for coercive military action to be taken on the basis of Security Council authorisation.[53] Arguably, therefore, authority for the creation of any peacekeeping operation with more extensive powers to apply military force can be implied from a combination of the objectives which underlie both Articles 1 (1) and 42.

The Council/Assembly division of authority

UNEF I, the first generally recognised UN peacekeeping operation, was created by the General Assembly under the terms of the *Uniting for Peace* resolution. The Assembly's powers in the peace and security realm are expressly provided to be inferior to those of the Security Council by virtue of Chapter IV of the UN

47 *Expenses* case, supra n13, at p.168.
48 For more detailed treatment of the implied powers doctrine, see White, supra n28, pp.44–49.
49 See, for example, Cox, supra n30, p.247.
50 Article 1 (1).
51 Article 2 (4).
52 Article 51.
53 While Article 42 contains the key power of action, Articles 43–50 created a detailed framework to govern such operations taken under the direction of the Council. As noted in Chapter 2, this has never been implemented in practice.

Charter.[54] However, in its Uniting for Peace resolution,[55] it purported to give itself the power to recommend measures for the maintenance or restoration of international peace and security when the Council was unable to act due to disagreement among its permanent members. The impact of the resolution was considered earlier and will not be revisited here,[56] suffice to note that the creation of UNEF I by the General Assembly under its terms did not trouble the ICJ in the *Expenses* case.[57] The role of the General Assembly in the creation of peacekeeping operations need not concern us in this book for three main reasons. First, only 'decisions' to take 'enforcement' action are expressly reserved to the Security Council by the Charter's provisions. At the very least, traditional peacekeeping of the kind practised throughout the Cold War period does not fall into this category, involving no use of force beyond self-defence and operating only on a consensual basis.[58] Second, in practice the legality of *Uniting for Peace* has come to be widely accepted even if not used very often.[59] Finally, post UNEF I, all peacekeeping operations have been created by the Security Council so the role of the General Assembly has come to take on no significant long-term relevance in respect of their creation and deployment.

Traditional peacekeeping operations

Limited functions

The functions of early peacekeeping operations were largely limited to the monitoring of ceasefire agreements and patrolling of demarcated boundaries between the parties to the dispute.[60] The role of this first generation of operations was essentially restricted to literally 'keeping the peace.' UNEF I, established by the General Assembly following the Suez crisis during which Israel, backed by the UK and France, had attacked Egypt,[61] was mandated to secure and supervise the cessation of hostilities and the withdrawal of foreign troops from Egyptian

54 See Chapter 2 for a more detailed exposition of the relevant provisions of Chapter IV, in particular Articles 10 and 12.

55 GA Res 377 (V).

56 See Chapter 3.

57 Supra n13. For discussion, see White, supra n28, pp.49–51; Schachter, O., 'Uses of law in international peacekeeping,' *Virginia Law Review*, 1964, v.50, n.6, pp.1096–1114, at pp.1102–1107.

58 This much was confirmed by the ICJ in the *Expenses* case, supra n13, at pp.166–168, which confirmed the legality of UNEF I even if it did not adjudicate on its legal basis.

59 See Chapter 3.

60 For an overview of first-generation operations, see Bothe, M. and Dorschel, T. (eds), *United Nations Peacekeeping: A Documentary Introduction* (Leiden: Brill, 1999); Bothe, supra n12, pp.665–667.

61 On the Suez crisis, see Louis, W.M. Roger, 'The Suez Crisis and the British dilemma at the United Nations,' in Lowe, V., Roberts, A., Welsh, J. and Zaum, D. (eds), *The United Nations Security Council and War* (Oxford: Oxford University Press, 2008), pp.280–297.

territory,[62] after which it came to serve as an effective buffer force between Egypt and Israel until President Nasser of Egypt withdrew his consent to its presence on Egyptian territory in 1967. While ONUC's mandate included taking offensive military action in support of governmental authorities,[63] the mandate of UNEF I served as a general template for subsequent operations during this first generation of peacekeeping. For example, the United Nations Force in Cyprus (UNFICYP) was created to prevent the recurrence of fighting between Greek and Turkish factions in Cyprus[64] through the performance of patrolling functions and, since Turkey's intervention in 1974, the supervision of a ceasefire and buffer zone.[65] The importance of UNFICYP is arguably evidenced by the fact that its mandate continues to this day.[66] UNIPOM was despatched in 1965 to supervise a ceasefire between India and Pakistan along their borders and the withdrawal of troops.[67] It remained until troops from both states had been withdrawn, its objectives having been achieved.[68] Created in the aftermath of the Yom Kippur war, UNEF II had similar functions to its predecessor, encompassing the supervision of the ceasefire between Egypt and Israel, the withdrawal of their forces and the patrol of a buffer zone.[69] Its role ceased following the conclusion of the Camp David peace agreement between Israel and Egypt. Also established in response to the aftermath of the Yom Kippur War, the United Nations Disengagement Observer Force (UNDOF) performed similar tasks in relation to a ceasefire between Israel and

62 GA Res 1000 (ES-1) (1956). See also GA Res 997 (ES-1) (1956). For discussion, see Sommereyns, R., 'United Nations peace-keeping forces in the Middle East,' *Brooklyn Journal of International Law*, 1980, v.6, pp.1–53, at pp.4–6. ON UNEF I specifically, see Diehl, P.F., 'First United Nations Emergency Force (UNEF I),' in Koops, J.A., MacQueen, N., Tardy, T. and Williams, P.D. (eds), *The Oxford Handbook of United Nations Peacekeeping Operations* (Oxford: OUP, 2015), pp.144–152.

63 See below.

64 SC Res 186 (1964).

65 UN Doc. S/11473; SC Res 361 (1974).

66 UNFICYP's mandate was most recently renewed by SC Res 2723 (2024). For discussion of the first two decades of its deployment, see Theodorides, J., 'The United Nations peacekeeping force in Cyprus (UNFICYP),' *International and Comparative Law Quarterly*, 1982, v.31, n.4, pp.765–783. For a longer-term view, see Asmussen, J., 'United Nations Peacekeeping Force in Cyprus (UNFICYP),' in Koops et al, supra n62, pp.197–213. In an early appraisal of UNFICYP, it was noted that it had been 'markedly successful … in preventing the escalation of hundreds of incidents to the point where serious consequences might follow'; see Popper, D.H., 'Lessons of United Nations peacekeeping in Cyprus,' *ASIL Proc*, 1970, v.64, pp.1–9.

67 For an overview, see Singh, P.K., 'United Nations India-Pakistan Observation Mission (UNIPOM),' in Koops et al, supra n62, pp.222–228.

68 SC Res 211 (1965). See Roy-Chaudhury, R., 'The Council and the India-Pakistan wars,' in Lowe et al, supra n61, pp.324–345, at pp.335–338.

69 SC Res 340 (1973). For an overview of UNEF II, see Bar-Yaacov, N., 'Keeping the peace between Egypt and Israel, 1973–1980,' *Israel Law Review*, 1980, v.15, pp.197–268; Diehl, P.F., 'Second United Nations Emergency Force (UNEF II),' in Koops et al, supra n62, pp.229–237.

Syria.[70] As with UNFICYP, it remains in place as a buffer force to this day.[71] Thus, ONUC aside, the first generation of peacekeeping operations followed a similar pattern: they performed limited supervisory functions where there was a ceasefire in place, they did not become parties to the disputes in question, and they are generally regarded as having played a key role in literally 'keeping the peace.' Observance of particular core principles arguably facilitated their success. That these operations were deployed where there was at least a substantial peace to keep was important, and the continued presence of UNFICYP and UNDOF is indicative of the success with which they are credited.[72]

Core legal principles

Although neither the General Assembly nor the Security Council explicitly advanced any specific legal basis for the creation of peacekeeping operations in the resolutions by which they were created during the Cold War period, their deployment took place in accordance with a series of principles first enunciated by Dag Hammarskjold in relation to UNEF I's creation,[73] and which can generally be applied to all subsequent Cold War operations with the possible exception of ONUC in the Congo.[74] Three principles were central to first-generation operations.[75] Firstly, as a consequence of the fact that UN peacekeeping was considered as a mechanism distinct from military enforcement action, peacekeeping forces were only deployed with the consent of the parties to the dispute that they were tasked to assist in the amelioration or settlement of.[76] Secondly, peacekeepers were to remain impartial in the performance of their mandate. Finally, peacekeepers were not to use force to implement their mandates other than in self-defence. In addition, as a result of the prevailing political climate of the Cold War, permanent members did not contribute forces to earlier peacekeeping operations, reflecting the status of early peacekeeping as an improvised attempt to bypass the

70 SC Res 350 (1974). UNDOF's most recent mandate was provided by SC Res 2766 (2024). See further Rudloff, P. and Diehl, P.F., 'United Nations Disengagement Observer Force (UNDOF),' in Koops et al, supra n62, pp.238–247.

71 On the status of these operations today, see their respective websites: http://www.unficyp.org/nqcontent.cfm?a_id=1, http://www.un.org/en/peacekeeping/missions/undof/.

72 Of course, a sceptic might argue that the fact that they remain necessary demonstrates that no long-term lasting peace has been achieved. However, a more positive perspective would be to assert that their continuation over such a lengthy period evidences relative success in the maintenance of peace, however fragile that may be.

73 UN Doc. A/3694. See also UN Doc. A/3943.

74 See below.

75 On these, see further Tsagourias, supra n43; Goulding, supra n2, pp.453–455.

76 As discussed above, consent to deployment is made legally necessary by fundamental norms of international law in the absence of a military enforcement mandate under the terms of Chapter VII of the Charter, in particular Article 42.

constraints imposed by the context of the period.[77] The participation of a major power would have made it difficult, arguably impossible, to obtain UN support for the deployment of the relevant operation. Over time, however, this principle became relaxed as major power cooperation increased and political disagreement among them ceased to be as significant an obstacle to action on the part of the Security Council.[78] Although UN peacekeeping operations are ordinarily created by the Security Council, they are nominally headed by the UN Secretary-General, to whom force commanders are directly accountable.[79]

An overview of peacekeeping operations created in the Cold War period demonstrates – with the exception of ONUC[80] – evidence of the observation of the aforementioned principles in their mandates and operations. This was arguably facilitated by the limited mandates conferred upon peacekeepers, which essentially involved them for the most part supervising ceasefire agreements, serving as buffer forces and supervising the withdrawal of troops. Maintaining impartiality was not particularly problematic given the limited functions assigned to peacekeepers in the mandates conferred upon them during the Cold War era. In environments in which parties had entered into ceasefire agreements and consented to the deployment of peacekeepers, there was an actual peace to keep and only a relatively limited risk of peacekeepers becoming partial in the discharge of their mandate. The success of early peacekeeping operations benefitted from the fact that they were only deployed with the consent of the respective parties, the centrality of this requirement being exemplified by U Thant's withdrawal of UNEF I from Egyptian territory in 1967 after President Nasser withdrew consent to its presence.[81]

Although all peacekeeping operations within this period were permitted to use force only in self-defence, this very concept underwent some development. While initially regarded as extending to the right of peacekeepers to use force in defence of their person, it came to embrace the use of force in defence of the peacekeeping mandate.[82] This conception of self-defence was applied to the mandate of UNFICYP, deployed to Cyprus in 1964,[83] to be followed in that of UNEF II, deployed to the Middle East in 1973.[84] However, there was never any suggestion that coercive force could be applied by peacekeepers – any exercise of force had

77 See Ali-Saab, supra n1.

78 As of 31 October 2024, all permanent members of the Security Council were contributing in some form to UN peacekeeping operations, ranging from China's sizeable 1,802 personnel to the US's mere 26.

79 See Bothe, supra n12, pp.687–688.

80 See below.

81 UN Doc. A/6730 and Add.1–3.

82 See Sloan, supra n3, pp.26–31; Cox, supra n30 at pp.249–56; Findlay, T., *The Use of Force in UN Peace Operations* (Oxford: SIPRI/Oxford University Press, 2002), pp.20–103.

83 See UN Doc. S/5960, 10 September 1964.

84 See UN Doc. S/11052/Rev.1, 27 October 1973.

to be essentially defensive in nature – and in practice the self-defence mandates of first-generation peacekeeping operations were interpreted restrictively.[85]

ONUC

The principles of traditional peacekeeping were only seriously challenged during the Cold War period by the actions of ONUC, deployed to the Congo in 1960 following internal unrest that accompanied its independence from Belgium and led to intervention by the latter.[86] The political environment within the Congo was markedly different from that in which other Cold War peacekeeping operations had been deployed. Findlay notes that ONUC 'was vastly different from UNEF. It was deployed in the middle of an incipient civil war overlaid with elements of foreign intervention.'[87] The initial mandate of ONUC was to facilitate the withdrawal of Belgian forces, maintain law and order and assist the new government,[88] there being no suggestion that it was empowered to resort to force other than in self-defence. However, as the situation within the country worsened amid the attempted secession of the Katanga province, aided by foreign mercenaries, ONUC's mandate was expanded to permit it to take 'all appropriate measures ... to prevent the occurrence of civil war in the Congo, including ... the use of force, if necessary, in the last resort.'[89] ONUC's resort to robust military measures effectively made it a party to the conflict, going beyond the established principles of peacekeeping at the time[90] and leading it to become embroiled in controversy as a result. As Bowett comments, 'It is difficult to avoid the conclusion that the Security Council by [resolution 161] abandoned a strict reliance on the principle of self-defence.'[91] None of the Council's resolutions made any reference to Chapter VII or any specific provision of the UN Charter, and officially the operation is regarded as a peacekeeping operation.[92] However, it appeared to cross the boundary into what might be considered military enforcement action.[93] Gray suggests that the language used in resolutions 161 and 169 appeared to echo Article 39 of

85 Findlay, for example, suggests that UNEF II only ever went as far as firing warning shots; Findlay, supra n82, pp.100–103.

86 For discussion of ONUC's experience, see Aksu, E., *The United Nations, Intra-State Peacekeeping and Normative Change* (Manchester: Manchester University Press, 2003), pp.100–129; Diehl, P.F., Druckman, D. and Mueller, G.B., *When Peacekeeping Missions Collide: Balancing Multiple Roles in Peace Operations* (New York: OUP, 2023), pp.104–121.

87 Findlay, supra n82, p.51.

88 SC Res 143 (1960).

89 SC Res 161 (1961), para.1. See also SC Res 169 (1961).

90 See Sloan, supra n3, pp.129–134.

91 Bowett, supra n4, pp.201–202.

92 The ICJ certainly did not consider ONUC to constitute an enforcement operation; *Expenses* case, supra n13, p.177.

93 For discussion, see Findlay, supra n82, pp.62–81.

the Charter.[94] While noting that most writers have based the operation on Article 40, Sloan argues that only Article 42 could provide any legal basis for the level of force applied by ONUC.[95] This contention is difficult to argue with, it being the only provision which envisages the application of coercive force. Whether Article 40 or 42 provides a better legal basis arguably depends upon whether ONUC's application of coercive force is considered on the scale which constitutes military enforcement action, which officially it has not been regarded as doing, or whether it is best seen as part of a series of provisional measures adopted to prevent further fighting within the Congo. However, notwithstanding the legal difficulties inherent in the ONUC experience, it was an isolated incident during the Cold War of a peacekeeping operation crossing the threshold into possible military enforcement and subsequent first-generation operations reverted to compliance with traditional principles. As one commentator on the operation has noted, ONUC fulfilled its mandate at a heavy cost,[96] which arguably provided an early indication of the dangers of departing from the principles which peacekeeping operations were supposed to observe.[97]

Second- and third-generation peacekeeping operations

Expanded functions (second generation)

As the Cold War began to come to an end, from the late 1980s onwards, a second generation of peacekeeping operations began to emerge which assumed a broader range of functions than their predecessors.[98] At the very time that new-found cooperation between the superpowers gave rise to new possibilities, the UN's broadened conception of security – as part of which threats to the peace were increasingly found to exist due to situations internal to states – found it faced with a number of intra-state conflicts or situations in which conflict had recently ended and some form of intervention was called for in order to build a lasting peace. As Gray notes, most post–Cold War peacekeeping operations were deployed in response to civil war situations, to support efforts to achieve their peaceful settlement and/or maintain ceasefires. Consequently, 'international intervention … had to go beyond the remit of earlier operations in order to assist in bringing about national reconciliation and re-establishing effective government.'[99] As a conse-

94 Gray, C., *International Law and the Use of Force* (2nd ed.) (Oxford: Oxford University Press, 2004), p.203.
95 Sloan, supra n3, pp.134–141.
96 Boulden, J., 'United Nations Operation in the Congo (ONUC),' in Koops et al, supra n62, pp.160–70, at p.168.
97 See Berdal, M., 'The Security Council and peacekeeping,' in Lowe et al, supra n61, pp. 175–204, at pp.182–184.
98 See, for example, Berdal, ibid, pp.184–185.
99 Gray, supra n94, p.210.

quence, 'peace-keeping operations became more numerous and complex, involving a wider set of political, military and humanitarian tasks.'[100]

This second generation of peacekeeping commenced with the deployment of operations of the kind despatched to Namibia,[101] Central America,[102] El Salvador[103] and Cambodia.[104] These operations were tasked with mandates which gave them a more direct role in the implementation of peace processes or ceasefire agreements. Their functions included the supervision of free elections,[105] human rights monitoring,[106] supervision of disarmament[107] and the verification of parties' compliance with obligations assumed under peace agreements. A particularly significant development occurred in respect of Cambodia, to which the United Nations Transitional Authority in Cambodia (UNTAC) was deployed. Established to create a peaceful and politically neutral environment for free elections to be held following the Paris peace talks between parties to Cambodia's long-running civil conflict, UNTAC ultimately came to assume much of the civil administration of the state in the interim period.[108]

While the emergence of a second generation of peacekeeping operations importantly demonstrated the ability of the UN collective security system to evolve to respond to new challenges in a changed environment, there was at first

100 Sens, A.G., 'From peace-keeping to peace-building: The United Nations and the challenge of intrastate war,' in Price, R.M. and Zacher, M.W. (eds), *The United Nations and Global Security* (Basingstoke: Palgrave Macmillan, 2004), pp.141–160 at p.143.

101 United Nations Transition Assistance Group (UNTAG), established by SC Res 632 (1989). See Howard, L.M., 'United Nations Transition Assistance Group (UNTAG),' in Koops et al, supra n62, pp.294–305.

102 United Nations Observer Group in Central America (ONUCA), established by SC Res 644 (1989). See Koops, J.A., 'United Nations Observer Group in Central America (ONUCA),' in Koops et al, supra n62, pp.306–313.

103 United Nations Observer Mission in El Salvador (ONUSAL), established by SC Res 693 (1991). For an overview of its performance of its functions, including its human rights and election monitoring mandate, see Howard, L.M., *UN Peacekeeping in Civil Wars* (Cambridge: Cambridge University Press, 2008), pp.98–126.

104 UNTAC, established by SC Res 745 (1991). See Widyono, B., 'United Nations Transitional Authority in Cambodia (UNTAC),' in Koops et al, supra n62, pp.395–407.

105 See White, N.D., *Keeping the Peace* (Manchester and New York: Manchester University Press, 1997), pp.270 et seq.

106 See White, ibid, pp.267–269. However, there is some evidence that earlier peacekeeping operations had performed functions related to the promotion and protection of human rights. See Mansson, K., 'The forgotten agenda: Human rights protection and promotion in cold war peacekeeping,' *Journal of Conflict and Security Law*, 2005, v.10, pp.379–403.

107 See White, supra n105, pp.263–267.

108 On UNTAC generally, see Ratner, S., 'The United Nations in Cambodia and the new peacekeeping,' in Warner supra n1, pp.41–67; Keller, L., 'UNTAC in Cambodia – From occupation, civil war and genocide to peace,' *Max Planck Yearbook of United Nations Law*, 2005, v.9, pp.127–178. For an assessment of its performance of its mandate, see Howard, supra n103, pp.143–173; Findlay, T., *Cambodia: The Legacy and Lessons of UNTAC* (Oxford: Oxford University Press, 1995).

no significant shift in terms of the legal principles which governed their deployment. The ability of UN peacekeeping to respond to new needs without compromising the legal principles upon which it was grounded is effectively summarised by Berdal. Second-generation operations

> pointed to the way in which the instrumentality of peacekeeping could, under new geopolitical circumstances, be expanded by the Council … Even so, all of the activities between 1987 and 1991 remained firmly predicated on the principles of consent,[109] minimum use of force, and impartiality.[110]

None of these operations was created by reference to Chapter VII of the UN Charter. There has certainly been no significant legal controversy over the initial post–Cold War expansion of peacekeeping to embrace a wider range of functions. Arguably, second-generation operations made an important contribution to the creation and strengthening of peace in most locations to which they were deployed. They were credited with having played a major role in ending long-standing conflicts in Central America, Southern Africa (Namibia, Angola and Mozambique) and Cambodia.[111]

'Robust' or 'militarised' peacekeeping (third generation)

UN peacekeeping became embroiled in controversy in the early to mid-1990s as operations found themselves deployed in environments where there was simply 'no peace to keep' and where the existence of the consent to their presence on the part of some of the parties to the conflict was at best questionable, and at worst simply non-existent. Whereas previous generations of peacekeeping operations had enjoyed the benefit of working in an environment where the parties to a dispute were at least substantially committed to its peaceful resolution, a new breed of conflict emerged for which it proved impractical for peacekeepers to perform their mandates in accordance with the long-standing principles of traditional peacekeeping. This led to a third generation of peacekeeping in which operations were entrusted with mandates which crossed the boundaries into military enforcement, as reference to the peacekeeping experiences of Somalia and former Yugoslavia illustrates particularly well.

109 Resolutions creating peacekeeping operations often referred to the consent of the parties, or their 'request' for the operation's deployment. See, for example, SC Res 626 (1988), pertaining to the United Nations Angola Verification Mission (UNAVEM) I; SC Res 782 (1992), preceding the establishment of the United Nations Operation in Mozambique (ONUMOZ).

110 Berdal, supra n97, p.185.

111 See, for example, Gray, supra n94, pp.211–215.

Somalia

Following Somalia's descent into civil war, the United Nations Operation in Somalia (UNOSOM I) was deployed in accordance with traditional peacekeeping principles and tasked with protecting the delivery of humanitarian assistance.[112] However, adherence to traditional principles proved problematic as it became clear that UNOSOM I could not perform its mandate in the hostile environment within which it had to operate, where breaches of ceasefires by the warring factions were commonplace.[113] A US-led military enforcement operation, the Unified Task Force (UNITAF), was authorised under Chapter VII to use 'all necessary measures' to establish a secure environment for the delivery of humanitarian assistance.[114] While considered to have had relative success in discharging its mandate,[115] it was only a temporary operation, following the conclusion of which a second UN operation, UNOSOM II, was created as its successor.[116] Its experience would prove controversial amid concerns over the extent to which it represented attempts to merge techniques of peacekeeping and military enforcement. With a broad mandate which involved responsibility for ensuring the delivery of humanitarian assistance to those in need,[117] the operation marked a departure from the traditional principles of consent, impartiality and restriction of the use of force to action taken in self-defence. In accordance with a recommendation of the secretary-general,[118] UNOSOM II was created under Chapter VII and empowered to take 'appropriate action' to enable the performance of its mandate. The invocation of Chapter VII should have left no doubt that the powers of the operation went beyond those of traditional peacekeeping. It marked the first occasion on which a peacekeeping operation was deployed by reference to Chapter VII, and the UN Department for Peacekeeping Operations notes that its mandate was 'to take appropriate action, *including enforcement measures*, to establish ... a secure environment

112 SC Res 751 (1992). See also the report of the Secretary-General, UN Doc. S/23829, paras.27–29. The mandate was expanded by resolution 775 (1992) to encompass the protection of humanitarian supplies outside of Mogadishu. For a discussion of UNOSOM I's experience, see Williams, P.D., 'United Nations Operation in Somalia I (UNOSOM I),' in Koops et al, supra n62, pp.408–415.

113 For discussion, see Ramsbotham, O. and Woodhouse, T., *Humanitarian Intervention in Contemporary Conflict* (Cambridge: Polity Press, 1996), pp.198–213; Lewis, I. and Mayall, J., 'Somalia,' in Mayall, J. (ed.), *The New Interventionism 1991–1994* (Cambridge: Polity Press, 1996), pp.94–126, at pp.107–110.

114 SC Res 794 (1992).

115 See, for example, Ramsbotham and Woodhouse, supra n113, p.208; Lewis and Mayall, supra n113, p.112.

116 See further Williams, P.D., 'United Nations Operation in Somalia II (UNOSOM II),' in Koops et al, supra n62, pp.429–442.

117 SC Res 814 (1993).

118 UN Doc. S/25354, at p.13.

for the delivery of humanitarian assistance.'[119] Any doubts that UNOSOM II was authorised to use force were dispelled by Resolution 837's expansion of its mandate to expressly authorise the arrest of those responsible for attacks directed against the operation,[120] clearly demonstrating that the line between peacekeeping and enforcement had been crossed. Although it has been noted that the actual use of force by UNOSOM II was in practice limited,[121] by acting upon this authority to pursue General Aidid, the leader of one of the main factions to the conflict, any suggestion that UNOSOM II might function effectively along the lines of earlier peacekeeping operations was shattered.[122] It had never enjoyed anything more than fragile consent to its presence on the part of some of the concerned parties and by entering into open conflict with one of the factions, any perceived impartiality was compromised.[123] As Bratt notes, this ended any credible role which the operation could play in resolution of the conflict.[124]

UN peacekeeping in Somalia has not generally been regarded in positive terms.[125] Although political factors played some part in this, the operation having been labelled 'under-manned, under-resourced and under-funded,'[126] the attempt to utilise 'robust' peacekeeping proved problematic.[127] While the appropriate circumstances were not present for a traditional peacekeeping operation to function, its conferment with enforcement powers while retaining the formal status of a peacekeeping operation introduced contradictions into its mandate and made confrontation even more likely.[128] As the situation in Somalia worsened, UNOSOM II began to collapse. The deaths of several US troops led to the withdrawal of its contingent, other contributing nations soon following course.[129] The operation was

119 UN DPKO website: http://www.un.org/en/peacekeeping/missions/past/unosom2mandate.html.

120 Para.5.

121 Sloan, supra n3, p.148.

122 Indeed, the very fact of the attack on troops deployed within UNOSOM II demonstrates the lack of sufficient consent to its presence on the part of the parties to the conflict, and the absence of a genuine peace to keep. While military enforcement may perform a function in such circumstances, peacekeeping as traditionally conceived is ill-suited to do so.

123 See further Lalande, S., 'Somalia: Major issues for future UN peacekeeping,' in Warner, supra n1, pp.69–99; Frederking, supra n5, pp.47–50; Thakur, R., 'From peacekeeping to peace enforcement: The UN operation in Somalia,' *Journal of Modern African Studies*, 1994, v.32, n.3, pp.387–410, at pp.394–401.

124 Bratt, D., 'Explaining peacekeeping performance: The UN in internal conflicts,' *International Peacekeeping*, 1997, v.4, n.3, pp.45–70, at p.64.

125 See, however, Crocker, C.A., 'The lessons of Somalia,' *Foreign Affairs*, 1995, v.74, n.3, pp.2–8.

126 Sloan, supra n3, p.147.

127 On the various lessons taken from the UNSOM II experience, see *The Comprehensive Report on Lessons Learned from United Nations Operation in Somalia (UNSOM)*.

128 Ibid, para.10.

129 As of May 1994, 12 member states had withdrawn their contingents. See the secretary-general's report of 24 May 1994, UN Doc. S/1994/614.

gradually reduced[130] and eventually withdrawn, leaving Somalia to suffer its fate, in March 1995.[131]

Former Yugoslavia

The break-up of Yugoslavia in the early 1990s gave rise to a number of related conflicts between Bosnian, Serb and Croatian factions, predominantly taking place on the territory of Bosnia-Herzegovina and Croatia.[132] The United Nations Protection Force (UNPROFOR) peacekeeping operation was deployed in 1992,[133] with a rapidly changing mandate which centred on three main tasks: the protection of the delivery of humanitarian assistance, the monitoring of a flight ban imposed in Bosnian airspace[134] and ensuring the protection against attack of a number of designated 'safe' areas. UNPROFOR's operations at first officially operated in accordance with traditional peacekeeping principles. Its founding resolution made no reference to Chapter VII, nor did the first 16 resolutions adopted by the Security Council in relation to the former Yugoslavia.[135] There was no suggestion of any authority to use force going beyond self-defence and the operation's deployment was expressly stated to be in support of a peace plan accepted by all relevant parties.[136] However, the commitment of the parties to peace fluctuated as ceasefire agreements were regularly broken, effectively meaning that there was no peace to keep. In response, UNPROFOR's mandate was adjusted on numerous occasions in response to developments on the ground and ultimately crossed the boundary which separates peacekeeping and enforcement.[137] While some Security Council resolutions referred to the consent of the parties to the presence of the operation,[138] this was not true of most resolutions. At best, consent was fragile or forthcoming

130 SC Res 897 (1994) amended the operation's mandate to exclude authority to apply coercive military measures.

131 SC Res 954 (1994), para.1, extended UNOSOM II's mandate for a final period until 31 March 1995.

132 For background to the conflict and an overview of its course, see Silber, L. and Little, A., *The Death of Yugoslavia* (2nd ed.) (London: Penguin, 1996). For an overview of the initial international responses, see Weller, M., 'The international response to the dissolution of the socialist Federal Republic of Yugoslavia,' *American Journal of International Law*, 1992, v.86, pp.569–607.

133 SC Res 743 (1992). For an overview and appraisal of UNPROFOR, see Diehl et al, supra n86, pp.121–141.

134 Introduced by SC Res 781 (1992).

135 Gray, supra n94, p.217.

136 UN Doc. S/23592.

137 See, for example, SC Res 769 (1992); SC Res 776 (1992); SC Res 819 (1993); SC Res 824 (1993); SC Res 836 (1993); SC Res 871 (1993); SC Res 908 (1994); SC Res 947 (1994); SC Res 982 (1995). For a summary of the evolution of the mandate, see its profile on the UN DPKO website, http://www.un.org/Depts/DPKO/Missions/unprof_p.htm.

138 See, for example, SC Res 762 (1992); SC Res 781 (1992); SC Res 824 (1993).

only from some parties.[139] To facilitate effective peacekeeping, the consent of all concerned parties is a 'practical necessity.'[140] Whereas traditionally peacekeeping had proceeded on the basis of the parties' commitment to a peace process, this was all too often lacking.[141]

Sloan suggests that it is a matter of debate as to when UNPROFOR crossed the line into the realm of military enforcement.[142] Although Chapter VII was first invoked in Resolution 807, it contained no language indicative of the conferral of authority to use force.[143] Sloan places emphasis on Resolution 836 as this not only invoked Chapter VII, but stated that UNPROFOR was authorised to take 'the necessary measures, including the use of force'[144] to effect its mandate,[145] leading Orakhelashvili to suggest that the authority therein conferred should be seen as grounded in Article 42's military enforcement provision.[146] However, while providing for the use of force, the same resolution gave some indication that this referred to measures taken in the exercise of a broad conception of self-defence.[147] On occasion, the use of force by UNPROFOR in support of its mandate was considerable.[148]

The legacy of UN peacekeeping in former Yugoslavia is not a happy one. The situation on the ground was not suited to peacekeeping, and the addition of an enforcement dimension to UNPROFOR's mandate, taken together with the conferral of NATO with authority to conduct air strikes in support of UNPROFOR's operations on the ground,[149] made it very difficult to function as an impartial force in the eyes of the parties to the conflict. That UNPROFOR was seen as an effective party to the conflict is perhaps best illustrated by a number of its personnel being taken hostage by Bosnian Serb forces. UN peacekeepers were unable to prevent the fall of safe areas created by the Security Council, the fall of the 'safe area' of

139 See Gray, C., 'Host-state consent and United Nations peacekeeping in Yugoslavia,' *Duke Journal of Comparative and International Law*, 1996–1997, v.7, pp.241–270.
140 Gray, ibid, p.250.
141 See further Ghebali, V.-Y., 'UNPROFOR in the former Yugoslavia: The misuse of peacekeeping and associated conflict management techniques,' in Warner, supra n1, pp.13–40.
142 Sloan, supra n3, pp.143–146.
143 Gray, supra n139, pp.257–262. However, if the resolution had not been intended to provide authority for coercive military measures, there would arguably have been no need to invoke Chapter VII.
144 Para.9.
145 Sloan, supra n3, pp.143–146.
146 Orakhelashvili, supra n28, pp.501–502.
147 Para.9, which specifically empowered UNPROFOR to use force, authorised it to do so 'acting in self-defence' in response to attacks upon the UN protected areas or the delivery of humanitarian relief supplies.
148 See Findlay, supra n82, pp.219–231.
149 SC Res 836 (1993), para.10. This confused the nature of UN efforts even more. In addition to peacekeeping mandates being injected with elements of enforcement, a pure enforcement operation was being waged by NATO at the same time as UNPROFOR sought to function, at least in some respects, as a peacekeeping operation.

Srebrenica to Bosnian Serb forces in 1995 representing perhaps the most obvious symbol of the inadequacy of peacekeeping measures.[150] The UN secretary-general himself noted

> the perils of crossing the line from peace-keeping to peace enforcement without first equipping the Force with the manpower, armament, logistic and intelligence capacity and command and control arrangements that would give the necessary credibility to its threat to use force.[151]

Put differently, peacekeeping and enforcement proceed from different assumptions and are reliant on different kinds of resources to be effectively implemented. This formed the basis for the assertion of one commentator on UN peacekeeping that 'The most egregious and fundamental failing of UNPROFOR was the attempt to use force in a supposedly peacekeeping context.'[152] The resources required for UNPROFOR to be able to effectively discharge its ever-changing and robust mandate were simply not there.[153] It was ultimately NATO air power and the subsequent Dayton peace talks that brought the conflict to a close. It is difficult to identify the contribution played by peacekeeping towards the eventual peaceful outcome.

The role of the traditional principles in third-generation operations

The experiences of peacekeeping in former Yugoslavia and Somalia, together with those of Rwanda where a lightly armed peacekeeping operation proved impotent in the face of genocide,[154] provoked a reassessment of the role to be played by UN peacekeeping. The late 1990s marked a decline in the presence of UN

150 For an account of developments leading to the fall of Srebrenica, see the reflective report of the secretary-general, UN Doc. A/54/549. Boutros Boutros-Ghali had suggested at one point that an additional 34,000 troops would be needed if full respect for the safe areas was to be ensured. See UN Doc. S/25939, p.3. See also Akashi, Y., 'The use of force in a United Nations peace-keeping operation: Lessons learnt from the safe areas Mandate,' *Fordham International Law Journal*, 1995, v19, n.2, pp.312–323.

151 UN Doc. S/1995/444, para.63.

152 Findlay, supra n82, p.271.

153 For example, at the time of the Security Council's adoption of Resolution 836 which expanded UNPROFOR's mandate, the secretary-general requested the provision of 34,000 peacekeepers. The Council only authorised 7,600: see *Background to UNPROFOR*, provided by the UN Department of Peacekeeping Operations, available at http://www.un.org/Depts/DPKO/Missions/unprof_b.htm.

154 See generally the *Report of the Independent Inquiry into the Actions of the United Nations during the 1994 Genocide in Rwanda*, UN Doc. S/1999/1257. It should be noted, however, that neither the United Nations Assistance Mission for Rwanda (UNAMIR) nor the UNAMIR II operation was tasked with a mandate under Chapter VII.

peacekeeping operations generally,[155] and their mandates were not as ambitious as those tasked upon UNOSOM II and UNPROFOR.[156] Indications at the time were that the third generation of UN peacekeeping operations, in which mandates appeared to contain elements of military enforcement, was coming to an end and that there would be a return to the types of operations which had comprised first- and second-generation peacekeeping, with the principles of consent, impartiality and non-use of force for purposes other than self-defence again being central. The Brahimi report, commissioned to make recommendations for reforms to UN peacekeeping operations, appeared to support the view that peacekeeping should remain distinct from enforcement, noting that 'consent of the local parties, impartiality and use of force only in self-defence should remain the bedrock principles of peacekeeping.'[157] The limitations of peacekeeping were also acknowledged, the report suggesting that 'there are many tasks which [peacekeeping operations] should not be asked to undertake, and many places they should not go.'[158] They should only be conferred with mandates that are 'clear, credible and achievable.'[159] Such remarks hint at the preservation of a clear divide between peacekeeping and military enforcement. However, the Brahimi report also implicitly acknowledged that the traditional principles applicable to peacekeeping may need to be reinterpreted in the context of contemporary conflict situations, arguing in favour of robust rules of engagement[160] and an understanding of the impartiality principle which can be distinguished from neutrality:

> Impartiality for such operations must therefore mean adherence to the principles of the Charter and to the objectives of a mandate that is rooted in those Charter principles. Such impartiality is not the same as neutrality or equal treatment of all parties in all cases for all time.[161]

155 It has been noted that whereas there were approximately 70,000 UN peacekeepers deployed in 1993, by 1998 this had declined to 10,000. See Guehenno, J.M., 'On the challenges and achievements of reforming UN peace operations,' *International Peacekeeping*, 2002, v.9, n.2, pp.68–80, p.71.

156 The Yugoslav and Somali episodes aside, Chapter VII authority was only conferred on a small number of operations. This was invariably for the relatively limited purpose of allowing operations to ensure their own safety and freedom of movement or to protect civilians under imminent threat of physical violence (for example, SC Res 1123 (1997), para 4; SC Res 1159 (1997), para.6; SC Res 1270 (1998), para.14).

157 *Report of the Panel on United Nations Peace Operations* (Brahimi report), UN Doc. A/55/305-S/2000/809, para.48.

158 Brahimi report, ibid, para.1.

159 Brahimi report, supra n157, pt.II. See also paras.56–63.

160 Brahimi report, supra n157, para.49.

161 Brahimi report, supra n157, para.50. On the evolution of the impartiality principle, see Rhoads, E.P., *Taking Sides in Peacekeeping: Impartiality and the Future of the United Nations* (Oxford: OUP, 2016), pp.46–91.

Furthermore, the report placed great emphasis on the role of peacekeeping in promoting human security.[162] The suggestion that peacekeeping could continue to operate in accordance with its original principles while adopting more robust mandates gave cause for concern on the part of some international lawyers, one commenting that 'the report still seems to be based on the untested assumption that peacekeepers can somehow act in a more muscular fashion without overstepping the line between peacekeeping and enforcement.'[163]

However, in the aftermath of Yugoslavia, Somalia and the Brahimi report, it appears to be the case that third-generation peacekeeping underwent refinement rather than disappeared. Arguably, a majority of mandates conferred upon operations subsequently contained express powers which went beyond those enjoyed by earlier peacekeeping operations, yet which did not amount to the scale of the peacekeeping/enforcement overlap seen in the mandates of UNPRFOR and UNOSOM II, and which appeared to afford at least some attempt to demonstrate respect for the 'bedrock' principles of peacekeeping.[164]

From peacekeeping to state-building?

Although the evolution of UN peacekeeping can be considered through the lens of three generations detailed above, some operations around the millennium pointed to the possible emergence of yet another form of peacekeeping which involved operations assuming greater responsibility for ensuring the long-term sustainability of peace, via its involvement in state-building initiatives. While elements of such a mandate can be seen in the role performed by UNTAC in Cambodia, where effectively 'for the first time ... a peacekeeping mission was governing a nation,'[165] it was a relatively short-term operation.[166] The role of UN operations in the administration of civil authority became firmly established in two later operations: UNTAET in East Timor and UNMIK in Kosovo, both created in 1999. As Breau comments, these two operations 'represented the "cross-over into comprehensive governance of territory."'[167]

162 See Peou, S., 'The UN, peacekeeping and collective human security: From *An Agenda for Peace* to the Brahimi report,' *International Peacekeeping*, 2002, v.9, n.2, pp.51–68, pp.55–60.

163 White, N.D., 'Commentary on the Report of the Panel on United Nations Peace Operations,' *Journal of Conflict and Security Law*, 2001, v.6, n.1, pp.127–146, p.130.

164 See below in the context of peacekeeping in the twenty-first century.

165 Breau, S., 'The impact of the responsibility to protect on peacekeeping,' *Journal of Conflict and Security Law*, 2006, v.11, pp.429–464, at p.457.

166 UNTAC was deployed from February 1992 to September 1993. For discussion of the role performed by UNTAC, see Findlay, supra n108; Keller, supra n108, at pp.154–170.

167 Breau, supra n165, p.458. On issues relating to the legal status of these territories while under UN administration, see Wilde, R., *International Territorial Administration: How Trusteeship and the Civilizing Mission Never Went Away* (Oxford: Oxford University Press, 2008), pp.144–146, pp.178–188.

Following East Timor's vote for independence in a UN-supervised referendum, UNTAET was created with a particularly ambitious mandate to assist East Timor in its advance towards statehood.[168] It assumed responsibility for security, law and order, the administration of the new state, the development of civil and social services and delivery of humanitarian assistance.[169] Effectively, through UNTAET, the UN assumed the administration of the emerging state and helped in the creation of its pillars of governmental administration.[170] It also enjoyed the capacity to issue legislative acts where necessary. Following the trend of most post–Cold War operations, UNTAET was created under Chapter VII and explicitly empowered to use all necessary measures to give effect to its mandate,[171] although in practice force was only exercised on a limited basis.[172] UNMIK performed a similar role in Kosovo following the end of the hostilities which gave rise to NATO intervention during 1999.[173] Pending resolution of Kosovo's 'future status,' UNMIK was tasked with providing interim administration for the province.[174] The UN role in both East Timor and Kosovo has been regarded positively,[175] there having been a generally successful transition to statehood in the case of the former and autonomous rule in the case of the latter.[176] The developments represented by the UN operations in East Timor and Kosovo arguably reflected the broadened conception of collective security which has increasingly dominated the UN agenda.

168 On UNTAET's role, see Diehl et al, supra n86, pp.143–171.

169 SC Res 1272 (1999).

170 See Kondoch, supra n43, pp.249–251. See also Howard, supra n101, Chapter 8.

171 Para.4.

172 See Findlay, supra n82, pp.287–296.

173 For an overview of UNMIK's mandate and structure, see Brand, M.G., 'Institution-building and human rights protection in Kosovo in the light of UNMIK legislation,' *Nordic Journal of International Law*, 2001, v.70, pp.461–488, at pp.462–465. For an overview of UNMIK's experience, see Caplan, R., 'United Nations Interim Administration in Kosovo (UNMIK),' in Koops et al, supra n62, pp.617–628.

174 SC Res 1244 (1999), paras.10–11.

175 See Wilde, R., 'Determining how the legitimacy of intervention is discussed: A case study of international territorial administration,' in Charlesworth, H. and Coicaud, J.-M. (eds), *Fault Lines of International Legitimacy* (Cambridge: Cambridge University Press, 2012), pp.327–359.

176 Whether, following its declaration of independence in 2008, Kosovo has made the transition to statehood is a point of some debate. Although the ICJ ruled that Kosovo's declaration of independence did not breach international law, significantly, it did not address the wider effects of the declaration. See *Accordance with International Law of the Unilateral Declaration of Independence in Respect of Kosovo*, Advisory Opinion, ICJ Rep 2010, p.403. The event of Kosovo's declaration provoked much academic commentary. For a collection of perspectives, see, for example, Summers, J. (ed.), *Kosovo: A Precedent?* (Leiden and Boston: Brill, 2011).

UN Peacekeeping in the Twenty-First Century: Changes and Challenges?

The scope of UN peacekeeping since the millennium

The problems encountered by UN peacekeeping operations during the 1990s led to a fresh appraisal of their very role within the UN collective security system, culminating in the Brahimi report, which investigated means of improving the efficiency of UN operations.[177] The Brahimi report stressed the need for operations to be rapidly deployable,[178] and encouraged the development of the UN's Standby Arrangement System (UNSAS) for peacekeeping.[179] The Brahimi report also stressed that it would be ideal if peacekeeping operations consisted of contingents from states which had been working together on the development of common standards.[180] A number of lessons were taken from the experiences in former Yugoslavia and Somalia, concerning important matters such as the provision of adequate resources for operations to perform their mandate and the existence of clear mandates in the first place. From the late 1990s onwards, improvements were seen in this respect,[181] and arguably the UN has not generated the kind of criticism for peacekeeping failures that followed the debacles of the early to mid-1990s. However, in reflecting the growing emphasis placed upon human security in UN responses to situations of concern, 'the Brahimi Report [was] forthright in arguing that peacekeepers "who witness violence against civilians should be presumed to be authorised to stop it, within their means, in support of basic UN principles."'[182]

In the earlier years of the twenty-first century particularly, UN peacekeeping operations have been tasked with an array of functions, one study suggesting that some missions have mandates to perform in excess of a hundred tasks.[183] However, while several large operations were established during the first decade post-millennium by resolutions adopted under Chapter VII of the UN Charter,[184] a retreat in peacekeeping began during the second decade, it having been noted that while no new large operations have been created since 2013, several large operations have come to a conclusion during the same period.[185] The UN peacekeeping

177 Brahimi report, supra n157. For discussion of the Brahimi report, see White, supra n163; Guehenno, supra n155; Peou, supra n162.

178 Brahimi report, supra n157, para.86.

179 Brahimi report, supra n157, para.117.

180 Brahimi report, supra n157, paras.114–116.

181 See Zacklin, R., 'The use of force in peacekeeping operations,' in Blokker, N. and Schrijver, N. (eds), *The Security Council and the Use of Force* (Leiden/Boston: Martinus Nijhoff, 2005), pp.91–106.

182 Rhoads, supra n161, p.68.

183 Wane, E.G., Williams, P.D. and Kihara-Hunt, A., *The Future of Peacekeeping, New Models and Related Consequences* (New York: United Nations, 2024), p.15.

184 See further below.

185 These have included operations in the Cote d'Ivoire, Darfur, Haiti, Liberia and Sierra Leone. See Karlsrud, J., 'Pragmatic Peacekeeping in Practice: Exit Liberal Peacekeeping, Enter UN Support Missions?,' *Journal of Intervention and Statebuilding*, 2023, v.17, n.3, pp.258–272, at p.258.

budget has declined during this time,[186] while the resourcing of operations has depended considerably on a number of smaller and medium states,[187] with China the only member of the P5 to have contributed significant numbers of peacekeeping personnel in the contemporary period.[188] At the time of writing, eleven UN peacekeeping operations remain active. Six of these have their origins broadly in the Cold War era,[189] most being relatively small-scale operations functioning in accordance with traditional peacekeeping principles,[190] while only three of the active operations could be classified as large-scale.[191]

There has clearly been a shift towards Chapter VII serving as the usual basis for the creation of peacekeeping operations ever since the 1990s. While nine of twelve operations established in the period 1998–2006 were created under a Chapter VII mandate,[192] later operations such as MONUSCO in the DRC and UNMISS in South Sudan were also grounded in this chapter.[193] The consequences of the blurring of any distinction between peacekeeping and military enforcement during the 1990s have been highlighted above,[194] but the subsequent creation of peacekeeping mandates does seem to have been influenced by the lessons learned therein and highlighted in the Brahimi report which, as noted, emphasised the importance of adhering to the traditional principles of peacekeeping. Nonetheless, the increased reliance upon Chapter VII mandates suggests that modern peacekeeping is doctrinally removed from first- and second-generation peacekeeping, necessitating some consideration of its exact nature and the consequences of this. That most recent peacekeeping operations have been created under Chapter VII does not of itself indicate that they ought to be considered enforcement operations – the Council is at liberty to make calls for provisional measures to be complied with

186 See, e.g., Kalsrud, ibid, p261, who points to a decrease from $8.5 billion to $6.6 billion in the period 2015–2023.

187 As of August 2024, Nepal, Bangladesh, Rwanda, India, Indonesia, Ghana and Pakistan all contributed larger numbers of personnel than the biggest contributor among the P5, China.

188 See Cho, S., 'China's Participation in UN Peacekeeping Operations since the 2000s,' *Journal of Contemporary China*, 2019, v.28, n.117, pp.484–498.

189 UNTSO, UNMOGIP, UNFICYP, UNDOF, UNIFIL and MINURSO.

190 Of the aforementioned operations, only UNIFIL is of significant size, standing at approximately 13,000 as of December 2024. See https://peacekeeping.un.org/en/mission/unifil.

191 MINUSCA, MONUSCO and UNMISS all had authorised personnel in excess of 15,000 as of December 2024. See their respective mission websites, at https://peacekeeping.un.org/en/mission/minusca, https://peacekeeping.un.org/en/mission/monusco, https://unmiss.unmissions.org/.

192 See Frederking, supra n5, pp.41–47. These included UNAMSIL (SC Res 1270 (1999), MONUC (SC Res 1291 (2000), UNMIL (SC Res 1509 (2003), UNOCI (SC Res 1528 (2004), MINUSTAH (SC Res 1542 (2004), ONUB (SC Res 1545 (2004), and UNMIS (SC Res 1590 (2005).

193 See SC Res 1925 (2010) and SC Res 1996 (2011) respectively.

194 See, for example, Gray, supra n139, pp.257–262; Cox, supra n30, pp.268–273; Berdal, M., 'The Security Council, peacekeeping, and internal conflict after the end of the cold war,' *Duke Journal of Comparative and International Law*, 1996–1997, v.7, n.2, pp.71–91, at p.86 et seq.

under Article 40, for example, which do not involve the application of any coercive measures – but when the mandates of peacekeeping operations are not only created by reference to Chapter VII but contain language of the kind which has traditionally been used to authorise the use of force, the implication is that they at the very least enjoy some form of military power exceeding a right of self-defence.

There is considerable support for the view that a distinction must be maintained between peacekeeping and enforcement, the preservation of the three core principles of peacekeeping being central to this. As early as the mid-1990s, Boutros Boutros-Ghali in his *Supplement to an Agenda for Peace* suggested that respect for these three principles was essential to the success of peacekeeping operations,[195] and that peacekeeping and the use of force should be seen as alternative techniques for responding to conflict resolution.[196] The blurring of the distinction between the two concepts, in his view, threatened to undermine the viability of peacekeeping operations and the safety of their personnel.[197] Much of the literature on early post–Cold War peacekeeping focused upon the need for peacekeeping to operate in accordance with its traditional principles if it is to prove successful.[198] The consequences of peacekeeping entering the realm of enforcement were plainly set out by Lalande, informed by the experience of UNOSOM II in Somalia.[199] First, obtaining the acceptance of peacekeeping operations by warring parties may prove more difficult if they became too closely associated with enforcement functions. One of the strengths of peacekeeping as traditionally conceived is that it involves low-intensity and impartial intervention into situations of tension, increasing its attraction to the parties. More robust intervention is less likely to enjoy such benefits. Second, states are less likely to commit troops and resources to operations that are to play a greater 'fighting' role. Third, on a related point, contributing states are forced to adopt a different kind of political analysis of the situation at hand. Perceptions of national self-interest are more likely to be at the forefront of considerations whether to participate in more 'robust' operations. Fourth, peacekeeping differs substantially from enforcement action in military terms. From a strategic or tactical perspective, the planning of each kind of operation must proceed from considerably different assumptions. Finally, relations between the UN and parties to a conflict are informed by the nature of any operation that is deployed to the trouble spot. Peacekeeping operations are traditionally cooperative ventures, involving a partnership between the UN forces and local parties. The operation effectively seeks to assist the parties in achieving predefined objectives. It plays a supervisory capacity in this respect. By contrast,

195 *Supplement to an Agenda for Peace*, UN Doc. A/50/60-S/1995/1, para.33.
196 *Supplement to an Agenda for Peace*, ibid, para.36.
197 *Supplement to an Agenda for Peace*, supra n195, para.35.
198 See, for example, Cox, supra n30, pp.168–173; Berdal, supra n194, at p.86 et seq; Azimi, N., *Humanitarian Action and Peacekeeping Operations* (London: Kluwer Law International, 1997).
199 Lalande, supra n123, pp.76–81. See also Sloan, supra n3, pp.282–285.

an enforcement action involves the direction of measures against specified actors. The UN does not have a military enforcement capacity, as originally envisaged by Article 43 and subsequent provisions of the UN Charter,[200] and confers enforcement authority upon able and willing actors when the Security Council considers that the need arises.[201]

Prima facie, many modern peacekeeping operations are not endowed with a mandate which draws a clear distinction between the techniques of peacekeeping traditionally understood and military enforcement. Blurring usually takes the form of a specific power within their mandate to resort to 'all necessary measures' or similar, usually in support of broadly humanitarian objectives, or to contribute towards the protection of civilians.[202] However, notwithstanding the difficulties of blurring the peacekeeping/enforcement distinction, it is perhaps unrealistic to expect many modern operations to be restricted to using force only on the basis of a narrow self-defence concept. Boutros-Ghali suggested that three factors had led to the traditional principles of peacekeeping being forfeited in operations during the 1990s: the increased humanitarian dimension of the operations, the need to protect civilians and the attempt to move peace processes at a pace faster than the parties are prepared to accept.[203] While twenty-first century peacekeeping operations have arguably sought to avoid the failings of the 1990s by operating more closely in accordance with the principles of traditional peacekeeping, the increased emphasis on human security at the core of the UN's conceptualisation of its collective security remit, influenced especially by the emergence of the *Responsibility to Protect* doctrine, has meant that peacekeeping operations now almost routinely come to include within their mandate a power to use force to protect not only themselves, but civilians subjected to or under the imminent threat of attack. The UN Security Council is in a no-win situation: while too eager a departure from the core principles of peacekeeping leads to charges of entering the realm of enforcement, the failure to respond to attacks on civilians simultaneously leads to a charge of inaction and irrelevance.

Specific, restricted powers to use force should not necessarily be equated with enforcement action. As noted earlier, a peacekeeping force's application of military measures is not intended to be its raison d'être: such powers are to be applied sparingly, without distinction, in the event of specified incidents – primarily in the current environment, to protect civilians from harm. By contrast, the use of force in a military enforcement action is the very raison d'être of such action: the operation exists specifically to use force in pursuit of designated objectives. Of course, parties to a conflict may consent to the presence of a peacekeeping operation

200 See Chapter 2.
201 See Chapter 7.
202 See below.
203 *Supplement to an Agenda for Peace* supra n195, para.34.

which enjoys powers to use force for purposes beyond self-defence, again distinguishing it from an enforcement operation. The point is, however, that as

> most missions since 1999 have been authorised through invocation of Chapter VII and thus do not formally require consent as a legal prerequisite for deployment or to undertake particular actions … [this stands] testament to the established dominance of the new understanding of the norm and, relatedly to a new role for UN peacekeepers.[204]

That said, it is argued that where operations rely for their presence upon the consent of the parties to the conflict, they are more successful than those which do not.[205] A mandate which allows for force to protect civilians is still clearly capable of being impartial. While peacekeepers will not retain strict neutrality in the event of one side reneging on its part of the agreement which serves as the basis for its deployment, they are capable of acting in accordance with the terms of their mandate without partiality to either side. The line between peacekeeping and enforcement may appear blurred to some degree, but it certainly exists. Third-generation peacekeeping can, arguably, function in accordance with reinterpreted versions of the core principles of peacekeeping. The re-conceptualisation of collective security as a concept which places human well-being at its very core necessitates that this is so. Nonetheless, questions remain as to the feasibility of 'robustness' within peacekeeping.[206]

The contemporary application of the principles governing UN peacekeeping

The importance of adherence to the core principles of peacekeeping continues to be reasserted time and again by studies undertaken into the performance of peacekeeping at the UN level. During 2015, the High-level Independent Panel on UN Peacekeeping Operations (HIPPO) stated that it was convinced of their importance,[207] while the more recent report of the Special Committee on Peacekeeping Operations similarly noted its belief that respect for these principles

204 Rhoads, supra n161, p.66.

205 As Bratt notes, those operations which have relied upon the consent of the parties – for example, in Namibia, Cambodia, El Salvador and Mozambique – have been more successful than those operations which have not; Bratt, supra n124, p.51. Bratt also notes that 'the best indicator of a successful peacekeeping operation is the existence of a Comprehensive Settlement Agreement which is adhered to by all of the parties' (at p.49).

206 See, for example, Tardy, T., 'A critique of robust peacekeeping in contemporary peace operations,' *International Peacekeeping*, 2011, v.18, n.2, pp.152–167, at pp.160–165.

207 *Report of the High-level Independent Panel on Peace Operations on Uniting Our Strengths for Peace: Politics, Partnership and People*, 2015, UN Doc. A/70/95-S/2015/446, para.125.

was essential to the success of a peacekeeping operation.[208] The importance of the existence of consent to the deployment of peacekeeping operations has continued to be referred to in Security Council resolutions,[209] up to the present day.[210] Rejecting Berdal's contention that there had been 'a real tendency on the part of the Security Council to weaken the requirement of consent as a basis for UN involvement,' Orakhelashvili argued that this is 'not really the case' and noted that operations such as UNAMID were premised on the consent of territorial states.[211] UNAMID is a particularly interesting case in point,[212] taking the form of a hybrid UN–African Union peacekeeping operation as a consequence of the fact that President Bashir of Sudan would not consent to the deployment of a solely UN force. Clearly, obtaining consent was considered important here. The existence of consent theoretically indicates the willingness of the concerned parties to engage in efforts to maintain or restore peace and underpins the prospective success of the peacekeeping operation in achieving its objectives.[213] Indeed, the Special Committee on Peacekeeping Operations stated that such operations should not be a substitute for addressing the root causes of conflict.[214]

Where political divisions exist within the Security Council on the appropriate response to a given situation, consent is a factor which can make it easier to achieve consensus on the deployment of a peacekeeping operation. It has, however, been a matter of debate as to whether an operation employing forcible measures can meaningfully respect the principles of consent and impartiality. Cox argues that 'the use of force is not compatible with consent and impartiality … it tends to jeopardize other parts of the mandate.'[215] At the same time, many consent-based operations have been conferred with authority to use all necessary measures under Chapter VII for the purpose of protecting civilians. Places of protection during conflict have also been created under UN authority with the consent of the warring parties.[216] Arguably, the factor which determines the extent to which consent may be compromised by a mandate which empowers the use of force is the extent to which force is permitted and the purpose thereof. Even where consent

208 *Report of the Special Committee on Peacekeeping Operations*, UN Doc. A/78/19, 2024, para.30.
209 See, for examples from the first decade of the twenty-first century, SC Res 1545 (2004); SC Res 1590 (2005); SC Res 1990 (2011).
210 See, eg., SC Res 2729 (2024), para.19 pertaining to UNMISS in South Sudan or SC Res 2759 (2024) pertaining to MINUSCA in the Central African Republic.
211 Orakhelashvili, A., *Collective Security* (Oxford: Oxford University Press, 2011), p.314.
212 SC Res 1769 (2007). See further Chapter 8 in the context of peacekeeping by regional bodies.
213 Indeed, the *Comprehensive Report on Lessons* learned from UNOSOM concluded that UN peacekeeping forces should not enter an area unless there existed political will towards reconciliation; supra n127, paras.88–89.
214 *Report of the Special Committee on Peacekeeping Operations*, supra n208, para.31.
215 Cox, supra n30, p.269.
216 See Oswald, B.M., 'The creation and control of places of protection during United Nations peace operations,' *International Review of the Red Cross*, 2001, v.83, n.844, pp.1013–1035, especially p.1016.

is given, it can be very unreliable and susceptible to withdrawal,[217] particularly where there are multiple parties involved, and the HIPPO report has observed that such factors have resulted in 'a growing number of missions operat[ing] in remote and austere environments where no political agreement exists.'[218]

It has also been argued that the conferment of peacekeeping mandates that include powers to apply military force do not necessarily compromise the principle of impartiality, which should be distinguished from a narrow understanding equating the term with neutrality.[219] One commentator has gone so far as to suggest that 'modern peacekeeping has lost its neutrality and for good reasons. However, peacekeeping should retain its impartiality.'[220] Impartiality was defined in the Brahimi report as loyalty to the mission mandate,[221] the 2008 principles and guidance on UN peacekeeping defining impartiality further as involving implementation of a mandate 'without favour or prejudice to any party' or 'even-handedness.'[222] Nonetheless, impartiality as now understood effectively permits a peacekeeping operation to 'actively pursue the implementation of their mandate even if doing so goes against the interests of one or more of the parties.'[223] Impartiality can no longer be equated with neutrality.[224]

Although all peacekeeping operations created in the twenty-first century have been given mandates under Chapter VII,[225] the Council has not always been clear or consistent in explaining the extent to which the use of force has been sanctioned, if at all. Authority to use force beyond self-defence has been most evident in those resolutions which have authorised the use of 'all necessary measures' or similar for objectives related to the protection of civilians.[226] On other occasions, although resolutions have been adopted under Chapter VII, they make no reference to such language,[227] making it unclear what the significance of the invocation of

217 Johnstone, I., 'Managing consent in contemporary peacekeeping operations,' *International Peacekeeping*, 2011, v.18, n.2, pp.168–182, at p.170.

218 *HIPPO Report*, supra n207, para.23.

219 See, for example, Yamashita, H., '"Impartial" use of force in United Nations peacekeeping,' *International Peacekeeping*, 2008, v.15, n.5, pp.615–630.

220 Tsagourias, supra n43, p.481.

221 Brahimi report, supra n157, p.617.

222 *United Nations Peacekeeping Operations: Principles and Guidance 2008* (New York: UN Department of Peacekeeping Operations, 2008). See Yamashita, supra n193, p.618.

223 Rhoads, supra n161, p.68.

224 For a critique of the attempted distinction between impartiality and neutrality, see Donald, D., 'Neutrality, impartiality and UN peacekeeping at the beginning of the 21st century,' *International Peacekeeping*, 2002, v.9, n.4, pp.21–38.

225 Howard, L.M. and Dayal, A.K., 'The Use of Force in UN Peacekeeping,' *International Organization*, 2018, v.72, Winter, pp.71–103, at p.71.

226 For example, SC Res 1270 (1999), para.14 (UNAMSIL); SC Res 1291 (2000), para.8 (MONUC); SC Res 1528 (2004), para.6 (UNOCI); SC Res 1545 (2004), para.5 (ONUB); SC Res 1590 (2005), para.16 (UNMIS); SC Res 1769 (2007), para.15 (UNAMID); SC Res 1925 (2010), para.12 (MONUSCO); SC Res 1990 (2011), para.3 (UNISFA); SC Res 1996 (2011), para.4 (UNMISS).

227 For example, SC Res 1509 (2003) (UNMIL); SC Res 1542 (2004) (MINUSTAH).

Chapter VII actually is. It has correctly been noted that within post–Cold War peacekeeping operations, 'the use of force … is primarily geared towards the ultimate goal of alleviating human suffering.'[228] Nonetheless, concern continues to be expressed at the danger that use of force mandates undermine claims to impartiality, open peacekeepers to attack and generate false expectations in respect of their abilities.[229]

Although undoubtedly early post–Cold War expansions in peacekeeping gave rise to some conceptual confusion in relation to the extent to which it remained distinct from military enforcement, it is nonetheless contended that in later years, force applied by peacekeepers has in practice generally been minimal and is best seen as a power of last resort, contrasting this from military enforcement operations which have been deployed specifically to use force.[230] As noted by Paddon Rhoads et al, 'in practice, the use of deadly force, particularly in a proactive or preventive manner, remains a relatively rare occurrence.'[231] The 2008 principles and guidance on UN peacekeeping distinguish the two concepts along the lines aforementioned, stating that:

> While robust peacekeeping involves the use of force at the tactical level with the consent of the host authorities and/or the main parties to the conflict, peace enforcement may involve the use of force at the strategic or international level, which is normally prohibited for member states under Article 2 (4).[232]

'Robust peacekeeping,' as peacekeeping operations tasked with mandates under Chapter VII have been labelled, ordinarily operates in accordance with the consent of the parties whose dispute or peace it is deployed to monitor.[233] The differentiation of 'robust' or 'militarised' peacekeeping from military enforcement has also been neatly summarised by Nasu. Whereas military enforcement entails the employment of armed force 'on [its] own initiative to achieve military objectives and thus to draw a military solution to a political dispute,' the use of armed force 'to respond in accordance with detailed rules and procedures to achieve non-military objectives pending a solution to a political dispute' does not reach that

228 Cox, supra n30, p.258.

229 Howard and Dayal, supra n225, pp.72–75.

230 Tsagourias defines enforcement as 'any action that involves the use of force that is directed against a state with the aim of overcoming its will'; supra n43, p.471. Where force is sanctioned by a mandate conferred upon an operation deployed with the consent of the parties, presumably this threshold is not reached.

231 Paddon Rhoads, E.P., Karlsrud, J., Labuda, P.I., Cusimano, S. and Duursma, A., 'Consent, impartiality and the (non-) use of force,' *International Peacekeeping*, 2023, v.30, n.4, pp.419–426.

232 *Principles and Guidance 2008*, supra n222, p.19.

233 See Tardy, supra n206.

level.[234] This aligns with the UN's own expression of extreme caution over any call for a peacekeeping operation to undertake enforcement tasks.[235]

While reflecting the increased emphasis within the UN system upon collective human security, the endorsement of the *Responsibility to Protect* doctrine arguably served to necessitate the creation of UN peacekeeping mandates which entailed authority to use force beyond self-defence all the more.[236] According to Tardy, 'some countries ... see a continuum between the "responsibility to protect" and robustness within peacekeeping missions in the protection of civilians.'[237] Accordingly, the protection of civilians has become a central theme of twenty-first century peacekeeping mandates. The importance of such an approach is emphasised by the HIPPO report, which acknowledged that the protection of civilians is now a core obligation imposed upon peacekeepers, but yet acknowledged that the expectations of them must converge with their resource capability.[238] Underlining the importance of the doctrine, it has been noted that even where the mandates of peacekeeping operations appear prima facie grounded in Chapter VI, several have by reference to Chapter VII conferred authority for all necessary measures to be taken for the protection of civilians.[239] Examples from the earlier part of the post-millennium era included UNAMSIL,[240] MONUC,[241] MINUSTAH,[242] UNMIS,[243] the United Nations–African Union Mission in Darfur (UNAMID)[244] and the United Nations Interim Security Force for Abyei (UNISFA).[245] A majority of twenty-first century peacekeeping mandates have contained such a protection of civilians function,[246] while as of October 2015, 98% of uniformed peacekeeping personnel were explicitly mandated to protect civilians.[247]

While the inclusion of a protection of civilians' power within peacekeeping mandates has been described as an 'insurance policy,'[248] existing to counter any

234 Nasu, supra n12, p.205.
235 *HIPPO Report*, supra n207, para.122.
236 For discussion of the doctrine's influence upon peacekeeping practice, see Breau, supra n165. See also Thakur, R., *The United Nations, Peace and Security* (Cambridge: CUP, 2006), pp.244–263.
237 Tardy, supra n206, at p.158.
238 *HIPPO Report*, supra n207, paras.82–85.
239 Johnstone, supra n217, at p.169.
240 SC Res 1270 (1999), para.14.
241 SC Res 1291 (2000), para.8.
242 SC Res 1542 (2004), para.7.
243 SC Res 1590 (2005), para.16.
244 SC Res 1769 (2007), para.15.
245 SC Res 1990 (2011), para.3.
246 Tardy, supra n206, at p.152. See also Holt, V., Taylor, G. and Kelly, M., *Protecting Civilians in the Context of UN Peacekeeping Operations: Successes, Setbacks and Remaining Challenges* (New York: United Nations, 2009), p.3.
247 Rhoads, supra n161, p.69.
248 By the Sierra Leonean representative within the Security Council in October 1999. See UN Doc. S/PV. 4054, at p.5.

hostile conduct on the ground which gives rise to humanitarian repercussions, it is not without its challenges. There is some risk that peacekeepers effecting such a mandate become more likely to be targeted by parties to a conflict,[249] a difficulty identified by the HIPPO report as having arisen in respect of the deployment of UN peacekeeping operations to as varied locations as Afghanistan, the DRC, Mali and Somalia.[250]

The place of peacekeeping in the peaceful settlement of disputes

As a tool of the collective security system, despite its military dimension, peacekeeping is arguably more closely aligned with peaceful settlement than the sanctions and military enforcement options open to the Security Council, which are undeniably predicated upon the use of coercion to pressure targets into accepting the will of the Council. The continued emphasis upon the core principles of peacekeeping affirms its connection with peaceful settlement.[251] It is true that there is no single template of what a UN peacekeeping operation looks like. However, in distinguishing peacekeeping from military enforcement, it is arguably important to ensure that each operation is conferred with a mandate which supports a process of pacific settlement. The dynamics of each situation will determine the specific role which peacekeeping plays within this. In low-key situations, it could be simply by patrolling a ceasefire agreement, whereas in more complex situations, particularly in the aftermath of internal conflict, it may involve the supervision or facilitation of the longer-term implementation of a more detailed peace agreement and involvement in peace-building measures. Although a situation in which peace is 'kept' implies the absence of conflict, where peacekeeping operations are deployed in the aftermath of long-standing violent conflicts, the threat of a return to violence is best protected against through a process that attempts to build confidence and stronger relationships between the relevant parties. Peacekeeping must not take place in isolation, but must serve the wider peace-building agenda.[252] Where this has been the case, for example, in the Central American peace process, the contribution of UN peacekeeping operations has been successful.

The importance of the relationship between peacekeeping and peace-building has been recognised by the UN itself,[253] noting in 2010 that 'UN peacekeep-

249 See, eg., Fjelde, H., Hultman, L. and Nilsson, D., 'Protection Through Presence: UN Peacekeeping and the Costs of Targeting Civilians,' *International Organisation*, 2019, v.73, Winter, pp.103–131.

250 *HIPPO Report*, supra n207, paras.24–26.

251 On this, see the discussion provided above.

252 See Fisher, R.J., 'The potential for peacebuilding: Forging a bridge from peacekeeping to peacemaking,' *Peace & Change*, 1993, v.18, n.3, pp.247–266. Peacebuilding does, however, present its own challenges. See Sens, supra n100, at pp.147–151.

253 *UN Peacebuilding: An Orientation* (New York: United Nations, 2010), pp.8–9.

ers increasingly play a significant role as early peacebuilders themselves. The mandates of multi-dimensional peacekeeping operations include many peacebuilding tasks.'[254] More recently, the HIPPO report emphasised the importance of the primacy of politics within processes involving the deployment of peacekeeping operations[255] and was critical of the tasking of operations with conflict management roles against a backdrop of violent conflict in which any viable peace process is absent.[256] Similarly, UN Secretary-General Antonio Guterres has described a UN peacekeeping operation as 'not an army, or a counter-terrorism force, or a humanitarian agency … [but] a tool to create the space for a nationally owned political solution.'[257] Consequently, at a minimum there should be agreement between the parties locally to the presence of a peacekeeping operation and the role that it is to perform. Indeed, the question can be legitimately asked of how an operation can play a role in mediating a conflict when one or more of the combatants do not even want it deployed.[258] While the absence of any such agreement does not preclude the adoption of robust measures by the UN to respond to human suffering, these would necessarily have to take the form of enforcement measures as opposed to techniques of peacekeeping.[259] While peaceful settlement may be aided by the imposition of non-military sanctions, for example arms embargoes in the context of attempting to end civil wars, military enforcement action cannot realistically form part of this process: its underlying assumptions and techniques differ from those of peacekeeping and where employed at the same time, problems arise, as the experiences of the 1990s in particular illustrated only too well. This reinforces the problems of blurring the distinction between peacekeeping and military enforcement too greatly.[260]

Supporting peacekeeping moving forward

Notwithstanding some of the conceptual difficulties which have arisen in respect of UN peacekeeping mandates, any operation can only succeed to the extent that the resources with which it is provided are adequate for the mandate to be

254 *UN Peacebuilding*, ibid, p.9.
255 *HIPPO Report*, supra n207, paras.43–48.
256 *HIPPO Report*, supra n207, para.113.
257 Quoted in Karlsrud, supra n185, at p.267.
258 Bratt, supra n124, p.63.
259 Force may be employed in defence of civilians in the course of a peacekeeping operation, where such a mandate is consented to by the parties concerned. However, where no such consent is forthcoming, such a mandate must be regarded as one of military enforcement given the practical inability of the operation to contribute towards any process of peaceful transition.
260 Some commentators, however, have suggested that peacebuilding measures as a key component of UN peacekeeping mandates have started to be deprioritised in favour of emphasis upon stabilisation measures. See, eg., Curran, D. and Hunt, C.T., 'Stabilization at the Expense of Peacebuilding in UN Peacekeeping Operations,' *Global Governance*, 2020, v.26, pp.46–68.

discharged. On a political level, UN peacekeeping has often come under criticism on the grounds that it is inadequately resourced, sometimes described as the 'commitment gap.'[261] This has most notably been the case in respect of some of the more ambitious operations, where mandates were arguably not supported with the provision of adequate resources. Peacekeeping capacities are dependent upon the provision of resources, most importantly, the very forces which will participate in peacekeeping operations, by member states. A number of considerations will exert influence over their willingness to commit these resources, inevitably including the nature of the mandates which they will be required to exercise. The reliance on ad hoc contributions of member states can make forward planning, rapid deployment and interoperability potentially difficult.

An early post–Cold War initiative to assist in this respect came in the form of the UN Standby Arrangements System (UNSAS), established to facilitate the efficient planning of peacekeeping operations, in the knowledge that specific resources could in principle be called upon by the Secretariat when a decision is taken to establish a peacekeeping operation. Under this system, states could enter into an arrangement with the Secretariat whereby they set out what resources they would in principle make available for use in peacekeeping operations. The purpose of UNSAS was to provide 'a precise understanding of forces and other capabilities' a state would have available 'at an agreed state of readiness, should it agree to contribute to a peacekeeping operation.'[262] If a state agreed to contribute, the forces were expected to be rapidly deployable and fully operational.[263] Other initiatives along these lines were also undertaken.[264] The UNSAS was credited by Kofi Annan with having proven helpful in the planning of a number of UN peacekeeping operations, deployed in a diverse range of situations,[265] while generating a measure of standardisation has also been attributed to the standby arrangements system.[266] Following recommendations made in the HIPPO report,[267] UNSAS was superseded from 2015 by the similarly designed Peacekeeping Capability Readiness System (PCRS).[268]

The PCRS does not, however, guarantee the availability of resources for peacekeeping operations. As the Canadian government's much earlier study on a

261 See Gray, supra n94, pp.278–280.

262 UN Doc. S/1994/777, para.2. Detailed information on numbers of personnel, size of units and related matters is expected; para.5.

263 Ibid, paras.3–4.

264 For example, the SHIRBRIG and FORD initiatives. For discussion, see Langille, H.P., 'Conflict prevention: Options for rapid deployment and UN standing forces,' *International Peacekeeping*, 2000, v.7, n.1, pp.219–253.

265 See UN Doc. S/2000/194, para.14; there the Secretary-General lists some situations in respect of which their existence has helped in the planning of operations.

266 See, for example, UN Doc. S/1995/943, para.20.

267 *HIPPO Report*, supra n207.

268 This system is detailed in its webpages: https://pcrs.un.org/SitePages/Home.aspx.

rapid reaction capability for the UN explained, 'As long as sovereign states retain the right to decide on the deployment of their national units, there will never be complete assurance that a UN force can meet an urgent situation on time or with sufficient capacity.'[269] The same point was made by then Dutch Foreign Minister Hans van Mierlo, who commented that as 'the units will remain part of the military forces of Member states … their deployment will remain subject to often time consuming, national decision making.'[270] On this matter, it is relevant to recall the UN's response to events in Rwanda at the height of 1994's mass genocide. In adopting Resolution 918, an attempted response on the part of the Security Council to the humanitarian crisis was to authorise the deployment of an enlarged UNAMIR peacekeeping operation. However, the operation could not be deployed due to the fact that no states were forthcoming with offers of contributions towards it, in spite of the fact that a number had entered into understandings with the UN under the UNSAS system in place at the time. As then Secretary-General Boutros Boutros-Ghali later wrote,

> [standby arrangements] provide no guarantee that troops will be provided for a specific operation … when in May 1994 the Security Council decided to expand [UNAMIR], not one of the 19 Governments that at that time had undertaken to have troops on stand-by agreed to contribute.[271]

The provision of physical resources aside, the financing of UN peacekeeping operations has also seen a state of relative decline over the course of the past decade or two, as alluded to above. Calls for a more comprehensive system of funding continue to be made,[272] but again the dependence on member states – and in particular, those responsible for making the biggest contributions to UN budgets – places limitations on progress in this respect.

Any evaluation of the success of UN peacekeeping as an enterprise is fraught with difficulties. Various factors inform the contribution that can be made by a peacekeeping operation in any given circumstances, ranging from the commitment towards the operation demonstrated by the Security Council to cooperation on the part of the local parties and the provision of adequate resources to support the operation's mandate.[273] However, notwithstanding the criticisms often hurled at peacekeeping, one major study on the future of peacekeeping has established that

269 Cited in Kinloch, S.P., 'Utopian or pragmatic? A UN permanent military volunteer force,' *International Peacekeeping*, 1996, v.3, n.4, pp.166–190, at p.169.

270 Cited in Kinloch, ibid, at p.169.

271 UN Doc. A/50/60-S/1995/1, para.43.

272 The HIPPO report made proposals in this respect; supra n207. See further Coleman, K.P., 'Extending UN Peacekeeping Financing Beyond UN Peacekeeping Operations? The Prospects and Challenges of Reform,' *Global Governance*, 2017, v.23, pp.101–120.

273 See Wane, Williams and Kihara-Hunt, supra n183, pp.45–49.

twelve of eighteen significant multidimensional peacekeeping operations active in the period 1960–2017 were successful in achieving the main objectives with which they had been tasked.[274] Informed by wider global developments which may come to bear on the prospects and challenges faced by UN operations, the *Future of Peacekeeping Operations Project* seeks to consider what future missions will look like.[275] Wane, Williams and Kihara-Hunt have suggested that the main contemporary challenge faced by peacekeeping is the intensification of geopolitical competition which has escalated as the twenty-first century has progressed,[276] while levels of resource/mandate compatibility continue to be commented on, there being 'widely shared concern that changes in conflict may be outpacing the ability of [UN peacekeeping operations] to respond.'[277]

Conclusion

In some respects, it is perhaps possible to conceive of UN peacekeeping as almost an accidental creation. As described by Berdal, 'the development of UN peacekeeping was a functional response to the fact that, during the Cold War, the United Nations could no longer rely on continued cooperation among the Allied powers.'[278] Nevertheless, UN peacekeeping ought to be seen as a remarkable creation on the part of the UN. Not mentioned anywhere in the UN Charter, 'It became a useful, arguably necessary, element of the restricted Cold War collective security function of the UN.'[279] During the first few decades of its application, peacekeeping allowed the UN to make an important contribution to the maintenance of international peace and security in fragile situations during a period in which the most robust tools of its collective security system – measures under Articles 41 and 42 – had effectively become paralysed. The apparently contradictory themes of the experience of the UN collective security system are seen clearly in the development and practice of UN peacekeeping. On the one hand, the poor resourcing of some peacekeeping operations and the unwillingness of states to commit troops to operations in some situations lend some credence to the realist critique of collective security and its dependence upon political circumstances which are not always favourable to its effective functioning. However, on the other hand and at the same time, the very creation of UN peacekeeping and its ability to evolve to meet new needs and challenges is evidenced by its transformation through subsequent generations of operations in which they have undertaken a wider range

274 Wane, Williams and Kihara-Hunt, supra n183, pp.6–9.
275 See https://peacekeeping.un.org/en/future-of-peacekeeping for the bank of publications and resources shared through this project.
276 Wane, Williams and Kihara-Hunt, supra n183, p.10.
277 *HIPPO Report*, supra n207, para.9.
278 Berdal, supra n194, at p.74.
279 White, supra n28, at p.43.

of tasks in accordance with an expanded conception of collective security. The humanitarian imperative in particular has come to influence the nature of modern peacekeeping operations, with the prevalence of protection of civilians mandates attached to all recently created peacekeeping operations serving as testament to the extent to which human security has come to form the very essence of collective security as practised within the UN system. Indeed, many of the modern challenges faced by the institution of peacekeeping are a consequence of this broadened conception of collective security, meaning peacekeepers contend with a wider range of functions and obstacles in discharging these than might historically have been the case.

Undoubtedly, peacekeeping continues to face a series of key challenges. The political environment within which the UN must function makes this inevitable. Central, however, to the continued relevance and effectiveness of peacekeeping is to ensure that it remains a mechanism that is distinct from military enforcement and is closely aligned to the willingness of concerned parties to participate within a process of peaceful settlement. Encouragingly, the fact that debates continue to take place centred on the improvement of the capabilities of UN peacekeeping demonstrates a desire for it to continue to sit at the heart of responses to tense post-conflict situations.

7

MILITARY ENFORCEMENT ACTION

Introduction

This chapter considers the use of military enforcement action as a tool through which the UN Security Council may respond to situations that constitute threats to or breaches of international peace and security.[1] This is undoubtedly the most robust means provided by the UN Charter framework for responding to such situations, involving as it does the utilisation of coercive military force. In this sense, it represents the most traditional conception of collective security, in which a collective military response is provided to situations of concern to the collective security system. While Chapter VII of the UN Charter provides detailed provisions to govern the taking of military enforcement action, it has never taken place in accordance with those provisions. Instead, the Security Council has been forced to rely upon the adoption of an 'authorisation model' where the application of coercive military measures is deemed necessary, whereby it confers authority upon willing actors to conduct military operations on its behalf. This approach has given rise to a number of consequences, including particularly the need for the Council to ensure that it exercises ultimate authority and control over action which it has authorised, as well as meaning that the existence of a viable military option will necessarily hinge upon the political considerations of those actors who are capable of discharging the functions which the Council wishes to entrust.

The chapter begins by explaining the 'authorisation' model that has been used by the Security Council in discharging its power to take military enforcement

1 The use of coercive military force by peacekeeping operations is not covered within this chapter, having been within the remit of the previous chapter.

DOI: 10.4324/9781003518105-8

action under Article 42 and the limitations which are placed upon the exercise of this power. We then outline a legal model by which it is contended military enforcement mandates ought to be created and exercised and consider the extent to which this has been complied with in the practice of the Council. The Council's practice in terms of the actors entrusted with military enforcement powers, their objectives and the targets of military action is then considered, before the problem of 'bypassing' the Council is addressed. Brief attention is then given to the military and political factors impacting upon the success of military enforcement measures, before we identify possible alternatives to the authorisation model approach. The chapter concludes with a brief reflection on the contemporary relevance of military enforcement action as a tool of the UN collective security system.

The 'authorisation' model for military enforcement action

The legality of the 'authorisation' model

The original Charter scheme for providing the Security Council with military forces through the conclusion of special agreements with member states has been detailed already.[2] We have also noted the failure of member states to conclude such agreements.[3] In the absence of any military enforcement capacity of its own, the Council has adopted a model for military enforcement measures whereby it confers authority in its resolutions for their application by willing states or organisations. While the provisions of Chapter VII envisaged that military enforcement action would be taken by the Council itself, using standby forces made available to it by member states in accordance with the special agreements provided for in Article 43, it is contended that the power conferred upon the Council to *take* military enforcement action embraces a power to *authorise* willing actors to take such action on its behalf. While not universally shared,[4] this expansive view of the Council's legal competence is now widely held among international lawyers.[5] If the Council has the power to take military enforcement action, it is logical that

2 See Chapter 2.

3 See Chapter 3.

4 See Quigley, J., 'The "privatization" of Security Council enforcement action: A threat to multilateralism,' *Michigan Journal of International Law*, 1996, v.17, pp.249–283, p.249.

5 See, for example, Sarooshi, D., *The United Nations and the Development of Collective Security* (Oxford: Oxford University Press, 2000), pp.143–153; McCoubrey, H. and White, N.D., *International Law and Armed Conflict* (Aldershot: Dartmouth, 1991), p.133, pp.144–145; Higgins, R., *Problems and Processes: International Law and How We Use it* (Oxford: Clarendon Press, 1994), pp.263–266; Corten, O., *The Law Against War: The Prohibition on the Use of Force in Contemporary International Law* (Oxford and Portland: Hart, 2010), pp.314–316; Blokker, N., 'Is the authorization authorized? Powers and practice of the UN Security Council to authorize the use of force by "coalitions of the able and willing,"' *European Journal of International Law*, 2000, v.11, n.3, pp.541–568, pp.547–555; Kirgis, F.L., 'The Security Council's first fifty years,' *American Journal of International Law*, 1995, v.89, pp.506–539, p.521.

it ought to have the lesser power to authorise others to perform this function on its behalf.[6] Several considerations can be invoked in support of this approach. First, given that express provision is made for the Council to authorise military enforcement action to be taken by regional arrangements in Article 53 of the UN Charter,[7] it would seem illogical to draw a distinction whereby the Council was unable to likewise authorise action to be taken by member states or groups of member states. Second, there is no reference in Article 42 to the subsequent provisions which were intended to provide the Security Council with the means to take military enforcement action, suggesting that the standby forces envisaged by Article 43 are best seen as simply one means which may be utilised for this purpose, but which are not a prerequisite for military enforcement action to be legally permissible. Reference to the doctrine of implied powers can also provide support for the Council being entitled to authorise other actors to apply military enforcement measures.[8] As Boutros Boutros-Ghali noted, '... when the Security Council entrusts enforcement tasks to groups of Member States ... this arrangement provides [it] with an enforcement capacity it would not otherwise have,'[9] thus enhancing its collective security capabilities. In light of the broad approach taken to implied powers by the ICJ in the *Expenses* case,[10] that conferring authorisation to conduct military enforcement action upon willing actors clearly furthers the UN's purposes and is not prohibited by any Charter provision militates in favour of its legality. The Security Council's flexible approach to its use of its military enforcement powers demonstrates again the evolutionary nature of the UN system and its ability to respond to the circumstances in which it finds itself.

Conditions applicable to the authorisation of military enforcement action

The Security Council enjoys broad discretionary powers with respect to its conferment of military enforcement powers on willing actors. Once one of the situations referred to by Article 39 has been determined to exist – a threat to the peace, breach of the peace, or act of aggression – the Council may proceed to sanction action under Article 42 involving the use of military measures. However, while the powers enjoyed by the Council in this regard are broad, they are not without any legal limitations.

6 For arguments based upon the law applicable to the delegation of powers, see Sarooshi, ibid, pp.16–19.

7 See Chapter 8 for further discussion of the regional military enforcement option.

8 See, for example, Blokker, supra n5, pp.547–549.

9 *Supplement to an Agenda for Peace*, UN Doc. A/50/60-S/1995/1, para.80.

10 *Certain Expenses of the United Nations*, ICJ Rep 1962, p.151. See Chapter 6.

Commentators such as Kelsen and Akehurst have suggested that the Council enjoys unlimited power in its determinations under Chapter VII.[11] However, the better view would appear to be that while the Council's power is discretionary and broad, it is still subject to some legal standards. There is support in practice for this. In the *Lockerbie* case heard by the International Court of Justice, while recognising the political discretion afforded the Security Council, Judge Jennings stated that actions of the Council were subject to a legal framework:

> that all discretionary powers of lawful decision-making are necessarily derived from the law, and are therefore governed and qualified by the law. This must be so if only because the sole authority of such decisions flows itself from the law. It is not logically possible to claim to represent the power and authority of the law, and at the same time, claim to be above the law.[12]

This was not the first time such a view had been expressed in the ICJ, it having been asserted in the much earlier *Admissions* case that the political character of the Council 'cannot release [it] from observance of the treaty provisions by which [it is] governed, when these provisions constitute limitations on [its] power.'[13] The ICTY drew a similar conclusion in the *Tadic* case, regarding the UN organs as being constrained by the constitutional framework provided by the UN Charter.[14] The Council itself has recognised that there are limits to its powers. For example, in the context of the adoption of Resolution 1483 on the occupation of Iraq, the president of the Security Council recognised that the powers exercised by the Council were not 'open-ended or unqualified' and 'should be exercised in ways that conform with the principles of justice and international law.'[15] Limitations on the Council's military enforcement powers may be found within the provisions of the UN Charter itself, which confer these powers, and under general international law.

Limitations imposed by the UN Charter

The Security Council may not authorise military enforcement action under Article 42 unless it has first determined that there exists a threat to the peace, breach of the peace or act of aggression under Article 39, there being a link between these two powers in Chapter VII of the UN Charter with Article 39 making explicit

11 Cryer R., 'The Security Council and Article 39: A threat to coherence?,' *Journal of Armed Conflict Law*, 1996, v.1, pp.161–95, p.165.

12 *Questions of Interpretation and Application of the 1971 Montreal Convention arising from the Aerial Incident at Lockerbie*, ICJ Rep 1998, p.110.

13 *Conditions of Admission of a State to Membership in the United Nations*, ICJ Rep, p.57, at p.64.

14 *Prosecutor v. Dusko Tadic (Jurisdiction)*, IT-94-1-AR72, 2 Oct. 1995, (1996) I.L.M 35.

15 UN Doc. S/PV.4761, pp.11–12.

reference to the Council's ability to follow such a determination by action under Articles 41 or 42.[16] The Council must also be satisfied that non-military sanctions have been, or are likely to be, ineffective in tackling the relevant threat to or breach of the peace.[17] The imposition of non-military sanctions is not a necessary prerequisite to military action, but the perception that they have been ineffective where applied, or are likely to be where they have not, is implicit in an authorisation of military enforcement measures.

It is widely recognised that decisions taken by the Council are of a political nature, and determining the existence of a threat to the peace or other situation referred to in Article 39 – thus paving the way for the possibility of military action – will be the product of political considerations on the part of the Council as opposed to the application of objective legal criteria. Legal restrictions upon the Council's ability to apply non-military sanctions were considered in Chapter 5 and broadly speaking, these are equally applicable to military enforcement action. It is not necessary to revisit these in significant detail, and instead we restrict ourselves to a recap of the key limitations. Under Article 25, member states agree to accept and carry out decisions of the Council 'in accordance with the present charter,' lending some support to the view that the Council must act in accordance with the provisions of the UN Charter. However, while this may represent a theoretical limitation on the powers of the Council, those powers are broad; it decides when a threat to the peace, breach of the peace or act of aggression exists and whether to initiate a military response. Furthermore, Article 25 may simply mean that member states are not obliged to comply with any decisions not taken in accordance with Charter provisions.[18] The Security Council is explicitly required to conform to the purposes and principles of the UN by Article 24(2) when discharging its duties. However, once again, it must be questioned as to what extent this practically restricts Council action. The purposes and principles listed in Articles 1 and 2 are sufficiently broad enough to serve as justification for most kinds of decisions and actions that can be envisaged on the part of the Council. Indeed, as the primary purpose of the UN is the maintenance of international peace and security[19] and the

16 Article 39 links these powers by providing that the Council 'shall determine the existence of any threat to the peace, breach of the peace, or act of aggression and shall … decide what measures shall be taken in accordance with Articles 41 and 42, to maintain or restore international peace and security.' This is further reinforced by Article 42's proviso that military action to be taken is 'as may be necessary to maintain or restore international peace and security.' See Frowein, J.A. and Krisch, N., 'Article 42,' in Simma, B. et al (eds), *The Charter of the United Nations: A Commentary* (2nd ed.) (Oxford: Oxford University Press, 2002), pp.749–759, at p.753; Corten, supra n5, pp.317–322.

17 Article 42 providing that the Council may initiate military enforcement action if it 'consider[s] that measures provided for in Article 41 would be inadequate or have proved to be inadequate.' See Frowein and Krisch, ibid.

18 Cryer, supra n11, p.167.

19 Article 1 (1).

authorisation of military measures can only come following a determination that there is at a minimum a threat to the peace, the military enforcement option can be seen as serving the very raison d'être of the UN. As Cryer noted, the purposes and principles are only likely to prove to be of much restriction on Security Council action in the most extreme of situations.[20] Thus, while under the UN Charter, the Security Council does not enjoy unlimited power, it is only possible to find any real restrictions upon this in rare incidences. Likewise, as discussed in Chapter 2, Article 2 (7), while proclaiming that 'nothing contained within the present Charter shall authorize the United Nations to intervene in matters which are essentially within the domestic jurisdiction of any state,' goes on to add that this 'shall not prejudice the application of enforcement measures under Chapter VII.' Therefore, this provision cannot be taken as constituting a limitation upon the powers of the Security Council to sanction military enforcement action, as when acting under Chapter VII, the domestic jurisdiction limitation places no restriction upon when the Council may sanction action. Furthermore, the broadened conception which has evolved over time of what the Council will deem to amount to 'threats to the peace' means that an increasing number of situations are considered to be of international concern and not reserved to the domestic jurisdiction of individual states. It is particularly pertinent to note that in its approach to the conceptualisation of threats to the peace and application of military enforcement measures, the Council does not require any prior use of force to have occurred, and certainly most military enforcement authorisations have not come in response to inter-state aggression.[21]

Limitations imposed by general international law

Under general international law, important potential limitations upon the Security Council's exercise of its powers can be found. The concepts of good faith, abuse of power and jus cogens have all been cited as potential restrictions upon the Council's exercise of its discretion.[22] The former two are somewhat similar in looking towards the motives that underlie particular actions. While there has been some suggestion that the notion of 'abuse of power' has yet to be firmly grounded as a principle of international law,[23] the need for 'good faith' to underpin the decisions and actions of international actors is based upon its recognition as a general principle of law within the meaning of Article 38 of the Statute of the ICJ,[24] the

20 Cryer, supra n11, pp.167–168.
21 See below.
22 Cryer, supra n11, p.169.
23 Cryer, supra n11, p.169.
24 Under Article 2 (2) of the UN Charter, member states are also obliged to fulfil their obligations under the Charter in good faith. See further De Wet, R., *The Chapter VII Powers of the United Nations Security Council* (Oxford and Portland: Hart, 2004), pp.195–198.

ICJ having declared it to be 'one of the basic principles governing the creation and performance of legal obligations.'[25] However, as with the limits to the Security Council's powers contained within the UN Charter, it is questionable whether this principle is likely to constitute a real restraint upon the Council in all but the rarest and most extreme cases. As Cryer noted, it would be difficult to show the presence of 'bad faith' behind a decision.[26] That decisions of the Council require the support of a qualified majority of its 15 members, including the acquiescence of all five permanent members to proceed, arguably offers a safeguard against this danger to some extent.

Perhaps the most significant limitation upon the Security Council's exercise of its Chapter VII powers is to be found in the concept of jus cogens, those peremptory norms of the international system from which no derogation is permitted.[27] Article 53 of the Vienna Convention on the Law of Treaties 1969 makes all treaties which conflict with jus cogens void, and any action taken which ran counter to recognised jus cogens would be unlawful. The relevance of jus cogens to the application of non-military sanctions has already been considered,[28] and the observations made in respect of Article 41 measures can equally be made in respect of military enforcement measures. Any resolution of the Security Council that sought to authorise military enforcement measures entailing massive human rights violations, genocide or some other violation of accepted peremptory norms of international law, would arguably be unlawful. However, while jus cogens serve as a crucial restriction on the exercise of Security Council powers, they are arguably likely to apply only in more extreme cases. It is difficult to see this collective body, endowed with the checks and balances found within its voting procedures, deciding to sanction such serious violations of international law.[29] As with non-military sanctions, military enforcement measures ought to be proportionate to the objectives that they are authorised to give effect to.[30] Actors discharging military enforcement mandates are also bound to respect the rules of international humanitarian law.[31]

Thus, while the Security Council is constrained by legal restrictions upon the purposes for which it chooses to authorise military enforcement action and the mandates which it confers upon those who are authorised to apply military

25 *Nuclear Tests Case (Australia v France)*, ICJ Rep, 1974, p.253, at p.268.

26 Cryer, supra n11, p.169.

27 For general discussion, see De Wet supra n24, pp.187–189; Hossain, K., 'The concept of jus cogens and the obligation under the U.N. Charter,' *Santa Clara Journal of International Law*, 2005, v.3, n.1, pp.72–98.

28 See Chapter 5.

29 See, however, Orakhelashvili, A., 'The impact of peremptory norms on the interpretation and application of United Nations Security Council resolutions,' *European Journal of International Law*, 2005, v.16, pp.59–88, at pp.59–60.

30 See Chapter 5.

31 UN Doc. ST/SGB/1999/13.

enforcement measures, these restrictions are likely to come into play in only the more extreme of cases. The Security Council clearly enjoys considerable discretion in its decision-making and action-taking in this respect.

A model for UN control of decentralised military enforcement action

It will be recalled that the original Charter scheme for military enforcement action envisaged a large degree of Security Council control over enforcement operations.[32] Using forces made available to it in accordance with special agreements made under Article 43, military action would be planned by the Council with the assistance of the MSC,[33] essentially the senior military officers of the permanent members.[34] Forces placed at the Security Council's disposal would come under the strategic direction of the MSC, which would in turn be responsible to the Council.[35] Clearly, the approach adopted by the Security Council when authorising member states to take enforcement action on its behalf differs markedly from this model. There are justifiable concerns that by merely authorising enforcement measures to be taken, an insufficient degree of control may be exercised by the Security Council over Chapter VII military action. As Delbruck argues, 'The needed allocation of law enforcement authority to decentralized law enforcement agents must not undermine the core principle of the international legal order, i.e., the monopolization, in principle, of forcible enforcement powers vested in the UN Security Council.'[36] Essentially, it is imperative that in authorising military enforcement action, the Council does not issue 'blank cheques' whereby it effectively stands back and abdicates any continuing responsibility for action taken by the ensuing operation.

The UN Charter attempts to centralise the use of force, making this the preserve of the Security Council. Even where states take action in pursuit of the theoretically independent right of self-defence, Article 51 obliges them to report to the Council upon the measures that they have taken.[37] Similarly, where regional arrangements conduct military enforcement action under the Council's authority, Article 54 requires that the Council 'shall at all times be kept fully informed

32 See Chapter 2.

33 Article 46.

34 See Article 47 (2), which provides that the MSC membership will comprise the chiefs of staff of the permanent members.

35 Article 47 (3).

36 Delbruck, J., 'The impact of the allocation of international law enforcement authority on the international legal order,' in Delbruck, J. (ed.), *Allocation of Law Enforcement Authority in the International System* (Berlin: Duncker & Humblot, 1995), at p.153.

37 Furthermore, the right of self-defence only exists until the Security Council has taken 'measures necessary' for the maintenance of international peace and security. For discussion, see Corten, supra n5, pp.472–479.

of activities undertaken or in contemplation under regional arrangements or by regional agencies for the maintenance of international peace and security.' It is therefore of crucial importance that action taken pursuant to a Security Council authorisation conforms to the objectives of the Council. As the body upon which the primary responsibility for the maintenance of international peace and security is conferred,[38] it is imperative that the Council be able to exercise a sufficient degree of control over any enforcement operation taken in the name of the UN. As Abass suggests, if the Security Council steps outside of the procedures intended to govern military enforcement action in the Charter provisions by authorising member states to conduct operations, it must then step back inside the provisions of the Charter by ensuring that such operations are subjected to the oversight of the Council, as 'failure to do this … makes the action liable to abuse and potentially an illegitimate one.'[39] Put simply, the Council cannot merely authorise military enforcement measures and then stand back. It must play a continuing role in their oversight and regulation.

It is also a generally accepted principle of the law governing delegation of powers that a body delegating its powers remains in a position to exercise overall authority and control over the use of these powers, making it important that the Security Council be capable of exercising some form of oversight of military enforcement operations authorised by it.[40] This means that in the context of military enforcement action, the Security Council may not delegate unrestricted command and control of operations to member states, but must remain in a position to exercise ultimate oversight of operations that it has authorised.[41] Member states willing to engage in enforcement action on behalf of the Security Council may have motives for doing so which go beyond the collective objectives of the Security Council, which could come into conflict with these and undermine the operation's level of fidelity to the Council's goals.[42] Reflecting one of the major criticisms of collective security – that states will only act where they perceive themselves as having interests at stake in doing so – this is an inherent political problem of a military enforcement model that relies upon the willingness of member states to provide the resources for action that is deemed necessary. Thus, a sufficient degree of control over any action they take is necessary to ensure that the national objectives of states participating in military enforcement operations do not result in action exceeding the mandate conferred upon them by the Security Council.

38 Article 24 (1).

39 Abass, A., *Regional Organisations and the Development of Collective Security: Beyond Chapter VIII of the UN Charter* (Oxford: Hart, 2004), p.78.

40 Sarooshi, supra n5, Chapter 1.

41 Sarooshi, supra n5, pp.32–35.

42 See below.

Experience has shown that the degree of control that the Security Council exercises over enforcement operations may be central to the willingness of its membership to support the adoption of military enforcement measures.[43] As the following discussion of meaningful tools of Security Council oversight will establish, broad international support is more likely to be forthcoming for operations that are subject to meaningful forms of UN oversight. A satisfactory method by which the Security Council can ensure that actors taking military enforcement action remain strictly committed to the objectives of the Council is through the adoption of a three-part approach to the authorisation of such action consisting of the following elements: (1) resolutions of the Security Council which authorise military enforcement action should be clear in providing that such measures are sanctioned and specifying the purposes for which they may be used; (2) authorisations contained in resolutions of the Council should not be open-ended, but rather should be of a fixed duration; and (3) the Security Council should make provision for adequate scrutiny of action taken by enforcement operations which it has authorised. Much emphasis has been placed upon these criteria in the relevant literature,[44] and as will become apparent, in the absence of a centralised UN military enforcement capacity, adherence to these requirements is crucial.

The provision of clear authority and objectives

The first essential element in ensuring that the Security Council is able to exercise adequate control over decentralised military enforcement action is to adopt resolutions which are relatively clear in setting out the objectives for which coercive military measures may be taken by those upon whom military enforcement powers are conferred. Resolutions should, first, be clear as to whether they are intended to serve as an authorisation to use military force. The Security Council's practice has demonstrated a tendency to omit any reference to the use of force, instead opting to authorise the use of 'all necessary measures,' 'all necessary means' or similar when conferring a military enforcement mandate. In the Council's first delegation of military enforcement authority, following North Korea's invasion of the Republic of Korea, it recommended member states 'furnish such assistance … *as may be necessary* to repel the armed attack and restore international peace and

43 To cite just two incidences, in respect of Resolution 770 concerning Bosnia, see the comments made in the Security Council by the representatives of India (pp.12–13), and Zimbabwe (pp.15–18); UN Doc. S/PV. 3106. On the authorisation granted by Resolution 940 for action in Haiti, see the comments of the Mexican (pp.4–5) and Cuban (p.6) representatives in the Council; UN Doc. S/PV. 3413.

44 See, for example, Blokker, supra n5, pp.560–567; White, N.D. and Ulgen, O., 'The Security Council and the decentralised military option: Constitutionality and function,' *Netherlands International Law Review*, 1997, v.44, pp.378–413, at pp.398–411; Wilson, G., 'The legal, military and political consequences of the "coalition of the willing" approach to UN military enforcement action,' *Journal of Conflict and Security Law*, 2007, v.12, pp.295–330, at pp.303–313.

security in the area.'[45] While making no reference to the *use of force*, by empowering states to provide assistance 'as may be necessary' to repel the armed attack by North Korea, there was little scope for doubt over the fact that the use of military force was sanctioned. This approach was repeated in the next significant military enforcement authorisation in response to Iraq's invasion of Kuwait,[46] the first occasion on which states acting under a Security Council mandate were empowered 'to use all necessary means' in carrying it out. Such language persisted in subsequent resolutions authorising military enforcement measures[47] through to the most recent authorisations of military measures, culminating in the action taken in respect of Libya, where member states were authorised to 'take *all necessary measures* … to protect civilians and civilian populated areas under threat of attack.'[48] The only exception to this practice is found in Resolution 221, adopted to permit the UK 'to prevent, by the *use of force* if necessary' vessels carrying goods to Southern Rhodesia in breach of the economic embargo imposed upon that state by an earlier resolution.[49] It is acknowledged that the omission of references to the use of force has on occasion probably been the product of diplomatic manoeuvres, sometimes designed to obtain China's acquiescence in the utilisation of military enforcement measures by the Security Council.[50] However, the most important consideration is that the Council adopts a consistent approach, allowing it to be clearly understood when it has sanctioned the use of military measures under Chapter VII. Arguably, the Council's approach to the authorisation of military enforcement measures has been relatively consistent, generally relying on the use of the universally recognised terms highlighted above for this purpose.

Resolutions authorising enforcement action should specify clearly the purposes for which it may be undertaken. Vague mandates risk those exercising them applying military measures to further objectives which were not within the contemplation of the Security Council, thus undermining its authority. This danger is acknowledged by Gaja when he writes that 'the objectives may be stated in the resolution in a way that leaves the intervening states a wide choice between

45 SC Res 8 (1950).

46 SC Res 678 (1990). Member states were authorised to '*use all necessary means* to uphold and implement resolution 660 and all subsequent resolutions and restore international peace and security in the area.'

47 With the exception of Resolution 221, all resolutions adopted by the Council authorising military enforcement measures have used the terms referred to or similar.

48 SC Res 1973 (2011).

49 SC Res 217 (1965).

50 China, more than any of the other permanent members, employs a relatively traditional approach to the matter of state sovereignty and is reluctant to support measures that constitute intervention in what it regards as internal affairs. It is, arguably, politically easier for China to abstain from voting on measures, as opposed to exercising its power of veto, where there is no express reference to the use of force. See Morphet, S., 'China as a permanent member of the Security Council,' *Security Dialogue*, 2000, v.31, n.2, pp.151–166; Gill, B. and Reilly, J., 'Sovereignty, intervention and peacekeeping: The view from Beijing,' *Survival*, 2000, v.42, n.3, pp.41–49.

the different kinds of military operation to be undertaken.'[51] He goes on to argue that 'the preservation of some essential elements of the Charter system appears to require that the Council refrain from giving "blank" authorizations, but keep a strict control over the objectives of the operation …'[52] Marrack Golding appears to agree, suggesting that the Council can avoid these kinds of problems by defining precisely the purpose for which force is authorised.[53] The desirability of clear mandates for the operations it authorises has been recognised by the Council itself.[54] The provision of clear objectives should also make it possible to identify when these have been achieved. The more specific they are, the easier this ought to be.

The Council's record in the provision of clear military enforcement mandates has been a mixed one. In the first military enforcement operation that it authorised, there was arguably a degree of ambiguity as to the scope of the mandate. Following North Korea's invasion of the Republic of Korea, Resolution 83 recommended that member states 'furnish such assistance to the Republic of Korea as may be necessary to repel the armed attack and to restore international peace and security in the area.' While the former part of the authorisation seems clear in envisaging action to expel North Korea from the Republic of Korea, this is unnecessarily complicated by the latter part, which gives rise to the possibility of a broader interpretation of the nature of the mandate based on its inclusion of the words 'to restore international peace and security in the area.' This was evidenced in the controversy over the decision of the participating forces to cross the 38th Parallel, separating the Republic of Korea from North Korea, which would appear to suggest a wider understanding of the mandate on their part.[55] While arguably an unreasonable interpretation of the resolution, which had been adopted in response to the armed attack by North Korea and explicitly made reference to the objective of repelling that armed attack, this could have been avoided with a more narrowly defined mandate focused solely upon the objective which it sought to achieve, removing any scope for disagreement over what it permitted.

Resolution 678, adopted to authorise a military enforcement operation to liberate Kuwait following Iraq's invasion, authorised:

> Member States co-operating with the Government of Kuwait, unless Iraq on or before 15 January 1991 fully implements … foregoing resolutions, to use all necessary means to uphold and implement Security Council resolution 660

51 Gaja, G., 'Use of force made or authorized by the United Nations,' in Tomuschat, C. (ed.), *The United Nations at Age Fifty: A Legal Perspective* (The Hague: Kluwer, 1995), at p.41.

52 Gaja, ibid.

53 Golding, M., 'The use of force by the United Nations,' *International Peacekeeping*, 1996, v.3, n.1, pp.1–18, at p.6.

54 See, eg., UN Doc. S/PRST/1998/35.

55 For discussion, see Withana, R., *Power, Politics, Law: International Law and State Behaviour During International Crises* (Leiden: Martinus Nijhoff, 2008), pp.101–105.

(1990) and all subsequent relevant resolutions and to restore international peace and security in the area.

While the reference to the need to uphold the earlier resolution, which had labelled Iraq's invasion a 'breach of the peace' and called for its departure, was difficult to misconstrue, the subsequent reference to the restoration of 'international peace and security in the area' led to its later invocation by states, principally the US and UK, as alleged authority for various military actions against Iraq in response to its failure to meet obligations in relation to weapons of mass destruction decommissioning, imposed by the terms of Resolution 687 which contained the ceasefire ending the Gulf conflict,[56] culminating in the full-scale invasion of the country in 2003. Essentially, the argument advanced by the states taking action against Iraq on each of these occasions was that as Iraq was in breach of terms contained in the ceasefire that ended the Gulf conflict,[57] the ceasefire was suspended, thus reviving the authority in Resolution 678 to restore 'international peace and security in the area,' which was once again threatened. There are various flaws with this reasoning. However, assessment of the merits of these legal arguments has been the subject of much spilled ink[58] and is not in need of further elaboration. While this author shares the view of most international lawyers that there was no legal basis in UN Security Council authorisation for the action, the key point for present purposes is that if Resolution 678 had been more specific, providing in clear terms that military action was authorised solely for the purpose of liberating Kuwait, it would have been difficult for it to be invoked as a basis for any of these later actions which it could not possibly have contemplated.

Although the Security Council can theoretically always resolve any uncertainty concerning the scope of an authorisation by amending it, in practice this is not satisfactory as any amendment to a mandate contained in an earlier resolution can be vetoed by a permanent member. A permanent member taking action on

56 For discussion of the legal issues raised by actions against Iraq during the 1990s, see Gray, C., 'After the cease-fire: Iraq, the Security Council and the use of force,' *British Yearbook of International Law*, 1994, v.65, pp.135–174; Lobel, J. and Ratner, M., 'Bypassing the Security Council: Ambiguous authorizations to use force, cease-fires and the Iraqi inspection regime,' *American Journal of International Law*, 1999, v.93, pp.124–154; White, N.D., 'The legality of the threat of force against Iraq,' *Security Dialogue*, 1999, v.30, n.1, pp.75–86.

57 Contained in SC Res 687 (1991).

58 See, for example, White, N.D., 'Self-defence, Security Council authority and Iraq,' in Burchill, R., White N.D. and Morris, J. (eds), *International Conflict and Security Law: Essays in Memory of Hilaire McCoubrey* (Cambridge: Cambridge University Press, 2005), pp.242–253; Sands, P., *Lawless World: America and the Making and Breaking of Global Rules* (London: Allen Lane, 2005), pp.174–203; Moir, L., *Reappraising the Resort to Force: International Law, Jus ad Bellum and the War on Terror* (Oxford: Hart, 2010), pp.83–106; Duffy, H., *The 'War on Terror' and the Framework of International Law* (Cambridge: Cambridge University Press, 2005), pp.197–209; Weller, M., *Iraq and the Use of Force in International Law* (Oxford: Oxford University Press, 2010), pp.144–173.

the basis of Security Council authorisation may prove unwilling to allow such an authorisation to be amended if this will serve to place limits upon its ability to pursue its own goals. Consider, for example, the difficulties which would have arisen had there been attempts to terminate or restrict the authority conferred by Resolution 678, given that its very existence formed a central plank of the legal justifications, however unconvincing, offered by the US, UK and their allies for various military actions against Iraq in the decade which followed the conclusion of the Gulf conflict.

Clear mandates should generate less disagreement as to the range of measures they sanction, and ought to make it easier for the Security Council to subject military enforcement action to scrutiny. To some extent, it is inevitable that Security Council resolutions authorising military enforcement action will have to leave some flexibility in the mandates that they provide, it being appreciated that the Council cannot foresee every possible eventuality which may arise. Indeed, on several occasions, the Security Council has had to adjust the mandates of operations in response to changing circumstances.[59] However, no broader authority should ideally be conferred upon those exercising military enforcement mandates than necessary at the time it is given.

While the examples of Korea and Iraq do not suggest an ideal approach to the conferment of clear military enforcement mandates, it is arguable that they represent outliers in the Security Council's approach to the authorisation of military enforcement measures, and there is evidence that on subsequent occasions the Council came to endow its resolutions with a greater degree of clarity.[60] For example, the resolutions authorising the presence of a multinational implementation force and a multinational stabilisation force in Bosnia to assist in the implementation of the Dayton peace agreement provided more detailed guidelines as to the range of purposes for which military force may be used.[61] The mandate conferred upon the Kosovo Force (KFOR) was also of a clearer nature, the purposes for which coercive measures could be used being specified in some detail.[62] The operation conducted by the multinational force deployed to the Democratic Republic of the Congo on the basis of Resolution 1484 was mandated to perform a number of specific functions which were clearly outlined in the resolution.[63] Likewise, the later multinational operation in Haiti was conferred with a clear,

59 The case of mandates conferred upon both NATO and the UNPROFOR peacekeeping operation during conflict in the former Yugoslavia during 1991–1995 is a prime example, as constant changes to the situation on the ground resulted in mandates being adjusted.

60 See, for example, Blokker, supra n5, pp.561–562; White and Ulgen, supra n44, pp.412–413.

61 SC Res 1031 (1995), paras.15–17; SC Res 1088 (1996), paras.19–21; SC Res 1174 (1998), paras.11–13; SC Res 1247 (1999), paras.11–13.

62 SC Res 1244 (1999), para.9.

63 Para.1.

limited mandate.[64] The mandate conferred upon the African mission in Mali was also detailed in clear terms.[65] Albeit just some examples, these nonetheless do indicate that the Security Council is capable of providing greater clarity in the resolutions it adopts to authorise military enforcement action. Considered alongside other patterns within the Council's practice relating to the elements of a desirable model of control over enforcement operations considered below, this is encouraging. Nonetheless, clear mandates cannot be assumed to have become the norm as disputes over the scale of force permitted by Resolution 1973 in relation to Libya evidenced. While the resolution's authorisation of the use of 'all necessary measures … to protect civilians and civilian populated areas under threat of attack'[66] was not particularly novel, the manner in which military action was conducted under its authority gave rise to some disagreements between states over what measures its terms permitted.[67] Although the resolution had sought to restrict military action to air strikes by providing that the mandate 'exclude[ed] a foreign occupation force of any form on any part of Libyan territory,'[68] the extent to which the authority to use force to protect civilians extended to combative action against the forces of the Gaddafi regime was the subject of some debate. The tensions arising from the wording of the salient parts of Resolution 1973 are laid bare by Wilmshurst's assertion that, 'It has to be acknowledged … that there may only be a thin line between repulsing government troops from civilian areas, on the one hand, and defeating those troops – leading to the fall of the government – on the other.'[69]

It seems apparent that the degree of clarity which resolutions are perceived to contain can be an important factor in determining the degree of support that they are able to obtain within the Security Council. For example, Resolution 770, authorising action in Bosnia, did not receive the backing of Zimbabwe, which considered that it left too much room for any states acting under it to define the scope of their acts.[70] China, which also abstained from voting on the adoption of the resolution, felt that its authorisation was so broad as to be tantamount to the

64 SC Res 1529 (2004), paras.2, 6.

65 SC Res 2085 (2012), para.9.

66 Para.4.

67 See Wilson, G., 'The United Nations Security Council, Libya and resolution 1973: Protection of civilians or tool for regime change?,' in Panara, C. and Wilson, G. (eds), *The Arab Spring: New Patterns for Democracy and International Law* (Leiden: Martinus Nijhoff, 2013), pp.101–121, at pp.108–113. See also Henderson, C., 'International measures for the protection of civilians in Libya and Côte d'Ivoire,' *International and Comparative Law Quarterly*, 2011, v.60, pp.767–778; Payandeh, M., 'The United Nations, military intervention, and regime change in Libya,' *Virginia Journal of International Law*, 2012, v.52, n.2, pp.355–405.

68 Supra n66.

69 Wilmshurst, E., 'The Use of Force,' in GeiB, R. and Melzer, N. (eds), *The Oxford Handbook of the International Law of Global Security* (Oxford: OUP, 2021), pp.821–836, at p.825.

70 UN Doc. S/PV.3106, at p.17.

issuing of a 'blank cheque.'[71] Similarly, Mexico, when abstaining on Resolution 940 pertaining to Haiti, expressed its view that 'a kind of carte blanche has been awarded to an undefined multinational force to act when it deems it to be appropriate.'[72] In the case of Resolution 1973 discussed above, pertaining to Libya, a number of states declined to support it and expressed their concerns over a lack of clarity regarding the scope for which the use of force had been authorised.[73] At the same time, those states voting in favour of resolutions authorising enforcement action have sometimes expressed their belief that the mandates conferred were clear. For example, Russia emphasised the clear mandate conferred upon the operation to be deployed to Rwanda on the basis of Resolution 929 in expressing its support for the resolution.[74]

Time limits

The second crucial means through which the Security Council can exert control over decentralised military enforcement operations is by imposing a time limit upon the duration of mandates conferred upon them, at the end of which the authorisation will cease. This provides the Council with a mechanism through which it can effectively respond to a situation in which it becomes apparent that an actor conferred with a military enforcement mandate is acting in a manner which exceeds or runs contrary to the authority with which it has been provided. The inclusion of a time limit allows the Security Council to retain overall control of military enforcement operations by facilitating the ready amendment or termination of a mandate, and its value in this regard has been recognised.[75] Theoretically, the Security Council can terminate or amend the parameters of any authorisation to take military enforcement action at any stage, yet as Golding notes, this is unlikely to be possible in a situation where an operation is conducted by a permanent member who may be inclined to veto such a change.[76] The case of Resolution 678 pertaining to Iraq is a case in point, where in addition to concerns over its lack of clarity, the absence of any time limit upon the authority to apply military enforcement measures against Iraq provided the US and other states with a basis upon which they would seek to justify actions taken against Iraq many years later. By specifying at the outset a date at which an authorisation will expire, the Council can ensure that it is able to bring to an end operations that do not remain committed to the objectives set for them or have served their purpose, or

71 Ibid, p.51.
72 UN Doc. S/PV.3413, at p.5.
73 UN Doc. S/PV.6498.
74 UN Doc. S/PV.3392, at p.2.
75 See Blokker, supra n5, pp.562–563; White and Ulgen, supra n44, pp.408–409.
76 Golding, supra n53, p.6.

change their mandates as it deems necessary. Of course, if the need for an operation remains, the duration of its mandate can be extended.[77]

In earlier authorisations of military enforcement action – for example, in Korea,[78] the Gulf,[79] Somalia,[80] the former Yugoslavia[81] and the first Haiti incident during 1994[82] – the Council did not impose any time limits upon the mandates that it created. The repercussions of this have been particularly noticeable in the case of Resolution 678. While part of the problem of this being later invoked for action that it could not have been designed to sanction stems from its ambiguous wording, the inclusion of a time limit within the resolution could have been of value in clearly restricting the duration for which the authorisation could have been invoked.

However, in its subsequent practice the Security Council came to more routinely place time limits upon the operations that it authorised. The first such situation was the restriction of the French-led Operation Turquoise in Rwanda by Resolution 929 to a two-month period.[83] This time limit was arguably important given concerns as to whether France was an appropriate actor to intervene in light of its historic involvement in Rwanda and was alluded to by other states during Security Council debates upon the adoption of the resolution.[84] Numerous resolutions thereafter contained time limits at the end of which mandates would expire, including in respect of military enforcement measures in Zaire,[85] Albania,[86] the Central African Republic,[87] Bosnia,[88] Côte D'Ivoire,[89] the Democratic Republic of the Congo[90] and Haiti.[91] Subsequent operations were authorised for time-limited

77 Indeed the Council has extended the duration of mandates on a number of occasions. Consider, for example, the mandate conferred upon the ISAF operation in Afghanistan. First authorised in SC Res 1386 (2001), its mandate was extended annually over a 13-year period until its conclusion in 2014. See, for example, SC Res 1776 (2007); SC Res 1833 (2008); SC Res 1890 (2009); SC Res 1943 (2010); SC Res 2011 (2011); SC Res 2069 (2012). The AU-led AMISOM is a similar case in point. First deployed on the basis of a six-month mandate (SC Res 1744 (2007)), its mandate was extended at periodic intervals until its eventual conclusion in 2022. See below.

78 SC Res 83 (1950).

79 SC Res 678 (1990).

80 SC Res 794 (1992).

81 SC Res 816 (1993), SC Res 836 (1993).

82 SC Res 940 (1994).

83 Para.4.

84 UN Doc. S/PV.3392, at p.2 (Russia) and p.11 (Oman).

85 SC Res 1080 (1996), para.8.

86 SC Res 1101 (1997), para.6; SC Res 1114 (1997), para.6.

87 SC Res 1125 (1997), para.4; SC Res 1136 (1997), para.5; SC Res 1152 (1998), para.6; SC Res 1155 (1998), para.5; SC Res 1159 (1998), para.7.

88 SC Res 1031 (1995), para.21; SC Res 1088 (1996), para.18; SC Res 1174 (1998), para.10; SC Res 1247 (1998), para.10.

89 SC Res 1464 (2003), para.9.

90 SC Res 1484 (2003), para.1.

91 SC Res 1529 (2004), para.2.

periods, often renewed. For example, AMISOM in Somalia was first authorised for a six-month period and renewed upon numerous occasions afterwards,[92] an EU operation in Chad and the Central African Republic was sanctioned for one year,[93] while the deployment of the African International Support Mission to Mali (AFISMA) was similarly endowed with a year-long mandate.[94] Although not all recent Security Council resolutions sanctioning the use of military enforcement measures have included time limits upon the duration of the relevant mandates – including those provided for forces in Kosovo[95] and East Timor[96] and that pertaining to Libya[97] – it has arguably come to represent the normal practice of the Council to impose them.

There is evidence to suggest that states do attach importance to the imposition of time limits upon military enforcement mandates, again suggesting the importance of their existence in obtaining support for the adoption of military enforcement measures. For example, in relation to the action in Haiti authorised by Resolution 940, the Cuban representative commented that, 'It is alarming to see the lack of any time-limits for the operation.'[98] By contrast, commenting upon the operation in Zaire authorised by Resolution 1080, the Egyptian representative considered it worth noting that it was a temporary force.[99]

Scrutiny by the Security Council

The third key element of an adequate model of Security Council control over decentralised military enforcement action is the existence of some form of scrutiny by the Council of operations while they are taking place. Clarity in mandates can prevent abuse or make it easier to identify when this occurs. The adoption of time limits for operations provides a means for responding to this without having to face the problem of the permanent members' veto power, which may be used to prevent the adjustment or termination of a mandate. The existence of meaningful

92 SC Res 1744 (2007), para.4. AMISOM was reauthorised at regular intervals for short periods. See, for example, SC Res 1772 (2007); SC Res 1801 (2008); SC Res 1831 (2008); SC Res 1863 (2009); SC Res 1910 (2010); SC Res 1964 (2010); SC Res 2010 (2011); SC Res 2036 (2012); SC Res 2073 (2012); SC Res 2182 (2014); SC Res 2221 (2015); SC Res 2297 (2016); SC Res 2355 (2017); SC Res 2372 (2017); SC Res 2415 (2018); SC Res 2431 (2018); SC Res 2472 (2019); SC Res 2520 (2020); SC Res 2563 (2021); SC Res 2568 (2021). Its final authorisation was provided by SC Res 2614 (2021).

93 SC Res 1778 (2007), para.6.

94 SC Res 2085 (2012), para.9.

95 SC Res 1244 (1999).

96 SC Res 1264 (1999).

97 SC Res 1973 (2011). However, for the first time, the Security Council took the step of expressly terminating the authority conferred by the resolution once its continuation was deemed no longer necessary. See SC Res 2016 (2011), para.5.

98 UN Doc. S/PV.3413, p.6.

99 UN Doc. S/PV.3713, p.17.

scrutiny by the Council serves as a necessary link between these two elements; it is crucial that a means exists by which the Security Council is in an informed position to enable it to assess the manner in which a mandate is being performed so that it is able to respond as it deems necessary.

Scrutiny of military enforcement operations can be achieved through the imposition of a requirement that the Council be provided with regular reports upon the manner in which they are being conducted. Much significance has been attached to the use of a reporting process as a means of enabling the Security Council to exercise sufficient control over the way in which powers of military enforcement are exercised by member states.[100] As Sarooshi notes, it is significant that regional arrangements and states acting in self-defence are required under express Charter provisions to report to the Council on action which they have taken,[101] making it logical to impose this requirement upon other actors engaged in military enforcement action.[102] By being provided with regular reports, the Council is theoretically provided with the information it needs to be able to draw conclusions in respect of the performance of military enforcement operations, placing it in an informed position to bring to an end, or adjust the mandates of, any operations where it considers this to be the most appropriate response to the manner in which they have been conducted. To strengthen the reliability of information supplied to the Council, it may request reports from parties other than those actors who are conducting the operations, such as the UN Secretary-General or one of his special representatives.[103]

Post–Cold War practice in this regard has been encouraging. It has become the norm for the Council to impose a reporting obligation upon those to whom it confers these powers.[104] Significantly, the requirements made by the Council with regard to the provision of reports gradually became more demanding. Resolution 678 merely required states acting pursuant to its authorisation to keep the Council informed of action taken, there being no timeframe stipulated for the submission of reports to the Council. Subsequent authorisations simply required the

100 See Blokker, supra n5, pp.563–565; White and Ulgen, supra n44, p.410.

101 By Articles 54 and 51 respectively.

102 Sarooshi, supra n5, pp.160–163.

103 See, for example, SC Res 1973 (2011), para.12, requiring the Secretary-General to report to the Council on action taken by member states to enforce the no-fly zone over Libya.

104 See, for example, SC Res 794 (1992), para.18; SC Res 929 (1994), para.10; SC Res 940 (1994), para.13; SC Res 1031 (1995), para.25; SC Res 1080 (1996), para.11; SC Res 1101 (1997), para.9; SC Res 1114 (1997), para.9; SC Res 1125 (1997), para.6; SC Res 1136 (1997), para.7; SC Res 1174 (1998), SC Res 1216 (1998), para.7; SC Res 1247 (1998), para.18; SC Res 1244 (1999), para.20; SC Res 1264 (1999), para.12; SC Res 1386 (2001), para.9; SC Res 1464 (2003), para.10; SC Res 1483 (2003), para.24; SC Res 1484 (2003), para.9; SC Res 1529 (2004), para.9; SC Res 1674 (2006), para.15; SC Res 1778 (2007), para.12; SC Res 1973 (2011), paras.4, 11; SC Res 2085 (2012), para.10; SC Res 2568 (2021), para.39.

provision of 'regular reports.'[105] Later, the Council came to specify more explicitly the intervals at which reports were required, often this being monthly[106] or even more frequently,[107] albeit not in all circumstances.[108] Significantly, however, the Council's prominent resolution on Libya required that states inform the secretary-general 'immediately' of any measures taken under the resolution.[109]

There are clear indications that the provision of reports upon the conduct of operations is again valued highly by states. Their comments during Security Council meetings at which military enforcement authorisations have been considered provide clear evidence of this. Take, for example, the adoption of Resolution 1031, which authorised the deployment of IFOR to oversee the implementation of the Dayton peace accord in Bosnia. At the time of its adoption, a number of states alluded to the importance of the imposition of a reporting obligation, which China believed was necessary so that IFOR could accept the control of and guidance from the Security Council,[110] and Ukraine felt served as an appropriate means of political monitoring by the Council.[111] Similar views had already been expressed by states on earlier occasions.[112] Later, in the Security Council debate upon the adoption of Resolution 1483 on the occupation of Iraq, it is interesting to note the comments of the representatives of France, Germany and Russia. All three states had opposed the US-led invasion of Iraq during 2003, yet in voting in favour of the resolution which conferred a mandate on the occupying powers in the process of reconstruction, all stressed the importance of the provision of reports to the Council in enabling the UN to play a meaningful role in the process.[113] The representative of France stated that 'the Security Council must ... continue to be closely involved ... in particular through the information which the Special Representative, the United States and the United Kingdom will regularly provide it.'[114] Similarly, the German representative noted that 'the Security Council is to be fully informed by the Secretary-General as well as [the US and UK],'[115] and Russia's representative stated that 'the Council will regularly monitor the entire process through consideration of reports ...'[116]

105 SC Res 794 (1992); SC Res 929 (1994); SC Res 940 (1994).
106 For example, SC Res 1031 (1995); SC Res 1136 (1997); SC Res 1247(1999). The Council has also imposed reporting requirements at 90-day intervals. See, eg., SC Res 2568 (2021), para.39.
107 For example, SC Res 1080 (1996); SC Res 1101 (1997).
108 For example, SC Res 1386 (2001), para.9.
109 SC Res 1973 (2011), para.4.
110 UN Doc. S/PV.3607, p.14.
111 UN Doc. S/PV.3607, p.29.
112 For example, UN Doc. S/PV.3413, p.20; UN Doc. S/PV.3145, pp.29–30.
113 Para.24.
114 UN Doc. S/PV.4761, p.4.
115 UN Doc. S/PV.4761, p.5.
116 UN Doc. S/PV.4761, p.8.

Practice under the 'authorisation' model

The actors entrusted with military enforcement mandates

Having outlined the legal framework that is arguably applicable to the authorisation of military enforcement operations, we now move to consider the practice of the Security Council under this model in terms of the actors to which it has entrusted these powers, the purposes for which military enforcement mandates have been conferred and the targets of these. Essentially, the application of military enforcement measures has been entrusted by the Security Council to its member states acting either individually, in small groups or in broader ad hoc coalitions of the willing, or to regional arrangements.[117] It is unusual for the Council to confer authority to take military enforcement upon a single state. Indeed, the only occasion on which the Council has entrusted a military enforcement mandate to a single state expressly named in its authorising resolution occurred in 1966 when Resolution 221 specifically 'called upon the ... United Kingdom ... to prevent, by the use force if necessary, the arrival at Beira of vessels reasonably believed to be carrying oil destined for Southern Rhodesia' in breach of the Council imposed embargo,[118] 'and to arrest and detain the tanker known as Joanna V.'

In the post–Cold War era, the Council has authorised military enforcement measures that it is envisaged will be principally conducted by the forces of a particular state, but has refrained from referring to that state by name in its resolutions. In response to situations existing in Somalia and Haiti, US-led military interventions were sanctioned. Resolution 794 implicitly conferred authority specifically upon the US by reference to an offer it had made to conduct the operation in question.[119] Resolution 940 conferred authority upon a US-led multinational force to restore to power the democratically elected government of President Aristide in Haiti. Strictly speaking, the relevant resolution referred to:

> Member States ... form[ing] a multinational force under unified command and control ... to use all necessary means to facilitate the departure ... of the military leadership ... the prompt return of the legitimately elected President and the restoration of the legitimate authorities ... and to establish and maintain a secure and stable environment that will permit implementation of the Governors Island Agreement.[120]

117 There is some debate over what constitutes a 'regional arrangement' in the sense of Chapter VIII of the UN Charter, on which see the next chapter. The term is used here broadly to encompass action taken by regionally based bodies or organisations.

118 SC Res 217 (1965).

119 Para.8. See UN Doc. S/24868.

120 Para.5.

However, this authorisation followed a US offer to lead such an operation and is best seen as the conferment of authority upon it for the purposes specified, although the more general language contained within the resolution left scope for other states to participate in the operation. Similarly, in respect of intervention in Rwanda, Resolution 929 referred to 'member states co-operating with the Secretary-General,'[121] yet followed a French offer to lead the operation,[122] and was clearly intended as providing authority for this initiative. Resolution 1101 again conferred authority on 'member states participating' in the multinational protection force to be deployed to Albania,[123] although the Council noted the willingness of Italy to lead the operation.[124] Resolution 1264 expressly conferred authority upon a 'multinational force under a unified command structure' to be deployed to East Timor, but this followed an Australian offer to lead such an operation,[125] indicating that Australia was envisaged as the principal actor that would act on the mandate.

On other occasions, the Council has crafted more general authorising resolutions which confer authority on states willing to participate in the relevant operations, acting through forums of their choosing. In a number of situations, this has followed, or given rise to, the formation of coalitions of the willing for the purposes of conducting the military operations. Following the invasions of the Republic of Korea and Kuwait, authority was conferred upon 'Members of the United Nations'[126] and 'Member States'[127] respectively, with action ultimately being taken by a US-led coalition comprising a substantial number of states.[128] While the US contributed the bulk of the forces, the wider participation of other states enhanced the perception of the operations as UN actions as opposed to US operations, potentially improving their legitimacy in the eyes of the wider international community. Similar language has been employed within a number of other resolutions authorising military enforcement measures. For example, Resolution 1386 authorised 'Member States participating in the International Security Assistance Force to use all necessary measures to fulfil its mandate.' Similarly, Resolution 1484 conferred enforcement authority upon 'Member States participating' in the interim emergency force authorised in the Democratic Republic of

121 Para.4.
122 UN Doc. S/1994/734.
123 Para.4.
124 Para.3. See UN Doc. S/1997/258.
125 UN Doc. S/1999/975.
126 SC Res 83 (1950).
127 SC Res 678 (1990).
128 The Korean operation comprised forces from 16 states. On the relevant numbers, see Bowett, D.W., *United Nations Forces* (London: Stevens & Sons, 1964), pp.43–77. Twenty-eight states contributed forces to the operation to liberate Kuwait. For details, see Foster, E. and Hollis, R., *War in the Gulf: Sovereignty, Oil and Security* (London: Royal United Services Institute for Defence Studies, 1991), pp.162–174.

Congo, as did Resolution 1529 in relation to the multinational operation authorised for Haiti.[129] Military enforcement powers were also conferred upon a multinational force in Iraq,[130] to which member states were urged to contribute.[131] The ad hoc coalitions that have been formed to undertake operations entrusted with military enforcement powers have ranged from small-scale coalitions involving a limited number of states to the larger coalitions that acted in the Korean and Gulf situations.

One benefit of naming specific states in resolutions authorising military enforcement measures is that taking action under the relevant mandates can be restricted to a limited number of states, which may be desirable where political considerations militate in favour of this or warrant the exclusion of certain other states from taking action on the basis of the Council's authority. Although the Security Council has implicitly referred in some of its resolutions to particular states upon whom military enforcement powers are being conferred, it has not availed itself of its power to exclude particular states from acting under general military enforcement mandates that are not formally conferred upon any particular state. Article 48 (1) of the UN Charter provides that action 'taken for the maintenance of international peace and security shall be taken by all the Members of the United Nations or by some of them, as the Security Council may determine.' This provision takes account of the fact that there may be legitimate pragmatic reasons why particular states ought not to participate in certain actions. Arguably, the only possible instance of the principle underlying Article 48 (1) being implemented is found in Resolution 678's conferment of authority upon states 'co-operating with the government of Kuwait.' These words restricted military enforcement authority to Kuwait's allies and prevented against the danger of Israel taking action against Iraq under Resolution 678's mandate,[132] which posed a risk of fracturing the coalition assembled to liberate Kuwait and giving rise to a fresh Arab–Israeli armed conflict. That the Council is not usually so prescriptive in tasking mandates upon willing states can be attributed to the fact that generally it will be known in advance who is to conduct a given operation. The Council's resolutions are principally a means of granting a seal of approval to action, rather than creating a mandate in the hope that an offer to discharge it will be subsequently forthcoming.[133]

129 Para.6.

130 SC Res 1511 (2003), para.13.

131 Ibid, para.14.

132 During the Gulf conflict, however, Israel was hit by missiles launched by Iraq, which would arguably have given it a right to take some form of action in self-defence, it having been the victim of an armed attack within the meaning of Article 51.

133 On the 'legitimising' function of the Security Council, see Claude, I.L., 'Collective legitimization as a political function of the United Nations,' in Kratochwil, F. and Mansfield, E.D. (eds), *International Organization: A Reader* (New York: Harper Collins, 1994), pp.192–201.

Military enforcement action conducted by regional arrangements is addressed specifically in Chapter VIII. There is clear authority in Article 53 for the Council's conferment of military enforcement powers upon these bodies. For present purposes, it will suffice to note that Security Council resolutions have conferred military enforcement mandates to be exercised by a number of regional organisations. As with mandates conferred upon member states generally, the Council has not traditionally referred to regional arrangements expressly by name, although it has become more common to do so over time. For example, Resolution 1464 conferred military enforcement authority on 'member states participating in ECOWAS [Economic Community of West African States].'[134] Following Resolution 1575's specific reference to 'member states acting through or in co-operation with the EU' in Bosnia,[135] the EU was later expressly authorised to deploy an operation to Chad and the Central African Republic, empowered under Chapter VII to use 'all necessary means' to perform its mandate.[136] The African Union has also been named in authorising resolutions.[137] On other occasions, however, resolutions have indirectly referred to the organisation that it is envisaged will act upon the authority conferred.[138]

On other occasions, resolutions have conferred a degree of choice upon would-be actors as to the forum through which they will act by conferring authority to take enforcement measures upon 'member states acting nationally or through regional arrangements or agencies,'[139] 'member states and relevant international organizations'[140] or states 'acting nationally or through regional organizations or arrangements.'[141] Arguably, the Council's approach to identifying the actors upon which it confers military enforcement mandates is essentially a pragmatic one that allows the most willing and able states or bodies to take action.

The objectives of military enforcement action

The Security Council's authorisation of military enforcement measures is related to responding to a threat to the peace, breach of the peace or act of aggression that the Council has determined to have arisen, although most determinations of the existence of a threat to the peace have not resulted in the adoption of military

134 Para.9.

135 Para.10. Note also SC Res 1671 (2006), which conferred authority on the EU-led European Union Force (EUFOR) operation.

136 SC Res 1778 (2007), para.6.

137 Pertaining to Somalia, beginning with SC Res 1744 (2007), para.4, which conferred authority on 'member states of the African Union.'

138 See, for example, SC Res 1031 (1995), para.14; SC Res 1088 (1996), para.18. Both provisions referred to an organisation named in an annex, which was NATO.

139 For example, SC Res 787 (1992), para.12; SC Res 816 (1993), para.4.

140 For example, SC Res 1244 (1999), para.7.

141 For example, SC Res 1973 (2011), para.4.

enforcement measures. Nor would this be appropriate in many situations, particularly where the source of the threat stems from, say, a natural environmental phenomenon or public health epidemic or pandemic. From a legal perspective, the objective of military enforcement measures is to remove the situation of concern which gave rise to their authorisation. However, it is possible to detect a number of underlying objectives that have given rise to the adoption of military enforcement measures, demonstrating the conceptualisation of collective security by the Security Council in terms which go beyond narrow traditional notions of the concept. These broadly fall under the following heads: reversing inter-state aggression, enforcing non-military sanctions, improving humanitarian conditions and/or protecting civilians at risk of harm, restoring a democratically elected government and supporting the implementation of peace agreements. It will be noted that when considering the objectives of military enforcement action, particularly in the post–Cold War era, we can identify an increased use of this tool to further a conception of collective security that has at its core human security.

Reversing inter-state aggression

Although traditional notions of collective security regarded it as an agreement among states that they would collectively respond to an attack against any one of their number,[142] only twice within the UN era has military enforcement action been sanctioned in response to one state's attack upon another. Many cases of inter-state aggression during the UN era have not even resulted in any determination under Article 39 by the Security Council due to the existence of the veto power and/or the presence of political interests of the P5 militating against such a determination. This has been most recently the case in respect of Russia's invasion of Ukraine in 2022. The first invocation of the Security Council's military enforcement powers came in 1950, when in Resolution 83, it called upon members to 'furnish such assistance to the Republic of Korea as may be necessary to repel the armed attack and to restore international peace and security in the area.' Similarly, Resolution 678 adopted following Iraq's invasion of Kuwait authorised member states to 'use all necessary means to uphold and implement Security Council Resolution 660 (1990) and all subsequent relevant resolutions and to restore international peace and security in the area,'[143] collectively understood as authority for a coalition of states to take military action to reverse the invasion and liberate Kuwait. In both cases, the Council's objectives were successfully implemented, with the Republic of Korea and Kuwait both being liberated following military action by a US-led coalition of states. However, although both actions were clearly authorised for the objective of reversing inter-state aggression, as noted above, problems within the

142 See Chapter 1.
143 Para.2.

authorising resolutions gave rise to wider interpretations by states than could possibly have been envisaged by the Council.[144]

Enforcing non-military sanctions

On a number of occasions, the Security Council has sought to strengthen the observance of non-military sanctions that it has imposed by authorising the application of military measures to prevent their violation. In the Council's only authorisation of military enforcement measures during the Cold War apart from the Korean action, the UK was given limited authority in Resolution 221 to use force if necessary to intercept a ship believed to be carrying goods in breach of the trade embargo that had earlier been imposed upon Southern Rhodesia.[145] In the early post–Cold War era, military enforcement powers were conferred upon relevant actors to ensure that non-military sanctions imposed against Iraq, the Federal Republic of Yugoslavia and Haiti were observed. Following the imposition of economic sanctions upon Iraq following its invasion of Kuwait,[146] in Resolution 665, the Council called upon:

> Member states co-operating with the government of Kuwait which are deploying maritime forces to the area to use such measures commensurate to the specific circumstances as may be necessary … to halt all inward and outward maritime shipping, in order to inspect and verify their cargoes and destinations and to ensure strict implementation of [the sanctions].[147]

Similar authorising language was employed in respect of measures to enforce an economic embargo imposed upon the Federal Republic of Yugoslavia by Resolution 757 and expanded by Resolution 787. Calling upon states acting nationally or through regional agencies or arrangements, identical language was used to that contained in Resolution 665 to permit the interception and inspection of maritime shipping to ensure sanctions were not being breached.[148] Similar authority was provided for the use of military measures to enforce an economic embargo that had been imposed on Haiti.[149]

The practice of strengthening non-military sanctions with the conferment of authority to take more robust measures to ensure their enforcement has continued up to the present day, although there has been a shift in the language adopted by the Security Council whereby member states are directed to 'take the necessary

144 See above.
145 SC Res 217 (1965). See above discussion.
146 SC Res 661 (1990).
147 Para.1.
148 SC Res 787 (1992), para.12.
149 SC Res 875 (1993), para.1.

measures' to prevent the transmission of arms or entry of individuals where these are subject to arms embargoes or travel bans respectively. Such authority can be detected, for example, in resolutions pertaining to sanctions regimes imposed in respect of South Sudan,[150] Somalia,[151] Haiti[152] and the Central African Republic,[153] over a period spanning into the 2020s. The use of military measures to enforce non-military sanctions arguably represents an innovative use of Article 42 and demonstrates the Security Council's willingness to recognise the relationship which can exist between measures under Articles 41 and 42, with limited action being taken under the latter provision to strengthen the effectiveness of action under the former.

Contributing to humanitarian goals/protecting civilians

The most common objective of UN-authorised military enforcement operations has concerned the advancement of humanitarian goals, in particular through the protection of civilians at risk of harm. This has marked a significant development within the UN collective security system. As noted in Chapter 1, traditional conceptions of collective security were very much concerned with the protection of states from external threats and paid no real attention to the well-being of individuals. The development of military enforcement action to the point where it is primarily sanctioned for humanitarian purposes exemplifies the evolution of collective security as practised within the UN Charter framework particularly well. It was noted in the previous chapter that it has become increasingly common for UN peacekeeping operations to be entrusted with a mandate that includes responsibility for the protection of civilians. At the same time, most military enforcement measures have also come to be authorised to effect humanitarian purposes in situations whereby threats to the peace are posed *within* states. While the exact formulation of these mandates has varied, they all have shared the common objective of the alleviation of humanitarian suffering by civilians during situations in which armed conflict has been present.

The first wave of military enforcement measures for humanitarian purposes was found in the responses to the conflicts that dominated the UN agenda in the early to mid-1990s: former Yugoslavia, Somalia and Rwanda. Beginning with its response to the consequences of civil war in Bosnia, the Security Council authorised 'all measures necessary to facilitate in coordination with the United Nations,' the delivery of humanitarian assistance to Sarajevo and wherever needed in Bosnia.[154] Subsequent resolutions built upon this by authorising the

150 See, e.g., SC Res 2206 (2015), para.9, SC Res 2428 (2018), para.5.
151 See, eg., SC Res 2713 (2023), para.4.
152 See, e.g., SC Res 2653 (2022), para.5, SC Res 2752 (2024), para.2.
153 See, eg., SC Res 2745 (2024), paras.2 & 4.
154 SC Res 770 (1992), para.2.

use of all necessary measures to ensure compliance with a flight ban in Bosnian airspace,[155] and to support the UNPROFOR peacekeeping operation in protecting a number of designated safe areas.[156] Around the same time, the Council responded to the humanitarian consequences of civil war in Somalia by authorising the US-led UNITAF 'to use all necessary means to establish as soon as possible a secure environment for humanitarian relief operations in Somalia.'[157] Following genocide in Rwanda, the French-led Operation Turquoise was authorised to use all necessary means to provide protection to those at risk and was specifically tasked with

> … the security and protection of displaced persons, refugees and civilians at risk in Rwanda, including through the establishment and maintenance, where feasible, of secure humanitarian areas; and provide security … for the distribution of relief supplies and humanitarian relief operations.[158]

This trend continued in later years. In 1996, the Council authorised action in eastern Zaire for the purpose of '[facilitating] the immediate return of humanitarian organizations and the effective delivery by civilian relief organizations of humanitarian aid.'[159] The multinational Operation Alba, deployed to Albania in the midst of a severe humanitarian crisis, was empowered to 'facilitate the safe and prompt delivery of humanitarian assistance, and to help create a secure environment for the missions of international organizations … including those providing humanitarian assistance,'[160] and INTERFET was similarly to take all necessary measures 'to facilitate humanitarian assistance operations' in East Timor.[161] In Resolution 1464, pertaining to the Côte d'Ivoire, we find one of the first explicit references within a mandate to the term 'protection of civilians' as a task conferred upon ECOWAS and French forces assisting them.[162] Around the same time, Operation Artemis in the Democratic Republic of the Congo was authorised to take all necessary measures to:

> contribute to the stabilization of … security conditions … improvement of the humanitarian situation in Bunia, to ensure the protection of the airport, the internally displaced persons in the camps in Bunia and … the safety of the

155 SC Res 816 (1993), para.4.
156 SC Res 836 (1993), para.10.
157 SC Res 794 (1992), para.10.
158 SC Res 929 (1994).
159 SC Res 1080 (1996), para.3.
160 SC Res 1101 (1997), para.2.
161 SC Res 1264 (1999), para.3.
162 Para.9.

> civilian population, United Nations personnel and the humanitarian presence in the town.[163]

As the first decade of the twenty-first century advanced, the African Union mission in Somalia was authorised to 'take all necessary measures' to fulfil a broad mandate which included 'the creation of the necessary security conditions for the provision of humanitarian assistance,'[164] and the EU operation in Chad and the Central African Republic enjoyed similar authority 'to contribute to protecting civilians in danger, particularly refugees and displaced persons [and] to facilitate the delivery of humanitarian aid.'[165]

This trend continued with the Security Council's conferment upon those states intervening in Libya following the uprising against the Gaddafi regime to take all necessary measures to 'protect civilians and civilian populated areas under threat of attack,'[166] while shortly thereafter the AFISMA operation deployed to Mali was tasked with a broad mandate that included 'to support the Malian authorities in their primary responsibility to protect the population … [and] … to create a secure environment for the civilian-led delivery of humanitarian assistance.'[167]

Restoring a democratically elected government

In addition to more general humanitarian mandates discussed above, the Security Council has expressly sanctioned military enforcement action to restore to power a democratically elected government. Following the seizure of power by a military junta in Haiti from the democratically elected president, Jean-Bertrand Aristide, Resolution 940 authorised relevant states to use 'all necessary means to facilitate the departure from Haiti of the military leadership … the prompt return of the legitimately elected President and the restoration of the legitimate authorities.'[168] That the objective of military action was the restoration of the democratically elected government was in no doubt, this being the clearly expressed objective of Resolution 940's mandate. In the event, a high-profile US delegation persuaded the military junta to relinquish power prior to the arrival of a US force,[169] suggesting the existence of the authority conferred by Resolution 940 was in itself sufficient to achieve the Council's objective. While the only formal invocation of

163 SC Res 1484 (2003), para.1.
164 SC Res 1744 (2007), para.4 (e).
165 SC Res 1778 (2007), para.6 (a) (i)–(ii).
166 SC Res 1973 (2011), para.4.
167 SC Res 2085 (2012), para.9 (d)–(e).
168 Para.4.
169 This comprised former President Jimmy Carter, the chair of the US Senate Armed Services Committee, Senator Sam Nunn, and former chair of the joint chiefs of staff, Colin Powell.

this purpose,[170] it is significant that the seizure of power by the military junta had given rise to a humanitarian crisis in Haiti that had been acknowledged by the Council. In this sense, action authorised by Resolution 940 can also be regarded as furthering humanitarian objectives: the humanitarian crisis was at the heart of the threat to the peace requiring redress, and the restoration of the deposed regime formed a key part of the solution.

Implementing peace agreements

From the mid-1990s, powers of military enforcement came to be conferred upon multinational forces conferred with responsibility for the implementation of peace agreements. This began with the mandates conferred upon the NATO-led Implementation Force (IFOR) and Stabilisation Force (SFOR) operations deployed to Bosnia-Herzegovina as part of the Dayton peace accords,[171] later followed by KFOR in Kosovo.[172] While the extensive use of force was not the objective of such mandates, military enforcement authority was essentially provided so that the use of force could be exercised if necessary to enable the relevant operations to discharge the humanitarian and security aspects of their mandates. The International Security Assistance Force (ISAF) deployed to Afghanistan post 9/11 was similarly empowered to use military enforcement measures in support of its mandate to support the new Afghan government in creating new governmental institutions and structures.[173]

Targets of military enforcement action

Unlike the actors entrusted with military enforcement mandates and their objectives, there has been no reference in authorising resolutions to the actors or entities which are the targets of military enforcement mandates, although this will usually be obvious by reference to the specified purposes of the authorised action. Identifying the targets of military enforcement action has been most

170 The Security Council has, however, issued military enforcement mandates in the aftermath of military coups in broader support of peacebuilding or stabilisation processes, that conferred upon the ECOWAS-led AFISMA force in Mali being a good case in point. See, e.g., SC Res 2085 (2012). It can be noted also that military enforcement action taken under UN authority has indirectly led to the overthrow of governments. The example of Libya is a case in point, where NATO military action in support of the protection of civilians weakened the military capacity of the Gaddafi regime and strengthened the position of the rebel forces that ultimately toppled the regime. See Wilson, supra n67.

171 SC Res 1031 (1995); SC Res 1088 (1996). The functions of the multinational force are outlined in Annex 1-A of the General Framework Agreement for Peace in Bosnia and Herzegovina, available at http://www.ohr.int/dpa/default.asp?content_id=380. The EU-led EUFOR operation replaced SFOR in 2004. See SC Res 1575 (2004).

172 SC Res 1244 (1999).

173 SC Res 1386 (2001), para.3.

straightforward in those cases where it has been sanctioned to reverse inter-state aggression, the aggressor being the obvious target of action. As collective security has increasingly come to be regarded in terms of human security, and military enforcement mandates have focused upon authorising action to create secure humanitarian environments and affording protection to civilians at risk of harm, action against non-state actors has become more common, where these are the source of threats posed to civilian populations.[174] However, the more general humanitarian tone of military enforcement mandates has meant that their targets are, arguably, less clear-cut than might historically have been the case given that their application is conceived to further objectives such as the creation of secure environments for civilians, where the focus becomes to make provision for effective responses to the actions of 'spoilers,' whether state forces or other armed factions, which endanger civilian welfare, and the identity of which may even shift over the period for which their authorisation is in force. That said, although in theory any number of actors could come to constitute legitimate targets under such mandates, they will invariably have been adopted with the conduct of specific actors or entities in mind. For example, while in adopting Resolution 1973, the Security Council authorised action to 'protect civilians and civilian populated areas under threat of attack' in Libya, irrespective of the source of that threat, the adoption of the resolution came against a backdrop of concerns in respect of the effects of military force deployed by the Gaddafi regime.[175]

Bypassing the Security Council

It is inevitable that on occasion the use of military force will be applied by states which has not been sanctioned by the Security Council and cannot be justified by reference to any accepted understanding of the right of self-defence, thus placing such action within the parameters of Article 2 (4)'s prohibition on the use of force by states against other states. This is a consequence of the inherent limitations of any system of law in regulating behaviour, as was recognised in Chapter 1.

174 See the various resolutions authorising military enforcement measures to serve humanitarian objectives, cited above. These came in response to situations of internal conflict, and to fulfil their mandates, forces acting under UN authority would be required to respond militarily to any factions whose conduct threatened the security of civilians or provision of humanitarian aid, as per the terms of the relevant resolutions.

175 See the Security Council's debate preceding the adoption of resolution 1973, UN Doc. S/PV.6498. For example, the French foreign minister referred to 'the murderous repression led by Colonel Al-Qadhafi's regime against his own people' (p.2), before proceeding to refer to the threat of attack against territories by the regime's forces (p.3). Lebanon's representative similarly cited 'violent acts and atrocious crimes being carried out by Libyan authorities against their people' (p.3), with assertions to the same effect made by representatives of the UK (p.4), Germany (p.5), the US (p.5), Brazil (p.6), Bosnia (p.7), Colombia (p.7), Portugal (p.8), Nigeria (p.9) and South Africa (p.10).

However, a distinction can be drawn between the more general use of force by states that takes place in contravention of international law, and that which the states concerned seek to ground in dubious assertions of UN authority while acting autonomously of the constraints of the UN system. While in the former kinds of situation, states will invariably seek to offer some form of legal justification for their actions[176] – typically, self-defence – in the latter they seek to ground their actions in the legitimacy which stems from UN authority, while effectively bypassing the norms of its collective security system. This is, arguably, a problem of the decentralised system of military enforcement and reinforces the need for the Council to endow its resolutions with sufficient clarity, backed up by time limits, to ensure that they cannot possibly be invoked to lend any legitimacy to action which has not been expressly sanctioned by the Council. However, the very fact that states seek to find support in Council resolutions for their actions demonstrates the unique legitimating status of the Council and the general overwhelming support which exists for the UN Charter system of collective security,[177] even if states do attempt to manipulate it on occasion. The legal arguments advanced by states for military actions grounded upon dubious claims of Security Council authorisation have sought to invoke either loose notions of implicit authority or the enforcement of the Council's will, or a 'revival of authority' whereby actions of the target states served to trigger the renewal of military enforcement mandates conferred previously in different contexts. There are three obvious cases in point which can be used to illustrate attempts to circumvent the proper strictures of the system of military enforcement action governed by the UN Charter: the Kurdish crisis, NATO intervention against the Federal Republic of Yugoslavia and the invasion of Iraq in conjunction with the various military actions taken against that state in the preceding decade.

Following the conclusion of the Gulf conflict in 1991, Iraq began a campaign of repression of its Kurdish population in northern Iraq which led to a humanitarian crisis in the region and to the Security Council determining that the situation constituted a threat to international peace and security,[178] demanding that Iraq end the repression[179] and allow access to international humanitarian organisations to those in need.[180] However, while condemnatory and outlining requirements which Iraq was expected to comply with, the language contained in Resolution 688 did

176 For example, Russia sought to invoke notions of self-defence and humanitarian impulses in support of its widely condemned invasion of Ukraine in February 2022. See, eg., Cavandoli, S. and Wilson, G., 'Distorting Fundamental Norms of International Law to Resurrect the Soviet Union: The International Law Context of Russia's Invasion of Ukraine,' *Netherlands International Law Review*, 2022, v.69, pp.383–410, at pp.387–388.

177 See Chapter 1.

178 SC Res 688 (1991).

179 Para.2.

180 Para.3.

not extend to sanctioning the application of military measures against Iraq, nor was it adopted by reference to Chapter VII. Nonetheless, following its adoption, a number of states joined in military action to create a safe haven for the Kurds in northern Iraq and enforce a no-fly zone over the affected area.[181] Although some consideration has been given to the action as a possible instance of the disputed doctrine of humanitarian intervention,[182] there was no real attempt on the part of the intervening states to justify it in such terms.[183] It would appear that intervening states regarded their action as being in support of the collective will of the Council, as expressed by Resolution 688. This has been labelled as an argument of effectiveness: Resolution 688 would only be effective if military action was taken to enforce its objectives.[184] Of course, the difficulty with such an argument lies in the fact that irrespective of its objectives, military action was not a method of achieving these that had been sanctioned by the Council. If states were legally entitled to take military action to enforce the Council's objectives irrespective of whether it has conferred any specific authority to do so, not only would this open the floodgates to all manner of possible actions, undermining the collective authority of the UN Security Council, but it would possibly lead to an excessively cautious approach on the Council's part to the adoption of condemnatory resolutions. Significantly, Resolution 688 only received the positive votes of ten states,[185] evidencing reluctance on the part of others to become involved in what was regarded by them as essentially an internal domestic matter.

NATO's bombing campaign against the Federal Republic of Yugoslavia was launched in response to a campaign of atrocities being perpetrated by FRY authorities against the Kosovar Albanian population of the province of Kosovo. In a series of resolutions adopted under Chapter VII, the Security Council had condemned the actions of federal authorities, demanded that they cease and determined the situation in Kosovo to constitute a threat to international peace and security.[186] However, there was no reference to the authorisation of 'all necessary measures' or similar such language which could be equated with the authorisation of military measures to enforce compliance with the terms of the relevant resolutions, and it was apparent that any attempt to include such authority would meet

181 For discussion, see Malanczuk, P., 'The Kurdish crisis and allied intervention in the aftermath of the second Gulf War,' *European Journal of International Law*, 1991, v.2, n.2, pp.114–132; White, N.D., 'Commentary on the protection of the Kurdish safe haven,' *Journal of Armed Conflict Law*, 1996, v.1, pp.197–204.

182 See, for example, Malanczuk, ibid; Adelman, H., 'Humanitarian intervention: The case of the Kurds,' *International Journal of Refugee Law*, 1992, v.4, pp.4–38.

183 See White, supra n181, at p.201.

184 White, supra n181, pp.202–203.

185 Cuba, Yemen and Zimbabwe voted against resolution 688, while China and India abstained.

186 SC Res 1160 (1998); SC Res 1199 (1998); SC Res 1203 (1998).

with the veto of Russia and China.[187] Following the failure of the Rambouillet peace talks, NATO began a campaign of air strikes against the FRY in order to compel compliance with the Council's demands, ultimately leading to a cease-fire and UN administration of Kosovo pending a final settlement of its status.[188] Although there were some attempts to justify the intervention by reference to the disputed doctrine of humanitarian intervention,[189] there were also suggestions that some NATO member states sought to justify their actions by reference to vaguely articulated claims that they were 'enforcing' Council resolutions, taking implicit authority from the demands advanced in them.[190] Disagreement among the permanent members over NATO's actions was reinforced by an attempt by Russia and China to obtain the Council's subsequent condemnation of it.[191] Although the draft resolution which they sponsored for this purpose was defeated by a vote of 12–3 in the Council,[192] lending some degree of legitimacy to the action, this cannot be taken as retrospective authorisation given the stance of those two permanent members, who would have vetoed any attempt to expressly sanction NATO's air campaign.

The aforementioned two examples concerned situations in which the relevant military actors essentially conceived of their actions as means of effecting the objectives of the Council's demands. Albeit not sanctioned by the Council, they nonetheless enjoyed significant levels of support within the international community, and express authorisation would not perhaps have been inconceivable if not for the existence of the veto power. The situation was, however, very different in respect of the US/UK-led invasion of Iraq in 2003, the legal arguments employed by the intervening states being more convoluted. The story of this episode is well-documented, and the legal arguments advanced by the intervening states were alluded to above.[193] Essentially, these revolved around the idea that authority contained in earlier resolutions can be revived if a state fails to abide by its obligations under those and subsequent resolutions. Such arguments are rejected by the prevailing weight of international legal opinion,[194] yet their advancement

187 That Russia and China introduced a draft resolution into the Council critical of NATO's actions reinforces this. See below.

188 On the basis of SC Res 1244 (1999).

189 On these, see Kritsiotis, D., 'The Kosovo crisis and NATO's application of armed force against the Federal Republic of Yugoslavia,' *ICLQ*, 2000, v.49, n.2, pp.330–359, at pp.339–344; Currie, J., 'NATO's humanitarian intervention in Kosovo: Making or breaking international law?,' *Canadian Yearbook of International Law*, 1998, v.36, pp.303–333, at pp.323–330.

190 For discussion of the legal arguments, see Kritsiotis, ibid, pp.343–344.

191 UN Doc. S/1999/328.

192 UN Doc. S/PV.3989.

193 A number of military actions taken against Iraq during the 1990s without express authority from the Security Council were based on broadly the same legal arguments by the relevant states. See supra n56 and accompanying text.

194 See the references cited in supra n56, n58.

reinforces the need for watertight authorising resolutions that leave no scope for invocation at a future date as authority for objectives that they could not possibly have contemplated.

While arguably not actions taken in conformity with the rules contained within the UN Charter system, nonetheless it is difficult to paint the former two examples considered here as genuine cases of subversion of the UN system. While acknowledging their illegality in terms of international law and the UN Charter framework, in both cases the proclaimed objectives of the intervening states were broadly in accordance with those set out in the Council's resolutions, evidencing the perceived unique legitimacy which emanates from UN authority. Even the Iraq scenario involved action being taken formally on account of the perceived threat posed by Iraq's failure to cooperate with a UN-created weapons inspection regime.[195] Collectively, however, these events reinforce the need for the Council to adopt resolutions that do not open themselves to alternative interpretations.

Outcomes of military enforcement action: Military and political influences

Structuring military enforcement mandates in appropriate terms is important in legal terms in order to subject those taking action under them to ultimate UN authority and oversight, and to minimise against the dangers of abuse. However, measuring the actual success of any application of military enforcement measures in achieving their objectives essentially calls for a judgement that is largely grounded in military and political perspectives. Decisions by the Security Council to sanction military enforcement action, and the purposes for which it is authorised, are essentially grounded in considerations that are political in nature. Their application then takes place through a military process. Whereas measuring success is not particularly difficult where the objective of action is clear and will be satisfied by a concrete outcome – for example, the reversal of aggression taking the form of the invasion of one state by another – the move towards mandates of an essentially humanitarian nature in the post–Cold War era can complicate assessments of success and inject degrees of relativity into judgements concerning the extent to which military enforcement measures have achieved their objectives. Where an operation is tasked with 'facilitating the delivery of humanitarian assistance' during an ongoing conflict, for example, there is scope for disagreement as to the extent to which the objective has been effected as long as the conflict continues. Even where some progress is made, the continuation of conflict may produce perceptions of failure. The case of Somalia is a case in point, where despite the

195 See SC Res 1441 (2002), para.1, in which the Security Council asserted that 'Iraq has been and remains in material breach of its obligations under relevant resolutions … in particular through Iraq's failure to cooperate with United Nations inspectors and the IAEA.'

fact that UNITAF was credited with having contributed to some improvements in the prevailing humanitarian situation,[196] that the conflict raged on and humanitarian conditions remained serious meant little credit was given for any successes. For the most part, military or political assessments of the outcomes of military enforcement action are better provided by scholars of military strategy and international relations. However, three observations are offered here on the outcome of military enforcement action as it has been practised under the authorisation model, by reference to the military and political factors that bear upon the utilisation of this approach to military enforcement under the UN Charter collective security system.

First, military enforcement action has enjoyed its obvious successes. Notwithstanding the later problems produced by the flawed wording contained in the resolutions which authorised the relevant actions, the reversal of North Korea's invasion of South Korea and Iraq's invasion of Kuwait are prime examples of the effective implementation of mandates conferred by the Security Council. The restoration of Haiti's democratically elected government in 1994 is another case in point,[197] as is the operation for the protection of civilians in Libya during 2011, the termination of military enforcement authority signalling the Council's recognition that the mandate had been successfully completed.[198] On various other occasions, operations tasked with humanitarian-inspired mandates,[199] or roles that involve their assistance with the implementation of peace agreements,[200] have been credited with at least some success in the performance of their mandates.

Second, there are practical military consequences of the decentralised model of military enforcement action that has been practised. Effective action in many circumstances will require the rapid deployment of forces to respond to a situation before it deteriorates, and it is also dependent upon effective interoperability between forces of different states that may be acting together as part of a larger

196 See Ramsbotham, O. and Woodhouse, T., *Humanitarian Intervention in Contemporary Conflict* (Cambridge: Polity Press, 1996), p.208; Lewis, I. and Mayall, J., 'Somalia,' in Mayall, J. (ed.), *The New Interventionism 1991–1994* (Cambridge: Polity Press, 1996), p.112.

197 Although in the event there was no need for the application of coercive military force due to the relinquishment of power by the military junta, it is arguable that the very existence of military enforcement authority had some bearing on this outcome.

198 SC Res 2016 (2011).

199 There are far too many assessments of military enforcement operations tasked with humanitarian functions to cite here. See, however, for some examples, Tripodi, P., 'Operation Alba: A necessary and successful preventive deployment,' *International Peacekeeping*, 2002, v.9, n.4, pp.89–104 (on intervention in Albania); 'DRC: EU calls Artemis operation "a big success,"' http://www.irinnews.org/report/46206/drc-eu-calls-artemis-operation-a-big-success (on the EU intervention in the DRC); Ludlow, D.R.L., 'Humanitarian intervention and the Rwandan genocide,' *Journal of Conflict Studies*, 1999, v.19, n.1, available at http://journals.hil.unb.ca/index.php/JCS/article/view/4378/5055 (on intervention in Rwanda).

200 See, for example, Smith, L.W., 'NATO's IFOR in action,' National Defense University Strategic Forum, 1999, n.154, available at http://www.dtic.mil/cgi-bin/GetTRDoc?AD=ADA394097.

coalition. As the authorisation model of military enforcement action relies upon the ad hoc provision of forces, a prompt response to those situations in respect of which the Security Council has decided to sanction action may not always be possible. Even assuming that there is a sufficient degree of political commitment on the part of member states towards taking action, it may be some time before states are practically able to deploy forces to the areas in which they are to operate. The consequences of such a delay could be very damaging, perhaps even meaning that by the time an operation commences, the threat it was established to tackle has receded.[201] This problem is arguably greater where an operation is comprised of contingents from a large number of states, especially if the operation's ability to function is contingent upon being at full strength. There may also arise practical difficulties in relation to command and control issues in any multinational operations comprising a number of states. This results from their ad hoc multinational nature.[202] There is admittedly a degree of irony in the proposition that the collective security ideal may be better practically served by the deployment of forces that are less collective in nature. However, although writing in the context of UN peacekeeping operations, the following observation of McCoubrey and White emphasises the problem: 'The principal dynamic … is that of the coordination of a multi-national force comprising units from countries with differing military and command structures and which … remain … answerable to their home governments.'[203]

Integrating forces from several states into a single unified operation, on an ad hoc basis, produces its challenges. There is also the possibility for disagreements to arise between different national contingents as to the management of the operation.[204] Other practical difficulties can include language barriers and differing capabilities, making it difficult to put into place an overall military command structure capable of ensuring that the operation functions in a coherent and integrated manner. For example, with reference to the Australian-led INTERFET operation in East Timor, although generally viewing it positively, Ryan has highlighted some

201 For example, the deployment of Operation Turquoise in Rwanda, authorised by Resolution 929 to take action to contribute to the security of those at risk, came only after the genocide that engulfed Rwanda in 1994 had taken place.

202 See McCoubrey and White, supra n5, Chapter 6, for discussion of the problems interoperability can give rise to and treatment of some of the difficulties which have arisen in historical incidents of multinational operations. They trace problems of interoperability as far back as the Peloponnesian War (p.121).

203 McCoubrey and White, supra n5, p.132.

204 This was a problem in World War II, according to McCoubrey and White, supra n5, p.122 et seq. Consider also the UNOSOM II operation in Somalia. While technically a UN operation, under the control of a UN commander, certain national contingents – including the US, but also covering French and Italian forces – began to take orders from their national authorities rather than the UN command of the operation; see Ostrower, G.B., *The United Nations and the United States* (New York: Twayne Publishers, 1998), pp.209–212.

of the problems of interoperability which can arise in a multinational operation as a result of different operational cultures and language barriers.[205] The role of major power participation is important in this regard, as in a situation whereby the bulk of forces are provided by one state, it should be easier to subject the operation to one unified command. The more diverse an ad hoc operation is in terms of participants, the more difficult it will become to exercise effective control over it.

Finally, as has been reinforced throughout this book, the practice of collective security hinges on political considerations and influences, and it is possible to detect in various instances of military enforcement action political calculations which underpinned the willingness or unwillingness of key actors to participate in the application of measures of military enforcement. The approaches of major powers are of particular significance in this respect, experience showing that most UN Security Council-sanctioned operations have been contingent upon the leadership of such states. The factors determining their attitudes towards participation in military enforcement operations have been considered by this author elsewhere,[206] but we might briefly note that perceived US interests were present in several of the situations in which it played a central role in spearheading military action: for example, a desire to prevent the spread of communism in the case of Korea,[207] economic interests in the case of the invasion of Kuwait[208] and domestic consequences caused by the humanitarian situation in Haiti following the overthrow of Jean-Bertrand Aristide's government.[209] At the same time, the reluctance of major powers to play a major role in major operations on the African continent is often attributed to the lack of key interests at stake for them in so doing.[210]

Alternatives to the 'authorisation' model

Some of the problems associated with the current approach to military enforcement action, whereby the Security Council authorises operations to be conducted by those actors willing to undertake them, might be addressed through the implementation of more centralised mechanisms for conducting military enforcement action. One option would be for the standby arrangements envisaged by Article 43 of the UN Charter to be implemented. Proposals for reform along such lines gained fresh interest in the early post–Cold War era,[211] although

205 Ryan, A., 'The strong lead-nation model in an ad hoc coalition of the willing: Operation Stabilise in East Timor,' *International Peacekeeping*, 2002, v.9, n.1, pp.23–44, at pp.32–34.

206 Wilson, supra n44, pp.316–327.

207 See Chapter 3.

208 See Wilson, supra n44, pp.317–320.

209 See Wilson, supra n44, pp.317–320 and references cited in footnote 100.

210 See, eg., Hawkins, V., 'Measuring UN Security Council Action and Inaction in the 1990s,' *African Security Studies*, 2003, v.12, n.2, pp.61–71.

211 See, eg., Rossman, J.E., 'Article 43: Arming the United Nations Security Council,' *New York University Journal of International Law & Politics*, 1994, v.27, pp.227–263.

they have subsided since. As noted in Chapter 2, Article 43 (1) provided for UN member states to make available to the Council military resources specified in special agreements concluded with the Council. Under Article 43 (3), those agreements could be concluded 'between the Security Council and Members or between the Security Council and groups of Members.' Furthermore, they would 'govern the numbers and types of forces, their degree of readiness and general location, and the nature of the facilities and assistance to be provided.'[212] Should the system envisaged by Article 43 ever be implemented, there would essentially be a centralised command and control system for military enforcement operations, in which the MSC, acting under the authority of the Security Council, could assume the role conferred upon it by Article 47 (3) to exercise strategic control over Chapter VII operations, and assist the Council with their planning as envisaged by Article 46. The Security Council would have a direct role in the control of operations, which should address concerns over the extent to which the Council is currently able to exercise ultimate authority and control over those operations that it authorises. From a legal perspective, this might be seen as a considerable improvement.

There are, theoretically at least, other potential practical benefits to the implementation of standby arrangements. Their principal purpose is to make available, by advance agreement, specified resources for the UN Security Council to be able to call on in the event of military enforcement action being taken. The implementation of special agreements on the basis of Article 43 would theoretically mean that the Security Council would have available to it when required those military resources covered by the agreements, which it could then utilise for Chapter VII military enforcement action. In this respect, the 'Article 43 option' appears to offer an improvement upon the current approach to military enforcement action. Rather than having to 'wait and see' whether actors willing to conduct military operations are forthcoming, the Council theoretically knows what forces and capabilities can be called upon. This assumes, however, that the introduction of standby arrangements does lead to significant military resources being placed at the Security Council's disposal. The commitment of very few resources would not constitute a significant advancement upon the present position. Furthermore, regardless of the legal nature of undertakings given by member states under Article 43 or on some other basis, standby arrangements will only provide the Security Council with a military enforcement capacity in a given situation if states do prove willing to supply the resources which they have already undertaken in principle to make available.

There are, arguably, advantages of a military nature that arise from the implementation of standby arrangements. Within the agreements by which forces are made available on standby for use by the Security Council, provision could be

212 Article 43 (2).

made for these to be maintained at a specified degree of readiness for action. If standby arrangements were accompanied by collective initiatives between states to enhance the operational capabilities of multinational operations, there would be greater scope to improve the preparedness of national earmarked forces for deployment. Such benefits have been identified within the context of the former UNSAS established for peacekeeping operations,[213] later replaced by the PCRS.[214]

While there are undoubtedly benefits to arise from the implementation of standby arrangements in terms of UN oversight of operations and their military preparedness and cohesiveness, they provide no guarantee that the Security Council will have available to it those resources necessary for military enforcement action to be effectively undertaken when it decides upon this course of action. This danger was considered in the context of the UNSAS and PCRS for UN peacekeeping operations in the previous chapter. As noted there, the response to events in Rwanda at the height of 1994's mass genocide is a clear indicator of this. Notwithstanding the existence of the fact that several states had entered into understandings with the Security Council, none were prepared to provide forces for an enlarged peacekeeping operation authorised by the Council.[215] This would appear to justify some scepticism as to the value of standby arrangements, and was central to that expressed by Brian Urquhart towards their merits.[216] Furthermore, there is little evidence to suggest that states are likely to be willing to conclude standby arrangements in the foreseeable future to govern the deployment of military enforcement operations.[217] Although there have been various collaborative initiatives between states designed to assist with the preparation of national forces for participation in multinational operations, such as the creation of UNSAS, PCRS and initiatives between states such as Friends of Rapid Deployment (FORD) and the Standby High Readiness Brigade (SHIRBRIG),[218] these have been more geared towards peacekeeping operations and are unlikely to extend to the implementation of the original UN Charter scheme for providing the Security Council with a military enforcement capacity.

A more radical alternative would be to provide the UN with its own permanent standing force, which would exist independently of the forces of individual states. An option along these lines has been mooted in various forms over the

213 UN Doc. S/2000/194, para.14. See further Chapter 6.

214 See Chapter 6.

215 SC Res 918 (1994).

216 Urquhart, B., 'Peacekeeping: We need serious rethinking,' *UN Chronicle*, 1998, n.3, p.36, at p.37.

217 See, eg., Rossman, supra n211, pp.242–249.

218 See Langille, H.P., 'Conflict prevention: Options for rapid deployment and UN standing forces,' *International Peacekeeping*, 2000, v.17, n.2, pp.219–253.

years,[219] including relatively recently.[220] In theory, an individually recruited UN force would enjoy clear advantages over the use of 'agents' authorised to conduct military enforcement action on an ad hoc basis. The military enforcement option would not be contingent upon states proving willing to commit forces in given situations and as a permanent UN body it would be subject to much closer Security Council oversight and control. However, the reality is that there is likely to be little political support, particularly from the major powers, for the creation of such an organ.[221] Obstacles such as determining the mode of recruitment to the force, reaching agreement upon locations for it to be based in and the mode of its financing, in addition to general concerns that such an initiative may enhance the power of the UN *vis-à-vis* that of nation states all suggest that, notwithstanding its apparent merits, to contemplate such a development as the creation of a permanent UN volunteer force is a utopian aspiration. As Kennedy and Russett ask, 'Are governments willing to let the world organization have its own army … making it appear to have acquired one of the attributes of statehood?'[222] There is no evidence to suggest that this question can be answered affirmatively. It might also be asked whether the practical benefits of a permanent UN force are easily overstated when often the barrier to the taking of military enforcement action will lie less in the non-existence of an available agent to task with such a mandate, but the inability of the Security Council to agree on the very principle of taking action due to the veto power.

Military Enforcement Action today

Of the core tools of the UN collective security system considered in this book, military enforcement action represents the least utilised in practice. There are

219 See Frye, W.R., *A United Nations Peace Force* (London: Stevens & Sons, 1957), pp.74–80; Bloomfield, L.P. et al, *International Military Forces* (New York: Little, Brown & Co, 1964), Chapter 7; The Report of the Commission on Global Governance, *Our Global Neighbourhood* (Oxford and New York: Oxford University Press, 1995), pp.110–112; Conetta, C. and Knight, C., *Vital Force: A Proposal for the Overhaul of the UN Peace Operations System and for the Creation of a UN Legion* (Cambridge, Massachusetts: Commonwealth Institute, 1995); Urquhart, B., 'For a UN volunteer military force,' *New York Review of Books*, 1993, June 10, pp.3–4; Kinloch, S.P., 'Utopian or pragmatic? A UN permanent military volunteer force,' *International Peacekeeping*, 1996, v.3, n.4, pp.166–190; Pattison, J., *The Responsibility to Protect* (Oxford: Oxford University Press, 2010), pp.229–236.

220 See, eg., Herro, A., 'The Elusive UN Agenda: Transactional Advocacy, Political Opportunities and the Latest Campaign to Establish a UN Standing Force,' *International Peacekeeping*, 2017, v.24, n.3, pp.388–409; Koops, J.A. and Novosseloff, A., 'United Nations rapid reaction mechanisms: Toward a global force on standby?,' *Contemporary Security Policy*, 2017, v.38, n.3, pp.427–442.

221 On obstacles, see, e.g., Koops and Novosseloff, supra n220, pp.435–438.

222 Kennedy, P. and Russett, B., 'Reforming the United Nations,' *Foreign Affairs*, 1995, v.74, n.5, pp.56–71, at p.63.

relatively few examples of major military enforcement mandates conferred by the Security Council, but since the earlier post–Cold War period when a wave of mandates were forthcoming, military enforcement action has come to feature seldom within the Council's contemporary repertoire. While a series of sanctions regimes and peacekeeping operations remain in place, the last notable military enforcement operation was that conducted by NATO against targets within Libya in 2011 on the basis of the Council's Resolution 1973. In respect of major instances in which the use of force is used by states, such as the Russia–Ukraine conflict or the situation between Israel and Hamas post-2023, the UN has been effectively excluded due to the prevailing positions of one or more of the permanent members. Where situations of grave concern have been taken up at the UN level, such as the Syrian conflict, pertinent P5 dynamics again have served to limit the scope for a meaningful response. For example, while the Syrian government's use of chemical weapons was condemned as a threat to the peace by the Security Council,[223] that the US responded unilaterally with air strikes supported by the UK and France demonstrated the non-viability of the UN-authorised military enforcement option.[224]

Conclusion

Clearly, the record of the UN in the successful utilisation of its military enforcement option is not a perfect one. It has never had its own forces with which to take military enforcement action, forcing it to rely upon the willingness of its member states to conduct operations under its authority. This has meant that on occasions, political factors have combined to deprive it of an adequate military capacity. On other occasions, the Security Council has failed to exercise sufficient oversight and control over the operations that it has sanctioned, risking those acting under its mandates abusing the powers that have been conferred upon them.

However, when we consider the initial failure to implement the special agreements envisaged by Article 43 by which forces would be made available to the Security Council on a standby basis, its subsequent achievements in respect of military enforcement action should not be dismissed. The development of the authorisation model approach has given it a military enforcement capability which it would not otherwise enjoy and while the political realities of the international environment place limits upon its potential which will vary from one situation to another, that military enforcement measures have been taken under UN Security Council authority even to the relatively limited extent to which they have ought to be regarded as an achievement. If anything, some of the criticisms levelled at the UN's military enforcement record are a result of its own success. Through its development of the concept of threats to the peace to embrace a far wider range

223 SC Res 2118 (2017).
224 See Wilmshurst, supra n69, pp.831–834.

of situations than might have been envisaged within, say, the League of Nations system, the UN Security Council has burdened itself with a more demanding workload amid greater expectations of the problems which it ought to effectively tackle. As noted earlier in this chapter, most instances of the employment of military enforcement measures have come in response to perceived threats that are essentially humanitarian in nature, generally the most difficult in respect of which the measurement of success can be achieved. Furthermore, over time, the UN Security Council has come to strengthen the oversight that it exerts over military enforcement operations that it sanctions through a more careful approach to the construction of mandates that are increasingly endowed with clarity, time limits and mechanisms for scrutiny. While its approach is still not as consistent as it might be, it has improved considerably in this respect.

8

REGIONAL ARRANGEMENTS AND THE UN COLLECTIVE SECURITY SYSTEM

Introduction

Chapter VIII of the UN Charter expressly provides for a role to be played by regional arrangements and agencies within the UN collective security system, although its provisions are relatively brief, restricting themselves to conferring regional arrangements with a role in taking enforcement action under the authority of the Security Council,[1] and effectively providing that regional arrangements assume primary responsibility for the peaceful settlement of disputes arising among their membership.[2] In the early post–Cold War era, attention was soon given to the role that these bodies may be capable of performing in supporting the UN Security Council in discharging its primary responsibility for the maintenance of international peace and security.[3] On a practical level, logic could be seen in such an approach stemming from the fact that most conflict situations are regional, if not national or local, in nature. At the outset of his term in office, UN

1 Article 53 (1).
2 Article 52 (2).
3 See for example, McCoubrey, H. and Morris, J., *Regional Peacekeeping in the Post-Cold War Era* (The Hague: Kluwer, 2000); Gray, C., 'Regional arrangements and the United Nations collective security system,' in Fox, H. (ed.), *The Changing Constitution of the United Nations* (London: British Institute of International and Comparative Law, 1997), pp.89–106; Farer, T.J., 'The role of regional collective security arrangements,' in Weiss, T.G. (ed.), *Collective Security in a Changing World* (Boulder: Lynne Rienner, 1993), pp.153–186; Morrison, F.L., 'The role of regional arrangements in the enforcement of international law,' in Delbruck, J. (ed.), *Allocation of Law Enforcement Authority in the International System* (Berlin: Duncker & Humblot, 1995), pp.39–55; Abass, A., *Regional Organisations and the Development of Collective Security: Beyond Chapter VIII of the UN Charter* (Oxford: Hart, 2004).

DOI: 10.4324/9781003518105-9

Secretary-General Boutros Boutros-Ghali placed considerable emphasis upon the role which regional organisations could play in the maintenance of international peace and security,[4] although as he would later acknowledge, the varying capabilities of regional arrangements make it difficult to adopt a universal model with regard to the role which they can play in the security arena.[5] Some years later, the Security Council expressed its 'determination to take appropriate steps to the further development of cooperation between the [UN] and regional and subregional organizations in maintaining international peace and security.'[6]

The purpose of this chapter is not to provide an overview of the numerous regional bodies that include a security remit among their functions, which has been done elsewhere.[7] Rather, this chapter seeks to provide an understanding of the role more generally of regional bodies within the UN Charter's collective security framework, and the legal and other factors which impact upon their viability and ultimate success in achieving their objectives. Particular attention is given to the legal framework applicable to the military enforcement role of regional bodies, as this has arguably been the source of the greatest controversy. The role of regional bodies in the other forms of action considered as part of the UN collective security apparatus has been less problematic, due to their lower level of intensity and the more flexible provisions applicable to their utilisation. After briefly setting out some observations upon the relative merits of regional action over that of the UN itself, the scope of 'regional arrangements and agencies' – the bodies afforded a role within the UN collective security system – is considered. There then follows examination of the role afforded by the UN Charter to regional arrangements and agencies within the areas covered by this book: pacific settlement, non-military sanctions, peacekeeping and military enforcement action. Much of the focus will necessarily centre on African and European bodies, these having been the most active in utilising these techniques, while Africa has also been the location of the largest number of conflict situations of any continent since the end of the Cold War.[8]

4 Boutros-Ghali, B., *An Agenda for Peace* (New York: United Nations, 1992), UN Doc. A/47/277-S/24111.

5 Boutros-Ghali, B., *Supplement to an Agenda for Peace* (New York: United Nations, 1995), UN Doc. A/50/60-S/1995/1, para.87.

6 SC Res 1636 (2005), para.1. See also 'United Nations, Regional Organizations to Agree on Stronger Partnerships in Facing Peace, Security Challenges,' Press Release, UN Doc. PI/1668.

7 See, for example, McCoubrey and Morris, supra n3; Tavares, R., *Regional Security* (London: Routledge, 2009).

8 This is borne out by the fact that there have been significantly more UN peacekeeping operations deployed upon the African continent than any other, while there have also been more sanctions regimes established in response to situations arising in Africa than elsewhere.

The relative merits of regional action

There are several reasons why action by regional bodies in response to security threats within their area of operation may be regarded as preferable to UN action,[9] at least in certain circumstances. In addition to the obvious benefit of relieving the burden placed upon the UN, states within a particular region may have closer ties based upon culture, history or politics, which provide them with a greater appreciation of problems arising within the region. This may mean both that regional actors are better suited to intervene and that the state that is the intended recipient of assistance will be more amenable to receiving this from its neighbours.[10] On a practical level, states within a region are also more likely to be directly affected by the consequences of conflict or a pervasive threat arising in a neighbouring state, whether taking the form of spill-over violence, refugee flows or economic, environmental or public health impacts of a situation of concern. If one subscribes to realist perspectives of states' behaviour,[11] with more at stake for themselves they are perhaps more likely to prove willing to take action than states in remote parts of the world. By virtue of their proximity, they will often also theoretically be in a better position to respond quickly where military action is considered the appropriate form of response to a situation of concern. However, while some considerations may serve to militate in favour of a regional over a global response to a situation of concern, there may be barriers to or concerns which stem from the prospects of a response led by a regional body due to contextual factors pertaining to the region in question or the particular organisation concerned.[12]

It should not be assumed that the states within a region will always have a great deal in common. Regions can be very diverse,[13] and where this is the case, a regional approach to a particular security threat may be no better than a more internationalised one. Regional bodies do not necessarily speak with one voice. The European Union is a good case in point. Notwithstanding its well-developed institutional structures for addressing peace and security issues, its membership has found itself divided over the most suitable responses to events ranging from the War on Terror to the invasion of Iraq, and from the Syrian Civil War to

9 See Tavares, supra n7, pp.13–14; Hollywood, D.M., 'It takes a village … or at least a region: Rethinking peace operations in the twenty-first century, the hope and promise of African regional institutions,' *Florida Journal of International Law*, 2007, v.19, pp.75–154, p.139.

10 A good case in point is that of Sudan, where a joint African Union-UN mission (UNAMID) was despatched because of the Sudanese regime's opposition to a purely UN mission.

11 See Chapter 1.

12 See Tavares, supra n7, pp.14–17; Hollywood, supra n9, pp.140–141.

13 This is, arguably, especially the case where regional bodies span entire continents. Consider, for example, the African Union, which enjoys among its membership a mixture of Christian and Muslim states with various ethnic and cultural groups, speaking numerous different languages, and with histories of colonial domination by different European powers (and in some cases, none).

the Russia–Ukraine conflict.[14] The African Union has on occasion encountered a similar lack of consensus.[15] Several regional bodies are also dominated by a small number of states assuming hegemonic status – for example, in the context of sub-regional African bodies, ECOWAS is heavily dominated by Nigeria,[16] the Southern African Development Community (SADC) by South Africa[17] – whose political priorities may mean that they are unsuitable to tackle some situations.[18] While the states of a region are theoretically more affected by a threat arising within that region, this may compromise their impartiality in taking appropriate action, particularly where the interests of a hegemonic power leading an action are at odds with the collectively agreed objectives it is intended to serve. The varying capacities of different regional bodies will also mean that regardless of the political suitability of action in a given situation, it may simply be impractical, particularly where the application of military force is required. Long-standing challenges to the development of an effective African collective security capability have included the limited military capabilities of many states on the continent, the internal instability experienced by a not insignificant number, and limited regional funds.[19] Thus, in considering the role of regional arrangements and agencies within the UN collective security system, it must not be assumed that a 'one size fits all' model can be utilised.

The scope of 'regional arrangements and agencies'

Although, as we have already noted, provisions of the UN Charter explicitly provide for a role to be performed by 'regional arrangements and agencies' within both the pacific settlement of disputes and enforcement action, nowhere in the Charter are these bodies defined. At the San Francisco Conference, attempts to incorporate a definition were rejected.[20] Former UN Secretary-General Boutros Boutros-Ghali suggested that there is

14 See, eg., Cachia, J.C. and De Battista, A.P., 'Political narrative, collective EU security and the State of the Union,' *European Politics and Society*, 2023, v.24, n.5, pp.703–719, at p.704 et seq.

15 Williams, P.D. and Boutellis, A., 'Partnership Peacekeeping: Challenges and Opportunities in the United Nations-African Union Relationship,' *African Affairs*, 2014, v.113, n.451, pp.254–278, at pp.259–264.

16 See Doktori, D., 'Minding the gap: International law and regional enforcement in Sierra Leone,' *Florida Journal of International Law*, 2008, v.20, pp.329–352, at pp.347–349.

17 See Tavares, R., 'The participation of SADC and ECOWAS in Military Operations: The Weight of National Interests in Decision-Making,' *African Studies Review*, 2011, v.54, n.2, pp.145–176.

18 See Hassan, H.A., 'Contending hegemony and the new security systems in Africa,' *African Journal of Political Science and International Relations*, 2015, v.9, n.5, pp.159–169.

19 See, eg., Fafore, O.A., 'The African Union's Collective Security Mechanisms and the Challenge of Armed Non-State Actors,' *Journal of African Union Studies*, 2020, v.9, n.3, pp.87–109, at pp.100–101.

20 UNCIO XII, 850, 857.

> deliberately ... no precise definition of regional arrangements and agencies, thus allowing useful flexibility for undertakings by a group of states to deal with a matter appropriate for regional action which could also contribute to the maintenance of international peace and security.[21]

Some bodies clearly consider themselves as constituting regional arrangements or agencies for the purposes of Chapter VIII.[22] For example, the OAS has explicitly referred to itself in such terms,[23] as has the OSCE.[24] Other bodies have generally been regarded as regional arrangements or agencies by the UN, for example the Arab League, the former Organization of African Unity (OAU) and the AU.[25] By contrast, NATO officially continues to regard itself as a collective self-defence alliance,[26] although in practice it has effectively been treated as a regional arrangement by the UN Security Council on those occasions when it has conferred it with a military enforcement mandate under the terms of its resolutions.[27] NATO has also adopted a broader conception of its remit over time which extends beyond that of a mere collective defence alliance.[28] Akehurst suggests that three criteria ought to be satisfied for an organisation to qualify as a regional arrangement or agency for the purposes of Chapter VIII: it should be consistent with the maintenance of international peace and security; it should be consistent with the purposes and principles of the UN; and it must be in some sense 'regional.' These do not appear particularly onerous standards to satisfy. However, it is argued that whether a body is expressly regarded as a regional arrangement or agency within the sense of Chapter VIII should not prevent its utilisation by the Security Council for the performance of functions envisaged for regional arrangements and agencies by the Charter's provisions. Three key considerations support such a view, with particular reference to military enforcement action.

21 *Agenda for Peace*, supra n4, para.61.
22 On the characterisation of regional organisations, see Abass, supra n3, pp.34–35.
23 Article 1, Charter of Organization of American States 1948.
24 Helsinki Declaration 1992 Pt. IV (2).
25 Ress, G. and Brohmer, J., 'Article 53,' in Simma, B et al (eds), *The Charter of the United Nations: A Commentary* (2nd ed.) (Oxford: Oxford University Press, 2002), pp.854–890, at p.862; Abass, supra n3, pp.34–42; Hummer, W. and Schweitzer, M., 'Article 52,' in Simma, B. et al (eds), *The Charter of the United Nations: A Commentary* (Oxford: Oxford University Press, 1994), pp.699–701.
26 Article 5, North Atlantic Treaty 1949.
27 Surprisingly, in a wave of resolutions concerning military enforcement measures to be applied by NATO in relation to former Yugoslavia during the early 1990s, the Council chose to adopt these under Chapter VII, as opposed to Chapter VIII, even though the relevant resolutions tended to confer authority on member states 'acting nationally' or through 'regional arrangements or agencies,' which could only possibly have referred to NATO, as it was the only organisation capable of taking action. See, for example, SC Res 770 (1992); SC Res 816 (1993); SC Res 836 (1993).
28 See below.

First, the absence of any definition means that where UN Security Council authority is required for regional action to proceed – as is the case for enforcement action under Article 53 (1) – the Council will effectively decide whether an organisation qualifies to take such action. That the body in question may not have been conceived as a regional arrangement or agency within the meaning of Chapter VIII need not prevent its utilisation for such functions if its membership is willing to undertake them.

Second, in relation to military enforcement action, as it is well established that the UN Security Council can authorise states acting within ad hoc coalitions to take such measures,[29] it is only logical that this power extends to groups of states acting through the forum of an organisation to which they collectively belong. Thus, even if an unduly restrictive definition were to be adopted of 'regional arrangements and agencies' for the purposes of Article 53 (1), other organisations could be authorised to take military enforcement action on the basis of this more general power of the Security Council. Such is the flexibility of the Council's power of authorisation based upon Article 42 that any organisation built upon geographical, political or economic ties could be conferred with military enforcement authority irrespective of its formal legal status.

Finally, the UN Security Council's practice has seen it adopt a flexible approach to the utilisation of regionally based bodies, having authorised military enforcement action to be taken by organisations not expressly established as regional arrangements or agencies under Chapter VIII. This approach was first witnessed at an early stage in the post–Cold War era when NATO was authorised to take military enforcement measures in the territory of former Yugoslavia by Resolutions 757, 816, 836 and 1031 during the civil war which raged there during the 1990s. Although most relevant resolutions during the course of that conflict conferred authority on states acting 'nationally or through regional arrangements or agencies,' this must have referred to NATO as it was the only organisation with the capacity to undertake some of the actions authorised by the resolutions, such as enforcing the ban on flights in Yugoslav airspace. While often resolutions were adopted only under Chapter VII, on some occasions Chapter VIII was also invoked.[30] Thus, NATO was arguably considered to constitute a regional arrangement for all practical purposes. Even if a particular organisation is not considered a regional arrangement or agency, it may take enforcement action on the same basis as ad hoc coalitions of states can under authorisation by the UN Security Council under Chapter VII.[31] Admittedly, the Council has not helped clarify the legal basis for mandates performed by regional bodies by authorising some

29 See Chapter 7.
30 For example, SC Res 787 (1992); SC Res 820 (1993).
31 Gray, C., *International Law and the Use of Force* (2nd ed.) (Oxford and New York: Oxford University Press, 2004), pp.204–206; McCoubrey and Morris, supra n3, p.233.

actions under Chapter VII and others under Chapter VIII. More generally, while the Council continues to make considerable reference in its proceedings to cooperation with regional arrangements and agencies in measures adopted to further the maintenance of international peace and security, explicit references to any specific Chapter VIII provisions are rare.[32] McCoubrey and Morris went so far as to suggest that military enforcement action by regional arrangements might be based upon a 'chapter seven and a half' basis, in the same way that traditional peacekeeping came to be regarded as a hybrid of Chapters VI and VII of the Charter.[33] Certainly, a basis in either chapter for regional enforcement action is conceivable.

The role of regional arrangements within pacific settlement

The legal framework

The UN Charter specifically directs member states to resolve their disputes through pacific means,[34] and directs them to attempt the pacific settlement of local disputes through regional arrangements or agencies before referring them to the Security Council,[35] thus conferring the regional bodies with primary responsibility in this respect.[36] As seen in Chapter 4, there is little by way of legal regulation of attempts to resolve disputes through pacific means. Regional arrangements and agencies thus enjoy a considerable amount of discretion in the efforts which they employ to address disputes among their membership where these do not take the form of enforcement measures under Chapter VII of the UN Charter. They may make use of any of the pacific modes of settlement in pursuit of the regional settlement of disputes.[37]

The constituent documents of most regional bodies provide no detailed provisions to govern their role in the pacific settlement of disputes and tend to confine themselves to reaffirming the UN Charter principle that states should resolve their

32 See, eg., *Repertoire of the Practice of the Security Council,* 26th Supplement, 2023, Part VIII, available at https://main.un.org/securitycouncil/sites/default/files/2024/26th_suppl_Part%20VIII_advance%20version.pdf#page=50. One rare instance of the invocation of Article 53 is found in SC Res 2719 (2023).

33 McCoubrey and Morris, supra n3, p.233.

34 Articles 2(3), 33.

35 Article 52 (2).

36 On the underlying logic, see Moerane, G.K., 'The United Nations Charter and the African Union Constitutive Act: The search for compatibility in addressing African peace and security,' *Global Change, Peace & Security,* 2023, v.35, n.2, pp.217–228, at p.220.

37 Although Article 33 provides a non-exhaustive list of peaceful means of dispute settlement, which refers to 'negotiation, enquiry, mediation, conciliation, arbitration, judicial settlement, resort to regional agencies or arrangements,' there is no reason why states might not be assisted by regional organisations in making use of the other listed means.

disputes peacefully.[38] However, a number of organisations have sought to establish a more detailed framework for their role in the area of pacific settlement. The OAS is one example of a regional organisation that has done this. Although the provisions of the OAS Charter are brief and largely reaffirm principles found in Chapter VI of the UN Charter,[39] these are supplemented by a special treaty created to govern pacific settlement procedures between OAS members.[40] SADC's Organ on Politics, Defence and Security is specifically empowered to take steps to attempt to resolve disputes between member states,[41] while ASEAN constitutes a rare case of an organisation which was very much founded upon the principle of pacific settlement to the exclusion of other methods of tackling threats to peace and security in its area of operation,[42] its treaty containing clear provisions to support the peaceful settlement of disputes,[43] built upon by later instruments.[44] The OSCE is similarly a body centred on the promotion of the peaceful settlement of disputes. With no experience in the most robust forms of intervention and coercion, the role of the political summit has been regarded as central to the advancement of its security objectives.[45] An innovative mechanism for brokering diplomatic solutions to disputes is found within ECOWAS's provision for a 'Council of Elders' of eminent persons whose good offices might be utilised for the purposes of serving as mediators, conciliators and facilitators in respect of disputes which may arise, where requested to do so by ECOWAS's Mediation and Security Council.[46] The Peace and Security Council created by the African Union also enjoys specific powers pertaining to the promotion of pacific settlement.[47]

The absence of an express legal framework for the peaceful settlement of disputes does not mean that an organisation cannot engage in making or facilitating

38 See, for example, Article 4 (e), Constitutive Act of the African Union 2000; Article 1, North Atlantic Treaty 1949; Article 21 (2) (c), Treaty on European Union 1992; Article 4, ECOWAS Treaty 1975; Article 2 (d), Treaty of Amity and Cooperation in Southeast Asia 1976; Article 4 (e), SADC Treaty 1992; Article 20, Pact of the League of Arab States 1945.

39 See Articles 24–27, Charter of the Organization of American States 1948.

40 American Treaty on Pacific Settlement 1948.

41 See also the SADC Protocol on Politics, Defence and Security Cooperation 2001, Article 11.

42 On the nature of ASEAN, see McCoubrey and Morris, supra n3, pp.161–166. As they note, ASEAN's 'security concepts and agendas must effectively deny [it] the capacity … to respond to a security crisis which had gone beyond the scope of discussion and consensus seeking' (at p.164).

43 Treaty of Amity and Cooperation in Southeast Asia 1976, Chapter IV.

44 See, e.g., Charter of the Association of South-East Asian Nations 2007, Chapter VIII. See also Desierto, D.A., 'The Association of Southeast Asian Nations and Southeast Asia's Regional Security,' in GeiB, R. and Melzer, N. (eds), *The Oxford Handbook of the International Law of Global Security* (Oxford: OUP, 2021), pp.947–62.

45 Greminger, T., 'The Organisation for Security and Co-operation in Europe,' in GeiB and Melzer, ibid, pp.1052–1070.

46 Protocol Relating to the Mechanism for Conflict Prevention, Management, Resolution, Peace-Keeping and Security 1999, Article 20.

47 See Protocol Relating to the Establishment of the Peace and Security Council of the African Union 2002, Articles 3–4.

efforts in this respect. As peaceful modes of settlement involve no application of coercive measures, regional organisations are at liberty to utilise them in response to disputes arising between their members. However, in the absence of any obligation contained within the constituent frameworks of the bodies to which they belong, states cannot be compelled to avail themselves of particular methods of peaceful settlement in order to resolve their disputes.[48]

Regional practice

A detailed treatment of regional efforts at the peaceful settlement of disputes is beyond our remit, and we necessarily confine ourselves here to some brief observations. It is worth noting, however, that the UN Security Council has routinely come to 'acknowledge ... and express ... support for the engagement of regional and subregional arrangements in the peaceful settlement of disputes.'[49] African bodies such as the AU and ECOWAS have featured prominently in such commendatory comments by the Council.[50] Whereas most regional bodies can claim to have initiated efforts to resolve disputes through diplomatic or pacific means to some extent, some specifically limit their remit to such courses of action. As previously noted, ASEAN is a good case in point. It has been credited with having fostered a culture of responding to disputes in such a way in South-East Asia and in so doing bringing greater stability to the region,[51] although its reluctance to foray into intra-state disputes has on occasion left it an effective bystander, for example in relation to conflict in East Timor and the repressive policies of the military junta in Myanmar.[52] This perhaps casts doubts over its capacity to play a meaningful role in tackling internal crises of a humanitarian nature which have come to dominate much of contemporary collective security discourse, although ASEAN has continued to be commended for its efforts to support democratic transition in Myanmar.[53]

There is no simple means of assessing the potential role which regional organisations are capable of performing in the peaceful settlement of disputes. This will vary from one situation to another in accordance with the political dynamics of the relevant organisation, the identity of the concerned parties and the nature of

48 See Chapter 4.

49 See *Repertoire of the Practice of the Security Council*, 24th Supplement, 2021, Part VIII, p.536, available at https://main.un.org/securitycouncil/sites/default/files/part_viii.pdf#page=17.

50 See, e.g., ibid, pp.536–537.

51 Nathan, L., *The Peacemaking Effectiveness of Regional Organisations* (London: Crisis States Research Centre, 2010), p.8. See also Leifer, M., *ASEAN and the Security of South-East Asia* (London: Routledge, 1989); Snitwongse, K., 'ASEAN's security co-operation: Searching for a regional order,' *The Pacific Review*, 1995, v.8, n.3, pp.518–530.

52 Nathan, ibid, p.8, p.17. ASEAN's norm that prohibits its interference in states' internal affairs has prevented it from addressing gross human rights violations and intra-state conflict situations.

53 See, e.g., UN Doc. S/PRST/2021/5, SC Res 2669 (2022).

the dispute. A Crisis States Research Centre (CSRC) project on the peace-making role of regional organisations concluded that their contribution towards the pacific settlement of disputes varies considerably, being influenced by the wider context within which the organisations have developed as well as the degree of intractability present in the situations with which they have sought to grapple.[54] During the Cold War period, it was observed that 'most of the difficult [peace and security] issues ... have not been settled at the regional level.'[55] A number of disputes were tackled through peaceful means with some success at the regional level by, for example, the OAU and OAS during the 1960s.[56] However, the limited contribution in this respect during this period has to be seen against the wider constraints imposed upon the operation of the UN collective security system by the geopolitical dynamics of the Cold War.[57]

The explosion in conflict that accompanied the end of the Cold War resulted in greater regional efforts to resolve situations constituting threats to peace and security. For reasons already detailed,[58] the consensual nature of peaceful settlement limits its success as an effective response to security threats. It is not possible to provide an overview of each regional attempt to apply techniques of peaceful settlement to situations of concern. However, it will suffice to note that although some regional bodies have played a very limited role in efforts at pacific settlement,[59] others have enjoyed some limited success. For example, if we consider security threats to have arisen on the African continent in recent years – the hotbed of more conflict than any other region in the post–Cold War era – we see obvious instances of this. The African Union took the lead in the brokering of a peace agreement in Kenya in 2008 following civil unrest in the aftermath of disputed elections,[60] while its predecessor organisation, the OAU, earlier facilitated the peace agreement which ended conflict between Ethiopia and Eritrea in 2000.[61] ECOWAS was specifically credited by the UN Security Council for the attempts it had undertaken to broker the settlement of the situation existing in Mali in the early 2020s following the coup which removed the leaders of the transitional government in

54 Nathan, supra n51, pp.19–20.

55 Wilcox, F.O., 'Regionalism and the United Nations,' *International Organization*, 1965, v.19, n.3, pp.788–811, at p.796.

56 See Wilcox, ibid, p.797 et seq. The OAU is regarded as having contributed positively to dialogue over border disputes between Algeria and Morocco, Mali and Mauritania, and Ethiopia and Somalia. The OAS assisted Guatemala in its dispute with Nicaragua and Honduras.

57 See Chapter 3.

58 See Chapter 4.

59 For example, the South Asian Association for Regional Cooperation (SAARC) or SADC.

60 See Lindenmayer, E. and Kaye, J.L., *A Choice for Peace? The Story of Forty-One Days of Mediation in Kenya* (New York: International Peace Institute, 2009).

61 The OAU role was praised by UN Secretary-General Kofi Annan. See UN Press Release SG/SM/7659.

place at the time.[62] The Intergovernmental Authority on Development (IGAD) was credited with having performed a key role in both the creation of a comprehensive peace agreement to end the conflict between the northern and southern regions of Sudan, culminating in the ultimate secession of South Sudan, and in the formation of transitional governmental institutions in Somalia. In both cases, the leadership provided by Kenya was of particular importance.[63] IGAD's diplomatic efforts in those locations continued to be commended in recent years.[64] Peaceful initiatives have not been restricted to Africa, the EU's mediation efforts in respect of the conflict that accompanied the break-up of the former Yugoslavia being a prime example,[65] while the OAS has also been credited with having aided the resolution of a number of disputes between its members, including those involving Belize and Guatemala in 2005 and El Salvador and Honduras in 2006.[66]

Regional sanctions

The legal framework

While the UN Charter provides a clear legal basis for the imposition of non-military sanctions by the Security Council, observation of which by member states is made mandatory,[67] there is no specific reference to the ability of regional bodies to impose collective sanctions. Article 53 refers simply to 'enforcement action' by regional arrangements and agencies and categorically makes such action conditional upon the authorisation of the Security Council. While undoubtedly military action involving the application of coercive force is considered to amount to enforcement action, it has been a matter of some debate whether non-military sanctions of the kind envisaged by Article 41 are likewise considered to come under this umbrella.[68] While there is some evidence to suggest that the UN's founders intended enforcement action to encompass all coercive measures,[69] in

62 UN Doc. S/PV.8794,

63 Nathan, supra n51, p.9.

64 See, eg., SC Res 2625 (2022), SC Res 2633 (2022), SC Res 2677 (2023), SC Res 2683 (2023), SC Res 2705 (2023), SC Res 2715 (2023).

65 See, for example, Wouters, J. and Naert, F., 'How effective is the European security architecture? Lessons from Bosnia and Kosovo,' *International and Comparative Law Quarterly*, 2001, v.50, pp.540–575, at pp.547–557.

66 See Herz, M., *Does the Organisation of American States Matter?* (London: Crisis States Research Centre, 2008), pp.25–26.

67 See Chapter 5.

68 See, for example, McCoubrey and Morris, supra n3, pp.46–52; Akehurst, M., 'Enforcement action by regional organisations with special reference to the Organization of American States,' *British Yearbook of International Law*, 1967, v.42, pp.175–227, at pp.185–197.

69 Akehurst, for example, considered all action covered by Chapter VII of the UN Charter to constitute 'enforcement action'; Akehurst, ibid, p.186.

practice it has not come to extend beyond military measures.[70] Paliwal notes that 'scholarly opinion typically concludes that economic sanctions or severance of diplomatic relations do not constitute enforcement actions.'[71] Similarly, White has observed that 'There is certainly practice by the regional organizations that suggest economic sanctions do not require the authorisation of the Security Council under Article 53.'[72]

The better view is that the term 'enforcement action' is in practice used to describe those measures that would be unlawful if taken in the absence of UN Security Council authority. UN Security Council's 'authorisation is only necessary to allow an action which, in the absence of such an authorisation, would be prohibited.'[73] The threat or use of force by states is outlawed by Article 2 (4) and is unlawful in the absence of either of the UN Charter exceptions being applicable,[74] hence the requirement for military enforcement action to proceed with UN Security Council authorisation. By contrast, states have long enjoyed the ability to impose non-military sanctions against other states, such as trade embargoes and diplomatic restrictions, on an individual or collective basis.[75] The power enjoyed by the UN Security Council under Article 41 is more extensive in that it empowers the Council to compel members to give effect to measures, but the non-utilisation of the sanctions weapon by the Council does not prevent states themselves choosing to effect such measures. Thus, if regional bodies wish to impose non-military sanctions, Article 53 should not be read as curtailing their actions in this respect to the extent that they do not conflict with any sanctions imposed by the Security Council.[76] This means that where sanctions have not been imposed by the Council, or imposed to a lesser extent than the states belonging to a regional body would wish, they might act through that organisation to impose measures which exceed those imposed by the Council. This can be a useful tool to employ where division

70 Hakimi, M., 'To condone or condemn? Regional enforcement actions in the absence of Security Council authorization,' *Vanderbilt Journal of Transnational Law*, 2007, v.40, pp.643–685, at pp.650–651.

71 Paliwal, S., 'The primacy of regional organizations in international peacekeeping: The African example,' *Virginia Journal of International Law*, 2010, v.51, n.1, pp.185–230, at p.193.

72 White, N.D., 'The EU as a regional security actor within the international legal order,' in Trybus, M. and White, N.D. (eds), *European Security Law* (Oxford: Oxford University Press, 2007), pp.329–349, at pp.340–341.

73 Villani, U., 'The Security Council's authorization of enforcement action by regional organizations,' *Max Planck Yearbook of United Nations Law*, 2002, v.6, pp.535–557, at p.539.

74 As provided for by Articles 42 (UN-authorised military enforcement action, which by virtue of Article 53 (1) covers action by regional arrangements or agencies) and 51 (the right of individual or collective self-defence).

75 Hickey, J.E., 'Challenges to Security Council monopoly power over the use of force in enforcement actions: The case of regional organizations,' *Ius Gentium*, 2004, v.10, pp.69–117, p.78.

76 Under Article 103 of the UN Charter, obligations assumed by member states under the terms of any other treaty arrangement are only permissible to the extent that they do not conflict with obligations arising from their membership of the UN.

between the P5 precludes action at the UN level, but for which strong regional support exists. The imposition of sanctions against Russia following its invasion of Ukraine is one such example.[77]

The constituent instruments of many regional bodies are silent on the issue of non-military sanctions. However, several of the more proactive regional bodies have created provisions to govern their application. African bodies have taken the lead in this respect. The African Union's Constitutive Act provides for sanctions to be imposed on states failing to comply with its decisions and policies,[78] and in response to unconstitutional changes of government,[79] governments coming to power through unconstitutional means face the sanction of being unable to participate in AU affairs.[80] The SADC treaty similarly provides for sanctions to be imposed for non-compliance with obligations under the treaty,[81] while ECOWAS is empowered under its 2001 protocol to impose sanctions in response to the removal of democratic governments.[82] Other bodies may base their imposition of sanctions on more general powers to take decisions or actions in pursuit of security-related objectives. This is not legally problematic. Where the imposition of sanctions fulfils an objective of a regional body, the absence of any express power is not a legal bar to such a course of action so long as its membership consents to take such action, an argument to which we return below in the context of regional military enforcement action. Where states can take such measures on an individual basis, they can logically do so collectively. Where targeted states enjoy close economic relations with their neighbours, regional economic sanctions are more likely to generate some impact, although whether this will translate into bringing about a change in the situation giving rise to the security threat is open to debate.[83]

Regional practice

During the Cold War, the OAS was the only regional arrangement to impose sanctions when it acted against the Dominican Republic and Cuba in the early 1960s.[84]

77 See below.

78 Article 23 (2).

79 Article 7 (1) (g), Protocol Relating to the Establishment of the Peace and Security Council of the African Union 2002.

80 Article 30, Constitutive Act of the African Union. See further Negm, N., 'The Sanctions Regime of the African Union in Response to Unconstitutional Changes of Government,' in Johnstone, I. and Ratner, S. (eds), *Talking International Law* (Oxford: OUP, 2021), pp.218–235.

81 Article 33.

82 Article 45, ECOWAS Protocol on Democracy and Good Governance 2001.

83 See Chapter 5 for discussion of the effectiveness of non-military sanctions in achieving their objectives.

84 For discussion see Brown-John, C. Lloyd, 'Economic sanctions: The case of the O.A.S. and the Dominican Republic, 1960–1962,' *Caribbean Studies*, 1975, v.15, n.2, pp.73–105; Akehurst, supra n50, pp.188–192.

As the more widespread imposition of sanctions by the Security Council commenced following the end of the Cold War,[85] their utilisation by regional arrangements has often been in support of or to complement measures that have been decided upon by the Security Council. However, on some occasions, sanctions have been applied by regional bodies in the absence of any UN measures having been applied, sometimes to effect wider objectives associated with the promotion of human rights and which evidence the evolution of collective security to embrace key human rights standards in the practice of the bodies taking action. The EU has been particularly active in this respect,[86] and has imposed sanctions in connection with the violation of international electoral standards in Belarus,[87] against members of the Egyptian government during the Arab Spring in connection with alleged misappropriation of state funds[88] and against Myanmar as a result of the domestic policies of its ruling military junta.[89] Significantly, the EU, like the Arab League, was able to impose wide-ranging sanctions upon Syria in response to human rights atrocities at a time when the Security Council was divided upon such measures,[90] and also imposed sanctions on Zimbabwe following human rights abuses by the Mugabe regime.[91] More recently, the EU has been responsible for the imposition of some of the most robust sanctions against Russia as a consequence of its invasion of Ukraine.[92] However, these have not been without their difficulties in terms of achieving consensus on their implementation as a result of the varied stances taken towards the conflict by EU member states.[93] A series of EU sanctions regimes have been imposed in response to situations existing in African states, sometimes in

85 See Chapter 5.

86 On the application of sanctions by the EU see Eeckhout, P., *EU External Relations Law* (2nd ed.) (Oxford: Oxford University Press, 2011), Chapter 12; Orakhelashvili, A., *Collective Security* (Oxford: Oxford University Press, 2011), pp.264–266; Giumelli, F., *How EU Sanctions Work: A New Narrative* (Paris: European Union Institute for Security Studies, 2013); Cardwell, P.J. and Moret, E., 'The EU, sanctions and regional leadership,' *European Security*, 2023, v.32, n.1, pp.1–21. For an overview of the various EU sanctions regimes currently in force, see https://data.europa.eu/apps/eusanctionstracker.

87 Council Decision 2010/639/CFSP (OJ L 280, 26.10.2010, p.18).

88 Council Decision 2011/172/CFSP (OJ L 76, 22.3.2011, p.63).

89 Council Decision 2010/232/CFSP (OJ L 105, 27.4.2010, p.22). See further Schembera, K., 'The rocky road of interregionalism: EU sanctions against human rights-violating Myanmar and repercussions on ASEAN-EU relations,' *Cambridge Review of International Affairs*, 2016, v.29, n.3, pp.1022–1043.

90 Council Decision 2011/782/CFSP (OJ L 319, 2.12.2011, p.56).

91 Council Decision 2011/101/CFS (OJ L 42, 16.2.2011, p.6).

92 See, e.g., Council Regulations (EU) 2022/259, 2022/260, 2022/261, 2022/262, 2022/263. These measures were adopted in the immediate aftermath of the Russian invasion, but have been added to on several occasions since. See, e.g., Council Regulations (EU) 2025/932, 2025/964.

93 See Portela, C., Pospieszna, P., Skrzypczynska, J. and Walentek, D., 'Consensus against all odds: Explaining the persistence of EU sanctions on Russia,' *Journal of European Integration*, 2021, v.43, n.6, pp.683–699, at pp.684–685.

support of UN measures. At the time of writing, Mali,[94] Guinea-Bissau,[95] Sudan,[96] South Sudan,[97] the Central African Republic,[98] DRC,[99] Libya,[100] Somalia[101] and Zimbabwe[102] are all subject to restrictive measures stemming from EU acts.[103]

The OAS has also proven itself willing to apply sanctions, having recommended its members adopt a series of measures in response to the military junta's seizure of power in Haiti some time before the UN Security Council adopted similar measures,[104] while later suspending Honduras' membership on account of the coup which took place there in 2009.[105] The African Union and ECOWAS, both organisations that have recently placed human rights at the centre of their conceptions of security, have imposed sanctions in response to incidents of concern stemming from human rights abuses or humanitarian crises. For example, both organisations imposed sanctions against the military junta that seized power in Mali during 2012.[106] Prior to its military incursions in those states,[107] ECOWAS sanctions against Liberia, Sierra Leone and Guinea-Bissau were particularly notable,[108] soon being supplemented by UN sanctions.[109] Responding to unconstitutional changes of government has been a key priority of both of these bodies, serving as the impetus for ECOWAS's imposition of sanctions against and suspension of Burkina Faso, Mali and Niger. The success of these measures might however be questioned due to the subsequent withdrawal from membership of the three states.[110] The African Union has also imposed sanctions in response to

94 See, e.g., Council Decision 2017/1775/CFSP.
95 See, e.g., Council Decision 2010/638/CFSP.
96 See, e.g., Council Decision 2014/450/CFSP.
97 See, e.g., Council Decision 2015/740/CFSP.
98 See, e.g., Council Decision 2013/798/CFSP.
99 See, e.g., Council Decision 2010/788/CFSP.
100 See, e.g., Council Decision 2015/1333/CFSP.
101 See, e.g., Council Decision 2010/231/CFSP.
102 See, e.g., Council Decision 2011/101/CFSP. See also Mutanda, D., 'EU sanctions on Zimbabwe: Rethinking Africa's economic and political security in the global age,' *Politikon*, 2023, v.50, n.4, pp.334–351.
103 See also Mutanda, ibid, pp.357–358.
104 See OAS MRE/RES.1, corr.1 (Oct 3, 1991).
105 See OAS General Assembly Resolution E—219/09, available at https://www.oas.org/en/media_center/press_release.asp?sCodigo=e-219/09.
106 See, for example, 'West African ECOWAS leaders impose Mali sanctions,' BBC News Online, 3 April 2012, available at http://www.bbc.co.uk/news/world-africa-17591322.
107 See below.
108 See Orakhelashvili, supra n86, pp.268–269.
109 ECOWAS sanctions against Sierra Leone were followed by UN sanctions imposed by SC Res 1132 (1997). See also UN Doc. S/PV.3822.
110 See Joint Communique from the Republic of Mali, Burkina Faso, and the Republic of Niger, 29 January 2025, available at https://maliembassy.us/joint-communique-from-the-republic-of-mali-burkina-faso-and-the-republic-of-niger/.

several unconstitutional changes of government within member states,[111] although often these have taken the form of suspension from participation in AU activities.[112]

A possible issue of concern arising from the EU's approach to sanctions is their application to states beyond its membership, in Africa and Asia,[113] making it the only regional body to have applied sanctions against targets outside of its own region. In fact, all of its sanctions have been applied against non-member states, leading some to question the legal basis for such action.[114] It is contended here that so long as a regional organisation's constituent provisions do not restrict its application of sanctions to its membership, there is no reason why it cannot apply them in respect of third states or actors if its members agree upon such a course of action. This may be in pursuit of values shared by that organisation's membership or to address perceived external threats to its number. As noted above, states have long enjoyed the power to adopt non-military sanctions on an individual basis and are thus entitled to do so collectively. That a group of states collectively constitutes an organisation should not prevent them from acting together in pursuit of common objectives simply because they involve the imposition of lawful measures against third states and actors. It must be remembered also that several of the sanctions regimes imposed by the EU have been in support of UN sanctions, which all members are obliged to respect; EU measures are compatible with such an obligation.

The difficulty of measuring the success of sanctions was noted in Chapter 5, and there is no relevant evidence to suggest that regional sanctions have been any more effective in achieving their objectives than those imposed by the UN.

Regional peacekeeping

The legal framework

We noted the difficulties of defining peacekeeping in Chapter 6. Where a peacekeeping operation follows the traditional principles that governed earlier generations of UN peacekeeping operations, there is no legal restraint from the UN Charter perspective on the ability of regional bodies to deploy such an operation. The deployment of a force which does not resort to military force other than in self-defence and is present with the consent of the state upon whose territory it is based, to perform agreed functions impartially, presents no challenge to the provisions of the UN Charter applicable to military intervention. Peacekeeping,

111 See Negm, supra n80, pp.228–234.

112 See Magliveras, K.D., 'The sanctioning system of the African Union: Part success, part failure?,' Paper presented at Expert Roundtable on 'The African Union: The First Ten Years,' Institute of Security Studies, Addis Ababa, October 2011, pp.15–29.

113 For full details of EU sanctions, see the list cited supra n86.

114 This issue has been largely overlooked by commentators on regional sanctions. See, however, White, supra n72, pp.338–342.

traditionally understood, differs from military enforcement action and is not based upon Chapter VII of the UN Charter.[115] UN authority for such operations is not necessary, as there is no prima facie violation of Article 2 (4). However, where an operation performs a mandate that is in line with those of operations which the Security Council has created under Chapter VII of the UN Charter, applying military measures which entail coercive force, it is likely that the Council's authority for such action is necessary as the boundaries of peacekeeping and military enforcement become blurred. This blurring has been particularly problematic within an African context where military operations undertaken by regional bodies are invariably described as peacekeeping missions, but which have on occasion employed such a broad conception of the term as to step into the realm of what is more appropriately considered military enforcement.[116] Any exercise of the use of force in legal terms constitutes an exception to Article 2 (4)'s general prohibition, and the integrity of this provision is served through narrowly defined exceptions. This requires that force other than that exercised in self-defence ought to be subject to the overall control of the Security Council, which it cannot be if its authority is not required for its application. Whereas the Council is legally entitled to adopt a broad conception of peacekeeping given its wide-ranging powers under Chapter VII, the subordination of regional bodies to the UN suggests that they ought not to be unless such operations receive the authorisation of the Council under Article 53.

Although a number of regional bodies' constituent instruments make provision for military operations to be undertaken,[117] few make specific reference to peacekeeping, and none actually define it.[118] Perhaps the clearest indication of any organisation's conception of peacekeeping appears in the Helsinki Summit document of the OSCE which, in providing for peacekeeping to be one of the OSCE's permitted functions,[119] expressly states that its peacekeeping operations will not entail enforcement action,[120] and reaffirms the principles of consent and impartiality,[121] thus removing them from the scope of Article 53 (1). Peacekeeping is also included in tasks which may be undertaken under the EU's common

115 See Chapter 6.

116 Williams and Boutellis suggest within an African Union context, for example, that there is a tendency to conceive of peacekeeping in broader terms than it has traditionally been understood within a UN context, effectively extending to enforcement. See Williams and Boutellis, supra n15, at pp.259–264. See also further below.

117 See below.

118 Writing in 1997, Gray notes that at that time the only express provision of a regional organisation's constituent framework providing for it to undertake peacekeeping was Article 6 of the Inter-American Treaty of Reciprocal Assistance 1947. See Gray, supra n3, at p.96.

119 CSCE Helsinki Summit Document 1992: The Challenges of Change, Pt.III, para.17.

120 Ibid, para.22.

121 Supra n119, paras.23–24.

foreign and security policy.[122] ECOWAS's 1999 protocol refers to peacekeeping as one of its functions, yet does not elaborate upon this in any real detail,[123] and the African Union's 2002 protocol refers to the power to conduct peace support operations,[124] with the envisaged African standby force's tasks to include observation and monitoring and peace support missions.[125] Importantly, partnership initiatives have been developed between the UN and some regional bodies to enhance peacekeeping capacities on a regional level,[126] a process encouraged by the HIPPO report.[127]

Again, as will be explained in greater detail below in reference to military enforcement action, there is no reason why the absence of any express provision to undertake peacekeeping tasks should act as a bar to an organisation so acting with the agreement of its members. As Gray explains, 'it seems to have been accepted by States that regional organisations have implied powers to establish peacekeeping forces … States can do together … what they could do separately.'[128]

Regional practice

A number of regional peacekeeping operations have been undertaken, although some operations labelled 'peacekeeping' by the relevant actors – perhaps the most prominent of which was the ECOWAS intervention in Liberia in the early 1990s – arguably belong in the category of military enforcement and are therefore considered below. As with UN peacekeeping, the relative success of these regional operations has varied in accordance with a number of factors.[129] Few regional peacekeeping operations took place during the Cold War and cannot be said to have made a major contribution towards the maintenance of international peace and security. Although an OAS peacekeeping force deployed to the Dominican Republic in the mid-1960s played a short-term role in stabilising and assisting the country through free elections, the extent to which it constituted a genuinely

122 Treaty on European Union 1992, Article 43 (1).

123 Protocol Relating to the Mechanism for Conflict Prevention, Management, Resolution, Peace-Keeping and Security 1999. See, for example, Articles 3, 6, 10, 19.

124 Protocol Relating to the Establishment of the Peace and Security Council of the African Union 2002. See, for example, Articles 6 (d), 7 (1) (c).

125 Article 13 (3). See also Jordaan, E., 'Collective Security in Africa: The Tension Between Theory and Practice,' *Strategic Review for Southern Africa*, 2017, v.39, n.1, pp.160–184.

126 See, e.g., Yamashita, H., 'Peacekeeping cooperation between the United Nations and regional organisations,' *Review of International Studies*, 2012, v.38, pp.165–186.

127 *Report of the High-level Independent Panel on Peace Operations on Uniting Our Strengths for Peace: Politics, Partnership and People*, 2015, UN Doc. A/70/95-S/2015/446, paras.53–60.

128 Gray, supra n3, p.97.

129 See Chapter 6.

impartial peacekeeping operation has been the source of some debate.[130] An Arab League force in Lebanon was heavily dominated by Syria and unable to make a significant contribution in the face of the intransigence of the parties to the conflict,[131] and an OAU force proved unsuccessful in ameliorating the consequences of civil war in Chad.[132] Although assessments of that operation vary,[133] it is apparent that it experienced significant difficulties. Only a third of its proposed strength was deployed; it only comprised contributions from three states,[134] and it relied on financial support from outside of the region, suggesting very few African states were able or willing to participate in an African-led operation without external support.[135]

Post–Cold War peacekeeping activity on the part of regional bodies has been essentially confined to Africa and Europe, although military activity taken under the auspices of regional organisations in these continents has often taken the form of enforcement. Significantly, several peacekeeping operations undertaken by regional bodies, whether acting alone or in partnership with the UN,[136] have proceeded on the basis of mandates conferred by UN Security Council resolutions. These resolutions have increasingly been adopted under Chapter VII, and while this may beg the question as to why Chapter VIII was not the preferred basis, this is in common with the position increasingly adopted in respect of UN peacekeeping operations. The conferment of a Chapter VII mandate, invariably containing authority to utilise 'all necessary measures' or similar in its discharge, provides a legal basis for those regional operations which may utilise a degree of coercive force in the manner of their operation. African Union peacekeeping operations established during the first decade post-millennium were deployed to Burundi,[137]

130 Although the UN includes the operation in its overview of peacekeeping operations: see https://peacekeeping.un.org/sites/default/files/past/domrepbackgr.html.

131 See McCoubrey and Morris, supra n3, p.198.

132 For discussion, see Naldi, G.J., 'Peace-keeping attempts by the Organization of African Unity,' *International and Comparative Law Quarterly*, 1985, v.34, pp.593–601; May, R. and Massey, S., 'The OAU intervention in Chad: Mission impossible or mission evaded?,' *International Peacekeeping*, 1998, v.5, n.1, pp.46–65.

133 Contrast, for example, Cot, J.-P., 'The role of the inter-African peacekeeping force in Chad, 1981–1982,' in Cassese, A. (ed.), *The Current Legal Regulation of the Use of Force* (Dordrecht, Boston and Lancaster: Martinus Nijhoff, 1986), pp.167–178; Naldi, ibid.

134 Nigeria, Senegal and Zaire.

135 For discussion, see Gray, supra n3, pp.97–100; Gray, supra n31, pp.300–301; May, R. and Cleaver, G., 'African peacekeeping: Still dependent?,' *International Peacekeeping*, 1997, v.4, n.2, pp.1–21, at pp.12–13; Naldi, supra n132, pp.593–595; Olonisakin, F., 'African "Homemade" peacekeeping initiatives,' *Armed Forces & Society*, 1997, v.23, n.3, pp.349–371, at pp.350–356.

136 For an appraisal of peacekeeping partnerships between the AU and UN, see Fafore, O.A., 'The African Union's Collective Security Mechanisms and the Challenge of Armed Non-State Actors,' *Journal of African Union Studies*, 2020, v.9, n.3, pp.87–109, at pp.98–99.

137 African Mission in Burundi (AMIB). AMIB was succeeded by ONUB, established by the UN Security Council acting under Chapter VII in SC Res 1545 (2004).

Somalia,[138] the Comoros[139] and Sudan,[140] an operation succeeded in turn by a hybrid innovative UN–AU partnership mission, UNAMID.[141] Although of potential benefit in supporting under-resourced African states taking responsibility for peacekeeping on the continent, UN–AU cooperation has not been without its challenges due to a divergence of views over the nature of peacekeeping.[142] Although ECOWAS has been active in deploying military operations to trouble spots in West Africa, its earliest 'peacekeeping' operations – in the likes of Liberia, Sierra Leone, Guinea-Bissau and the Côte d'Ivoire – invariably amounted to enforcement actions due to the scale of force exercised by them and are thus considered in the next section.[143] However, as with some AU operations, the UN Security Council has also conferred Chapter VII mandates upon peacekeeping operations led by ECOWAS, for example AFISMA in Mali.[144]

The EU has conducted a number of operations ranging from low-key policing missions to military enforcement action. Its first real peacekeeping operation was Operation Concordia in Macedonia, which replaced a NATO operation and is considered to have been a general success.[145] It has also deployed a range of lower-key missions, including those tasked with policing functions,[146] as well as acting outside of the region, the naval 'Operation Atalanta' off the Somali coast being a prime example.[147] Other regional organisations have undertaken peacekeeping or related deployments on a smaller scale. For example, the OSCE has deployed various field missions in support of peace and security objectives, albeit

138 African Mission in Somalia (AMISOM). While created by the African Union in January 2007, from February 2007 it operated under a mandate conferred by the UN Security Council acting under Chapter VII. See SC Res 1744 (2007). This mandate was extended periodically thereafter, succeeded in turn by the AU-led ATMIS. See SC Res 2628 (2022).

139 Security Assistance Mission in the Comoros (MAES).

140 AMIS.

141 Established by SC Res 1769 (2007). On the earlier African Union operations, see Omorogbe, E.Y., 'Can the African Union deliver peace and security?,' *Journal of Conflict and Security Law*, 2011, v.16, n.1, pp.35–62. See also Tavares, supra n7, pp.21–34.

142 See Williams and Boutellis, supra n15. See also Badmus, I.A., 'The African Mission in Burundi (AMIB): A Study of the African Union's Peacekeeping Success and "Triangular Area of Tension in African Peacekeeping",' *India Quarterly*, 2017, v.73, n.1, pp.1–20.

143 See Tavares, supra n7, pp.35–45.

144 SC Res 2085 (2012).

145 On EU operations, see Naert, F., 'ESDP in practice: Increasingly varied and ambitious EU security and defence operations,' in Trybus and White, supra n72, pp.61–101, at pp.65–86; Tsagourias, N., 'EU peacekeeping operations: Legal and theoretical issues,' in Trybus and White, supra n72, pp.102–133, at pp.107–110.

146 For an overview, see the relevant part of the EU website, https://www.eeas.europa.eu/eeas/missions-and-operations_en.

147 Established by Council Decision (CFSP) 2024/3186. An overview of the mission's mandate can be found at https://eunavfor.eu/mission.

not reaching the scale of peacekeeping operations,[148] while the Commonwealth of Independent States (CIS) has undertaken peacekeeping operations in several former Soviet states.[149]

Regional military enforcement action

The legal framework

Military enforcement action by regional organisations has taken place on several occasions during the post–Cold War era, as a number of regional bodies – particularly within Europe and Africa – have placed increased emphasis on developing such a role for themselves in terms of both the provisions of their constituent frameworks and their military infrastructure. Controversy has arisen, however, where regional organisations have acted in a manner which appears at odds with the UN Charter requirements applicable to regional military enforcement action, and developments within the African Union and ECOWAS especially have come to challenge the continued relevance of those very requirements, at least as applicable to the actions of those organisations. The UN Charter explicitly provides for enforcement action to be taken by regional arrangements in Article 53, which states that 'The Security Council shall, where appropriate, utilize such regional arrangements or agencies for enforcement action under its authority. But no enforcement action shall be taken under regional arrangements or by regional agencies without the authorization of the Security Council.' In attempting to understand the scope of this provision, four issues arguably require attention: the question of when it is 'appropriate' to utilise regional arrangements and agencies for military enforcement purposes, as required by Article 53; the nature of the authorisation that must be provided by the Security Council; the legal competence of regional arrangements and agencies within the terms of their own constituent frameworks; and the matter of regional accountability to the Security Council in light of developments which appear to have undermined this.

When is it 'appropriate' to utilise regional arrangements and agencies?

The requirement that regional arrangements and agencies utilised for enforcement action be 'appropriate' for this has not received much attention and is best seen as recognition of the political judgement which the Security Council must exercise when considering whether to authorise regional action in each situation. Although not strictly a legal requirement, it is suggested that the perceived legitimacy of regional operations warrants that three important considerations are borne in mind by the Security Council before sanctioning action. First, the

148 For an overview, see *Survey of OSCE Field Operations*, OSCE Secretariat Prevention Centre, OSCE Doc. SEC.GAL/84/13, 7 May 2013.

149 Note also the deployment of a CTSO operation to Kazakhstan in 2022.

military capacities of the relevant organisations are central to the practical role that they can play in conducting military operations. The very legitimacy of an operation becomes undermined if it is not perceived to be led by a credible actor. While an organisation like NATO boasts a permanent, highly developed and institutionalised military capability that it can call on, most relevant organisations have traditionally lacked permanent, readily available resources, instead relying on ad hoc formations. Recent developments within organisations such as the EU, the African Union and ECOWAS have sought to enhance their military capabilities, principally through the creation of standby arrangements.[150] Second, an understanding of the legal framework and political agenda of each organisation is central in considering its possible role as a military enforcement actor. Whereas some organisations clearly envisage themselves performing military functions, others do not, and ultimately it is these political objectives that will determine the role which they discharge in support of the UN collective security system. Finally, to make the use of a regional arrangement 'appropriate,' it is important to ensure that it is not politically unsuited to the situation at hand. While states in a region may be more willing to act in response to local situations by virtue of being more directly affected, their involvement in responses to certain conflicts or disputes may form part of broader objectives to advance individual goals of their own which are incompatible with the collective objectives specified in the relevant Security Council resolutions authorising military enforcement action. Particular danger arises in situations whereby a regional operation is heavily under the influence of a single state in respect of which there are serious concerns as to its suitability to act in the circumstances. As noted earlier in this chapter, hegemony is a potential problem in a number of organisations where a region is dominated by the existence of one major regional actor, in contrast to the UN's global membership.

The requirement of UN Security Council authorisation

Article 53 (1)'s final requirement is that enforcement action receives Security Council authorisation. There has been some discussion as to whether this authorisation must precede action, or whether it may be granted subsequently.[151] It is contended that the better view holds that authorisation should be obtained before any military enforcement action is taken.[152] The insertion of Article 53 (1) by the UN's founders reflected a genuine concern at the time that regional bodies might act for their own ends.[153] The UN Charter aims to centralise the use of

150 See below.

151 See, for example, Abass, supra n3, pp.52–59; Akehurst, supra n68, p.214.

152 Morrison, supra n3, p.50.

153 Hickey, supra n75, p.76. See also Harrell, P.E., 'Modern-day "guarantee clauses" and the legal authority of multinational organizations to authorize the use of military force,' *Yale Journal of International Law*, 2008, v.33, pp.417–446, at p.423.

force under the ultimate authority and control of the Security Council. Only prior authorisation fully ensures effective Security Council control of operations. As Ress and Brohmer argue, 'effective control … requires the means and possibility to exert influence over the concrete enforcement actions planned by the regional arrangement, for example to review their proportionality. This is only possible if Art[icle] 53 is read as demanding prior authorization.'[154] Villani makes the same point, arguing that 'when it authorizes an enforcement action by regional organizations, the Security Council must keep effective control over such an action.'[155] The danger of permitting subsequent authorisation is that otherwise illegal uses of force are encouraged in the hope that they will be authorised afterwards,[156] risking placing operations in a legal 'no-man's land,' whereby they are potentially lawful or unlawful depending upon when and if the Security Council ever decides to authorise them ex post facto.[157] Consider, for example, NATO's bombing of the Federal Republic of Yugoslavia that lacked any express UN Security Council authorisation. A subsequent Russian-sponsored draft resolution condemning the action was defeated in the Security Council by a 12 to 3 vote.[158] Thus, although lacking legal justification, the rejection of a condemnatory resolution lent at least an air of legitimacy to it, even if not ex post facto authorisation. The prior authorisation of enforcement action ensures that its legality is in no doubt.[159]

A number of writers have, however, taken the view that retroactive authorisation satisfies the requirements of Article 53 (1). One such commentator, Paliwal, writes that 'sufficient scholarly opinion indicates that approval or commendation of a regional enforcement action after it has taken place satisfies the authorization requirement of Article 53 (1).'[160] It is certainly possible to identify situations in which the Security Council has expressed its approval or commendation of regional military action.[161] The first such example is found with the ECOWAS intervention in Liberia, commended by the Security Council in Resolution 788. This was followed by similar retroactive commendation of ECOWAS military action taken in respect of Sierra Leone[162] and the African Union's deployment of

154 Ress and Brohmer, supra n25, at p.864.

155 Villani, supra n73, p.552. See also Nowrot, K. and Schabacker, E.W., 'The use of force to restore democracy: International legal implications of the ECOWAS intervention in Sierra Leone,' *American University International Law Review*, 1998–1999, v.14, pp.321–412, at pp.363–364; Doktori, supra n16, p.339.

156 See Akehurst, supra n68, p.214; Villani, supra n73, p.552.

157 See Ress and Brohmer, supra n25, pp.867–869; Gray, supra n31, pp.37–42.

158 *UNYB* 343.

159 Subject to the action taking place in accordance with the parameters of the mandate conferred upon it.

160 Paliwal, supra n71, p.194.

161 See Paliwal, supra n71, pp.198–213.

162 See SC Res 1162 (1998). See also UN Docs. S/PV.3857, S/PV.3902.

the AMIB operation to Burundi.[163] However, commendation cannot be assumed to constitute retroactive authorisation. It could simply reflect an expression of the Council's satisfaction, whereas authorisation entails the conferment of legal authority for an action.[164] Importantly, commendation can also be issued as a means of expressing support for non-coercive regional activities, for example ECOWAS's mediation efforts in Mali.[165] Some distinction should arguably be retained between the means of expressing support for legally non-contentious measures and those requiring express UN authority. Furthermore, to accept 'commendation' or similar such language as amounting to authorisation effectively opens the door to allowing implicit, as opposed to express, authorisation. This is dangerous in that any Security Council statement of support, however loosely articulated, for any course of action may potentially be seized upon as providing legal authority for action that the Council may not have even envisaged. This risk was considered in the previous chapter. It is submitted that the better view remains that for the purposes of ensuring legal certainty and ultimate UN oversight of regional action and the accountability of regional actors to the Security Council, its prior express authorisation is required for enforcement action taken by regional arrangements.

References to Article 53 by the Security Council have been sparse,[166] which is not particularly helpful when attempting to find authority within its resolutions for military action taken by regional organisations which might cross the threshold of enforcement action. The absence of any reference to Article 53 or Chapter VIII more broadly does not preclude the conferment of an enforcement mandate on a regional organisation. Where enforcement authority has been conferred upon regional bodies, it has typically been done with reference to Chapter VII generally and invariably without naming specific organisations entrusted with a Security Council mandate. One such recent example of this approach is found in the conferment of authority upon states acting individually or through regional organisations to use the necessary measures to enforce the inspection of vessels off the coast of Libya.[167] However, whether expressly sanctioned under Article 53/Chapter VIII or under Chapter VII, either basis would be indicative of the conferment of enforcement powers. Perhaps of greater concern has been the suggestion that certain regional organisations have attempted to develop an autonomous

163 SC Res 1545 (2004).

164 See Abass, supra n3, pp.54–57; Ress and Brohmer, supra n25, p.864.

165 See, e.g., UN Doc. S/PV.8794.

166 See, e.g., *Repertoire of the Practice of the Security Council*, supra n49, pp.547–551. No resolutions referred explicitly to Article 53 during 2021, while during 2023 only one resolution did so (SC Res 2719 (2023)).

167 First authorised in SC Res 2292 (2016), this authority has been extended periodically, including recently through SC Res 2780 (2025).

right to take military action that is not contingent on prior UN Security Council authorisation, an issue which is considered in the following sections.

The legal competence of regional arrangements and agencies

There is no indication that any significant attention has been given from the UN perspective to the question of whether the organisations utilised for enforcement action under Chapter VIII are legally competent to do so within the terms of their own constituent frameworks. The main debate has centred on the compatibility of regional action with the UN Charter framework.[168] Article 103 provides that 'in the event of a conflict between the obligations of the Members of the United Nations under the present Charter and their obligations under any other international agreement, their obligations under the present Charter shall prevail.' If states were obliged to take enforcement action on the direction of the Security Council, Article 103 would render any provisions of an organisation's constituent framework prohibiting this irrelevant. However, it is generally accepted that the absence of the special agreements between the Council and member states envisaged by Article 43 means that the Council cannot compel states to participate in military operations. As Higgins states, 'the consequence of the failure to conclude agreements under Article 43 was that UN members could not be compelled to provide forces and assistance.'[169] If states cannot be compelled to participate in action, it would be a strange interpretation of the UN Charter which found that regional arrangements could be so compelled, given that regional organisations are simply groups of states.[170]

Ress and Brohmer argue that the absence of Article 43 agreements means that regional arrangements can only be used for enforcement action with their consent.[171] On a practical level, it would be wise for the Security Council to have regard to the internal legal frameworks of regional arrangements when considering their utilisation for military enforcement purposes. It is doubtful whether it would be appropriate to attempt to make use of regional arrangements for actions prohibited by their own legal frameworks, and in practice, the Council does not appear to have authorised regional action when this would appear to obviously

168 Gray, supra n3, p.97; Lumsden, E., 'An uneasy peace: Multilateral military intervention in civil wars,' *New York University Journal of International Law and Politics*, 2002–2003, v.35, pp.795–838, p.815.

169 Higgins, R., *Problems and Processes: International Law and How we Use it* (Oxford: Clarendon Press, 1994), at p.265.

170 White N.D., *Keeping the Peace: The United Nations and the Maintenance of International Peace and Security* (Manchester and New York: Manchester University Press, 1997), pp.116–117; Malancuk, P., *Akehurst's Modern Introduction to International Law* (7th ed.) (London and New York: Routledge, 1997), p.389.

171 Ress and Brohmer, supra n25, p.863.

contravene the relevant organisation's internal legal framework.[172] The constituent frameworks of regional arrangements reflect to a large extent their political agendas and values, and to make use of a regional arrangement for action which was perceived as running counter to its core principles would be problematic. The perceived legitimacy of regional arrangements will hinge upon the manner in which they operate, and participation in military enforcement action may be difficult if considered to run counter to their legal frameworks.

While the legal frameworks governing some regional organisations appear to include provisions that might be taken to confer upon them the power to undertake military enforcement action, the frameworks of many do not contain such express provisions. This has not, however, always been a bar to their participation in military enforcement measures. For example, although NATO's treaty only expressly provides for defensive military action in response to an attack on one of its members in a specifically defined geographical area,[173] its members have willingly taken non-defensive military measures on the basis of Security Council authorisation. This began with action in support of UN peacekeeping operations in the former Yugoslavia,[174] while NATO also applied coercive military force against targets in Libya on the basis of authority provided in Security Council resolutions.[175] The lack of any military enforcement provision within an organisation's governing treaty should not prevent it from being utilised for this purpose if its membership consents to this. As McCoubrey and Morris argue, with specific reference to NATO:

> other operations may, subject to general norms of international law, still be undertaken with [the members'] consent in their sovereign capacities using the infrastructure which they themselves have created ... peace support beyond its core remit is in effect undertaken as a pre-existing and highly organised 'coalition of the willing.'[176]

It is difficult to see any legal objection to the members of an arrangement mutually agreeing to use its resources for additional purposes. Although they cannot be required to undertake such obligations, they can agree to assume them.[177] Although it is difficult to justify the adoption of coercive military measures by

172 Abass, supra n3, p.63.
173 Articles 5 and 6, North Atlantic Treaty 1949.
174 See, for example, Gazzini, T., 'NATO's role in the collective security system,' *Journal of Conflict and Security Law*, 2003, v.8, n.2, pp.231–263.
175 SC Res 1973 (2011).
176 McCoubrey and Morris, supra n3, p.231.
177 Nordquist, M.H., *What Color Helmet?* (Newport: Naval War College, 1997), p.63; White, N.D., *The Law of International Organisations* (Manchester and New York: Manchester University Press, 1996), p.205.

organisations where their constituent frameworks expressly prohibit enforcement action on their part, to cite merely the absence of express provision for enforcement action to prevent them from participating in military enforcement measures is an unduly legalistic approach.

Significantly, however, a number of regional organisations have sought to develop normative and institutional provisions which build upon their original constituent frameworks in order to provide stronger potential legal bases for their conducting military enforcement action, evidencing a willingness to evolve to respond to new challenges arising in their areas of operation. This has particularly been the case in respect of key European and African bodies, which we focus our attention on here in illustrating the normative and institutional evolution of regional bodies as military enforcement actors.

NATO, the organisation enjoying the strongest military capacity, was established as a Western collective self-defence alliance to counteract the Soviet threat at the outset of the Cold War period,[178] and its treaty makes no reference to Chapter VIII of the UN Charter. However, while NATO's treaty has not been amended and the organisation has continued to regard collective self-defence as remaining its core remit notwithstanding the expanded scope of the operations which it will conduct,[179] its members have made it clear that they are prepared to use NATO's military infrastructure for additional purposes such as military enforcement action ever since NATO conducted operations in the former Yugoslavia during the 1990s, in support of Security Council objectives. This wider use of NATO resources was first formally approved by NATO's Council at Washington in its 1999 Strategic Concept.[180] NATO's Strategic Concept has been revised on several occasions since, but continues to assert a willingness to undertake a wider range of operations than those taken in self-defence.[181] The most recent iteration is clear in articulating a role for NATO which encompasses three core tasks: deterrence and defence, crisis prevention and management and cooperative security.[182]

The EU has likewise constitutionally evolved as a body that can be utilised within the terms of its own internal legal framework for enforcement action under UN Security Council authority. Although originally a primarily economic organisation,[183] the Treaty on European Union introduced a common foreign and

178 See further Smith, M.A., 'At arm's length: NATO and the United Nations in the cold war era,' *International Peacekeeping*, 1995, v.2, n.1, pp.56–73.

179 See, for example, the NATO Council's Washington Declaration of April 1999, para.2, text in *NATO Review*, 1999, v.47, n.2, at p.D1. NATO's core remit was reaffirmed by the Riga Summit Declaration of 29 November 2006, *Press Release (2006) 150*.

180 Ibid, pp.D7–13.

181 See most recently, the NATO 2022 Strategic Concept, available at https://www.nato.int/nato_static_fl2014/assets/pdf/2022/6/pdf/290622-strategic-concept.pdf.

182 Ibid, paras.20–46.

183 See Arnull, A., Dashwood, A., Dougan, M., Ross, M., Spaventa, E. and Wyatt, D., *Wyatt and Dashwood's European Union Law* (5th ed.) (London: Sweet & Maxwell, 2006), Chapter 1.

security policy.[184] The Treaty of Nice developed its military role by amending the Treaty on European Union, Article 43 (1) of which now provides for EU action taken under its common foreign and security policy to include 'humanitarian and rescue tasks, military advice and assistance tasks, conflict prevention and peace-keeping tasks, tasks of combat forces in crisis management, including peace-making and post-conflict stabilisation.' The broad range of activities covered by this provision may be taken as providing a legal base on which military enforcement action could be based. Significantly, under its common defence and security policy, the EU is expressly permitted to utilise its civilian military assets for 'missions outside the [EU] for peace-keeping, conflict prevention and strengthening international security in accordance with the principles of the United Nations Charter.'[185] Thus, an internal EU legal basis is also provided for those operations which it conducts beyond the geographic boundaries of the EU – in practice, all operations it has undertaken to date. A Political and Security Committee also exists as part of the EU's CFSP framework,[186] to which the Council of the EU may confer responsibility for the political control and strategic direction of crisis management operations. Unlike some other regional bodies,[187] the EU appears prima facie to have displayed a strong level of commitment to observance of the strictures of the UN Charter principles pertaining to the centralisation of enforcement action under the authority of the Security Council. On several occasions, the European Council has expressly stated that its contribution to international peace and security will be 'in accordance with the principles of the United Nations Charter' or has recognised the 'primary responsibility of the ... Security Council for maintaining peace and ... security.'[188] Core provisions of the EU's CFSP also emphasise the importance of conducting action in accordance with the UN Charter.[189]

With a disproportionate share of threats to international peace and security arising on the African continent, two of the region's organisations in particular have evidenced a willingness to develop their constitutional frameworks to provide them with a legal basis to function as military enforcement actors.[190] Arguably

184 Title V, Treaty on European Union. Text available on the EU website at https://eur-lex.europa.eu/resource.html?uri=cellar:2bf140bf-a3f8-4ab2-b506-fd71826e6da6.0023.02/DOC_1&format=PDF See McGoldrick, D., *International Relations Law of the European Union* (London and New York: Longman, 1997), Chapter 7.

185 Article 42 (1).

186 Article 38.

187 See below on the African Union and ECOWAS, for example.

188 See, for example, the Presidency Conclusions at Santa Maria Da Feira, Annex I, para.1, text available at https://www.europarl.europa.eu/enlargement_new/europeancouncil/pdf/feira_en.pdf and the Presidency Conclusions at Nice, Annex VI, text available at https://www.europarl.europa.eu/summits/nice1_en.htm.

189 See, e.g., Article 42 (1).

190 Note also, however, the provisions of the SADC's Protocol on Politics, Defence and Security Cooperation 2001. Article 11 (3) (d) allows it to resort to enforcement action as 'a last resort' and only with the authorisation of the UN Security Council under Article 53 of the UN Charter.

influenced by the explosion of civil conflict, and accompanying humanitarian crises, upon the continent in the post–Cold War era, the African Union sought from the point of its inception to confer itself with express powers to undertake enforcement operations which went beyond those enjoyed by its predecessor.[191] Its Constitutive Act has been subject to much analysis.[192] While reaffirming the OAU principles of sovereignty and non-intervention in Articles 3(b) and 4(g), Article 4(h) expressly affirms 'the right of the Union to intervene in a Member State pursuant to a decision of the Assembly in respect of grave circumstances.'[193] Initially, 'grave circumstances' were restricted to war crimes, genocide and crimes against humanity, but later broadened to include 'a serious threat to legitimate order,'[194] thus apparently providing a legal basis upon which enforcement action could be taken in a number of circumstances and reflecting a broadened conception of collective security which embraces respect for the protection of human rights.[195] The military architecture of the African Union was enhanced further with the adoption of the protocol relating to the establishment of its Peace and Security Council,[196] which significantly made provision for an African standby force to undertake peace support operations on behalf of the Union,[197] a long-standing aspiration on the continent.[198] However, more controversially, the protocol proclaimed that the African Union enjoyed the 'primary responsibility for promoting peace, security and stability in Africa.'[199] This appears to run counter to the UN Charter's allocation of primary responsibility for the maintenance of international

191 While the OAU's provisions did not expressly prohibit it from taking military enforcement action, arguably Articles III (2) and (3) of its charter suggested this was precluded in respect of intra-state situations with their emphasis upon the principles of non-interference in internal affairs and respect for the sovereignty and territorial integrity of each state.

192 Abass, A. and Baderin, M.A., 'Towards effective collective security and human rights protection in Africa: An assessment of the constitutive act of the new African Union,' *Netherlands International Law Review*, 2002, v.XLIX, pp.1–38; Magliveras, K.D. and Naldi, G.J., 'The African Union: A new dawn for Africa?,' *International and Comparative Law Quarterly*, 2002, v.51, n.2, pp.415–425; Packer, C.A.A. and Rukare, D., 'The new African Union and its constitutive act,' *American Journal of International Law*, 2002, v.96, n.2, pp.365–378.

193 Text available at https://au.int/sites/default/files/pages/34873-file-constitutiveact_en.pdf Article 4(j) also provides for 'Member states to request intervention from the Union in order to restore peace and security.'

194 By the Protocol on Amendments to the Constitutive Act of the African Union 2003, text in *Netherlands International Law Review*, 2004, v.LI, p.233.

195 Abass and Baderin, supra n192, pp.13–24; Abass, supra n3, pp.162–171; Maluwa, T., 'Fast-tracking African Union or making haste slowly? A note on the amendments to the constitutive act of the African Union,' *Netherlands International Law Review*, 2004, v.LI, pp.195–236, at pp.215–220.

196 For text, see https://www.peaceau.org/uploads/psc-protocol-en.pdf.

197 Article 13.

198 See, eg., Franke, B., 'A Pan-African Army: The evolution of an idea and its eventual realisation in the African Standby Force,' *African Security Studies*, 2006, v.15, n.4, pp.1–16.

199 Article 16 (1).

peace and security to the UN Security Council,[200] as well as the protocol's explicit acknowledgement of the UN Security Council's primary responsibility for the maintenance of international peace and security.[201] It has been suggested that the effect of Article 4(h) of the African Union's Constitutive Act was to empower the African Union to take military action without the authorisation of the UN Security Council.[202] This appears to be supported by statements at the time from the director of the African Union's Peace and Security Department.[203] The extent to which this development has undermined the ability of the UN Security Council to exert ultimate authority and control over regional action is considered further in the subsequent sections where we assess the level of regional accountability to the UN which exists and regional military enforcement practice.

The organisation most active on a military level within Africa has been ECOWAS. Like the EU, its origins were essentially economic,[204] but its members soon concluded protocols on Non-Aggression in 1978 and Mutual Assistance on Defence in 1981.[205] Article 4 of the latter protocol committed ECOWAS to take appropriate measures in the event of an armed conflict between member states, or an internal conflict supported by outside powers and likely to endanger peace and security in the community, including the possibility of military action under Article 6(3), although it was expressly provided that ECOWAS forces should not intervene in conflicts remaining internal to states. Article 13 also provided for earmarked forces to be made available by member states. However, an enhanced military role which extended to military enforcement action became possible under the terms of the *1999 Protocol Relating to the Mechanism for Conflict Prevention, Management, Resolution, Peacekeeping and Security*.[206] Essentially designed to serve as ECOWAS's key peace and security mechanism, this protocol allowed ECOWAS's use of force and established organs such as the Mediation and Security Council that under Article 10 (2) is empowered to 'authorise all forms of intervention [and] the deployment of political and military missions.' Under Article 25, a broad range of situations suffice to bring the mechanism introduced by the protocol into play, ranging from conflict between states, to serious human rights violations and overthrows of democratically elected governments. It is thus potentially applicable to situations internal to states and again evidences a broadened human rights-centred conception of security. Like the African Union,

200 Article 24 (1).
201 Preamble and Article 17 (1)
202 Abass, supra n3, pp.162–171.
203 In correspondence with Ademola Abass, he stated that 'we will not wait for the UN to authorise an action we intend to take.' Cited in Abass, supra n3, p.166.
204 See the ECOWAS Treaty, text in *ILM*, 1975, v.14, p.1200.
205 Contained in Weller, M. (ed.), *Regional Peace-keeping and International Enforcement: The Liberian Crisis* (Cambridge: Grotius Publications, 1994), at pp.18–19.
206 For discussion, see Abass, A., 'The new collective security mechanism of ECOWAS: Innovations and problems,' *Journal of Conflict and Security Law*, 2000, v.5, n.2, pp.211–229.

there are clear indications that ECOWAS envisaged itself able to undertake military enforcement action in the absence of a UN mandate. Abass points to Article 10 of its 1999 protocol, under which its Mediation and Security Council is given power to 'authorise all forms of interventions and decide … on the deployment of political and military missions,'[207] while the director of ECOWAS's legal department at the time was quoted as stating that it will not feel obliged to seek UN Security Council authorisation for its military interventions.[208] As with developments within the African Union, the extent to which this undermines the ultimate authority of the UN Security Council within the military enforcement realm is considered in the sections that follow.

Regional accountability to the UN Security Council

As explained in Chapter 7, the UN Charter system of collective security attempts to centralise the use of force by subjecting it to the ultimate authority and control of the Security Council. Except when exercised in self-defence, the use of force by states requires the sanction of the Security Council. The Charter provisions do not distinguish in this respect between action taken by states acting in ad hoc coalitions and that taken through regional forums of which they are members. Article 53 (1) provides that the Council shall utilise regional arrangements for enforcement action 'under its authority,' emphasising the importance of the Council's ultimate authority over such action. Article 54's requirement that regional arrangements keep the Council informed of their action reinforces the importance of its ability to exercise oversight of decentralised operations by mandating some form of reporting to the Council on the part of regional arrangements. UN control is important given the risk of participating states seeking to advance goals of their own which do not accord with those of the Security Council. As Farer comments, 'unlike the UN, regional organizations could be dominated by a single state or ideological bloc.'[209] The cases of Nigeria in ECOWAS, South Africa in SADC, the US in the OAS and Russia in the CIS are just some such examples.[210]

However, ensuring sufficient UN oversight over regional operations requires both that the Security Council strives to exert firm control over authorised actions and that regional arrangements themselves are amenable to the Council's overall control and willing to act strictly within the authority conferred upon them. There is some cause for concern that the Security Council has struggled to adequately

207 See Abass and Baderin, supra n140, pp.13–24; Abass, supra n3, pp.162–171; Maluwa, supra n143, pp.215–220.

208 Cited in Abass, supra n3, pp.166–167.

209 Farer, supra n3, p.164.

210 See also Weiss, T.G., Forsythe, D.P. and Coate, R.A., *The United Nations and Changing World Politics* (2nd ed.) (Boulder: Westview, 1997), p.41.

subject operations which it has authorised to its ultimate oversight.[211] Although more recent military enforcement authorisations by the Council have witnessed a stricter imposition of clear objectives, time limits and reporting requirements,[212] doubts over the Council's ability to exercise adequate control stem not from the nature of the resolutions in which it has clearly authorised enforcement action, but from situations in which it appears to have played no role in the initiation of enforcement action yet acquiesced in it, as well as evidence that some organisations have attempted to develop a degree of autonomy for themselves which might effectively result in the Council having little role in the oversight of the operations which they conduct.

The standard example routinely invoked of insufficient oversight by the Security Council of regional military enforcement is found in the already cited case of ECOWAS's 'peacekeeping' operation deployed to Liberia in the early 1990s.[213] It is generally accepted that the ECOWAS Monitoring Group (ECOMOG), the regional force deployed, took action going beyond traditional peacekeeping, involving the application of military force.[214] Thus, in accordance with the terms of Article 53 of the UN Charter, it should have received the prior authorisation of the Security Council. However, the force was not deployed pursuant to any UN military enforcement mandate. Initially, the Council seemed content to leave ECOWAS to its own devices in respect of initiatives taken in response to the ongoing civil war in Liberia, before adopting a resolution in which it commended ECOWAS for its efforts.[215] Initial ECOWAS intervention in Sierra Leone at a later stage also lacked any prior Security Council authorisation despite strong suspicion that it involved the application of coercive measures,[216] yet again received commendation from the Council.[217] Arguably, such an approach is unsatisfactory. The Security Council effectively appears to have acquiesced in the use of coercive military measures without actually sanctioning them. The importance of prior authorisation for regional enforcement action, and the dangers of permitting retroactive authorisation, was highlighted earlier. If the Council is willing to permit a regional body to undertake an enforcement role, it should authorise such action

211 See Chapter 7.

212 Ibid.

213 See Gray, supra n3, pp.100–109; Gray, supra n31, pp.294–297, pp.302–309; Howe, H., 'Lessons of Liberia,' *International Security*, 1996–1997, v.21, n.3, pp.145–176; May and Cleaver, supra n135; McCoubrey and Morris, supra n3, pp.141–145; Olonisakin, supra n135, at pp.356–365; Sesay, M.A., 'Collective security or collective disaster? Regional peace-keeping in West Africa,' *Security Dialogue*, 1995, v.26, n.2, pp.205–222.

214 See the references cited, ibid.

215 See SC Res 788 (1992), para.1. Commendation of ECOWAS became a common feature of a catalogue of subsequent resolutions. Examples include SC Res 813 (1993); SC Res 911 (1994); SC Res 972 (1995).

216 See, for example, Nowrot and Schabacker, supra n155.

217 See Gray, supra n31, pp.218–224.

prior to its commencement, in unambiguous terms, and make efforts to ensure that the action is subject to its ultimate control through the nature of the mandate conferred.[218] Any other approach suggests a degree of disinterest on the Security Council's part and a possible abdication of its primary responsibility in the arena of military enforcement action.

Arguably, as discussed in Chapter 7, the Security Council's utilisation of tools of control and oversight appears to have improved over time, and its approach to the Liberian episode involving ECOWAS should not be taken as a template for how it will typically respond to such situations. However, of greater consequence for the issue of regional accountability to the Security Council are developments within some regional organisations themselves – ECOWAS and the African Union, specifically – by which those organisations purport to enjoy an autonomous right to take military enforcement action regardless of whether UN Security Council authority has been provided for them to do so. These developments were outlined abovc. The right of autonomous action asserted by the African Union and ECOWAS cannot be reconciled with the UN Charter collective security system. Hakimi suggests that an 'operational system' has sprung up which operates alongside that of the Charter. While officially states continue to recognise the UN Charter norms, it is suggested that some regional bodies have taken action which is difficult to justify by reference to UN Charter legal norms, but which the international community has repeatedly, but discreetly, acquiesced in.[219] The powers asserted by the African Union and ECOWAS might be based upon the idea of consent to intervention:[220] the states parties to the relevant constituent instruments of those organisations, through their acceptance of those instruments, consent to military intervention within their territories in accordance with the applicable norms and procedures. The natural logic of this line of reasoning is that because any military force applied pursuant to these powers is effectively consensual, there can be no prima facie violation of Article 2 (4)'s prohibition on the use of force, meaning that there is therefore no requirement for UN Security Council authorisation. This is not without its problems. To accept the 'consent to intervention' basis for the autonomous powers asserted by ECOWAS and the African Union implies that states provide advance consent to military intervention within their territory for all manner of purposes in the future that they cannot possibly envisage. While the African Union does not have a significant track record of taking military enforcement action in the absence of UN Security Council authorisation, Abass and Baderin note that 'ECOWAS had regularly been usurping this vital power of the Security Council before finally encoding it as part of is legal norms

218 Abass, supra n3, pp.157–161; Gray, supra n3, pp.100–109.
219 Hakimi supra n70, p.645 et seq.
220 Abass, supra n3, pp.188–208.

in its … adopted Protocol.'[221] The actual practice of these organisations as military enforcement actors is addressed in the next section.

Regional practice

There was relatively little regional practice in respect of military enforcement action during the Cold War period, being essentially restricted to action taken under the auspices of the OAS in respect of Cuba[222] and the Dominican Republic,[223] and US reliance on the Organization of Eastern Caribbean States' (OECS) authority for its intervention in Grenada,[224] although it might also be argued that the Arab League force deployed to Lebanon in 1976 crossed the boundary into enforcement in some aspects of the performance of its functions.[225] None of these uses of force took place on the basis of UN Security Council authority, which in the context of the Cold War paralysis of the Security Council is perhaps unsurprising. While there appears to have been a considerable degree of international toleration of the OAS-sanctioned measures to enforce an embargo against Cuba imposed during the Cuban Missile Crisis,[226] the US-led intervention in Grenada, which relied in part on OECS authority for its purported legal justification, was widely condemned as unlawful,[227] as was OAS sponsored intervention within the Dominican Republic.[228]

In the post–Cold War era, military enforcement action at the regional level has been notably conducted by four organisations. Our brief overview of regional military enforcement practice is therefore confined to these bodies. NATO is unique among regionally based organisations in terms of the well-developed, robust military infrastructure which it enjoys and which makes its capabilities superior to those of other regional organisations. It has also sought to enhance these military capabilities yet further over time, for example through the creation of the NATO Response Force to respond to rapidly emerging crises.[229] NATO also plans regular exercises to strengthen military cooperation and capabilities, in the aftermath of Russia's invasion of Ukraine using its 2022 Strategic Concept to commit members to further training exercises.[230] NATO has played a significant role in conducting

221 Abass and Baderin, supra n192, p.22.

222 See Hickey, supra n75, pp.87–93; Hakimi, supra n70, pp.653–660; Harrell, supra n153, pp.433–436; Akehurst, supra n68, pp.197–203.

223 Lumsden, supra n168, pp.808–811; Akehurst, supra n68, pp.203–213.

224 See Hickey, supra n75, pp.94–96; Hakimi, supra n70, pp.660–666; Harrell, supra n153, pp.436–438.

225 See Hickey, supra n75, pp.93–94.

226 Hakimi, supra n70, pp.653–660.

227 See references in n223, supra.

228 See references in n224, supra.

229 On other initiatives see the Riga Summit Declaration, supra n179, paras.23–24.

230 See Strategic Concept 2022, supra n181.

UN-authorised military enforcement action and was the first to lead enforcement operations pursuant to express Security Council authorisation.[231] As noted above, it has proven willing to act beyond its core Article 5 remit,[232] as its actions in the former Yugoslavia evidence: first conducting air strikes in support of Security Council resolutions, followed by its role in leading the IFOR and SFOR operations in Bosnia[233] and KFOR in Kosovo.[234] NATO also conducted air strikes against the FRY in 1999 in response to the Yugoslav regime's treatment of the ethnic Albanian population of Kosovo, albeit without prior UN Security Council authorisation, yet again evidencing a willingness to take action going beyond self-defence.[235] NATO later led the International Security Assistance Force in Afghanistan, a Chapter VII operation,[236] in a country outside the area to which its treaty provisions apply, a practice repeated when it participated in air strikes against targets in Libya following the uprising against the Gaddafi regime, on the basis of UN authority.[237] NATO continues to be involved in various security-related initiatives on an ongoing basis, ranging from naval operations to combat piracy, providing training and support to national forces and bodies in places such as Iraq and Kosovo and providing operational support to the African Union.[238] Given its unrivalled military capacity and experience of enforcement action to date, NATO prima facie appears a capable military actor for military enforcement purposes. While its use of force against the FRY in response to events in Kosovo lacked UN Security Council authorisation,[239] NATO has not expressly asserted any autonomous right to apply

231 For discussion, see Gazzini, supra n174.

232 NATO only first invoked Article 5 of its treaty in the wake of 9/11 terrorist attacks. See *Press Release (2001) 124*, available at http://www.nato.int/docu/pr/2001/p01-124e.htm. On operations conducted in pursuance of this remit in the Mediterranean, see the NATO website at https://www.nato.int/cps/en/natohq/topics_7932.htm#:~:text=Under%20Operation%20Active%20Endeavour%2C%20NATO%20ships%20patrolled%20the,against%20the%20United%20States%20of%2011%20September%202001.

233 Established by SC Res 1031 (1995) and SC Res 1088 (1996) respectively. On their functions, see the SFOR website, http://www.nato.int/sfor. For discussion, see Laugen, T., *Stumbling into a New Role: NATO's Out-of-Area Policy After the Cold War* (Oslo: Institutt for Forsvarsstudier, 1999), pp.69–87.

234 Established by SC Res 1244 (1999). On its functions, see the KFOR website, https://jfcnaples.nato.int/kfor.

235 For discussion of the legal issues raised see Kritsiotis, D., 'The Kosovo crisis and NATO's application of armed force against the Federal Republic of Yugoslavia,' *International and Comparative Law Quarterly*, 2000, v.49, pp.330–359; Wheatley, S., 'The Foreign Affairs Select Committee report on Kosovo: NATO action and humanitarian intervention,' *Journal of Conflict and Security Law*, 2000, v.5, n.2, pp.261–273; White, N.D., 'The legality of bombing in the name of humanity,' *Journal of Conflict and Security Law*, 2000, v.5, n.1, pp.27–43.

236 See SC Res 1386 (2001); SC Res 1413 (2002); SC Res 1444 (2002); SC Res 1510 (2003); SC Res 1563 (2004); SC Res 1623 (2005).

237 SC Res 1973 (2011).

238 For an overview of current and previous NATO operations and missions, see the NATO website, https://www.nato.int/cps/en/natohq/topics_52060.htm.

239 On the legal implications of the NATO action, see Chapter 7.

military force in the absence of UN Security Council authority and that particular episode should not be taken as setting a precedent for future unilateral military actions on its part.

Initiatives within the EU beginning in the early post–Cold War era sought to enhance its collective military capabilities. At the Helsinki Summit in December 1999, EU members expressed their intention to establish a Rapid Reaction Force to be comprised of contingents held on standby by member states.[240] Stating their 'determination to develop an autonomous capacity to take decisions and, where NATO as a whole is not engaged, to launch and conduct EU-led military operations in response to international crises,'[241] member states were required to be able by 2003 to deploy up to 60,000 personnel within 60 days.[242] A major milestone was reached in May 2025, when the EU announced that its rapid reaction force was finally fully operational.[243] The European Council has also established permanent bodies to steer military responses by the EU to crisis situations, including the Political and Security Committee, the Military Committee and the Military Staff.[244] It is also possible that should the EU decide to take military action, it could make use of NATO assets. NATO has, for some time, displayed a positive attitude in regard to this matter.[245]

The EU has built up a degree of experience in conducting military enforcement operations.[246] Its first significant operation was a UN-authorised Chapter VII operation in the Democratic Republic of the Congo during 2003,[247] significantly an operation conducted outside of its own region. Soon thereafter, an EU force was also deployed to Chad and the Central African Republic, with a Chapter VII mandate of a broadly humanitarian nature conferred by the UN Security Council

240 See Gordon, P.H., 'Their own army?,' *Foreign Affairs*, 2000, v.79, n.4, pp.12–19; Van Ham, P., 'Europe's common defense policy: Implications for the trans-Atlantic relationship,' *Security Dialogue*, 2000, v.31, n.2, pp.215–228.

241 Helsinki European Council, Presidency Conclusions, para.27, text available at https://www.europarl.europa.eu/summits/hel1_en.htm.

242 Ibid, para.28.

243 See 'Common Security and Defence Policy: EU Rapid Deployment Capacity becomes operational,' 20 May 2025, available at https://www.eeas.europa.eu/eeas/common-security-and-defence-policy-eu-rapid-deployment-capacity-becomes-operational_en.

244 See Annexes III–V of the Presidency Conclusions, supra n242.

245 See, for example, the NATO Council's Washington Summit Communique, para.10, supra n130, at pp.D2–7. See also the NATO Council's Madrid Declaration of 1997, para.18, text in *NATO Review*, 1997, v.45, n.4, Special Insert, pp.1–4.

246 See Duke, S., 'Setting the agenda: Is CFSP at a watershed?,' in Duke, S. (ed.), *Between Vision and Reality: CFSP's Progress on the Path to Maturity* (Maastricht: European Institute of Public Administration, 2000), pp.3–33; Menon, A., 'From crisis to catharsis: ESDP after Iraq,' *International Affairs*, 2004, v.80, n.4, pp.631–648; Wessel, R.A., 'The state of affairs in EU security and defence policy: The breakthrough in the Treaty of Nice,' *Journal of Conflict and Security Law*, 2003, v.8, n.2, pp.265–288.

247 On the basis of SC Res 1484 (2003). See further Abass, A., 'Extraterritorial collective security: The European Union and Operation ARTEMIS,' in Trybus and White, supra n72, pp.134–156.

in 2007.[248] The EU has also taken over operations in the former Yugoslavia from NATO[249] and has conducted a number of police missions.[250] Albeit not enforcement actions, the EU currently deploys a series of naval operations, as well as a robustly equipped force which ensures compliance with the Dayton Accords in Bosnia-Herzegovina.[251] Thus, there is every indication that recent developments reflect the emergence of a more active EU, extending to the military enforcement sphere, although some caution is necessary. EU member states do not always share the same foreign and defence policy objectives, as divisions over the 2003 operation to topple the regime of Saddam Hussein illustrated only too well.[252] As alluded to above, notwithstanding the EU's adoption of comprehensive sanctions against Russia following its invasion of Ukraine, there remain tensions between some member states in respect of the approach which the EU should adopt in terms of its relationships between these two states.[253] More generally, there have long existed tensions between those states wishing to prioritise the role of NATO in peace support operations, and those who prefer to see the EU become the primary European-based body in this respect.

The African Union and ECOWAS have also demonstrated potential as viable regional military actors. That the African Union has envisaged itself playing a leading role in matters pertaining to regional security is apparent from the initiatives which it has undertaken to enhance its military capabilities, as referred to above. A degree of caution is, however, necessary. The limited military capabilities of many African states,[254] as well as the fact that many continue to have domestic security priorities of their own to reckon with, may limit in turn their capabilities and necessitate assistance from actors outside the region, something encouraged by the High-Level Panel report upon UN reform published not long after the AU was established.[255] Most of the AU's own deployments have taken the form of relatively limited operations,[256] with one commentator suggesting that only its

248 SC Res 1778 (2007).

249 EUFOR succeeded SFOR in Bosnia, commencing activities under a Chapter VII mandate conferred by SC Res 1575 (2004). The EU also succeeded NATO in conducting a military mission in Macedonia. For details see the operations section of the EU website, https://www.eeas.europa.eu/eeas/missions-and-operations_en#11927.

250 See EU website, ibid. On EU military operations generally, see Naert, supra n145; Tsagourias, supra n145.

251 For details of EU missions and operations in place see https://www.eeas.europa.eu/eeas/missions-and-operations_en#11927.

252 See Menon, supra n246, pp.87–88; Wessel, supra n246, pp.637–647.

253 See supra n93 and accompanying text.

254 On which, see May and Cleaver, supra n135, pp.8–11; Hollywood, supra n9, pp.152–153.

255 UN Doc. A/59/565, para.272. See also Ramsbotham, A., Bah, A.M.S. and Calder, F., 'Enhancing African peace and security capacity: A useful role for the UK and G8?,' *International Affairs*, 2005, v.81, n.2, pp.325–339.

256 To, eg., Burundi, Somalia and Comoros. See Paliwal, supra n71, pp.201–206.

action in Comoros might be considered to amount to enforcement action.[257] On a positive note, the African Union was involved in the response to the severe crisis in the Darfur region of Sudan which arose as a consequence of internal conflict in the area, resulting in mass atrocities, fatalities and displaced persons.[258] It initially deployed relatively low-key military missions to assist in the implementation of peace agreements concluded between the parties to the conflict, a contribution recognised and supported by the UN Security Council.[259] However, subsequently, UNAMID was authorised by the Security Council to deploy to Darfur to assist in the implementation of the peace process with a Chapter VII mandate.[260] With an initial authorised strength of 26,000, this is the largest operation to date in which the African Union has been involved, although it never reached its envisaged size,[261] suggesting political commitment towards its role may be lacking. That the operation constituted a joint effort with the UN and depended upon a significant number of contributions from non-African states might add support to such a view. While including a mandate under Chapter VII that empowered it to use force for the purpose of protecting civilians, it was essentially a robust peacekeeping operation. Nonetheless, UNAMID may come to serve as a template for sizeable, robust operations where deployment within an African state is concerned, depending for their viability on the supplementation of regional forces with the input of extra-regional actors.

ECOWAS quickly gave an indication of its desire to strengthen its capacity to conduct military operations within West Africa when it made provision for ECOMOG, the force first despatched to the conflicts in Liberia, Sierra Leone and Guinea-Bissau, to become a standing force.[262] ECOWAS's track record lends support to the view that it is an organisation with much potential as a military enforcement actor in West Africa. Its earliest significant military endeavour was its despatch of the ECOMOG 'peacekeeping' force to oversee the implementation of peace initiatives in Liberia,[263] notably commended by the UN Security Council,[264] implying that an important contribution was made. Although difficult to regard

257 Jordaan, supra n125, p.175.

258 For basic background to the situation in Darfur, see the UNAMID website at https://unamid.unmissions.org/.

259 See, for example, SC Res 1556 (2004); SC Res 1590 (2005); SC Res 1591 (2005); SC Res 1627 (2005). See also Zwanenburg, M., 'Regional organisations and the maintenance of international peace and security: Three recent regional African peace operations,' *Journal of Conflict and Security Law*, 2006, v.11, n.3, pp.483–508, at pp.493–498.

260 SC Res 1769 (2007).

261 For details of the deployed forces, see supra n258.

262 See Abass, supra n247, pp.217–220.

263 For discussion, see Howe, supra n213; May and Cleaver, supra n135; Olonisakin, supra n135; Sesay, supra n213.

264 See, for example, SC Res 788 (1992).

as an unqualified success,[265] it nevertheless evidences a willingness on the part of ECOWAS to conduct peace support operations. ECOWAS followed up shortly afterwards with actions in Sierra Leone[266] and Guinea-Bissau,[267] reinforcing perceptions of its prospects in discharging a significant future military enforcement role. ECOWAS forces were deployed at a later stage in the Côte d'Ivoire on the basis of a Chapter VII UN Security Council authorisation,[268] while it also deployed the AFISMA military operation to Mali to assist its government in responding to the threat posed by rebel forces, a mission which received UN Security Council authorisation.[269] In more recent times, ECOWAS forces have also been deployed to Gambia over several years as part of *Operation Restore Democracy* to support the constitutional transfer of power and subsequently provide training and assistance to Gambian forces.[270] This intervention did not take place on the basis of UN authority. The evident willingness of ECOWAS forces to undertake action which goes beyond the application of traditional peacekeeping measures suggests such a capacity to undertake robust operations, although it does raise questions concerning the appropriateness of the role performed by ECOWAS in situations where it has not been provided with UN Security Council authority to act.[271] Furthermore, ECOWAS's ability to take action has always been heavily dependent upon the role played by Nigeria, possibly undermining any perception of it as a genuinely collective forum for regional action.

Conclusion

While no generalisations ought to be made about the contribution which individual regional organisations can make to the collective security agenda of the UN, it is apparent that a number of organisations have actively sought to develop both their legal and physical capabilities in order to enhance their capacity to effectively perform collective security functions. Developments in respect of some African organisations have been particularly encouraging given the disproportionate levels of conflict on the continent. This evolution has taken a number of forms: the development of more explicit legal bases for regional action, the strengthening of collective regional military capacities, and increased utilisation of the resulting

265 Problems included a lack of consent to its deployment and cooperation from some parties to the conflict, notably Charles Taylor's NPFL faction.

266 See Gray, supra n31, pp.312–318; McCoubrey and Morris, supra n3, pp.143–144. The Security Council commended its activities in Sierra Leone; see, for example, SC Res 1162 (1998), para.2.

267 Also commended by the Security Council; SC Res 1233 (1999), para.3.

268 SC Res 1464 (2003). See Zwanenburg, supra n259, pp.496–500.

269 SC Res 2085 (2012).

270 See Ateku, A-J., 'Regional intervention in the promotion of democracy in West Africa: A analysis of the political crisis in the Gambia and ECOWAS' coercive diplomacy,' *Conflict, Security and Development*, 2020, v.20, n.6, pp.677–696.

271 See above.

legal and military apparatus for action in support of the UN collective security agenda.

From a UN perspective, the legal framework applicable to regional efforts involving pacific settlement, sanctions and peacekeeping is relatively generous and affords regional bodies considerable flexibility in making use of these tools to the extent that their activity does not contradict or undermine similar actions being undertaken at the UN level. Generally speaking, the conclusions drawn upon the merits and drawbacks of these tools of the collective security system in previous chapters can be applied as much to action taken on a regional level as that which takes place under the auspices of the UN. Military enforcement action taken by regional actors, however, is potentially more controversial. While the better view holds that the strictures of the UN Charter system require that regional enforcement action is preceded by the clear conferment of authority by the UN Security Council, in practice there has been some departure from this mode. This is a matter of concern especially in light of the fact that some regional organisations appear prepared to claim a right of intervention upon their own initiative. It is too soon to conclude that the UN Charter norms applicable to the use of force have been directly challenged on any significant scale: only time will tell whether this ultimately proves to be the case.

There is no suggestion that regional organisations are any more effective in their efforts to resolve situations threatening international peace and security than the UN. However, on some occasions, they may be a preferred source of action and the developments which recent years have witnessed arguably warrant the conclusion that despite the shortcomings of a number of organisations, the prospects of regional action making an important contribution to the advancement of collective security are better than they were when Boutros Boutros-Ghali made his plea for a greater use of their resources over three decades ago.[272]

272 *Agenda for Peace*, supra n4.

CONCLUSION

In a world in which conflicts continue to exist, long-running tensions are yet to receive any permanent resolution, and the actions of some international actors appear immune from international sanction, it is all too easy to paint the United Nations as a failure. Its primary purpose, the maintenance of international peace and security, remains at best only partially achieved. Prima facie, the extensive legal powers conferred upon the UN's organs, particularly the Security Council, for utilising a range of mechanisms for responding to situations threatening international peace and security provide it with the tools necessary for the effective implementation of collective security. However, collective security is not singularly a legal concept, and the extent to which effective action has been possible in any given case has been primarily determined by political factors. Most significant among these have been the willingness of the Security Council's membership, in particular the P5, to authorise relevant measures in response to situations of concern; the commitment of the UN membership to actually implement those measures; and the amenability of the situation at hand to the action taken. For such reasons, the Security Council's approach has not been a consistent one. The state of international relations, particularly as these pertain to interactions between the P5, also fluctuates over time and the parameters within which effective UN action can take place invariably shift. While the Security Council was largely paralysed in terms of its capacity to adopt Chapter VII measures during the Cold War period, its end created new opportunities and gave rise to optimism rooted in newfound cooperation between the Council's major powers. That period has, in

DOI: 10.4324/9781003518105-10

turn, been succeeded by the current era in which profound tensions exist between those same powers.

This book has never shied away from the fact that collective security suffers from its limitations. However, the UN story has also been a remarkable one of the creative establishment and evolution of a collective security system capable of responding flexibly to changing needs and circumstances. In Chapter 1, we noted the potentially broad nature of the concept of collective security, and the UN experience has seen it take on a form in which a wide range of situations are considered to be of concern to the international community at large, and which increasingly places human security at its very core, with phenomena such as climate change and public health epidemics brought within its remit in recent times. The UN Charter was designed to permit the implementation of a broad and flexible system of collective security. While building in protection for the interests and positions of the major powers by virtue of the veto afforded to the Security Council's permanent members, the Charter provisions facilitate a number of responses to be provided under UN auspices to a range of situations of concern. This framework has made possible the application of a more comprehensive form of collective security in the practice of the UN than was ever conceivable under the narrower and more legalistic provisions found in the League of Nations Covenant. While the geopolitical realities of the Cold War restricted the UN's potential during that period, the period since has seen considerable activity in respect of all the tools of the collective security system considered in this book. The UN membership has also proven itself willing to evaluate its collective security practices and priorities on several occasions through its endorsement of recommendations for the improvement of the UN system's functioning contained in documents such as the *Agenda for Peace*, the Brahimi report on UN peacekeeping operations, the Responsibility to Protect doctrine, and the High-level Independent Panel on UN Peace Operations.

In each of the collective security mechanisms considered by this book, there is demonstrable evidence of a creative and flexible use of Charter provisions to respond to changing needs and circumstances, although the utilisation of some mechanisms appears to have stagnated somewhat in recent years. Diplomacy under UN auspices has arguably benefitted the most from the existence of a flexible, enabling framework located in UN Charter provisions, imposing few real barriers to efforts along these lines. In particular, the diplomatic role of the UN Secretary-General has been developed by those who have held the position through an interpretation of the powers conferred upon the office-holder that has afforded him an independent right of action in pursuit of efforts to further the resolution of disputes or conflicts. This has, arguably, led to the good offices of the Secretary-General becoming the most high-profile form of peaceful response associated with the UN. Although the extent to which non-military sanctions can ever be an effective tool for coercing their targets to adjust behaviour giving rise to threats to international peace and security is a contentious matter, the

UN's experience of sanctions in the 1990s and criticisms levelled at their harmful effects nonetheless provoked reconsideration of their use. Following various initiatives taken to enhance understanding of the workings of sanctions regimes, the Security Council is now primarily focused upon a policy of targeted sanctions grounded in the perceived need to influence decision-makers without generating negative humanitarian effects on civilian populations at large. The move towards greater emphasis upon human security has arguably had some bearing upon this development, the negative humanitarian effects of wide-scale economic sanctions being at odds with the values advanced in prominent provisions of international human rights and humanitarian law. Peacekeeping represents a truly remarkable 'invention' of the UN system and creative use of the Charter framework to plug a gap left by the deadlock that paralysed the Security Council during the Cold War. Its evolution through later generations of operations to undertake new functions and adapt the principles by which it works reinforces yet further the responsiveness of the UN system, principally by addressing needs associated with the protection of civilians. It is noted, however, that relatively few new peacekeeping operations have been created in the course of the past decade when contrasted with the wave of new operations created in the period running from the end of the Cold War to the time of the 'Arab Spring.' The Security Council's development of the 'authorisation' model for military enforcement action taken under its authority, while bringing its own problems, again represented a sensible adaptation of the original Charter scheme for military enforcement action. Difficulties in ensuring that ultimate UN control is exercised over operations sanctioned by the Council have been addressed to some extent through a more cautious approach to the construction of its resolutions that provide military enforcement mandates. However, while always the least utilised tool of the collective security system, the military enforcement option does not appear to be a priority response considered by the Security Council in the current climate.

The use of regional organisations as collective security actors to relieve some of the burden placed upon the UN has been facilitated by Charter provisions that are generous to the role which these bodies may play within the UN system, conferring them with considerable freedom in efforts for the peaceful settlement of disputes, non-military sanctions and peacekeeping. Although the legal frameworks and political agendas of regional bodies vary considerably, several have endeavoured to develop these to facilitate an enhanced legal and military capacity to apply military enforcement measures, particularly important within an African context given the disproportionate prevalence of, and amount of time spent by the Security Council in discussing, conflict situations on that continent. The UN framework for military enforcement action has apparently been challenged by the attempts of some organisations to create for themselves an autonomous right to take military action regardless of whether Security Council authority has been provided for so doing. Although too soon to establish what long-term effect this may have, there is a very real danger that over time this may serve to undermine or even destroy the Council's primary responsibility for the maintenance of international peace and security.

The major shortcomings of the UN collective security system are inherently political. The legal model of collective security enshrined within the UN Charter facilitates a number of responses to situations of concern insofar as political circumstances make this possible and has adapted to meet new needs as these have changed.

INDEX

Note: Page numbers followed by 'n' indicate note number (s).

For Product Safety Concerns and Information please contact our EU representative GPSR@taylorandfrancis.com Taylor & Francis Verlag GmbH, Kaufingerstraße 24, 80331 München, Germany